Conversation: From Description to Pedagogy

CAMBRIDGE LANGUAGE TEACHING LIBRARY

A series covering central issues in language teaching and learning, by authors who have expert knowledge in their field.

In this series:

Affect in Language Learning *edited by Jane Arnold*

Approaches and Methods in Language Teaching second edition *by Jack C. Richards and Theodore S. Rodgers*

Beyond Training *by Jack C. Richards*

Classroom Decision-Making *edited by Michael Breen and Andrew Littlejohn*

Collaborative Action Research for English Language Teachers *by Anne Burns*

Collaborative Language Learning and Teaching *edited by David Nunan*

Communicative Language Teaching *by William Littlewood*

Developing Reading Skills *by Françoise Grellet*

Developments in English for Specific Purposes *by Tony Dudley-Evans and Maggie Jo St John*

Discourse Analysis for Language Teachers *by Michael McCarthy*

Discourse and Language Education *by Evelyn Hatch*

The Dynamics of the Language Classroom *by Ian Tudor*

English for Academic Purposes *by R. R. Jordan*

English for Specific Purposes *by Tom Hutchinson and Alan Waters*

Establishing Self-Access *by David Gardner and Lindsay Miller*

Foreign and Second Language Learning *by William Littlewood*

Group Dynamics in the Language Classroom *by Zoltán Dörnyei and Tim Murphey*

Language Learning in Distance Education *by Cynthia White*

Language Learning in Intercultural Perspective *edited by Michael Byram and Michael Fleming*

The Language Teaching Matrix *by Jack C. Richards*

Language Test Construction and Evaluation *by J. Charles Alderson, Caroline Clapham and Dianne Wall*

Learner-Centredness as Language Education *by Ian Tudor*

Learners' Stories: Difference and Diversity in Language Teaching *edited by Phil Benson and David Nunan*

Managing Curricular Innovation *by Numa Markee*

Materials Development in Language Teaching *edited by Brian Tomlinson*

Motivational Strategies in the Language Classroom *by Zoltán Dörnyei*

Psychology for Language Teachers *by Marion Williams and Robert L. Burden*

Research Methods in Language Learning *by David Nunan*

Rules, Patterns and Words: Grammar and Lexis in English Language Teaching *by Dave Willis*

Second Language Teacher Education *edited by Jack C. Richards and David Nunan*

Society and the Language Classroom *edited by Hywel Coleman*

Task-Based Language Teaching *by David Nunan*

Teaching Languages to Young Learners *by Lynne Cameron*

Teacher Learning in Language Teaching *edited by Donald Freeman and Jack C. Richards*

Testing for Language Teachers second edition *by Arthur Hughes*

Understanding Research in Second Language Learning *by James Dean Brown*

Using Surveys in Language Programs *by James Dean Brown*

Vocabulary: Description, Acquisition and Pedagogy *edited by Norbert Schmitt and Michael McCarthy*

Vocabulary, Semantics and Language Education *by Evelyn Hatch and Cheryl Brown*

Voices from the Language Classroom *edited by Kathleen M. Bailey and David Nunan*

Conversation: From Description to Pedagogy

Scott Thornbury and Diana Slade

CAMBRIDGE UNIVERSITY PRESS
Cambridge, New York, Melbourne, Madrid, Cape Town, Singapore, São Paulo

Cambridge University Press
The Edinburgh Building, Cambridge CB2 2RU, UK

www.cambridge.org
Information on this title: www.cambridge.org/9780521891165

First published 2006

Printed in the United Kingdom at the University Press, Cambridge

A catalogue record for this publication is available from the British Library

Library of Congress Cataloging-in-Publication Data
Thornbury, Scott, 1950–
   Conversation : from description to pedagogy / Scott Thornbury and
Diana Slade.
      p. cm. – (Cambridge language teaching library)
   Includes bibliographical references and index.
   ISBN 0-521-89116-7 (pbk. : alk. paper) – ISBN 0-521-81426-X
(hardback : alk. paper)
   1. Conversation analysis. 2. Discourse analysis. 3. Language and
languages–Study and teaching. 4. Communicative competence. I. Title.
II. Series.
P95.45.T49 2006
371.102'2–dc22   2006023282

ISBN-13 978-0-521-81426-3 hardback
ISBN-10 0-521-81426-X hardback
ISBN-13 978-0-521-89116-5 paperback
ISBN-10 0-521-89116-7 paperback

Contents

Thanks and acknowledgements   viii

    Introduction   1

1   **Characterizing conversation**   5
    Introduction   5
1.1 The nature of conversation   5
1.2 Approaches to the analysis of conversation   27
    Summary   37

2   **The vocabulary of conversation**   40
    Introduction   40
2.1 Lexical size   42
2.2 Lexical density and lexical variety   43
2.3 Lexical frequency   45
2.4 Lexical repetition   49
2.5 Vague language   54
2.6 Fillers   56
2.7 Discourse markers and other inserts   57
2.8 Routines and lexical phrases   62
2.9 Appraisal and involvement   65
2.10 Implications   69

3   **The grammar of conversation**   73
    Introduction   73
3.1 Complexity   75
3.2 Heads and tails   80
3.3 Grammatical incompletion   83
3.4 Ellipsis   83
3.5 Deixis   85
3.6 Questions   86
3.7 Tense and aspect   90
3.8 Modality   94
3.9 Reporting   98
3.10 What do learners need to know?   100

Contents

4	**The discourse features of conversation**	107
	Introduction	107
4.1	Cohesion in conversation	108
4.2	Interaction in conversation	113
4.3	Topic management: Topic development, topic change and topic choice	127
4.4	Discourse strategies	130
	Summary	137
5	**Genres in conservation: Storytelling and gossiping**	142
	Introduction	142
5.1	Chat and Chunks in conversation	142
5.2	Genre theory	145
5.3	Storytelling genres	151
5.4	Lexico-grammatical features of storytelling genres	159
5.5	Storytelling genres: Summary	168
5.6	Gossip	170
5.7	Lexico-grammatical features of gossip	177
5.8	Gossip genre	180
5.9	Classroom implications	180
	Summary	182
6	**Acquiring L1 conversational competence**	186
	Introduction	186
6.1	Conversational competence	186
6.2	Turntaking	188
6.3	Child-directed speech	190
6.4	Formulaic language	192
6.5	Repetition	194
6.6	Scaffolding	196
6.7	Syntax: Vertical constructions	197
6.8	Cohesion	198
6.9	Coherence	199
6.10	Functions, genres and speech acts	200
6.11	Pragmatics	203
6.12	Educated discourse: Talk at school	204
6.13	Sociocultural theory and 'instructional conversation'	206
7	**Acquiring L2 conversational competence**	214
	Introduction	214
7.1	Fluency	214
7.2	Formulaic language	218
7.3	Communication strategies	219

7.4   Pragmatic competence   223
7.5   Transfer   224
7.6   Acquisition vs learning   230
7.7   Classroom talk   238

8   Teaching conversation: A history   247
      Introduction   247
8.1   Pre-reform and reform   247
8.2   Direct method: Learning-through-conversation   249
8.3   Audiolingualism: Drills, dialogues and the conversation
      class   251
8.4   Situational English: Conversation in context   252
8.5   Oral English: Conversation as speaking practice   254
8.6   CLT: Conversation as communication   255
8.7   Task-based learning: Conversation as a task   266

**9   Teaching conversation: Approach, design, procedure
      and process**   274
      Introduction   274
9.1   Approach   275
9.2   Design   281
9.3   Procedure   295
9.4   Process   307
      Conclusion   318

Task key   326
References   342
Author index   358
Subject index   361

Thanks and acknowledgements

The idea of co-authoring a book on conversation emerged, appropriately enough, out of a conversation. Through conversation, we discovered a mutual interest *in* conversation – and in its description and its teaching. The combination of our two specialisms – linguistic description, on the one hand, and teacher education, on the other – seemed to represent a plausible, even original, vantage point from which current research into spoken language could be surveyed and evaluated. That initial conversation has been prolonged and nourished over many years, albeit mostly at a distance, and against the backdrop of our separate, and often demanding, professional and personal lives. Credit for encouraging us to keep talking the talk, and for helping turn the talk into a book, must go to Mickey Bonin, previously of Cambridge University Press, for whose enthusiasm, support and extraordinary patience, we owe an incalculable debt. We would also like to thank the publishing team at CUP, and Jane Walsh in particular, as well as our indefatigable editor, Sylvia Goulding. Special thanks are due, too, to Jane Evison for her careful reading of the manuscript and for her insightful suggestions: these were an invaluable aid in the preparation of the final draft.

Diana Slade would also like to thank the following: Christian Matthiessen, who has been a constant source of support and inspiration about spoken language; Susie Eggins, the co-author of her previous book on conversation, for the many insights that she gained from her; and Helen Joyce, who read and commented in detail on drafts of some of the chapters: Helen has always been very generous with her time and made many helpful suggestions. She would also like to thank four other colleagues for their support and the many discussions on aspects of applied linguistics: Hermine Scheeres, Tim McNamara, Erich Steiner and Solange Vereza. And she thanks her colleagues both within and outside the University of Technology, Sydney, and her friends, for their endless patience and for putting up with conversations about this book for far too many years.

Both authors are grateful to the UTS and Macquarie University's OZTALK team for their permission to use the spoken language corpora, and especially to Penny Biggins, for her painstaking work on the transcriptions.

Thanks and acknowledgements

Scott Thornbury thanks his colleagues at International House, Barcelona, as well as the many students and trainees who have unwittingly helped both shape his thinking and pilot many of the activities. Particular thanks are due to Jessica Mackay and Patrick Obregon for permission to use transcripts of their classes.

On a more personal note, the writing of this book would not have been possible without the unconditional support of Piet, Philip, Olivia, Georgia, and Gwen: we thank you all.

The authors and publishers are grateful to the following for permission to use copyright material. While every effort has been made, it has not been possible to identify the sources to all of the material used and in such cases the publishers would welcome information from the copyright owners. Apologies are expressed for any omissions.

The publishers are grateful to the following for permission to reproduce copyright material.

For the text on p.6: 'Hail Shatters City' which appeared in *The Sydney Morning Herald* 15 April 1999. Used by permission of *The Sydney Morning Herald*.

For the text on pp.23–4: 'Andy and Lisa's multimedia Wedding Album'. Taken from the website http://www.quantumenterprises.co.uk, © 1996–2006 Andy & Lisa Hunt and Quantum Enterprises.

For the text on p.153: 'Bag in Turkey'. Used by kind permission of Dr Neal R Norrick, © 2000.

For the text on p.170: Short extract from Episode 2, Scene 1. *The Royle Family: The Complete Scripts*. Written by Caroline Aherne, Craig Cash and Henry Normal. Published by Andre Deutsch, © 2002.

For the text on p.246: 'Bad Habits' taken from *Understanding Language Classrooms*, by David Nunan, © 1989; for the text on p.266: 'Conversation between Student A and Student B' taken from *Cutting Edge, Intermediate Student's Book*, by Cunningham and Moore, © 1998; for the text on pp.272–3: 'Thinking about learning' from *Intermediate Choice Student's Book*, by Mohamed and Acklam, © 1995; for the text on p.284: 'Input 30 Some British (middle class) conversational and cultural dos and don'ts' from *Conversation and Dialogues in Action*, by Dörnyei and Thurrell, © 1992; for the text on pp.292–3: 'Thinking about learning: conversation patterns' from *Intermediate Choice Student's Book*, by Mohamed and Acklam, © 1995; for the text on pp.293–5: 'Role Play: asking favours' from *Cutting Edge, Intermediate Student's Book*, by Cunningham and Moore, © 1998; for the text on p.301: 'Buying time: fillers' from *Conversation and Dialogues in Action,* by Dörnyei and Thurell, © 1992; for the text on pp.320–21: 'Attitude Words' taken from *Upper Intermediate Matters, Student's Book,* by Bell and Gower, © 1992; for the text on p.323: 'Role Play: getting to know you' from *Cutting Edge, Intermediate Student's Book,* by Cunningham and Moore, © 1998. All reproduced by permission of Pearson Education Limited.

For the text on pp.258–9: 'Seeing the Good side' from *Conversation Gambits, Real English Conversation Practices, 1ˢᵗ edition,* by RECGEN CANADA. © 1988; for the text on p.299: 'What are you doing here?' from *Innovations Elementary Workbook without answer key, 1ˢᵗ edition,* by Dellar and Walkley, © 2005; for the text on p.319: 'Telling a story' from *Innovations Upper Intermediate: A Course in Natural English, 2ⁿᵈ edition,* by Dellar, Walkley and Hocking, © 2004. Reprinted with permission of Heinle, a division of Thomson Learning: www.thomsonrights.com.

For the text on p.261: 'Closing a conversation' and for the text on p.322: 'Changing the topic', from *Beach Street: An English Course for Adults (Student's Book 2),* © NSW Adult Migrant English Service, 1998.

For the text on p.263: 'Asking people to do things' from *Meanings into Words Intermediate,* by Doff, Jones and Mitchell, © 1983; for the text on pp.263–4: 'Speaking: small talk' from *English Panorama Student's Book* by O'Dell, © 1997; for the text on p.271: 'It's terrible' from *Cambridge English Course 1,* by Swan and Walter, © 1984; for the text on p.282: 'Goals for a direct approach to teaching conversation' from *The Language Teaching Matrix,* by Richards, © 1990; for the text on pp.314–15: 'Classroom interaction and discourse options' from *Studies in Second Language Acquisition 7,* by Kramsch, © 1985. Reproduced by permission of Cambridge University Press.

For the text on p.260: 'Good news, bad news' from *Fast Forward 1 Classbook,* © Oxford University Press 1986 and for the text on pp.321–2: 'Hesitation strategies' from *Handshake Student's Book,* © Oxford University Press 1996. Reproduced by permission of Oxford University Press.

For the text on pp.271–2: 'Task 2 Conversation' from *Platform 2 Student's Book,* by Betterton and Leigh, © 2005. Reproduced with permission of McGraw-Hill Interamericana de España.

For the text on p.289: 'The long goodbye' from *Inside Out Upper Intermediate Student's Book,* by Sue Kay and Vaughan Jones, © 2001. Used with permission of Macmillan Education.

For the text on p.306: Common European of Reference for Language: learning, teaching assessment, © Council of Europe.

To the memory of John Slade

Introduction

Casual conversation is a fundamental human activity, and one in which most of us engage many times a day. It may take the form of small talk about the weather at the supermarket check-out, or gossip about colleagues around the office coffee machine, or an extended phone conversation with a close friend about the meaning of life. Before getting down to the business at hand, sales reps chat with their clients, doctors chat with their patients, waiters with diners, and teachers with their students. Strangers at a bus stop will start up a conversation to vent their frustration about the service. Taxi drivers famously air their opinions, seldom solicited. Your dentist will chat away even when your responses are reduced to grunts. Fellow passengers on a long-haul flight will exchange pleasantries before settling in to watch the movie. Listeners will phone a radio talk show to sound off about local crime, and teenagers will talk for hours on their cell phones about matters of apparently enormous consequence. Even very young children chat away with their parents, and by the age of three are able to have fairly sustained conversations with their playmates.

Conversational talk crosses age groups, gender, class, culture and ethnicity. Levelt (1989) calls it 'the canonical setting for speech in all human societies'. Indeed, the stylistic features of conversation have extended beyond spoken talk itself and 'crossed over' into other modes and media, such as the popular press and advertising, a process called *conversationalization* by Fairclough (1992). And the advent and rapid expansion of the use of email, text messaging and online chat have further blurred the distinction between spoken and written language, while underscoring the ubiquitous role of conversation in human affairs.

The centrality of conversation to human discourse owes to the fact that it is the primary location for the enactment of social values and relationships. Through talk we establish, maintain and modify our social identities. The role that conversation plays in our formation as social beings starts at an early age. Stubbs (1983: IX) asserts that 'infants learn, as it were, to engage in conversation before they learn language', and Hatch (1978: 404) claims that 'language learning evolves out of learning how to carry on conversations, out of learning how to communicate'. Even as far back as the 1930s, Harold Palmer argued that all language

1

use is based on, and is an extension of, conversation, adding that conversation must therefore be the start of any study of language. In Palmer's day, this meant prioritizing the teaching of pronunciation. The nature of spoken language itself was barely understood and for a long time spoken language was taught as if it were simply a less formal version of written language. This is a view that has been rectified only recently, with the advent of corpus linguistics and the consequent amassing of corpora of spoken data. Findings from such data now heavily inform the content of learner dictionaries, such as the *Cambridge Advanced Learner's Dictionary* (second edition 2005), and descriptive grammars, such as the *Longman Grammar of Spoken and Written English* (Biber *et al.*, 1999).

Finally, sociocultural theories of learning, such as those that derive from Vygotsky's research into children's cognitive development, foreground the role of conversation as the medium for *all* learning, and have contributed to the notion that effective teaching is, essentially, a 'long conversation' (Mercer, 1995). Recent research into second-language acquisition also supports the view that the learning of second languages may be successfully mediated through conversational interaction (van Lier, 1996). Such a view not only reinforces the arguments for an approach to language teaching that systematically deals with spoken English, but would seem to vindicate the intuitions of those legions of learners who consistently demand inclusion of more 'conversation' in their language courses.

For all these reasons, an account of how conversation works is therefore essential in the development of a pedagogy for second-language learning. This book aims to meet this need by providing the reader with first an overview of the features that characterize conversation and distinguish it from other spoken and written genres (Chapter 1), followed by a systematic description of conversational English, including its vocabulary (Chapter 2), its grammar (Chapter 3), its discourse structure (Chapter 4), and its characteristic generic patterning (Chapter 5), and then an informed account of its development in both first- and second-language acquisition (Chapters 6 and 7). On this basis, and after a review of teaching approaches to date (Chapter 8), an integrated approach to the teaching of conversation will be outlined, along with practical classroom applications (Chapter 9).

In short, the book aims:

- to introduce practising teachers to the nature and structure of conversation in English, drawing from a range of theoretical models;
- to equip readers with analytical techniques necessary to analyse authentic conversation at the level of vocabulary, grammar, discourse and genre;

- to outline how first-language conversational competence develops, and to relate this research to the development of second-language conversational competence;
- to identify and analyse the kinds of difficulties that learners of English encounter when participating in conversation;
- to outline a range of methodological approaches, procedures and techniques for teaching English conversation and to illustrate these approaches by reference to current materials;
- and, finally, to argue for an interactive, 'integrated' model of instruction, informed by the description of conversation and the learning theories outlined in the preceding chapters.

A note on transcription conventions

Wherever possible the data used as examples in this book come from authentic sources, i.e. from spontaneous and naturally occurring conversations recorded in a variety of contexts. (The few instances of invented data are identified as such.) In transcribing these conversations we have tried to capture their spontaneity and informality, but not at the expense of their readability. This has sometimes meant ignoring the finer details of transcription, such as length of pauses, pitch direction and other paralinguistic phenomena, unless these features have been expressly singled out for discussion. In cases where we cite data that employ different transcription conventions from our own, we have modified these transcriptions so as to bring them into line. Where this has not been possible, an explanation of any variant conventions will be found alongside the data.

The transcription devices that we use are the following:

- **full stops**: these indicate completion, usually realized by falling intonation
- **commas**: these are used to separate phrases or clauses in order to make utterances more readable
- **question marks**: these are used to indicate utterances that, in their context, function as questions, irrespective of their grammatical form or their intonation
- **exclamation marks**: these are used conservatively to indicate the expression of surprise or shock
- **capital letters**: words in capital letters are used conservatively to indicate emphasis
- **quotation marks**: double quotation marks are used to signal that the speaker is directly quoting speech; single quotation marks are used to signal that the speaker is saying what they or someone else thought

- **empty parentheses**: non-transcribable segments of talk are indicated by ( )
- **filled parentheses**: words within parentheses indicate the transcriber's best guess as to a doubtful utterance
- **square brackets**: information about relevant non-verbal behaviour is given within square brackets [ ]
- **dots**: three dots indicate a hesitation within an utterance: . . .
- **dash**: a dash represents a false start:

  Speaker: Did you ever get that – I mean in French what is it?
- **equals sign**: a double equals sign is used to represent overlap phenomena, such as
  - **simultaneous utterances**, i.e. where two speakers are speaking at the same time:

    Speaker 1:   Is it still going, Studebakers?
    Speaker 2:   = =I don't know
    Speaker 3:   = =No it's got a new name
  - **overlapping utterances**: the point where the second speaker begins talking is shown by = = preceding the point in the first speaker's turn:

    Speaker 1:   Can you dance now= =Rod, can you?
    Speaker 2:   = =I can do rock'n' roll and Cha Cha and Rumbas and Sambas and waltzes
  - **contiguous utterances**: i.e. when there is no interval between adjacent utterances produced by different speakers:

    Speaker 1: they had to move out of the flat because the whole= =
    Speaker 2: = =roof collapsed.

1   Characterizing conversation

Introduction

Conversation accounts for the major proportion of most people's daily language use but despite this (or perhaps because of it) it is not that easily defined. Compare, for example, these three dictionary definitions:

- If you have a conversation with someone, you talk with them, usually in an informal situation (*Collins' COBUILD English Dictionary*).
- Informal talk in which people exchange news, feelings, and thoughts (*Longman Dictionary of Contemporary English*).
- An informal talk involving a small group of people or only two; the activity of talking in this way (*Oxford Advanced Learner's Dictionary*).

While all three definitions highlight the informal and the spoken nature of conversation, only one singles out group size as a defining feature, while another focuses on topic. The distinction between *a conversation* (i.e. conversation as a countable noun) and *conversation* (uncountable) is either ignored or blurred in the first two definitions. Finer distinctions between conversation and, say, *chat, small talk, discussion* and *gossip*, are not dealt with. And, as we shall see in Chapter 8, the term *conversation* with special reference to language-teaching methodology has been enlisted for a wide variety of uses – ranging from *speaking* and *communication* to *dialogue* and *role play*. In this chapter we shall attempt to characterize conversation, first by contrasting it with other kinds of language, and then by listing its distinguishing features. By way of conclusion, we will offer a working definition of conversation that will serve as the starting point for a more detailed description in subsequent chapters.

1.1   The nature of conversation

In April 1999 a freak storm devastated parts of the city of Sydney. Here is how the storm was reported in *The Sydney Morning Herald* the following day:

Text 1.1

Hail shatters city

A freak hail storm swept across Sydney last night, causing damage worth hundreds of millions of dollars and triggering a massive rescue and repair effort by emergency services.

Thousands of homes were damaged as roofs caved in and windows and skylights were smashed. Thousands more cars were wrecked or badly damaged in the storm, which struck with no official warning.

The ambulance service said dozens of people were treated for cuts and lacerations after being hit by falling glass or hail stones, which witnesses described variously as being as big as golf balls, lemons, cricket balls and rock melons.

. . . At Paddington, Ms Jan Mourice said all houses on one side of Prospect Street had windows smashed. Mr Lucio Galleto, of Lucio's Restaurant at Paddington, said: 'I had five windows in the restaurant smashed. Water flooded in and patrons' cars have been smashed.'

(*The Sydney Morning Herald*, 15 April 1999)

On the day after the storm a radio talk show host interviewed a spokesman from the Weather Bureau:

Text 1.2

(1) PC: . . . here on 2BL. Well what went wrong? Why didn't the Weather Bureau tell us what was happening? You have heard earlier this morning reports that the Bureau thought er saw the storm but thought it would go back out to sea. It didn't. Steve Simons, a senior forecaster with the Bureau, joins me on the line this morning. Good morning Steve.

(2) SS: Good morning Philip.

(3) PC: So what went wrong?

(4) SS: What went wrong was that the storm developed down near Wollongong and we had it on the radar and we were tracking it and the track at that stage was showing it going out to sea and then very suddenly it developed into what we call a 'supercell' which is the beginning of a severe thunderstorm and these supercells have a habit of doing some rather crazy things. It changed direction very suddenly – this was down near Otford Bundeena way = =

(5) PC: = =Yes all right so er what was the time interval between you first discovering this storm and then discovering that it was in fact heading for the the city?

(6) SS: The time that we realised that it was heading for the city . . .

(Radio 2BL, Philip Clark Breakfast Presenter, 15 April 1999)

A couple of days later four friends were talking about how they were affected by the storm. Here is the transcript of part of that conversation:

Text 1.3: Hailstorm

(1) Odile: . . . No I think I don't know many people who have been affected except you and I. That much.
(2) Rob: You don't know?
(3) Odile: Well you know except for the neighbours.
(4) Rob: Oh a friend of ours in Paddington, they had to move out of the flat= =
(5) Grace: = =Mm.
(6) Rob   because the whole= =
(7) Grace: = =roof collapsed.
(8) Rob: The tiles fell through the ceiling= =
(9) Grace: = =Mm
(10) Rob: into the room and they've actually had to move out completely.
(11) Odile: Oh really?
(12) Dan: And there was the little old lady over the road who . . .
(13) Rob: Oh yeah. [laughs] She was sitting in her living room and a hail stone fell through the skylight, this old Italian woman. She had corrugated iron but it fell through the skylight. It fell through the ceiling and landed in her lap when she was sitting= =
(14) Odile: = =Mm.
(15) Rob: watching television.
(16) Dan: Watching *The X-files* probably.
(17) All: [laugh]
(18) Odile: I'm so glad the kids were not there because you know that hole is just above Debbie's head.
(19) Rob: Yeah.
(20) Grace: Oh yeah.
(21) Rob: No, it is amazing more people weren't injured.
(22) Grace: Mm.
(23) Rob: So erm they go back to school tomorrow?
(24) Odile: Not tomorrow = =
(25) Rob: = =Monday.
(26) Odile: It's Sunday.
(27) Rob: Monday.
(28) Grace: Monday.
(29) Odile: Monday.
(30) Rob: Mm.

(31)	Odile:	Yeah.
(32)	Grace:	Is the school OK?
(33)	Odile:	You mean, general damage?
(34)	Grace:	Yeah.
(35)	Odile:	I don't know.
(36)	Rob:	The school's closed next to us, yeah.
(37)	Grace:	I was speaking to erm . . .
(38)	Odile:	Oh my god I hadn't thought about that . . .

(Authors' data)

Each of these three texts deals with the same topic – the storm – but each deals with it in a very different way. These differences derive partly from the different channels of communication involved, partly from the different purposes that motivated each text, and partly from the different kinds of roles and relationships existing in each of the communicative situations. While all three texts encode instances of spoken language (Text 1.1 both reports and directly quotes what witnesses are supposed to have said), only Texts 1.2 and 1.3 exhibit the 'jointly-constructed-in-real-time' nature of talk, and only one of these texts – Text 1.3 – is a *conversation* in the sense that we will be using in this book.

In order to arrive at a workable definition of conversation, then, it will be useful to look at the differences between these three texts in more detail. By highlighting the differences, first between written and spoken English, and then between formal and informal spoken English, the following defining characteristics of conversation, and their implications, will be discussed:

- that (to state the obvious) it is *spoken*, and
- that this speaking takes place *spontaneously*, in *real time*, and
- that it takes place in a *shared context*;
- that it is *interactive*, hence *jointly constructed* and *reciprocal*;
- that its function is primarily *interpersonal*;
- that it is *informal*; and
- since, it is the critical site for the negotiation of social identities, it is *expressive* of our wishes, feelings, attitudes and judgements.

1.1.1 *Conversation is spoken*

Conversation is spoken (or primarily so, since computer-mediated communication now allows conversation to take place by means of writing – see Section 1.1.8 below). Hence the most obvious difference between Texts 1.1, 1.2 and 1.3 lies in the choice of *mode*: Text 1.1 is – and was always – written, whereas Texts 1.2 and 1.3 are written transcriptions of what was originally spoken. The transfer from one mode (speaking) to another (writing) means that most of the prosodic features of the spoken language, i.e. sentence stress, intonation, tempo and articulation rate, rhythm and voice quality, are lost in transcription. In order to redress this omission, here is a transcription of Text 1.3 with prosodic features represented, using the system adopted by Crystal and Davy (1975), as outlined in the glossary below:

|| tone-unit boundary
| first prominent syllable of the tone-unit
`   falling tone
´   rising tone
-      level tone
^   rising-falling tone
ˇ   falling-rising tone
'   the next syllable is stressed
↑   the next syllable is stressed and also steps up in pitch
"   extra strong stress
SMALL CAPITALS   the word, or words, containing the nuclear syllable in a tone-unit

-      pauses, from brief to long
- -
- - -

Text 1.3 – Phonological transcription

(1) Odile: . . . |no Ì 'think || I don't |know ↑many 'people 'who have been AFFÈCTED || except |you and ↑Ì || |THÀT 'much || - - -

(2) Rob: you |don't KNŎW ||

(3) Odile: |WÈLL you KNÓW || ex'cept for the ↑NÈIGHBOURS ||

(4) Rob: oh a ↑friend of 'ours in PÅDDINGTON || |they 'had to 'move 'out of the ↑FLÂT ||

(5) Grace: |M` M ||

(6) Rob: be|cause the WHÓLE ||

(7) Grace: |roof COLLÀPSED ||

(8) Rob: the ↑tiles 'fell through the CÊILING ||

(9) Grace: |M`M ||]

(10) Rob: |into the ↑RÒOM || and they've |actually had to 'move 'out COMPLÈTELY ||·

(11) Odile: oh |RÈALLY ||

(12) Dan: and |there was the little old 'lady over the RÓAD who || -

(13) Rob: |oh YÈAH || [*laughs*] |she was 'sitting in her LÎVING 'room || and a |hail stone 'fell through the SKŶLIGHT || this |old ITÂLIAN 'woman || |she had

                        'corrugated ÎRON ‖ but it 'fell through the
                        SKŶLIGHT ‖ it 'fell through the 'ceiling and
                        'landed in her · ↑LÁP ‖ |when she was SÌTTING ‖

(14)	Odile:	|M-M ‖
(15)	Rob:	|watching TELEVÍSION ‖---
(16)	Dan:	|watching the ↑X-FÌLES ‖ PRÒBABLY ‖
(17)	All:	[*laugh*]
(18)	Odile:	|I'm ↑so 'glad the ↑KÌDS were not THÉRE ‖ be|cause you KNÓW ‖ that |HÓLE ‖ is 'just above 'Debbie's HÈAD ‖
(19)	Rob:	|YĒAH ‖
(20)	Grace:	|oh YÊAH ‖
(21)	Rob:	|no it ↑ÌS a'mazing ‖ more |people weren't ÌNJURED ‖
(22)	Grace:	|MM ‖---
(23)	Rob:	|SÓ erm ‖ |they go back to 'school TOMÓRROW ‖
(24)	Odile:	not |TOMǑRROW ‖
(25)	Rob:	MÒNDAY ‖
(26)	Odile	it's |SÙNDAY ‖
(27)	Rob:	|MÒNDAY ‖
(28)	Grace:	|MÒNDAY ‖
(29)	Odile:	|MÒNDAY ‖
(30)	Rob:	|MM ‖
(31)	Odile:	|YEAH ‖--
(32)	Grace:	is the |school ÓK ‖
(33)	Odile:	|you MÉAN ‖ |general DÂMAGE ‖
(34)	Grace:	|YÊAH ‖
(35)	Odile:		Î don't 'know ‖
(36)	Rob:	the |SCHÒOL'S 'closed ‖ |next to ÙS ‖ |YÈAH ‖
(37)	Grace:	|I was SPÈAKING to erm ‖
(38)	Odile:	↑oh my GÒD ‖ I hadn't ↑THÓUGHT about 'that ‖

It would be impossible to convey the full extent of the conversational 'work' that is achieved through prosody, but among the features that are worth noting in the above extract – and which are either completely absent or only notionally represented in written text (e.g. by the use of punctuation) – are the following:

- The use of intonation (i.e. changes in pitch direction), and specifically a rising tone to signal questions, where no other grammatical markers of interrogation are present, as in Rob's utterances (2) and (23);
- The use of high 'key' – i.e. a marked step up in pitch – to indicate the introduction of a new topic: (4) oh a ↑friend of 'ours in PĂDDINGTON ‖;
- The way intonation is used to contrast information that is considered to be shared by the speakers ('given') and that which is being proclaimed as 'new', for example, in Odile's utterance (18):

‖I'm ↑so 'glad the ↑KÌDS were not THÉRE‖ be|cause you KNÓW‖ that ‖HÓLE‖ is 'just above 'Debbie's HÈAD¶

She uses a falling tone on 'kids' to introduce a new topic (or to 'pro-claim' it, in Brazil's (1997) terminology), and a rising, or 'referring' tone, on 'there' and on 'hole' to refer to what is common ground. The other speakers have already been shown the hole, a fact that is sug-gested by the deictic expressions 'there' and 'that' which assume a shared perspective, not to mention the explicit reference to shared knowledge in the expression 'you know'. On the other hand, the new information about the proximity of the hole to Debbie's head is 'pro-claimed' using a falling tone.

- The use of high key to maintain a speaking turn, contrasted with a fall to low key as the speaker prepares to relinquish the turn, as in Rob's turn 10.
- The use of high key to signal 'high involvement', as in Odile's turn 38.

The extract demonstrates what Dalton and Seidlhofer (1994: 89) call the 'crucial and all-pervasive' role that intonation – and *key* in particular – plays in conversation management, influencing the management of topics and of turns, the identification of information status and the sig-nalling of degree of speaker involvement. One has only to imagine a con-versation between two Daleks (the robotic characters in *Dr Who*, who speak in an uninflected monotone) to appreciate the importance of these prosodic features, and how they are implicated both in the interactive nature of conversation, and its interpersonal function.

1.1.2 Conversation happens in real time

'I had five windows in the restaurant smashed. Water flooded in and patrons' cars have been smashed.'

Notice how in the newspaper article even the quoted speech follows the conventions of written language, in that each sentence forms a complete entity, consisting of clauses that combine a single subject and its predi-cate in ways that do not deviate from the norms of written grammar. Moreover, there are no *erms* or *ahs* or false starts and back-trackings. Compare this to:

(4) Rob: Oh a friend of ours in Paddington, they had to move
            out of the flat= =
(5) Grace: = =Mm.
(6) Rob   because the whole= =
(7) Grace: = =roof collapsed.

11

Even without the addition of prosodic features, this is clearly transcribed speech. It conveys the sense of being locally planned in real time. Compare this to the news article, where the production process has been elaborated through several stages of drafting, re-drafting, editing and publication. 'The main factor which distinguishes written from spoken language . . . is time' (Crystal and Davy, 1975: 87). The real-time spontaneity of talk accounts for a number of features that distinguish it from writing. The most obvious of these are 'dysfluency' effects, which occur 'when the need to keep talking . . . threatens to run ahead of mental planning' (Biber *et al.*, 1999: 1048). Texts 1.2 and 1.3 include several instances of such dysfluency:

- hesitations: *So erm they go back to school tomorrow?*
- word repetition: *it was in fact heading for the the city*
- false starts: *No I think I don't know many people who . . .*
- repairs: *the Bureau thought er saw the storm*
- unfinished utterances: *they had to move out of the flat because the whole* [. . .]
- ungrammaticality (in terms of written norms, at least): *except you and I*

Other devices that 'buy' planning time, and thereby help avert the more distracting effects of dysfluency, include the use of *fillers* (as in: *Well you know except for the neighbours*), and the repetition of *sentence frames* (*but it fell through the skylight* it fell through the *ceiling . . .*). Repetition may also take the form of 'borrowing' chunks of the previous speaker's utterance, as in Text 1.2:

> PC: So what went wrong?
> SS: *What went wrong* was that the storm developed down near Wollongong (. . .)

More generally, it is now thought that a great deal of spoken language is borrowed, in the sense that it is retrieved in 'chunk' form, not simply from other speakers' utterances, but from the speaker's own store of pre-fabricated and memorized items (Nattinger and DeCarrico, 1992; Wray, 1999). One class of such 'second-hand' chunks are *utterance launchers*, examples of which include:

> *and there was the* little old lady over the road who.
> *it is amazing* more people weren't injured
> *I'm so glad* the kids were not there . . .
> *you mean*, general damage?
> *I was speaking to* erm . . .

The ability to achieve fluency by stringing chunks together accounts for one of the basic constructional principles of spoken language, which is that talk is built up clause by clause, and phrase by phrase, rather than sentence by sentence, as is the case with written text (see Chapter 3). This explains why utterance boundaries are less clearly defined in spoken language, and why coordination is preferred to subordination (the use of subordinate clauses). Spoken language consists of frequent sequences of short clauses joined by *and, but, then, because*. For example:

> what went wrong was that the storm developed down near Wollongong *and* we had it on the radar *and* we were tracking it *and* the track at that stage was showing it going out to sea *and* then very suddenly it developed into what we call a 'supercell' which is the beginning of a severe thunderstorm *and* these supercells have a habit of doing some rather crazy things

The 'layering' of phrase on phrase, and of clause on clause, allows for a looser form of utterance construction than in written sentences, with their canonical subject–verb–object structure. Thus, in order to foreground the *theme* of an utterance (i.e. the point of departure of the message), information in the form of a noun phrase can be placed at the *head* of the utterance, in advance of the syntactic subject: a friend of ours in Paddington, *they had to move out*. Likewise, retrospective comments can occupy a *tail* slot that does not exist in written sentences: *I don't know many people who have been affected except you and I. That much.*

Another characteristic of spoken language which is attributable to its spontaneity is the fact that information is relatively loosely packed. One measure of this density is the proportion of content words (such as nouns and verbs) per clause. Spoken texts are not as lexically dense as written texts. So, for example, in Text 1.1 above, of the 142 words in all, 88 are lexical words – that is nouns, verbs, adjectives, and – *ly* adverbs – giving a *lexical density* (Halliday, 1985) figure of 62 per cent. In the spoken Text 1.3, however, the lexical density is just 36.5 per cent. This lower lexical density is partly a consequence of production pressure, but the more thinly spread occurrence of propositional content, as represented in lexical words, also helps make spoken language easier to process by listeners, who, like speakers, are also having to work under the constraints of real-time processing.

The lower lexical density of talk is balanced by the fact that it is often deceptively intricate, as speakers construct 'elaborate edifices' (Halliday, 1985: 330) of loosely linked clauses and phrases (as in the extract about the storm, quoted above). Halliday describes this as 'the ability to "choreograph" very long and intricate patterns of semantic movement while maintaining a continuous flow of discourse that is 'coherent without being constructional' (1985: 202). It is these 'long and intricate patterns' that can often tax the processing ability of listeners, especially non-native-speaker listeners.

1.1.3 Conversation takes place in a shared context

> A freak hailstorm swept across Sydney last night, causing damage worth hundreds of millions of dollars and triggering a massive rescue and repair effort by emergency services.

In the newspaper text, few assumptions are made about the reader's present state of knowledge. Even the city (*Sydney*) is named, although most readers of the paper will be Sydney residents, and many will have experienced the storm themselves. The writer cannot assume, however, that this is the case, hence most referents (that is, the people, places and things that the content words refer to) have to be made explicit. The only reference that a reader who is removed from the events in both space and time may have trouble identifying is *last night*. Compare this to:

(18) Odile: I'm so glad *the kids* were not there because you know *that hole* is just above *Debbie's* head.
(19) Rob: Yeah.
(20) Grace: Oh yeah.
(21) Rob: No it is amazing more people weren't injured.
(22) Grace: Mm.
(23) Rob: So erm *they* go back to school *tomorrow*?
(24) Odile: Not tomorrow = =
(25) Rob: = =Monday.
(26) Odile: It's Sunday.

In the conversation, where the context is both shared and immediate, Odile can take it for granted that her listeners will be able to identify the referents of *the kids*, *there* and *that hole*, and that they know who *Debbie* is. By the same token, Rob can safely assume that *they* in turn 23 will be taken to refer to *the kids*, and that everyone knows that *tomorrow* is Monday (although in fact it is Sunday, as the others are quick to point out). This heavy reliance on the shared knowledge of the participants, including knowledge of the immediate temporal and spatial context, accounts for a number of features of talk that distinguish it from most written text. For example:

* the frequent use of pronouns: for example, there are 25 pronouns (including the possessive form *her*) in Text 3, compared to only one in Text 1;
* the frequency of deictic items (that is, words that 'point' to features of the physical context, such as *this*, *that*, *there*, *now*, *then* etc);

- ellipsis, where what is omitted can be reconstructed from the context, as in:

> (2) Rob: You don't know [*many people who have been affected*]?
>
> (3) Odile: Well you know [*I don't know many people who have been affected*] except for the neighbours.

- non-clausal expressions that can stand alone, and whose interpretation relies on situational factors, such as

> (19) Rob: *Yeah.*
>
> (20) Grace: *Oh yeah.*
>
> (21) Rob: *No it is amazing more people weren't injured.*
>
> (22) Grace: *Mm.*

In summary, in face-to-face interactions participants share not only the physical context (so that explicit mention of referents is often not necessary) but also the institutional, social and cultural contexts, as well. This sharing of contextual knowledge – resulting in, among other things, a high frequency of pronouns, the use of ellipsis and substitute pro-forms – means that the interpretation of the conversation is dependent on the immediate context. By contrast, in written communication, where writers cannot instantly adapt their message according to their ongoing assessment of their readers' comprehension, greater explicitness is needed to ensure understanding.

1.1.4   Conversation is interactive

Conversation is speech but it is not *a* speech. It is dialogic – or, very often, *multilogic* – in that it is jointly constructed and multi-authored. It evolves through the taking of successive (and sometimes overlapping) turns by the two or more participants, no one participant holding the floor for more time than it is considered appropriate, for example to tell a story (as in Rob's turn 13 in Text 1.3). Conversation is co-constructed reciprocally and contingently: that is to say, speakers respond to, build upon and refer to the previous utterances of other speakers. Thus, Rob's question (in Text 3)

> (23)   So erm they go back to school tomorrow?

while marking a shift of topic, nevertheless makes reference back to Odile's utterance, several turns back:

> (18)   I'm so glad the kids were not there

At the same time, Rob's question produces an answer (Odile: (31) Yeah), but only after a side-sequence in which Rob's *tomorrow* is corrected by other participants (and himself) to *on Monday*. Meanings are jointly constructed and negotiated to form a complex and textured semantic network. As van Lier puts it:

> Progression is fast, unpredictable, and turns are tightly interwoven, each one firmly anchored to the preceding one and holding out expectations (creating possibilities, raising exciting options) for the next one.
>
> (van Lier, 1996: 177)

This dual nature of utterances, whereby they are both retrospective and prospective, is a condition that van Lier calls *contingency*. In order to anchor contingent utterances, and to signal the direction the 'fast, unpredictable' talk is heading, certain words and phrases occur frequently at the beginning of speakers' turns, or at transition points in the flow of talk, such as *yes*, *yeah*, *yes all right*, *no*, *oh*, *well*, *so*, etc. These are known variously as *discourse markers* and *interactional signals* (see Chapter 2). So, in this extract from Text 1.3, such signalling devices are italicized:

(18)	Odile:	I'm so glad the kids were not there *because you know* that hole is just above Debbie's head.
(19)	Rob:	*Yeah*.
(20)	Grace:	*Oh yeah*.
(21)	Rob:	*No* it is amazing more people weren't injured.
(22)	Grace:	*Mm*.
(23)	Rob:	*So* erm they go back to school tomorrow?

Take away the interactional signals and the conversation doesn't seem to hold together nor flow so easily:

Odile:	I'm so glad the kids were not there. That hole is just above Debbie's head . . .
Rob:	It is amazing more people weren't injured. [pause]
Rob:	erm they go back to school tomorrow?

Of course, written language employs discourse markers, too, but usually not with anything like the frequency they are used in interactive talk. At the same time, there is a greater variety of discourse markers in written language. The following, for example, would be rare in spoken language but are frequent in certain kinds of texts, such as academic prose: *moreover, therefore, however, whereas, by the same token* etc. Talk has a narrower range of markers, but uses them more frequently: McCarthy (1998) notes that the words *yes*, *no*, *so*, *well*, *oh* and *right* occur significantly more frequently in collections of spoken data (*spoken corpora*) than in collections of written data (*written corpora*).

The fast and unpredictable nature of conversation means that it is not always plain sailing. Occasionally, ambiguities need to be resolved, as in this exchange:

> (32) Grace: Is the school OK?
> (33) Odile: You mean, general damage?

Such repair work is possible because of the reciprocal nature of conversation. Speakers are either physically or audibly present and can provide immediate feedback on each other's utterances, by, for example, agreeing (*yeah*), 'back channelling' (*mm*), showing interest (*oh really?*), clarifying (*you mean. . .?*), or responding to questions. At the same time, speakers are having to constantly adapt their message according to their interlocutors' reactions, both verbal and paralinguistic. Tannen observes that conversation is less a matter of two (or more) people alternating between the roles of speaker and listener, but that it is more a joint production in which 'not only is the audience a co-author, but the speaker is also a co-listener' (1989: 12). She uses the term *involvement* to characterize this quality, and identifies features such as the rhythmic and repetitive nature of much conversation as being indicative of its high-involvement style. We also saw, earlier, how the use of pitch – and high key in particular – contributes to a high-involvement conversational style.

1.1.5   *Conversation is interpersonal*

So far we have contrasted Text 1.1 – the newspaper story – with the spoken Texts 1.2 and 1.3. But what distinguishes the two spoken texts? Why is one 'conversation' and the other not? To answer this question, we need to identify differences in the channel, the purpose and the tenor of each exchange.

Text 1.2 is spoken but it is mediated both by telephone and by radio: this fact alone does not disqualify the talk as being conversational. Telephone talk, as we shall see, very often falls within the parameters of conversation, despite not being face-to-face communication. Radio talk-back programmes share many of the features of casual conversation, especially when more than two interlocutors are involved. Nevertheless, the purpose of Text 1.2, however informal the language, is essentially informative. The roles of the speakers are established from the outset as interviewer and interviewee, the interviewee having been contacted because of his expertise, and the purpose of the interviewer's questions being to elicit information (and perhaps with the ulterior motive of assigning blame: *What went wrong?*). Hence, the direction of the questioning is entirely one-way: it would not be appropriate for the interviewee to ask questions of the interviewer. The management of the discourse is very much in the control of the interviewer, therefore. Even when a third speaker joins the talk her questions to the expert are directed through and by the interviewer:

    (1) PC: Erm just hang on there for a second because Emilia wants to ask a question about that. Yes Emilia, good morning.

    (2) E: Good morning Philip. Look I was at the Ethnic Communities' Council meeting with Angela as well. Some of the stuff that I saw was actually bigger than than a cricket ball, I mean it was like a big huge orange, you know?

    (3) PC: Mm.

    (4) E: But the interesting thing about it was I mean I've seen hail before and even big hail and normally it comes down fairly compact and it looks white and it's got smooth edges but some of the stuff that was coming down last night it . . . you could see the crystals and it actually had ragged edges, it wasn't even smooth, and I just wondered whether that was a particular type of hailstorm that had come over you know and formed differently to others?

    (5) PC: Yeah, all right. Steve? What's the answer to that? I have heard reports that that too not all the hail that fell was in a in a ball.

    (6) SS: No hail very often isn't in a ball. It comes down in all sorts of jagged shapes and lumps because very often the various hailstones aggregate together . . .

Thus, even with more than two participants involved, the interview structure, and the roles inherent in this, are still in place: the interviewer (PC) manages the interaction in a way that in casual conversation between friends would seem out of place and extremely assertive. It is hard to imagine, for example, that the conversation between friends could have gone like this:

    Rob: So erm they go back to school tomorrow?
    Odile: Yeah.
    Rob: Erm just hang on there for a second because Grace wants to ask a question about that.
    Grace: Is the school OK?
    Odile: You mean, general damage? . . .

It is clear that the conversation in Text 1.3 is not managed in the same way as the interview in Text 1.2, where an asymmetrical relationship exists between the interactants. In other words, the right to initiate, to ask questions, to direct the flow of talk is not equally distributed. In casual conversation, however, such as in Text 1.3, such rights are equally distributed: the relationship between speakers is said to be *symmetrical*. This is not the same as saying that the relationship is one of equality, as van Lier points out:

> Equality refers to factors extrinsic to the talk, such as status, age, role, and other social and societal factors that decide one person has more power or is 'more important' (or more knowledgable, wiser, richer, and so on) than another. Symmetry refers purely to the talk and the interaction itself . . . symmetry refers to the equal distribution of rights and duties *in talk*.
>
> (van Lier, 1996: 175)

In Text 1.3 there are a number of what are called *initiating moves*, as opposed to *responding moves*. Typically, these initiating moves can take the form of questions, as in

(23) Rob: So erm they go back to school tomorrow?

but they can also take the form of statements:

(18) Odile: I'm so glad the kids were not there

Even in the brief segment that has been transcribed (Text 1.3) all four of the speakers (Odile, Rob, Dan and Grace) make initiating moves, suggesting that, even if their contributions are not exactly equal, their right to initiate is equally distributed. The equal distribution of rights in conversation contrasts with the situation in other spoken genres such as interviews (as we have seen), and service encounters (such as those that take place in shops). The function of service encounters is primarily *transactional*: the speakers have a practical goal to achieve, and the success of the exchange depends on the achievement of that goal. Typical transactional exchanges include such events as buying a train ticket, negotiating a loan or returning a damaged item to a store. To a certain extent it could be argued that the radio interview is transactional, too, but, rather than the transaction of goods or services, it is the transaction of information that is the objective. The same argument might apply also to the interaction that characterizes classrooms (including language classrooms), another context in which rights are not equally distributed and where information is being transacted – typically in the form of facts.

The storm conversation in Text 1.3, however, does not have as its objective the trading of either goods and services, nor of information. That is to say, the satisfactory achievement of the goals of the encounter is not product-oriented. These goals can be partly inferred from what participants themselves often say after a conversation: *We had a nice*

19

chat or *The conversation really flowed*, or, less positively: *No one had very much to say to each other* or *Graham went on and on.*

What is at stake in casual conversation is the social well-being of the participants, the aim being essentially *phatic*, i.e. to signal friendship and to strengthen the bonds within social groups. Rather than being directed at the achievement of some practical goal, the talk is primarily directed at the establishing and servicing of social relationships. For this reason conversation has been labelled *interactional* as opposed to *transactional*. Brown and Yule further refine the distinction between these two purposes:

> We could say that primarily interactional language is primarily *listener-oriented*, whereas primarily transactional language is primarily *message-oriented*.
>
> (1983: 13)

Because it emphasizes the personal element, we will use the term *interpersonal* in preference to *interactional*. This is also consistent with Halliday's use of the term to identify one of language's *metafunctions*: 'Interpersonal meaning is meaning as a form of action: the speaker or writer doing something to the listener or reader by means of language' (1985: 53). The 'something' that a speaker is doing in conversation is social 'work'– the establishing and maintaining of social ties.

It is important to emphasize that talk is seldom purely transactional or purely interpersonal, but that both functions are typically interwoven in spoken language: even the most straightforward transactions are tempered with interpersonal language (such as greetings) and chat amongst friends would be ultimately unrewarding without some kind of information exchange taking place (as in Text 1.3). Nevertheless, the *primary* purpose of a shopping exchange is not social, and nor is the primary purpose of the storm conversation to exchange factual information about storm damage.

1.1.6   Conversation is informal

Partly because of its spontaneous and interactive nature, and partly because of its interpersonal function, conversation is characterized by an informal style. An *informal* (or *casual*) style contrasts with the style of more formal spoken genres, such as speeches and recorded announcements, where *formal speech* is defined as 'a careful, impersonal and often public mode of speaking used in certain situations and which may influence pronunciation, choice of words and sentence structure' (Richards and Schmidt, 2002: 209). Informality in speech is characterized by lexical choices – such as the use of slang, swearing and colloquial language – and by pronunciation features, such as the use of contractions. Examples of an informal style in the hailstorm conversation include:

> *lexical*:   Is the school OK? (rather than *undamaged*, for
> example) Yeah. (instead of the more formal *yes*)
> Oh *my god* I hadn't thought about that . . .
> (swearing)
>
> *pronunciation*:   You *don't* know? (rather than *do not*) The
> *school's* closed next to us (rather than *school is*)

A feature of conversation's informal style is the frequent use of *vernacular grammar* (Biber *et al.*, 1999), that is, the use of stigmatized forms that are often associated with a particular regional variety. Examples cited by

> He's left now, *ain't* he?
> Oh yeah. Whatever they want they *gets*.
> *Me and Jody* had a contest for the ugliest pictures.
> Don't say I *never* gave you *nothing*.

(Biber *et al.*, 1999: 112–5)

1.1.7   Conversation is expressive of identity

The use of vernacular language, mentioned above, underlines the fact that conversation is a critical site for the negotiation of social identities. It is through informal talk that people establish and maintain their affiliation with a particular social group, and 'vernacular features of grammar can be highly prized because of their role in establishing and maintaining social solidarity among the speakers in selected groups' (Biber *et al.*, 1999: 1121). In fact, it has been claimed (e.g. by Dunbar) that language, in the form of conversation, originally evolved as a kind of 'vocal grooming' in order to facilitate the bonding of large groups. 'In a nutshell . . . language evolved to allow us to gossip' (Dunbar, 1996: 79). Dunbar argues that language fulfils this social (or *interpersonal*) function more effectively than physical grooming because:

> It allows us to reach more individuals at the same time; it allows us to exchange information about our social world so that we can keep track of what's happening among the members of our social network (as well as keeping track of social cheats); it allows us to engage in self-advertising in a way that monkeys and apes cannot; and, last but not least, it allows us to produce the reinforcing effects of grooming . . . from a distance.

(Dunbar, 1996: 192)

Conversation is marked, therefore, by continual expressions of likes, dislikes and emotional states. Interactants express their attitudes about each other, about others who are not present and about the world. There are also constant expressions of politeness, such as *please, thank you, sorry; would you . . .?; do you mind* etc. There is also a lot of humour in conversation: funny stories are told, jokes are exchanged, and participants tease one another. Consider this transcript below from an authentic conversation between four men during a coffee break at work:

1.	A:	It'd be good practice
2.	B:	That's a good idea Jim – the best suggestion I've heard you make all this year – then maybe we can understand you Jim – I don't know how Harry understands you
3.	A:	Who?
4.	B:	Harry
5.	A:	Who's Harry?
6.	B:	Harry Krishna
7.	All:	(laugh)
8.	C:	Who's Harry: Harry Krishna
9.	All:	(laugh)
10.	B:	Didn't you say you were going there?
11.	A:	(laughs) I've told you – I'm breaking away from them now
12.	D:	He's changed
13.	A:	I've changed
14.	B:	You're giving it away?
15.	C:	He's shaved his 'mo' off
16.	B:	He's only getting too lazy to carry his upper lip around
17.	C:	Harry Krishna
18.	All:	(laugh)

(Authors' data)

Here the men's use of mutual teasing serves to ensure (on the surface) that they have a laugh and enjoy the coffee break. But the purpose of casual talk such as this is also to help construct cohesive relationships between a group of people who are not necessarily friends but see each other on a daily basis.

Text 1.3 also had examples of humour, such as Dan's reference to *The X-files* – a popular television series about the paranormal:

Rob:	. . . it fell through the ceiling and landed in her lap when she was sitting [Odile: Mm] watching television.
Dan:	Watching *The X-files* probably.
All:	[laugh]

Also highly frequent in conversation is the occurrence of *appraisal language* (see Martin, 2000), including evaluative vocabulary (*awful, wonderful, ugly, weird*, etc) and formulaic expressions (*What a joke; He was the laughing stock . . .* etc). There are a number of other linguistic ways that speakers encode attitude, including swearing (*bloody hell!*); the use of nicknames and familiar address terms (such as *love, mate*) and the use of interjections (*wow, cool*) (see Eggins and Slade, 1997).

To summarize, the fact that the conversation is both interpersonal and expressive of personal and social identity is linguistically encoded in a variety of ways, many of which are exemplified in the storm conversation:

- the use of supportive back-channelling (such as *Mm*);
- the frequency of appraisal language (that is, language that expresses the speaker's attitude to, or evaluation of, what he or she is saying): *completely, probably, I'm so glad, oh my God*, etc;
- many sentences have human agents, and the speaker is often the subject of the sentence: *I'm so glad the kids were not there*; *I was speaking to erm . . .*;
- the telling of stories (Rob's long turn 13);
- a preference for informal rather than formal or specialized lexis, e.g. *they had to move out of the flat* rather than *they had to vacate their apartment*;
- the use of humour;
- the use of swearing (*bloody hell!*);
- the use of nicknames and familiar address terms (such as *love, mate*)

(Lexical and grammatical features encoding the interpersonal purposes of conversation will be explored in more depth in Chapters 2 and 3.)

1.1.8 Conversation in other modes

So far, we have been working under the assumption that conversation is necessarily spoken. However, this assumption needs to be qualified in the light of the development of computer-mediated communication (CMC), such as that which occurs in internet chat rooms, where, although communication takes place in real-time (it is *synchronous*), it is written. That is to say, chat participants key in utterances at their 'home' terminal that are then almost immediately available for all other participants to read and respond to. Quite often, CMC shares many of the kinds of features of talk between friends that we have identified. Here, for example, is an extract of internet chat. The first 'speaker's' turns are indicated by the time at which they were posted (e.g. [12:40]); the second speaker's are marked >:

Session Start: Sun 26 May 1996 12:40:29

> [12:40] How are you?
> good.
> fine here

[12:41] Please tell me more about you :)
> like what
[12:42) Ok, just to refresh memories, I'm 32,
divorced, English, 8 old son . . .
[12:42] test beds for a living :)
> well, I've never really talked to you before so no
refreshing was necessary – this is all new
[12:42) Ok :)
[12:43] What about you?
> I'm 40, single, American, no children
> and I'm an interior designer
[12:43] Whereabouts in America? . . .
> In Palm Beach, Florida
[12:43) I'm in southwest England
> whereabouts?
[12:44] Sounds nice. . . .
[12:44] :)
[12:44] Wellington, Somerset.
> I've been there. It's beautiful country
[12:45] Really? :)
[12:45] It is lovely here
[12:45] I was chatting with Lee yesterday . . .
[12:45) but she always seems to be busy
> yes, she's a friend of mine
[12:46) :)
[12:46] She is nice
[12:46] very sweet . . .
[12:46] but very busy
> she is. We've known each other for lots of years
[12:47] You live close by?
> about an hour from her
[12:47) That's nice :)

This text shares a number of the features of conversation that we have isolated in our analysis of Text 1.3 (the storm conversation). Speakers take turns; they respond to previous turns; questions are distributed between participants; topics are introduced, developed, dropped; there are opening moves (*how are you?*), and presumably closing ones; there are evaluative responses (*that's nice*), checking moves (*really?*) and confirming moves ([*but very busy*] *she is*). And, as a consequence of the constraints of real-time processing, the language is syntactically relatively simple, elliptical (*sounds nice; about an hour from her*), and often produced in clause- or phrase-length chunks: *she is nice/very sweet/but very busy*. Discourse markers and interactional signals are used to mark shifts in the direction of the talk, and to manage the interaction: *ok, well, yes, but* . . . There is humour (*test beds for a living*). Even paralinguistic indicators of involvement are signalled using emoticons: ☺, in order to compensate for the lack of visual or intonational information. Hillier characterizes such texts as 'writing to be read *as if heard*' (2004: 213).

Similar features have been identified in *asynchronous* electronic communications, such as in newsgroups and email exchanges, where there is a time lapse between the sending of the message and its reception. Text message exchanges may be either synchronous or asynchronous, but, either way, they are characterized by a highly informal and interpersonal style. Thus, the electronic medium has had the effect of dissolving many of the traditional distinctions between written and spoken interaction: interactants are less writers than co-participants in an exchange that resembles live talk. It is too early to say to what extent these proto-genres will develop their own idiosyncratic features, both linguistic and pragmatic (but see Crystal, 2001). As interesting and as suggestive as these developments are, they are outside the scope of this present study. Suffice it to say that *spoken* conversation remains the interactional type from which these electronically mediated interactions derive many of their characteristics.

1.1.9 Defining conversation

To summarize: conversation is (primarily) spoken and it is planned and produced spontaneously, i.e. in real time, which accounts for many of the ways it differs linguistically from written language, or from spoken language that has been previously scripted (as in news broadcasts, for example). In Halliday's formulation: 'Writing exists, whereas speech happens' (1985: xxiii). Conversation is the kind of speech that happens informally, symmetrically and for the purposes of establishing and maintaining social ties. This distinguishes it from a number of other types of communication, as shown in Table 1.1, although it is important to stress that there is considerable variation within categories. There are sections of news broadcasts that are unscripted, for example; and not all emails serve a transactional function, nor is all classroom talk dialogic.

On the basis of Table 1.1, we can now offer a more comprehensive definition of conversation than those with which this chapter began:

> Conversation is the informal, interactive talk between two or more people, which happens in real time, is spontaneous, has a largely interpersonal function, and in which participants share symmetrical rights.

(Note that, because we have defined conversation as being informal, we will use the terms *conversation* and *casual conversation* interchangeably.)

Table 1.1. *Characteristics of different communicative events*

	spoken	unscripted, spontaneous	dialogic/ multilogic	synchronous	interpersonal (vs transactional) function	symmetrical relationship
email exchange	✗	✓	✓	✗	✗	✓?
news broadcast	✓	✗	✗	✓	✗	✗
interview	✓	✓	✓	✓	✗	✗
service encounter	✓	✓	✓	✓	✗	✗
classroom talk	✓	✓	✓	✓	✗	✗
chat room exchange	✗	✓	✓	✓	✓	✓
conversation	✓	✓	✓	✓	✓	✓

1.2 Approaches to the analysis of conversation

Spoken language, and conversation in particular, has only recently started to receive the same kind of detailed linguistic attention as written language. Moreover, many approaches to the analysis of conversation have been partial, focusing on particular features of conversation through the lens of a single theoretical construct. The approach we will be adopting in subsequent chapters is a more eclectic one, on the grounds that a more comprehensive, and hence potentially more useful, analysis should draw on a variety of theoretical models. Our starting premise, and one of the basic assumptions shared by all the different models to be discussed below, is that conversation is structurally patterned, and displays an orderliness that is neither chaotic nor random but, rather, is tightly organized and coherent. It follows that, if this organization can be described in ways that are accessible to teachers and learners, there are likely to be practical classroom applications. (This does *not* mean, of course, that one such application would simply be to 'deliver' the description to learners without some form of pedagogical mediation.)

Conversation, then, has been analysed from the perspective of a number of different academic disciplines. The most important of these are sociology, sociolinguistics, philosophy and linguistics.

Figure 1.1 below provides a typology of these different approaches to the analysis of conversation.

1.2.1 Sociological approaches

Perhaps the most significant contribution to the study of conversation has come, not from linguistics, but from sociology. A fundamental concern of sociologists is to account for the organization of everyday life, including the way that social activities are structured and ordered. The sociological approach to analysing 'talk-in-interaction' has come to be known as Conversation Analysis (CA), a branch of sociology which posits that it is in and through conversation that most of our routine everyday activities are accomplished. CA is represented primarily in the studies of Sacks, Schegloff and Jefferson (see, for example, 1974). The objective of CA is to describe and explain the orderliness of conversation by reference to the participants' tacit reasoning procedures and sociolinguistic competencies. To take the 'hailstorm' conversation as an example, a researcher within the CA paradigm would be particularly interested in showing how the speakers are oriented to the rules of turntaking and how they accomplish this in an

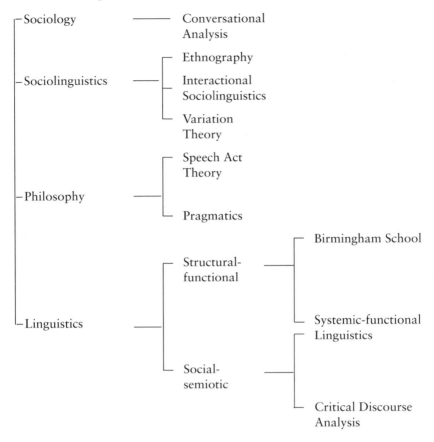

Figure 1.1 Different approaches to analysing conversation (from Eggins and Slade, 1997)

orderly manner, as when Grace 'takes over' Rob's turn and finishes it for him:

(6) Rob: because the whole= =
(7) Grace: = =roof collapsed.

Conversation analysts are also interested in how conversational 'repairs' are achieved, and how these repairs also illustrate the participants' orientation to the basic rules of turntaking, as in this instance when Rob uses the word *tomorrow* to ask about an event that will in fact take place the day after tomorrow:

(23) Rob: So erm they go back to school tomorrow?
(24) Odile: Not tomorrow = =
(25) Rob: = =Monday.
(26) Odile;   It's Sunday.
(27) Rob: Monday.
(28) Grace: Monday.
(29) Odile: Monday.
(30) Rob: Mm.
(31) Odile: Yeah.

The repair sequence is interpolated into another sequence, which is the simple, two-part, question-and-answer sequence of turns 23 and 31. The question and the answer would normally constitute what is called an *adjacency pair*, that is a two-part exchange, the second part of which is functionally dependent on the first – as in greetings, invitations, requests, and so on. In this case, a repair sequence is inserted (i.e. it forms an *insertion sequence*) in the adjacency pair, because the first element of the pair – the question – cannot be answered until the question has been 'repaired'. (Another example of an insertion sequence occurs at turn 33.) Conversational analysts are particularly interested in what such sequences demonstrate about the orderliness of conversation, and how the conversational 'work' is co-operatively managed. (In Chapter 4 we will return to the subject of conversation management.)

1.2.2   Sociolinguistic approaches

Sociolinguistic approaches have emerged from the theoretical common ground shared by sociology, anthropology and linguistics. These are especially concerned with the analysis of language in its social context, and the way that language use varies according to contextual and cultural factors. Hymes (1972a), one of the foremost proponents of what is called the *ethnography of speaking*, proposed a rubric for investigating the contextual factors that impact on any speech event. These factors include, among others, the *setting*, the *participants*, the *ends* (or purpose) of the speech event, its *key* (i.e. its 'tone, manner, or spirit', such as whether it is serious or jokey), and its *genre*, or type. Like an anthropologist, an ethnographer, armed with this rubric, would seek not only to describe the speech event under study, but to explain it, particularly in relation to the culture in which it is embedded. An ethnographer observing – or, better, *participating in* – the hailstorm conversation, for example, might be interested in this comment by Dan, in response to Rob's mentioning that the woman who received the hailstone in her lap was watching television:

(16) Dan: Watching *The X-files* probably.

The fact that this throwaway line not only effectively ends Rob's narration, but elicits laughter all round, despite the fact that it would seem rather flippant in the light of the seriousness of the situation (after all, the woman could have been killed), suggests that this particular speech event has ends other than the simple relaying of disaster stories, and that these ends are mutually understood. The use of humour (a feature of the speech event's *key*) serves to create a sense of group membership, and this has cultural implications that an ethnographer might be keen to explore. Is this light-hearted key a distinguishing feature of this kind of conversation in this particular culture, irrespective of the seriousness of the topic, for instance? And what cultural assumptions are shared by the mention of a television programme that dramatizes supernatural events?

Sociolinguists would also be interested in the *variation* that the speakers display in, for example, their pronunciation or their choice of words, and would attempt to correlate these linguistic factors with social variables – such as class, ethnicity or gender. The fact that Odile is of French origin, for example, might be reflected not only in her pronunciation, but in her interactional style – and the study of such variation is the province of *interactional sociolinguistics* (see Tannen, 1984, 1989). Proponents of *variation theory* (see, for example, Labov, 1972) are interested in tracking language change and variation as evidenced in such discourse units as spoken narratives. Narratives exhibit relatively stable structures, but allow for a great deal of linguistic variation within these structures, not least because of the tendency of speakers to adopt a vernacular style when narrating, all of which makes them an ideal site for the study of patterns of linguistic variation and change. The narrative that Dan and Rob collaborate in telling (in the hailstorm conversation) displays a number of the generic features of narratives that Labov and Waletzky (1967) identified in their seminal study of the narratives of urban Afro-Americans. These include an *abstract* (or brief announcement of the topic of the story):

(12) Dan: And there was the little old lady over the road . . .

an *orientation* (to the situational context and the participants):

(13) Rob: Oh yeah [laughs] she was sitting in her living room . . .

a *complication*:

. . . and a hailstone fell through the skylight . . .

which is in turn typically followed by some form of *resolution* (although not in the case of the hailstorm story) and a *coda*:

(16) Dan: Watching *The X-files* probably.

There is also a seam of *evaluative* language running through the story, such as *little old lady*, *this old Italian woman*, which serves to convey the speakers' (amused) attitude to the events they are relating. (Spoken narratives will be described in more detail in Chapter 5.)

1.2.3 Philosophical approaches

Speech Act Theory, which grew out of the philosophical study of meaning, has been influential in the way it has added to our understanding of how speakers' intentions are expressed in language. Philosophers such as Austin (1962) and Searle (1969) re-conceptualized speech as 'action' and attempted to describe how (a potentially infinite number of) spoken utterances can be classified according to a finite – and relatively limited – set of functions. By ascribing communicative functions to utterances, and by attempting to describe the conditions under which an utterance can fulfil a specific function, speech act theory helped pave the way for a communicative – rather than purely formal – description of spoken language. The hailstorm conversation provides at least two examples of utterances that might be interesting to analyse from the perspective of speech act theory, since their function is not transparent in terms of their form. That is, they are declarative sentences in terms of their grammatical form, but are nevertheless interpreted as being questions:

> (2) Rob: You don't know?

and

> (23) Rob: So erm they go back to school tomorrow?

Note that in the transcript the two utterances have been punctuated as if they *were* questions but, of course, in spoken language there are no such things as 'question marks'. Nor is rising intonation necessarily a reliable indicator of a question: many statements (especially in Australian English) are uttered with a rising intonation. And many utterances that are both intended and interpreted as questions are uttered with a falling intonation. According to speech act theory, to count as a question an utterance must fulfil a number of conditions, or rules. These include the condition that the speaker does not know the answer, that the speaker sincerely wants to know the answer, and that the answer is not likely to be forthcoming without the question being asked. But, with regard to the first 'question' (*You don't know?*), the previous speaker (Odile) has already said that she doesn't know, suggesting that Rob's question may have some other function, such as expressing his surprise – or even his disbelief – at her not knowing many people who have been affected by

31

the hailstorm, i.e. the utterance has an *expressive* function, rather than a purely representative one.

Closely related to speech act theory, and sharing a similar philosophical background, is *pragmatics*. Like speech act theory, pragmatics is concerned with elucidating speaker meaning, especially where speaker meaning seems to be at variance with semantic meaning, that is, the literal meaning of the words and grammatical forms of an utterance. Moreover, pragmatics goes further and seeks to answer the question as to how the speaker's meaning is retrieved by listeners, rather than being interpreted literally or nonsensically. So, for example, Odile's utterance:

> (18) Odile: I'm so glad the kids were not there because you
>   know that hole is just above Debbie's head . . .

would make very little sense to anyone who had not been privy to the conversation up to this point. There is no inherent logical connection between Odile's being glad the kids were not there, and the hole being just above Debbie's head. And even with access to the co-text (the previous utterances) the significance of the hole is not obvious. Nevertheless, the others seem to have no problem interpreting the statement as meaning *the hole where the hailstone came through is just above the place where Debbie's head would have been had she been there*. They are able to make this interpretation partly through recourse to shared contextual knowledge (they have just been shown the hole). But they are also interpreting the utterance through adherence to a mutually accepted set of principles for the conduct of talk, without which coherent conversation would be impossible. These principles were first outlined by Grice (1975), who expressed them in terms of four 'maxims':

1. *Maxim of quantity*: Make your contribution just as informative as required.
2. *Maxim of quality*: Make your contribution one that is true.
3. *Maxim of relation*: Make your contribution relevant.
4. *Maxim of manner*: Avoid obscurity and ambiguity. Be brief and orderly.

Thus, in accordance with the maxim of relation, and given all the possible meanings that Odile's utterance could have had, her listeners were disposed to select the interpretation that was most relevant, that is the one which (according to *relevance theory*, Sperber and Wilson, 1990) required the least processing effort in order to make sense. This assumption of relevance is fundamental to the maintenance of conversational coherence. It accounts, for example, for Odile's outburst:

> (38) Odile: Oh my god I hadn't thought about that . . .

as she suddenly sees the relevance of Rob's comment about the school next door being closed, which in turn relates to Grace's question: *Is the school OK?* – a question that at first Odile couldn't quite see the relevance of. (She asks: *You mean, general damage?*). Only three turns later does she see the point: that her own children's school may also have been closed because of hailstorm damage. Pragmatics, then, offers insights into how speakers and listeners co-operate in order to achieve coherence, making sense of each other's utterances by searching for relevance in the co-text and the context.

1.2.4   Linguistic approaches

Originating more in linguistics than in any other discipline, both the *Birmingham School* of Discourse Analysis and *Systemic Functional Linguistics* have made major contributions to the description and analysis of spoken language.

The *Birmingham School*, influenced by the work of Firth (1957), was established primarily by Coulthard and Sinclair, whose earlier work focused on the analysis of classroom discourse (see, for example, Sinclair and Coulthard, 1975, and Sinclair and Brazil, 1982). They were interested in identifying the 'grammar' of interaction, and in particular the way a speaker's discourse choices are pre-determined by the immediately preceding utterance, analogous to the way that the choice of a word in a sentence is determined. This 'discourse grammar' was described in terms of a hierarchy, from the largest units (e.g. a lesson) to the smallest, these being the individual *acts* of which a lesson might be composed. These acts are not to be confused with *speech acts*, as mentioned above, rather, they are defined in terms of their interactive function, such as *eliciting, informing* and *evaluating*, or their turn-taking function, such as *cueing* and *nominating*. Intermediate categories in the hierarchy include *exchanges* and it was the structure of exchanges which was the focus of particular interest. The identification of the three-part exchange structure that characterizes classroom interaction – *initiation, response, follow-up* – is one of the best-known findings of this School (see Chapter 7). But discourse consists of larger units too, such as *transactions*, and these are often identifiable by the discourse markers that *frame* them. In the hailstorm conversation, there is a clear division between two transactions at turns 22 and 23:

> (22) Grace: Mm.
>   [pause]
> (23) Rob: So erm they go back to school tomorrow?

Rob's *so* serves to frame the introduction of a new topic, and the transaction that follows is composed of a number of exchanges about this topic, each exchange realized in the form of question-and-answer moves. The fact that exchange structure allows considerable flexibility – more so than, perhaps, sentence grammar allows – is evidenced by the way that the exchanges are interrupted by insertion sequences, as we noted above.

Systemic Functional Linguistics (SFL) is largely derived from the work of Halliday (see Halliday, 1985; Halliday and Matthiessen 2004; Eggins, 1994). The central concern of SFL is, in a systematic way, to relate language to its social context and, in particular, to the functions it performs in that context. Such a concern leads to a focus on the analysis of actual language in use: of texts considered in relation to the social context, both cultural and situational, in which they occur. Systemic Functional Linguistics stresses the centrality of the study of conversation to the study of language, because conversation is the most important vehicle by means of which social reality is represented and enacted in language. Moreover, 'to understand the nature of text as social action we are led naturally to consider spontaneous conversation, as being the most accessible to interpretation' (Halliday, 1978: 140).

Systemic Functional Linguistics is a *functional* approach to language description. Functional descriptions seek to explain the internal organization of language in terms of the functions that it has evolved to serve. As a functional approach, SFL argues that language should be thought of as real instances of meaningful language in use. In turn, because language – in the form of written or spoken *texts* – always occurs in social contexts, SFL argues for the need for a descriptive framework whereby language and context are systematically and functionally related to one another.

It is well known that different contexts predict different kinds of language use. SFL argues that there is a systematic correlation between context and language, and, specifically, that three different aspects of context correlate with the three different kinds of meaning expressed in language. Halliday (1985; Halliday and Matthiessen, 2004) identifies the determining context factors as being:

- the *field* of discourse (what is being talked or written about);
- the *tenor* of discourse (the relationship between the participants); and
- the *mode* of discourse (whether, for example, the language is written or spoken).

The significance of field, tenor and mode is that these three contextual dimensions are then encoded into three types of meanings represented in language. The three types of meaning are:

1. *ideational meanings*: meanings about the world. These are a reflection of field;

2. *interpersonal meanings*: meanings about roles and relationships. These are a reflection of tenor; and
3. *textual meanings*: meanings about the message. These are a reflection of mode.

Most significantly, these three types of meaning occur simultaneously in every clause or text. Take as an example, a clause from the hailstorm conversation, Rob's comment:

(21) Rob: No it is amazing more people weren't injured.

simultaneously expresses meanings about the world (*more people weren't injured*) and about the relationship with the participants in the conversation, through the exaggerated expression of attitude (*it is amazing*). This has an interpersonal function in that, not only does it serve to validate Odile's relief that the kids weren't injured, but it captures the general feeling of amazement shared by the participants, and reinforces the sense of solidarity that their talk instantiates. Finally, the discourse marker *No* has a textual function in that it connects Rob's utterance with the preceding talk, signalling an agreement to the negative implication of Odile's comment, i.e. that people weren't injured.

Together the field, tenor and mode of the situation constitute the *register variables* of a situation. Texts whose contexts of situation co-vary in the same way are said to belong to the same *register*. The concept of register is a 'a theoretical explanation of the common-sense observation that we use language differently in different situations' (Eggins and Martin, 1997: 234). It is a useful way of explaining and predicting the relationship between features of context and features of text. Thus, the three texts about the hailstorm cited at the beginning of this chapter (the newspaper account, the radio interview and the friendly conversation) all share the same field, in that they are all about the hailstorm. But they differ with regard to their tenor and mode. It is these tenor and mode differences which are reflected in different kinds of grammatical and lexical choices, and which account for such different wordings as the following:

> At Paddington, Ms Jan Mourice said all houses on one side of Prospect Street had windows smashed. [newspaper report]

> Steve Simons, a senior forecaster with the Bureau, joins me on the line this morning. [radio interview]

> Oh a friend of ours in Paddington, they had to move out of the flat [conversation]

The way that, within specific cultural contexts, register variables influence how particular texts (whether spoken or written) are structured and have become institutionalized is captured in the concept of *genre* (see Chapter 5). A genre is a recognizable language activity, such as a news report, or a conversational story, whose structure has become formalized over time. Speakers of a language know how to perform these language activities in ways that are appropriate to their cultural contexts. For example, they know how to make stories interesting, entertaining or worth listening to. *Genre theory* provides semantic and grammatical tools for grouping texts with similar social purposes into text-types. For example, the hailstorm conversation contains a story (in turns 12, 13 and 16) that has its own internal structure (an orientation and a complicating event) and which, in turn, is embedded within the larger conversation. As we will see in Chapter 5, in conversation speakers weave in and out of telling stories and gossiping, and these genres are nested within highly interactive talk consisting of shorter exchanges.

Sharing with SFL a concern for the social context of language in use, proponents of *Critical Discourse Analysis* (CDA), such as Fairclough (1995), view discourse as a form of social practice. They argue that discourse, including conversation, can be properly understood only in relation to the social structures that it both shapes and is shaped by, and in particular the relations of power inherent in these social structures. A job interview and a friendly chat, for example, while sharing many superficial features, manifest very different relations of power, and these differences will determine the kind of language choices that the participants make, including the way turns are taken and distributed. At the same time, the language choices they make are socially *constitutive*, in that they help to sustain and reproduce the existing social structures, as when the job interviewee has to be *invited* to ask questions, rather than simply being allowed to ask them unsolicited. But even conversation, which on the surface would seem to be one of the most egalitarian forms of interaction, can itself be the site for significant interpersonal work as interactants enact and confirm their social identities. This is particularly the case when conversation is used as a way of 'disguising' inequalities of power, as when a boss might say to an employee: 'Let's have a little chat about your future plans . . .'

The hailstorm conversation, if examined through the lens of Critical Discourse Analysis, would not reveal significant inequalities amongst the participants, perhaps, but their choice of language to talk about – and to position themselves in relation to – parties who are not present may shed some light on unstated but shared ideological values. The fact, for example, that Dan's neighbour is first characterized as *a little old lady*, rather than, say, as *an elderly pensioner*, and then as *this old Italian woman*, construes her not only as an object of mirth, but tends to reinforce cultural stereotypes of age, gender and race, all at the same time. CDA is particularly effective at unmasking this kind of ideological 'sub-text'.

Finally, the analysis of conversation has been immeasurably enhanced by the advent of two technological innovations: the invention of the tape recorder and the computer. The former allowed the recording and transcription of authentic data, which in turn paved the way for descriptions of spoken English that describe attested use, rather than basing their descriptions on invented examples. The computer enables researchers to compile and consult databases (called *corpora*) of spoken language, and has given rise to the science of *corpus linguistics* (see Chapter 2). Much of the authentic spoken data we use in this book comes from different spoken corpora. For example, the Australian data comes from a spoken-language corpus called OZTALK, a joint Macquarie University and University of Technology, Sydney, project (referred to hereafter as OZTALK).

Among other things, corpora permit the analysis and comparison of word frequency counts across a number of different contexts. For example, a word frequency analysis of the hailstorm text, using a software program, shows that over 85 per cent of the words in the text are in the most frequent 1000 words in English. Words that are not in this frequency band include *hail, corrugated, ceiling, skylight, injured, tiles* and *X-files*. Moreover, 50 per cent of the words in the text are *function words*, such as *a, about, am, and*, etc. Of these, the most frequent is the definite article *the* (12 occurrences, compared to only one of the indefinite article *a*). A *concordance* of the examples of *the* in the text (Table 1.2 overleaf) shows just how many references – to people, places, things, TV programmes – the speakers share. This in turn underlines the way that their conversation both reflects and reinforces the commonality of their different but interconnected worlds.

Summary

This chapter has aimed to provide a working definition of conversation. To do this, we have attempted to answer these questions: *How is conversation different from other related forms of communication?* and *How are these differences realized in terms of language?* In the chapters that follow we will take conversation to mean spontaneous, spoken, dialogic (or multilogic) communication, taking place in real time and in a shared context, whose function is primarily interpersonal, and in which the interactants have symmetrical rights.

We have also looked at some of the different theoretical constructs that have provided tools for analysing and describing conversation, and which will inform our analysis in the chapters that follow. In the next

Table 1.2   *Concordance of occurrences of* the *in the hailstorm text*

	THE	tiles fell through
tiles fell through	THE	ceiling into
ceiling into	THE	room and theyve actually had to move out
ove out completely. Oh really? And there was	THE	little old lady over
little old lady over	THE	road who . . . Oh yes she was sitting in her
er living room and a hail stone fell through	THE	skylight, this old Italian woman. She had
She had corrugated iron but it fell through	THE	skylight it fell through
skylight it fell through	THE	ceiling and landed in her lap when she was
he was sitting watching television. Watching	THE	X-files probably. Im so glad
X-files probably. Im so glad	THE	kids were not there because you know that
Its Sunday. Monday. Monday. Monday. Yes. Is	THE	school OK? You mean, general damage? I
l OK? You mean, general damage? I dont know.	THE	schools closed next to us, yes. I was

four chapters, we will take a closer look at the linguistic features of conversation, specifically its vocabulary and grammar, its discourse structure (i.e. the way it is constructed sequentially and reciprocally), and the way its larger structures have become generalized into certain culturally-embedded patterns – or genres. A description of conversation at these different levels clearly has implications for teaching, and these implications will be explored in the second half of the book.

Task

In the transcription of spoken English below, can you identify features that are evidence of (a) spontaneity; (b) its interactive nature (i.e. reciprocity); and (c) its interpersonal function?

Mary:	I discovered that Adam used to be my neighbour yesterday.
Fran:	Oh really?
Mary:	Yes. In the conversation. Over a year, oh, well over a year ago.
Adam:	Yes we used to be neighbours about, about a year ago. About yeah well over a year ago we used to be neighbours in Glebe.
Fran:	But you never actually, did you know people in common?
Mary:	Yes.
Adam:	Yes definitely. We knew the peop . . . person who moved in there afterwards.
Mary:	Well he moved in while I was moving out. He lived with me for about four or five weeks but I was never there. But I couldn't believe it.
Adam:	[laugh] It's incredible.
Mary:	We used to think there were these strange people next door. And Adam used to think there were these strange people next door.
All:	[laugh]
Adam:	And now we KNOW there were strange people next door.
Mary:	No doubts yeah.

(Authors' data)

---

2 The vocabulary of conversation

Introduction

What characterizes the vocabulary of conversation? For example, how many words do speakers typically use? What distinguishes the lexis of casual conversation from more formal and less spontaneous forms of spoken language, and from written language? How many – and which – words do you need, to be able to take part in conversations in a second language? These are some of the main issues dealt with in this chapter. The point needs to be made, however, that the notion of *vocabulary item* is going to be stretched to include not only *single* words, but groups of words, and not only *lexical* items (such as those that would be included in a learner's vocabulary list) but items that have a grammatical or discoursal function. This expanded notion of lexis is in keeping with current thinking that views the boundaries between grammar and lexis, and between discourse and grammar, as fuzzy in the extreme. Nevertheless, for convenience, this chapter groups a variety of conversational phenomena under the general term *vocabulary*.

Much of the evidence for the description that follows draws on the findings of *corpus linguistics* and so a brief outline of the principles and goals of this discipline is in order. A *corpus* (plural *corpora*) is a collection of actually occurring texts (either spoken or written), stored and accessed by means of computers, and available for study and analysis by grammarians, lexicographers, teachers and language learners. Corpora can vary in size from fewer than a million words to several hundreds of millions (as is the case with both the COBUILD corpus and the British National Corpus (BNC)). Whereas in the early days of corpus compilation the size of the corpus was a major priority (the bigger the better), nowadays the corpus's representativeness is considered more important. Specialized corpora that target a particular discourse community (such as teenagers or language learners) or particular registers (such as academic, legal, or business texts) are now common. The first corpus to collect naturally occurring spoken data on a large scale was the Longman Spoken and Written English Corpus (the LSWE corpus). Biber *et al.* (1999) describe how the data were collected:

The sampling for the conversation subcorpus was carried out along demographic lines: a set of informants was identified to represent the range of English speakers in the country (UK or USA) across age, sex, social group and regional spread. Then these informants tape-recorded all their conversational interactions over a period of a week, using a high-quality tape recorder. All conversations were subsequently transcribed orthographically, for use in lexicographic and grammatical research.

(1999: 29)

Nearly one thousand speakers were recorded, each producing on average around 7,000 words per hour (or a little under 120 words a minute) and thereby yielding approximately 6.5 million words of text. This represents roughly a sixth of the total LSWE corpus, on which the *Longman Grammar of Spoken and Written English* (Biber *et al.*, 1999) was based, an important source of data for this and the following chapters.

One of the first corpora to target only spoken language was the CANCODE (Cambridge and Nottingham Corpus of Discourse in English) corpus (see McCarthy, 1998). This corpus aims to gather data representative of specific contexts, both professional and social, in which unrehearsed, non-formal spoken language is produced. It currently consists of around 5 million words of transcribed conversation (Adolphs and Schmitt, 2003). This project has generated a great number of research studies on the subject of spoken language (including its lexical characteristics), a bibliography for which can be found in McCarthy (1998). A smaller corpus of spoken language is OZTALK, jointly held at Macquarie University and the University of Technology, Sydney – a source of many of the examples in this current study. Analysis of corpus data is facilitated by the use of *concordancing* software, such as Scott's *WordSmith Tools* programme (Scott, 1999).

Corpus data is particularly fruitful as a source of information about the *frequency* of individual items (whether of lexis or of grammar), and about an item's typical co-textual environments, including its *collocations*. In this way, they are able to uncover recurrent patterns in the language. For example, corpora show that the sequences *nice and* [adjective] and *good and* [adjective] often serve to intensify the force of the adjective, as in these examples (from OZTALK):

<S 01> You should have it at night so you go in bed *nice and clean.*
<S 03> *Nice and fresh.*

Glow zones are *good and heavy.*

Corpus data show that *nice and* [adjective] is far more frequent than *good and* [adjective]. Moreover, *good and* tends to combine with adjectives that have negative connotations (*good and sorry*), while *nice and* combines with favourable and unfavourable adjectives alike (data from Biber *et al.*, 1999). Moreover, as Hoey points out, 'corpora are not just important for the study of the minutiae of language – they are central to a proper understanding of discourses as a whole' (2005: 150), a point he demonstrates with this example:

> In 51 examples of *I know* drawn from a small corpus of casual conversation . . ., 26 are either the first words of a turn or within one or two words of the beginning of a turn (e.g. *Yeah I know, No no I know*), suggesting that *I know* is typically primed positively for turn beginnings; none are conversational-initial [i.e. no examples of *I know* begin a conversation].
>
> (Hoey, 2005: 150)

Hoey concludes that 'there is no aspect of the teaching and learning of a language that can afford to ignore what corpus investigation can reveal' (*ibid.*). In that spirit, much of what follows is informed by corpus linguistics.

2.1 Lexical size

In terms of the number of words they need to control, the demands placed on speakers and listeners are considerably fewer than they are for writers and readers: 'From the small amount of evidence available, it seems that about half the words needed to understand written English are needed to understand spoken English', notes Nation (1990: 85). Schmitt cites an analysis of a corpus of Australian English (Schonell *et al.*, 1956) which suggests that 'a person can largely function in every-day conversation with a vocabulary of 2000 words' (Schmitt, 2000: 74). On the basis of computer counts of word frequency, McCarthy notes that 'there is usually a point where frequency drops off rather sharply, from hard-working words which are of extremely high frequency to words that occur relatively infrequently' (1999: 7). The drop-off point, according to McCarthy, is situated around about 2000 words down in the frequency ratings, leading him to conclude 'that a round-figure pedagogical target of the first 2000 words in order of frequency will safely cover the everyday core' (*ibid.*). However, Adolphs and Schmitt (2003), in comparing the Schonell *et al.* word list with one derived from the CANCODE corpus, found that the top 2000 word families in fact provide only around 95 per cent coverage, rather than the near 100 per cent claimed by Schonell *et al.* (Note that the researchers refer to word *families*, not individual words. A *word family* is a base word plus its inflexions and its most common derivations, a concept that correlates more or less with the *headwords* of a typical dictionary.) Adolphs and

Schmitt admit, though, that 'there is almost no research which explores the percentage of words which need to be known in order to operate successfully in a spoken environment' (2003: 432). They therefore tentatively suggest that 2000 word families may be a useful starting point but that '3000 word families (providing coverage of nearly 96 per cent) is a better goal if learners wish to minimize their lexical gaps' (2003: 433).

This figure, however, is based on a broad cross section of native speaker contexts, including professional and academic registers, in the UK and Ireland, and does not necessarily represent the lexical needs of most learners, especially those learning English as an International Language (McKay, 2002). For such learners, the 95 per cent coverage of a native speaker's lexical coverage represented by 2000 words would seem to be more than sufficient, and the effort involved in learning a further 1000 words in order to gain one percentage point extra coverage seems out of all proportion to the gains in communicative efficiency that might be made. In fact, the target need not even be as high as 2000 – West (1960) developed a minimum adequate speech vocabulary for learners of English of just 1200 words (compared to the minimum 2000 words for dealing with written language). This, he argued, would be sufficient for learners to say most of the things they would need to say. Moreover, even fewer words would still give the learner (theoretically at least) an advantage, since, in spoken language, a little goes a long way: McCarthy and Carter (1997) point out that whereas the 50 most frequent words in written text cover 38.8 per cent of all written text, the top 50 spoken words cover 48.3 per cent – that is to say almost *half* – of spoken text.

Nation (1990), while recommending a basic speaking vocabulary of 2000 words (equivalent to the *General Service List* [West, 1953]), points out that 'to speak English it is not necessary to have a large vocabulary. In developing learners' spoken English vocabulary it is best to give learners practice in being able to say a lot using a small number of words.' (1990: 93). One way of economizing on vocabulary size is the use of *vague language* (Channell, 1994), such as *thing, stuff, . . . and things like that, . . . or so, . . . or something, . . . or whatever* (see below). Repetition is also more tolerated in informal speech than in written language. Repetition has both an interpersonal and a textual function (see below), but it also allows learners to achieve an acceptable degree of conversational competence using limited lexical means.

2.2 Lexical density and lexical variety

Repetition, combined with a reliance on a relatively limited number of high frequency words, accounts for the fact that there is typically a lower *lexical density* and less *lexical variety* in conversation than in other registers. (We are using the term *register* here in the sense that it is used in Biber *et al.* (1999) to mean 'particular kinds of text', such as fiction, academic prose and newspaper language; in Chapter 5 we will refine this definition somewhat.) As we saw in Chapter 1, lexical density is a measure of the ratio of the text's *content* words to its *function* words. Content words are words that carry a high information load, such as nouns, adjectives and lexical verbs. Function words are those that serve mainly a grammatical purpose, such as articles, auxiliary verbs and prepositions, to which should also be added *inserts*, i.e. words like *hmm*, *yeah*, *yuk* and so on, that are inserted freely into talk and which primarily serve an interactional and interpersonal purpose (see below). The fewer the content words, in proportion to function words and inserts, the lower the lexical density. Of all registers, both spoken and written, conversation has by far the lowest lexical density. This is because talk tends to carry a much lower information load than written text, an effect in large part due to the spontaneity of most speaking compared to the planned nature of most writing. Also, as Stubbs (1996) points out, talk is not only produced in real time but has to be understood in real time. Hence, conversational language must be more predictable. Because there are many fewer function words than content words in a language, the former are more predictable: 'We would expect, therefore, that written texts have a higher proportion of unpredictable lexical words, and that spoken texts have a higher proportion of more predictable grammatical words' (Stubbs, 1996: 73). Moreover, recourse to the immediate context using deictic language (i.e. words, such as *here, that, now*, which 'point' to the temporal or spatial context) and pronouns (*I, you, they*) may render explicit mention of referents redundant. Biber *et al.* (1999) note that, in conversation, pronouns are by far the most frequent class of function words.

Low lexical density is particularly the case in what Ure (1971) called 'language-in-action' – that is '[spoken] language being used directly in support of actions that are taking place at the moment' (McCarthy and Carter, 1997: 33). In the following segment of language-in-action talk, in which two people are playing a computer game, of the 142 total words (counting contractions as single words), only 49 are content words. (The content words are in bold and inserts in italics):

<S 01>   *No* **wrong way wrong way. Go** that **way** now **jump**
         over. 'B' **over** now **press** now **go down** there **get down**
         there. *No* **jump jump** through that **gap. Jump** and **get**
         up there. = = *Oh oh* you're **dead.**
<S 02>   = = *Oh . . . oh . . .* why?
<S 01>   Don't you **dare touch** that **thing** you'll **die.**

44

<S 02>	Did. Now what?
<S 01>	Well no just **wait** 'til that **comes** now **get** that. **Get** that one. . . . *See* just **get** it.
<S 02>	Now what do I do?
<S 01>	**Get** the **feather**. You've **won**.
<S 02>	*Yes*. There you go. How do you **fly**?
<S 01>	I'll **show** you. Now!
<S 02>	Now what do I do?
<S 01>	I'll do it.
<S 02>	*No no no no* just **tell** me. Which **way**? . . . This **way**?
<S 01>	*No* that **way**.
<S 02>	Now what **way**?
<S 01>	**Get down** there. [4 secs] Now *yeah* like that. Now **walk**. *Oh* **turn back turn back**. *Oh*. You're **dead**.
<S 02>	Oh.

(OZTALK: UTS Macquarie University Spoken Language Corpus)

Lexical variety is the measure of the different words in a text. In the conversational extract quoted on page 7, in which a hailstorm is being discussed, there are 205 'running words' or 'tokens' (that is, 205 words altogether) but, owing to the repetition of a number of these, only 111 different words, or 'types'. *Monday*, for example, is repeated four times. The 'type – token ratio' is therefore 0.54: this is the measure of the text's lexical variety. The extract from the newspaper about the same hailstorm, on the other hand, with 142 tokens and 98 types, has a type–token ratio of around 0.70. Ure (1971) found that spoken texts generally had much lower ratios than written texts, confirming that the former show less lexical variation than the latter.

2.3 Lexical frequency

We have already noted (on page 43) that the 50 most frequent word types in a corpus of spoken text comprise nearly 50 per cent of all the word tokens in that text. That is to say, nearly half of all conversation consists of just 50 words, endlessly recycled. What are these 50 most frequent words – and are they the same as the 50 most frequent words in written corpora? McCarthy and Carter (1997) compared a 330,000 word corpus of written data with a similar-sized corpus of spoken data and found significant differences (see Table 2.1). For example, the list of the 50 most frequent words of written text consists entirely of function words: *the, with, but, are, when*, etc. The spoken list, on the other hand, appears to include some content words as well: *know, well, got, think, right*. A closer look at the data reveals that these words are elements of

Table 2.1. *Fifty most frequent words from 330,000 words of Cambridge International Corpus (CIC) written date (mostly newspapers and magazines) and 330,000 words of spoken data (CANCODE).*

	Written	Spoken
1	the	the
2	to	I
3	of	you
4	a	and
5	and	to
6	in	it
7	I	a
8	was	yeah
9	for	that
10	that	of
11	it	in
12	on	was
13	he	is
14	is	it's
15	with	know
16	you	no
17	but	oh
18	at	so
19	his	but
20	as	on
21	be	they
22	my	well
23	have	what
24	from	yes
25	had	have
26	by	we
27	me	he
28	her	do
29	they	got
30	not	that's
31	are	for
32	an	this
33	this	just
34	has	all
35	been	there
36	up	like
37	were	one
38	out	be
39	when	right
40	one	not
41	their	don't

Table 2.1. (cont.)

	Written	Spoken
42	she	she
43	who	think
44	if	if
45	him	with
46	we	then
47	about	at
48	will	about
49	all	are
50	would	as

discourse markers (*you know, I think, well* . . .). *Well*, for example, occurs nine times more frequently in spoken text than in written text. Other common discourse markers and inserts include *and, yeah, but, oh, so,* and *yes* (which are, respectively, the 4th, 8th, 17th, 18th and 24th most frequent words in the spoken corpus).

As an example, here is a short conversational extract (in which a woman describes the experience of being massaged by her physiotherapist). It consists of 121 running words, of which 76 (italicized here) are in the top 50 words of spoken English, according to the CANCODE corpus (McCarthy, 1998: 122–3). That is to say, over 60 per cent of the talk comprises words that are in this high-frequency band.

<S 01>　　So *what's, what's this* physio?
<S 02>　　Mummy.
<S 03>　　Shh Sarah. Go *and* = = read your book.
<S 04>　　= = *To to to* talk *no I just* feel *like it's like* um . . .
　　　　　I can, *I* now *know what* sado-masochists feel *like you know*. *It's* kind *of there's a* . . . *there's a* sense *in* which *it's* pleasurable *to be* tortured . . . because *you know it's* doing, *not for* sexual pleasure *in this* case, *but* because *you know it's* doing *you* good 'cause *I I* lie *there and it's like* someone's *got a* knife *in* my back = = *and is just*
<S 02>　　= = Mummy.
<S 04>　　absolutely *just* gently pulling *it right* along *for* bit after bit *you know and I just* moan *and* groan.

　　　　　　　　　　　　　　　　　　　　　　　(OZTALK)

However, the fact that it would be all but impossible to sustain a coherent conversation using *just* these words suggests that frequency alone is not an adequate criterion on which to base the design of a lexical syllabus. Since many of the high-frequency words are function words or inserts and hence carry little informational load, a speaker knowing only such words would be severely constrained in terms of the topics at his or her command.

Nevertheless, a common core of frequently occurring words might provide learners with a critical mass on which they can then build for their own particular purposes. McCarthy (1999) argues the case for the 2000 most frequent words forming such a 'core lexicon'. He also points out that these 'heavy duty words' can be grouped into at least nine significant categories (excluding function words, which he groups separately as grammatical rather than lexical items). These nine equally important categories are:

- **modal vocabulary** – the modal auxiliaries (*would, can, might,* etc) and other ways of expressing degrees of certainty or necessity, such as *seems, possible, certain, maybe, apparently,* etc;
- **delexical verbs** – i.e. such high-frequency verbs as *do, make, take* and *get* that form common collocations with nouns, prepositions and particles, such as *take a break, make a mistake, get back,* etc;
- **interactive words** – i.e. words that signal the speaker's attitude or stance, such as *just* (as in *it was just amazing*), *actually, really, quite, literally;*
- **discourse markers** – whose function it is to organize the flow of talk and to manage its interactivity: *so, anyway, right, ok?* (see below for more on discourse markers);
- **basic nominal concepts** – 'such as *person, problem, life, noise, situation, sort, trouble, family, kids, room, car, school, door, water, house, TV, ticket,* along with the names of days, months, colours, body parts, kinship terms, other general time and place nouns such as the names of the four seasons, the points of the compass, and nouns denoting basic activities and events such as *trip* and *breakfast . . .'* (McCarthy, 1999: 8);
- **general deictics** – i.e. words that situate the talk in terms of time and place, such as *now, then, here, there, this* and *that;*
- **basic adjectives** – especially those that have an evaluative function, such as *nice, lovely, different, good* and *bad;*
- **basic adverbs** – especially those referring to time and frequency (*today, yesterday; normally, generally*); to manner and degree (*suddenly, fast; totally, especially*), as well as sentence adverbs (*basically, hopefully,* etc) – a category that overlaps with both the modal and interactive categories;
- **basic verbs for actions and events** – such as *sit, give, say, leave, stop, put, enjoy,* etc.

McCarthy argues that the above categories might provide useful organizational principles in the design of a lexical syllabus.

48

Other features of spoken language relating to lexical frequency that have been noted by researchers include the higher incidence of adverbial phrases (Crystal, 1980), and the lower incidence of nouns (Biber *et al.*, 1999) in spoken data. Whereas nouns tend to outnumber verbs in written text (e.g. in academic and news texts there are three to four nouns per lexical verb), in conversation the ratio between verbs and nouns is roughly 1:1.

2.4 Lexical repetition

A distinctive characteristic of conversation is repetition, at the level of words, of grammatical structures, and of discourse features. In this section we look at repetition at the word and phrase level, and in particular at the way the repeated use of *keywords* serves to make talk both cohesive and coherent. In the following extract the topic of the conversation (*renin/ rennet*) is explicitly signalled in the repeated use of these two words – four and eight mentions respectively in fewer than a hundred words.

Text 2.1: Junket

Kath:	I made junket when I was in the first year of secondary school. It's the only time I've ever come across renin in my life. Is it something to do with rabbits?
Simon:	It's weird. No, it's cows' stomachs.
Nick:	What?
Kath:	Cows' stomachs? Renin?
Simon:	The setting factor. The jelly factor.
Kath:	you put it = = in junket.
Scott:	= = in junket
Simon:	= = in cheese. You put it in cheese.
Kath:	Now have you ever eaten a junket?
Simon:	It's the same stuff as rennet. Rennet = =
Nick:	= = rennet? = =
Simon:	= = rennet.
Kath:	= = Oh rennet.
Simon:	Rennet
Kath:	Is rennet rennet or renin?
Hilda:	Is it something = =
Kath:	= = no renin is some pills aren't they?
Simon:	That's 'Rennies'.

(Authors' data)

Listeners are likely to be in no doubt as to what the conversation – at this point – is *about*. The more than usual frequency of the words *renin* and

Table 2.2.   Keywords in **Pigs** *text (data extracted using* WordSmith Tools *[Scott, 1999])*

Word	Number of occurrences in Pigs text	% of Pigs text	Number of occurrences in BNC sample	% of BNC sample	'Key-ness'
pig	9	4.27	22	>0.01	28,492.0
dead	5	2.37	302	0.01	656.5
they	10	4.74	13,015	0.61	52.5
was	11	5.21	16,138	0.76	49.8

rennet in this text (neither word occurs once in the two-million-word British National Corpus [BNC] sampler CD-Rom) suggests that these are *keywords* – that is, those words 'whose frequency is unusually high in comparison with some norm' (Scott, 1999). (The norm is typically a large corpus of text.) Their unusual frequency makes the keywords in a text reliable indicators of that text's topic.

In the following extract (from Crystal and Davy, 1975), a frequency comparison between the words in the text and the two-million word corpus on the British National Corpus Sampler CD-ROM shows that the words that appear with more than usual frequency are: *pig, dead, they, was* (see Table 2.2). In fact, these four words capture the essence of the story the speaker is telling:

Text 2.2: Pigs

A: Oh and one pig died because it ate too much.
B: Oh really?
A: Oh it was revolting. They were terrible, the pigs.
C: Oh.
A: They made a dreadful row in the morning when it was feeding time and one pig it was, erm a young pig about that size you know, middling and erm it was dead and it was lying there. I'd never seen a dead pig before. Absolutely stiff.
B: The children saw it, did they?
A: Oh they were engrossed you know.
C: Oh yes.
A: It was marvellous. Erm they thought this was wonderful and erm they they asked why it was dead and er the farmer apparently didn't want his wife to know because he'd overfed them before and she'd been furious and of course he was trying to keep it from her but all the kids were agog about the dead pig. And *** was telling them not to tell the farmer's wife = =

D: = = Yeah
A: and all this. So, this pig was absolutely dead, so they put it
      on, they have a sort of smouldering heap that smoulders all
      the time so they went to burn the pig and all the kids
      [laughs]
C: [laughs]
A: hanging over the gate watching this pig and they were very
      er very taken that the pig had died because it had eaten too
      much, you know.
D: What a marvellous death.

The statistical information shows that the word *dead*, for example, occurs five times in the Pigs text, comprising 2.37 per cent of the total words in the text, whereas the same word occurs 302 times in the two-million word BNC corpus, a mere 0.01 per cent of the total corpus. The calculation of how unusual the frequency of *dead* is in the Pigs text is done by a software program (Scott, 1999) that cross-tabulates the two frequencies and performs a test of significance on them. This yields the word's 'key-ness' i.e. 656.5. By comparison, the frequency of the word *pig* is hugely significant, with a key-ness rating of 28,492. Knowing which words are *key* in a text can help the language teacher make decisions about which words may need to be given special attention – e.g. by being pre-taught – in order to ensure an understanding of the gist of a text.

The reiteration of lexical items is an important means of achieving discourse cohesion. So far we have been talking about direct repetition – but there are other ways in which a lexical item can be re-introduced into discourse. Categories of lexical repetition that have a cohesive function, according to the model of cohesion propounded by Halliday and Hasan (1976), include:

1. direct repetition, e.g. *a pig* → *the pig*;
2. use of a derived form, e.g. *smouldering* → *smoulders*; *dead* → *died* → *death*; *ate* → *eaten*;
3. use of a synonym, or near-synonym, including a hyponym, e.g. *engrossed* → *agog* → *very taken*; *children* → *kids*;
4. use of a superordinate, e.g. *pig* → [*animal*];
5. use of an item from the same lexical set, e.g. *ate* → *feeding time* → *overfed*.

The net effect of these different ways of repeating an item, along with the use of referring pro-forms (e.g. *it, they*), makes the Pigs text extremely cohesive. Moreover, the core propositional content of the text is instantiated in synonymous clusters such as *pig died* and *dead pig*. These are in turn repeated, forming a *lexical pattern* (Hoey, 1991) that

51

ripples throughout the text. Two patterns that serve to connect the Pigs text are, respectively: *pig + die + overfed*, and *children + engrossed*. Thus:

> one *pig died* because it *ate too much* → *it* was *dead* → a *dead pig* → *overfed them* → *it* was absolutely *dead* → the *pig* had *died* because it had *eaten too much*

and

> [the *children*] *they* were *engrossed* → *they* thought this was *wonderful* → the *kids* were *agog* → *they* were *very taken*

An accurate summary of the story can be constructed simply by combining these two propositions: *one pig died because it ate too much; the children were engrossed.* The reiteration of these two notions helps the listener construct an accurate *schema* for the story, that is, a mental representation of the sequence of events and their relation to one another. Hence this reiteration can be said to contribute to the text's *coherence* (i.e. its capacity to make sense) as much as its *cohesion* (its property of being connected). Proof of the success of this strategy in the Pigs story is speaker D's comment: *What a marvellous death!* which serves to combine elements of both of the text's dominant themes.

Repetition, then, serves a *textual* function, contributing to both the cohesion and coherence of a text. But it also has an *interpersonal* function – what Tannen (1989) refers to as its interactional function. This typically occurs across speaker boundaries, as in this example (where a group of four people are talking about the arrangements for a wedding), where direct repetitions of another speaker's utterances (or parts of utterances) are italicized:

Text 2.3: Wedding arrangements

Female 1:	And who's the other person?
Female 2:	His sister-in-law.
Male:	My *sister-in-law*.
Female 1:	Who's she this one = =?
Male:	= = Jenny.
Female 2:	Jenny. She's she's awful. She's the . . .
Male:	A pain.
Female 2:	Sit them together.
Female 3:	*Sit them together.*
Female 2:	That's what we were thinking.
Male:	Yeah.
Female 2:	*Sit them together.*
Female 3:	Yeah.
Female 1:	Would they get = = along?
Female 2:	= = That would give Wolfgang a clear message.

Male:	[laughs] Mmm?
Female 1:	Would they get along I mean as as [inaudible]
Male:	No I don't think so no they *would*n't *get* = = *along.*
Female 1:	= = Not at all?
Male:	I don't think so.
Female 2:	The only thing is Margaret will realise about = = you know . . .
Female 1:	= = How does she, does she know that's the way you feel? = =
Female 2:	= = I don't I'm not sure I mean, I = = don't and um I have to . . .
Male:	= = What?
Male:	She knows I don't like her.
Female 1:	Aaah.
Female 2:	Oh *she knows*.
Male:	*She knows.*

(OZTALK)

The above is a good example of Tannen's contention that 'repetition not only ties parts of discourse to other parts, but it bonds participants to the discourse and to each other, linking individual speakers to a conversation and in relationships' (1989: 51–2). Carter argues convincingly that repetition – including the re-arrangement of elements in a repeated pattern – is an inherent characteristic of talk, and creates 'what might be termed an affective convergence or commonality of viewpoint' (2004: 8). In this short example, a group of women, anticipating a meal, celebrate their shared female-ness:

<S03>	Well here's to, here's to a nice = = dinner.
<S01>	= = Here's to the girls.
<S03>	Secret women's business.
<S04>	Oh.
<S03>	Or women's secret business or whatever.
<S01>	Or women's business secrets.
<S04>	Mmm. Women's business full stop.
<S01>	[laughs]

(OZTALK)

McCarthy (1988) identifies a further feature of lexical repetition across turns, which he calls *relexicalization*. This occurs when speakers do not repeat each other verbatim but instead use paraphrase or a (near-) synonym, as in the extract about the wedding arrangements quoted above:

Female 2:	Jenny. She's she's awful. She's the . . .
Male:	*A pain.*

53

McCarthy and Carter comment that 'this taking up of one's own and others' lexis is the very stuff of conversational progression; it is one of the principal ways in which topics shade almost imperceptibly one into another, while interpersonal bonds are simultaneously created and reinforced by the "sharing" of words' (1997: 35).

2.5 Vague language

Vagueness is a feature of spoken language that is often censured in the false belief that it is evidence of woolly thinking. It is true that the demands of spontaneity may account for some instances of vagueness – for example, the substitution of specific lexical items by words like *thingummy* or the over-use of *sort of* to fill pauses. However, vagueness – and specifically *hedging* – has, primarily, an interpersonal function. Hedging is a form of deliberate imprecision so as to avoid either committing oneself, or imposing on one's interlocutors. (Holmes [1995] suggests that this function may be more characteristic of women's talk – see the section on gender in Chapter 4.) In the following extract, in which the topic (women who swear) is potentially sensitive, the speaker may be hedging so as not to sound dogmatic or to give offence (hedges are italicized):

> You know you're considered really rough, if you swear. You know you're *sort of* one of the girls that work in the bar or you know like in some of the Asian countries you know? You certainly don't come from a good family *and stuff like that*. [. . .] Like if you're working in a small industry? Um – or in a small office *or something* then it's considered anti-social to swear, to carry on like that.

> (Authors' data)

Note the use (in this last extract) of the tags *and stuff like that* and *or something* – what Channell (1994) calls *vague category identifiers*. In the following extract vague category identifiers are italicized (but note also other expressions of vagueness, including the use of the indefinite pronouns *something* and *somebody*):

> Di: I'd like to just go out and find something a bit unusual that wasn't off the rack of sixty of the same dress and do like my sister did the dress that she wore, *something like that*, and um standing out in a field *or something*, you know? Just a nice setting, you know?
> Jess: Mmm.
> Di: And go back to somebody's place and have a cup of tea or scones *or something*.

Jess: Right, yes.
Di: You know? None of this hooha . . .
Jess: Quite sort of simple and . . .

(Authors' data)

Other vague tags include: *and things*; *and/or stuff like that*; *and all that sort of thing*; *or what have you*; *and this, that and the other*.

Words like *stuff* and *thing* are highly productive in that they can substitute for almost anything. In the following extract a researcher uses *stuff* in reference to the conversational material she has been recording, where to use a more technical term (such as *data*) might have distanced her from her interlocutors:

> And I turned it [the tape recorder] off and all that *stuff* is what would have been great in terms of language and *stuff* like when you because it was just like when you two had already relaxed and forgotten that I was there. You know when you were talking about all that *stuff* about being vindictive and all that sort of *stuff*.

(Authors' data)

Vagueness, then, serves the interpersonal function of conversation, and is considered perfectly acceptable. In fact, not to be vague about facts and figures might be considered inappropriately pedantic. In this extract the time expressions (italicized) are made approximate by the use of vague quantifiers (*a few, around*):

Sue: How long have Mark and Jenny been together for?
Judy: *A few years, quite a few years.*
Sue: Have they managed to keep that private?
Judy: Yeah.
Sue: That's pretty amazing that they've sort of yeah.
Judy: They're only young. It's *probably around 6 months* before it got out.

(Authors' data)

Other common ways of expressing vague quantities include *loads of*, *a lot of*, *a bit of*, *umpteen*, *some*, *several*, *a few*.

Placeholder words (Channell, 1994) such as *thingy, thingummy, whatsisname* and *whatsit* are used to substitute for more specific terms that the speaker either has forgotten or does not wish to mention. Again, the use of these can have an interpersonal function in gossip sequences, signalling a shared lack of respect for a third party:

Fran: Well Anne-Marie gets mistaken for a man all the time.
Mary: Oh yes, all the time *What's her face* in Bed Allocations.
Fran: Leonie, yeah.

(Authors' data)

For language learners vague language – such as the use of words like *stuff* and *whatsit* – has an obvious attraction, as it allows them to compensate for gaps in their lexical knowledge, including those created by online processing demands. In this sense, vagueness devices provide the means for realizing a useful production strategy (see p. 200). It is important, though, that learners do not overgeneralize such devices to registers where they would not be thought appropriate.

2.6 Fillers

Some instances of vague language – like *sort of* – double as *pause fillers*, that is, those linguistic devices used to fill a momentary hesitation occasioned by the demands of real-time processing pressure. The most frequent pause fillers (also called *hesitators*) are *er* and *erm* (conventionally transcribed as *uh* and *um* in American English). In Text 2.2 (Pigs), the following short segment contains three instances (in italics):

> it was marvellous *erm* they thought this was wonderful and *erm* they they asked why it was dead and *er* the farmer apparently didn't want his wife to know

Filling a pause (as opposed to leaving it unfilled) is a convenient way of signalling that the speaking turn is not yet finished. Had the speaker not filled the pause after 'marvellous' (above) her interlocutors might have concluded she had finished her turn. Hence fillers tend to occur at potential transition points in the talk, especially those which happen to be the site of online planning pressure, such as (as in the above example) at the beginning of a clause.

Verbal fillers (Stenström, 1994), such as *well I mean, well erm you know*, are typically used to buy time at the beginning of a speaking turn. Female 2's turn, from the conversation about wedding arrangements quoted in Section 4 above, contains a number of hesitation devices, including verbal fillers and repeats, before she is finally interrupted:

> Female 2:   I don't, I'm not sure, I mean, I don't and = = um
> I have to . . .
> Male: = = What?

Note that *I mean* is classified here as a verbal filler, but (as we shall see in the next section) it can also function as a discourse marker to signal the speaker's pragmatic intentions. This double function is shared by a number of other common expressions, such as *actually, obviously* and *you know*. Stenström (*op. cit.*) comments that, from a discourse-strategic point of view, they often operate as *stallers*, as the speaker 'buys time' in order to plan what to say next.

2.7 Discourse markers and other inserts

As we shall see in Chapter 4, conversations are more than the simple layering of successive independent utterances, one upon the other. Just as sentences in written text are sequenced and organized into larger thematic units such as paragraphs, talk, too, is segmented into loose topically coherent macrostructures. Topics are broached, commented on, developed, extended, replaced, retrieved . . . and all this conversational flux is continuously shaped and negotiated by the interactants. Crucial to this collaborative organizational 'work' is the inserting of *discourse markers* and other *interactional signals* into the stream of talk.

Discourse markers (Schiffrin, 1987) serve to show how what is being said is connected to what has already been said, either within a speaker's turn or across speaker turns. This relation works at the local level, by connecting adjacent utterances (with *and*, *but*, *so*, for example), and at the global level, by segmenting the flow of talk into its larger chunks (or macro-structures) such as signalling the opening or closing of a conversation, or the introduction or resumption of a topic, through the use of markers like *firstly*, *finally* or *anyway*. In this extract, discourse markers are italicized:

> Di: Is she on holidays? I haven't seen her since I've been back.
> Judy: No no she's not. [laughs]
> Di: *Actually* it's really ridiculous. *I mean* – I think she's made
>   an absolute fool of herself, *because* there is a girl who rings
>   him every afternoon from Canberra. He originally comes
>   from Canberra this guy *and* I often used to pick up the
>   phone. Now it's not her.
> Sue: *So* you don't know what's going on?
> Di: I think she's atrocious.

> (Authors' data)

In the above extract, by preceding an utterance with *actually*, the speaker signals that what follows is not only evident to her but may not be evident to other parties, including her immediate interlocutors. In this instance, the speaker uses it globally, to signal the (re-)introduction of a topical thread that has been temporarily interrupted. *I mean* signals that what follows re-states, clarifies, or otherwise elaborates what has just been proclaimed. (As we saw in the last section, both *actually* and *I mean* also have a strategic function as stalling devices.) *Because* indicates a causal connection between what has just been stated and what follows. *And* simply indicates that what follows is thematically relevant to what has preceded it, without making the logical connection explicit. (In this case *and* picks up the thread of the narrative after a parenthetical aside.) *So* implies that what follows is a consequence of what has just been said. In this extract *I mean, because, and* and *so* are all used to make connections at the local level – that is, across or within adjoining utterances.

Interactional signals (Stenström, 1994), on the other hand, are those devices that function to facilitate the cut-and-thrust of online talk. They are analogous to the signals (both gestural and mechanical) that car drivers make to one another in order to indicate their intentions (and their reactions to the intentions of other drivers) as they negotiate heavy traffic: 'I'm turning in this direction', 'I'm going to cut in here', 'You go ahead . . .', 'Sorry, my mistake', 'That was dumb!' etc. Interactional signals include attention signals (*hey!*), response elicitors (*right? OK? eh?*), and their associated response forms (*yes, no, OK*). These also include *back-channel devices* such as *mm, uh huh*, which function as feedback to the speaker, signalling that the message has been understood and confirming that communication is on course. Carter and McCarthy (2006) use the term *pragmatic markers* for all of the above categories, i.e. verbal signals that both monitor and stage the unfolding talk.

Here are some common pragmatic markers, and their respective functions:

- *right, now, anyway*   These are global discourse markers in that they each provide a *frame* to the discourse, i.e. they mark the beginning or closing of a segment of talk. Stenström notes that, while all three have this framing function, 'generalizing somewhat, *right* looks backward, *now* looks forward, while *anyway* looks both ways' (1994: 64).

- *well*   This is a very common way of initiating a turn and linking it to the preceding turn, with the general function of deliberation, i.e. 'let me think about that'. Often *well* serves to mark the onset of a contrast, e.g. a difference of opinion.

- *oh*   This is typically used either to launch an utterance or to respond to the previous speaker's utterance, and signals a shift in the speaker's orientation to the ongoing flow of talk, often with implications of surprise or unexpectedness – hence it can stand alone as an *interjection* – and

	often combines with other inserts, as in *oh yeah*, *oh no*, *oh well* etc.
• *and, but, or*	The discourse function of these conjunctions parallels their grammatical function in that they are used to connect discourse, both within and across speaker turns – *and* marking some kind of continuity, *but* marking a contrast, and *or* marking an option. *And* and *but* are used globally to connect whole discourse units when, for example, they signal the return to a previously mentioned topic.
• *so, because*	These conjunctions can also be used to signpost discourse moves, both locally and globally, and signal that what follows is (respectively) the *result* or the *cause* of what has been mentioned.
• *y'know, I mean*	These markers serve to gain and maintain attention on the speaker – the first by appealing to the hearer's shared knowledge, and the second by signalling that some kind of clarification is going to follow.

As in the case of *y'know* and *I mean*, discourse markers may consist of more than one word. Longer expressions that function to signal conversational transitions include such fixed or semi-fixed phrases as *in (actual) fact, that reminds me, by the way, speaking of which, I tell you what*. Biber *et al.* (1999) use the term *overtures* for longer expressions that serve to launch utterances, of which they list the following examples:

I would have thought
Like I say
The question is
There again
What we can do is
You mean to say
Going back to . . .

(For more on lexical phrases, see below.) In this extract, topic shifts are signalled by conventionalized overtures (in italics):

Judy: *Reminds me of* my Mum with a Christmas tree every year. We've got pine trees along the back fence. Mum gets up the barbie or whatever she can stand on, she just yanks off a branch and there's the tree.

All: [laugh]

> Di: Your Mum lives in Newcastle doesn't she?
> Judy: *Getting back to, getting back to* this business . . .
> Di: Oh yes. [laughing]
> Judy: How come he phoned your mother?

(Authors' data)

Other inserts often grouped along with discourse markers because of their role in marking transitions, signalling speaker attitude, or in managing interactions are the following:

- greetings and farewells (*hi, bye bye*)
- interjections (*oh!, wow!, ugh!*)
- polite formulae (*thank you, sorry, please*)
- hedges (*I think . . ., . . . actually*)
- expletives (*shit!, bloody hell!*)

It is important to note that there is considerable overlap in the functions of discourse markers, and that the overlap extends to other categories of inserts, such as vague language and fillers (see above).

Discourse markers typically occur at the beginning of speaker turns, because they are signalling devices. *Tails* (sometimes called *tags*), on the other hand, come at the end of an utterance and serve either to qualify the utterance or to solicit listener involvement. Typical tails of the former type are *actually, really*, as well as vague category identifiers (mentioned above) such as *and stuff like that*, while involvement solicits include *you know? ok?* and question tags: *does she? isn't it?* etc. Tails are dealt with in more detail as a feature of the grammar in Chapter 3; for the moment we are concerned primarily with the way they are realized lexically.

In the following extract, in which a group of women co-workers are having their lunch break, different inserts, including discourse markers and tails, are highlighted, numbered and categorized:

Text 2.4: Flowery shirts

> Sue: (. . .) *'cause*[1] he had really flowery shirts on and jeans.
> Di: *Mmm*[2].
> Sue: *I mean*[3] he looks respectable *but*[4] it's not the sort of == get up for a hospital.
> Di: == *No*[5].
> ?: Tailored pants?
> Di: Tailored pants and sports shoes.
> Sue: *I just thought*[6] that Jerry knows that he doesn't want to wear any sneakers.
> Di: *Mmm*[7]
> Sue: Runners *and*[8] *I just thought*[9] Jerry wears jeans and em,

running shoes *and*[10] I think they might check him too, I'm just letting you know == *so that*[11] you might make a mention to him

Di: == *Right*[12].

Sue: *Mmm*[13].

Di: They'd like tailored slacks.

Sue: *That's right*[14]

?: *Mmm*[15].

Di: Slacks. *'Cause*[16] I don't think Jerry's got a great deal of money at the moment?

Judy: No I don't.[17] == A bit unfair *really*[18]

Di: == He was unemployed for a while.

Sue: *It is*[19].

Di: *'Cause*[20] tailored slacks are a bit expensive.

Sue: *They are*[21]. *I mean*[22] Jerry looks quite respectable too *you know*[23] it's nothing

Judy: He is neat *isn't he*[24].

Sue: *Oh well*[25] *Anyway* [26]*I just thought*[27] we'd let you know that they're on the look out *anyway*[28].

Di: *Okay*[29]. I'll tell him. It's a wonder they'll let you wear your sweatshirt.

Sue: *Yeah*[30] it's a wonder *isn't it*[31] [. . .] *Anyway*[32] they're on the lookout

Judy: *Okay*[33], *fine thanks*[34]

Di: *Well*[35], at least Mark's got that in his favour. Mark does dress exceptionally well *doesn't he*[36]?

(Authors' data)

1 = discourse marker, signalling a causal relation
2 = interactional signal – a backchannel device, conveying agreement
3 = discourse marker, signalling elaboration, explanation
4 = discourse marker, signalling a contrastive relation
5 = interactional signal, a response form, conveying agreement (to a negative statement)
6 = overture (utterance launcher), signalling personal stance
7 = as 2, i.e. interactional signal – a backchannel device, conveying agreement
8 = discourse marker, signalling thematic connection
9 = as 6, i.e. overture (utterance launcher), signalling personal stance
10 = as 8
11 = discourse marker, signalling purpose
12 = interactional signal, a response form, conveying agreement
13 = as 2
14 = as 12
15 = as 2
16 = as 1
17 = as 5
18 = tail, qualifying preceding statement
19 = interactional signal, response form conveying agreement
20 = as 1
21 = as 19
22 = as 3
23 = discourse marker – appeal to shared knowledge
24 = question tag, soliciting agreement

25 = discourse marker, signalling closure of one topic and onset of a shift in conversation flow
26 = discourse marker, signalling return to a prior topic
27 = as 6
28 = tail, similar function to 26
29 = as 12
30 = as 12
31 = as 24
32 = as 26
33 = as 12
34 = interactional signal, polite formula for thanking
35 = discourse marker, initiating a contrast (from talking about Jerry to talking about Mark)
36 = as 24

2.8   Routines and lexical phrases

No discussion of the vocabulary of conversation would be complete without considering the important role played by fixed and semi-fixed multi-word phrases (or lexical *chunks*) in the achievement of conversational fluency. We have seen already how many discourse markers and 'overtures' consist of more than one word and are formulaic in nature: *I mean to say, to be frank, I take your point but . . ., on the other hand . . .* Similarly, many expressions of vagueness are multi-word units: *sort of, something like that, what's her face.* Pawley and Syder (1983) propose that speakers have at their command a repertoire of literally hundreds of thousands of such items – what they called 'lexicalized sentence stems' – and Nattinger and DeCarrico note that 'a significant amount of conversational language seems to be highly routinized as prefabricated utterances' (1992: 114). Sorhus (1976, quoted in Aijmer, 1996) estimates that fixed expressions come at the rate of one every five words in spoken English.

Multi-word phrases, lexical chunks, lexicalized sentence stems, prefabricated utterances: the wide range of terms used to identify this feature of language attests to the difficulty of defining exactly what characterizes a lexical phrase. Wray's definition (of what she calls a *formulaic sequence*) seems as good as any:

> a sequence, continuous or discontinuous, of words or other meaning elements, which is, or appears to be, prefabricated: that is, stored and retrieved whole from memory at the time of use, rather than being subject to generation or analysis by the language grammar.
>
> (Wray, 2000: 465)

For the purposes of studying the language of conversation it is useful to distinguish between those multi-word items that constitute a single grammatical unit (such as a verb, noun or adjective) but have no specific pragmatic function, and those that are both grammatical units *and* pragmatically functional. The former (which, following Nattinger and DeCarrico (1992), we will call *lexical phrases*) are perhaps best thought of as being 'big words' – i.e. items in the user's mental lexicon, stored alongside, and to all intents and purposes indistinguishable from, single-word items – what Wray (2000) calls 'standard phrases with simple meanings'. The second type of chunk, which we will call *conversational routines* – or just *routines* (after Aijmer, 1996) – include multi-word versions of the kinds of sentence add-ons and inserts that we have been looking at in this chapter, i.e. fillers, discourse markers, utterance launchers, tags, expletives etc. So, while lexical phrases such as *out of the blue*, *bits and pieces*, *curry favour* etc. can be assigned a part-of-speech category and a 'dictionary meaning', they do not perform a specific socio-interactional function (Wray, 2000). Phrases like *how do you do* and *on the other hand* do have a socio-interactional function (Wray, 2000). *How do you do?* functions as a formal greeting; *on the other hand* signals that what follows contrasts with what preceded it.

Wray (2000) points out that the storage and deployment of what we are calling lexical phrases facilitates production, in that they save valuable processing time that might otherwise be spent on generating utterances 'from scratch'. Thus, as fluency facilitators, they are primarily speaker–oriented. Conversational routines, on the other hand, are aimed at achieving efficient comprehension in the interests of social and interactional objectives, and hence are more hearer–oriented. In classroom terms, therefore, learning a stock of lexical phrases is likely to improve fluency, while learning conversational routines will have positive effects on overall intelligibility.

Many multi-word items are *idiomatic* (*so long, on the other hand, out of the blue*) while others are *non-canonical*, that is, they do not follow orthodox grammatical constructions: *long time no see, the sooner the better, God willing*.

Multi-word items can also be divided into at least two types on the basis of their form: those that are fixed, and those that allow some degree of variation. Examples of fixed routines are: *how do you do?*, *at any rate*, *what on earth!*, *I beg your pardon?* Examples of routines which contain elements that allow substitution and which are therefore variable, or semi-fixed, include: *have a nice day, it seems to me (that), frankly speaking, would you like a . . .? Have a nice day* is a semi-fixed salutation, in that it allows such variations as *Have a nice morning/ evening/time* and *Have a good/fabulous/pleasant day. Would you like a . . .* functions as an invitation or offer and is followed by an open slot. This latter kind of construction is called by Nattinger and DeCarrico a *sentence builder*, that is 'a lexical phrase that provides the framework for whole sentences'

(1992: 42). The category of sentence builder includes what we have referred to earlier as *utterance launchers*. Common conversational examples of sentence builders that serve to launch utterances include:

that reminds me of X
speaking of X
it seems to me that X
I remember X-ing
as far as I can X
the thing is that X

Such phrases regularly appear in materials designed for the teaching of conversation, and have been described as *conversational gambits*. Keller and Warner (1988), for example, distinguish between *opening gambits* (such as *guess what!* . . .; *the truth of the matter is* . . .), *linking gambits* (such as *in fact, that's why* . . .), and *responding gambits* (such as *you're joking!*; *poor you*).

A further distinction can be made to include those (usually fixed) routines that are conventionalized social formulae, particularly greetings (such as *good morning, so long, have a nice day*), as well as ritualized ways of thanking, apologizing, making requests and making offers. Examples include (after Aijmer, 1996):

thanking	*thank you very much*
	many thanks
	thank you ever so much
	thanks a million
apologizing	*I'm sorry*
	I'm awfully sorry
	beg your pardon
	excuse me
requests	*would you mind . . .?*
	how about . . .?
	do you think you could . . .?
	I wonder if you could . . .
offers	*I'll . . .*
	shall I . . .?
	would you like to . . .?

In the following extract, conversational routines, including sentence builders and social formulae, are in bold, while other lexical phrases are in italics:

> Judy: I had this friend and she came to me and she's saying, she was talking about, **you know**, she understood **sort of** problems of a mixed marriage and **I thought she**

	meant, **you know,** an inter-racial **sort of** marriage, **you** **know** and **all she meant was** between a Roman Catholic and an Anglican
Jes:	Really?
Judy:	Yeah. **I mean** *in this day and age*! **It's just** = =
Jess:	= = Incredible, **isn't it?**
Di:	But some people are really *back in the Ark.*
All:	Yeah.
Di:	Because **I mean to say** his parents are a mixed marriage.
Deidre:	**Bye bye.**
Judy:	Bye.
Di:	Bye.
Jess:	**See you later.**

(Authors' data)

Using corpus data, Biber *et al.* (1999) identify a form of extended collocation that they term a *lexical bundle*. Lexical bundles are defined as sequences of three or more words that show a statistical tendency to co-occur in particular registers. They are distinguished from the other kinds of multi-word units that we have been looking at by their lack of idiomaticity, by their frequency, and by the fact that they are often structurally incomplete. Some common lexical bundles that occur in conversation are:

> *do you want me to*
> *going to be a*
> *I said to him*
> *I don't know what*

(Biber *et al.*, 1999: 989)

Lexical bundles are more common in conversation than in other registers: about 30 per cent of the words in conversation occur in a recurrent lexical bundle, or 45 per cent if two-word contracted bundles (such as *I don't, you can't*) are taken into account, compared to just over 20 per cent in academic prose (Biber *et al.*). Figure 2.1 overleaf (Categories of multi-word items) provides a summary of the different phrase types mentioned in this section.

---

lexical phrases – "standard phrases with simple meanings": *time out*; *black and blue*; *head over heels*; *the bitter end*; *missed the boat* etc.

---

conversational routines – phrases that perform a socio-interactional function, including:

- fillers: *I mean, sort of*
- discourse markers: *on the other hand, by the way*; *in other words*
- sentence builders and utterance launchers: *would you like a . . . ? the thing is . . . ; do you mind if I . . . ? that reminds me of . . .*
- tags/tails: *. . . and so on*; *. . . or something*; *. . . you know what I mean?*
- expletives: *bloody hell*; *holy smoke*
- social formulae
  - greetings: *nice to see you*; *have a nice day*
  - thanks: *thanks a lot*
  - offers: *would you like a lift?*
  - etc

---

lexical bundles – frequently recurring word sequences: *have a look at . . . yeah I know but . . . if you've got a . . .*

Figure 2.1 Categories of multi-word items (or *chunks*)

2.9 Appraisal and involvement

The interpersonal nature of conversation requires speakers to demonstrate their involvement in, and commitment to, the flow of talk, by expressing their personal stance and attitude towards what they themselves are saying (or what their interlocutors are saying or have just said). Given the social function of conversation, speakers also need to demonstrate their 'membership' credentials to the immediate social group. This accounts for the prominence, in conversational data, of the language of *appraisal* and *involvement*. Martin and Rose (2003) have developed an evaluative framework for the analysis of attitudinal meanings in text. In this section we will look at two of their categories, *appraisal* and *involvement*.

Appraisal refers to the language 'resources used to negotiate emotions, judgements and valuations, alongside resources for amplifying and engaging with these evaluations' (Martin, 2000: 144). It includes a range of expressive devices, such as the use of highly coloured adjectives (*stunning, awful, hideous, amazing* etc.) which are in turn frequently intensified by the use of adverbs such as *incredibly, totally, really, just,* etc. It can also be realized through the use of verbs that express likes and dislikes, such as *hated, adored, loathed, loved*, etc. Martin and Rose (2003) describes three categories of appraisal: *affect* (the expression of personal feelings, such as pleasure and satisfaction, and their opposites); *judgement* (the expression of social sanctions and social esteem) and *appreciation* (the expression of opinions).

Tables 2.3 to 2.5 (after Martin, 2000) expand these categories and provide both positive and negative examples of each.

Involvement refers to the language resources used for indexing group membership, and includes the use of names and other address terms (such a *mate, darling, sir*), slang, swearing and taboo language, jargon, foreign expressions, catchphrases, and anything else that is likely to be recognized as 'in-group' language by the other members of the group.

Eggins and Slade (1997) have extended the analysis of involvement to include an analysis of humour in casual conversation. Their authentic all-male workplace conversations contain many examples of involvement language. In the following extract, involvement lexis is italicized:

John: [eating lunch]
Harry: You've got a mouthful of *bloody* apple-pie there. I know that. He can't speak now even if he wanted to. You're a *guts*, Casher.
John: Oh yeah?
Keith: You're getting fat too. You'd better watch that heart.
Harry: You know when you're a – when you become a *bloody blackfella* you gotta share all these *goodies* with your bloody *mates*.
John: Yeah? == You want some?
Harry: == Your Aussie *mates*. No no

Table 2.3.   Categories of affect (after Martin 2000: 151)

Affect: How do you feel about it?

Category	Meaning	Positive examples	Negative examples
un/happiness	How happy did you feel?	*happy, cheerful, over the moon*	*down, sad, miserable, distraught*
in/security	How secure did you feel?	*together, confident, composed*	*uneasy, anxious, freaked out, worried*
dis/satisfaction	How satisfied did you feel?	*interested, absorbed, caught up in, engrossed, like*	*tired, fed up, hate, exasperated*

Table 2.4.   *Categories of judgement (after Martin 2000: 156)*

Judgement			
Category	Meaning	Positive examples	Negative examples
social sanction	How moral?	*good, right, moral, upright, ethical*	*immoral, wrong, cruel*
	How believable?	*credible, believable*	*deceitful, dishonest*
social esteem	How strongly committed?	*brave, strong, self reliant*	*cowardly, weak*
	How usual/ destined?	*lucky, blessed, fortunate, extraordinary, normal, outstanding, remarkable*	*unfortunate, unlucky, cursed, ordinary, peculiar, odd*
	How able?	*skilful, competent*	*incompetent*

Table 2.5.   *Categories of appreciation (after Martin 2000: 160)*

Appreciation: What do you think of it?			
Category	Probe/test	Positive examples	Negative examples
reaction	What did you think of it? Mental process of cognition: I think/know/ understand it was . . .	*nice, neat, wonderful, fascinating, stunning lovely, beautiful, splendid, great, exhilarating*	*uninviting, repulsive horrible, boring, dull plain, ugly, awful, revolting, irritating, depressing*
composition	How did it go together?	*harmonious, simple, elegant, spacious, restrained*	*complex, extravagant, cramped, overdone*
valuation	How did you judge it?	*deep, meaningful, challenging, daring, relevant, profound, touching*	*shallow, meaningless, insignificant, irrelevant*

This short extract contains six involvement lexical items, all based on one interactant teasing another. Friendly ridicule in the all-male group, in these particular cultural contexts, appears to serve the function of creating solidarity and expressing 'mateship'. Far from being considered offensive, it is considered a hallmark of group membership, and with people new to the group it is a way of establishing shared ways of seeing the world, and shared perceptions. The function of teasing is, therefore, to establish similarity and in-group membership in these contexts.

Appraisal is a grading system, a cline from negative to positive where the speaker invites a response by evaluating. It is, in a sense, open to negotiation whereas involvement (for example swearing) is an indexical system: it is a system of inclusion or exclusion where there is no space for negotiation. An analysis of these evaluative, interpersonal meanings provides a picture of how the participants in conversations build up solidarity and how they position and reposition listeners.

In the following extract (a continuation of the workplace conversation cited above) one speaker, John, is quizzed by his workmates about his recent naturalization. Instances of both appraisal and involvement language are highlighted:

John: Well I went there and this, eh this *pretty* girl come in. She's *beautiful.*
Steve: What she said?
John: She said, 'Come in'. Started to talk, you know? She's Italian. *Only this big* – she had *beautiful* eyes, *mate.* My wife next me, she's *only* talking to me.
All: [laughter]
John: I said she can answer the question.
Keith: Was she *Eyetalian Eyetalian* descent was she?
John: Yeah. Oh she's been here ten years she said.
Steve: She's naturalized too.
John: She said, 'I'm, I'm *very happy* here in Australia but *only one thing.*'
Keith: What'd she *wanted?*
John: She said, 'We've got no relatives here.'
Harry: You should have told her to have some *bambinos* . . .

(after Eggins and Slade, 1997: 117–8)

2.10 Implications

With regard to the classroom, the implications of the above discussion of the vocabulary of conversation might include the following:

- Learners need to acquire a critical mass of high-frequency words – around 1,500 – to equip them for the productive demands of casual conversation.
- This spoken 'lexicon' will need to include a high proportion of modality terms and deictic expressions, as well as the vocabulary to express basic nominal, verbal, adjectival and adverbial concepts.
- Learners need a range of common lexical items used to express emotion and attitude (appraisal lexis).
- Conversational fluency can be enhanced by the use of a range of fillers, lexical repetition devices, vague terms, and routinized lexical phrases.
- In order both to negotiate the flow of talk and to signal involvement, a basic repertoire of discourse markers and interactional signals is essential.
- Techniques for hedging, such as the use of vague language, are important if the interpersonal goals of conversation are not to be compromised.
- A memorized bank of fixed phrases, including social formulae and 'conversational routines' (or gambits) will provide the means to achieve a range of conversational purposes.

With regard to this last point, it is probably fair to say that basic conversational competence, including the management of openings and closings, turn-taking, relinquishing turns and so on, in a foreign language revolves principally around having a store (or 'tool-box') of appropriate routines – what we will call *lexical phrase knowledge*. Richards suggests that 'conversational routines typically have to be learned and used as fixed expressions' (1990: 75). And the sooner the better, as Nattinger and DeCarrico point out:

> Lexical phrases are integral to conversation, for they provide the patterns and themes that interlace throughout its wandering course. These phrases are essential, even for rudimentary 'communicative competence', yet texts that present conversational language do not do so in any systematic way that would permit learners to form connected, functional discourse.
>
> (1992: 121)

A systematic approach to the teaching of conversational routines would involve categorizing these routines according to their discourse functions, and selecting exemplars according to criteria of frequency and coverage (i.e. the range of contexts in which an item is encountered). In Chapter 9 we will look at ways this might be done.

Task

In the following extract (*Feature Walls*) four women are talking about home decoration. The speakers are:

<S01> Female, aged 41, Anglo-Australian, sister of <S04>, daughter of <S03>;

<S02> Female, aged 38, Anglo-Australian; her partner's mother is <S03>;

<S03> Female, aged 74, Anglo-Australian, mother of <S01> and <S04>; and

<S04> Female, aged 47, Anglo-Australian, sister of <S01>, daughter of <S03>.

Read the transcript and

1. estimate the lexical density (i.e. proportion of content words to function words);
2. estimate the lexical variety (i.e. the proportion of types to tokens: see page 45);
3. identify any words that you think are low frequency, i.e. not within the 2,000 most frequent words band. (You can check using a recently published learners' dictionary, most of which tag words for frequency);
4. identify any *keywords*, i.e. any words whose frequency is unusually high in the extract;
5. identify instances of indirect repetition, e.g. derived forms, synonyms and antonyms, co-hyponyms, or items from the same lexical set (see page 51);
6. identify any instances of speakers repeating (parts of) a previous speaker's utterance;
7. identify any instances of vague language;
8. identify any fillers and stallers;
9. identify any discourse markers and interactional signals;
10. identify any possible lexical phrases and conversational routines;
11. identify any likely lexical bundles; and
12. identify any instances of appraisal language.

Feature Walls

<S01> I think it's a nice blue.
<S04> I quite like it.
<S03> I think I find it too too.

\<S01\>	Mother's = =
\<S04\>	= = I'm going to paint my new room, like I wanted I'm going to paint the side wall a colour.
\<S01\>	Well I think, cause I I'm, it's lovely this terrific bold bright. Lesley's Lesley's = = got that.
\<S04\>	= = Lesley's, oh Lesley's house is = = gorgeous.
\<S01\>	= = That um you know = =
\<S04\>	= = Pink and yellow and = =
\<S01\>	= = She's got this, you know this terrific one wall which is just hot pink and it looks = =
\<S04\>	= = And it's great.
\<S01\>	And then she's got a beautiful royal blue couch right in front of it. It's the most uncomfortable couch in the world but it's, it looks terrific.
\<S02\>	Gorgeous.
\<S01\>	[laughs] But um
\<S04\>	Well that's what I thought I'd do in that room. I thought I'd just paint = =
\<S01\>	= = something bold yeah.
\<S04\>	something fairly bold along that middle wall = = that's you know that's
\<S03\>	Back to the fifties.
\<S04\>	What do you mean 'back to the fifties'?
\<S03\>	That's what you used to do in the fifties. Feature = = walls.
\<S02\>	= = Feature wall yes. = =
\<S01\>	= = Yeah but then they = =
\<S03\>	Darling just, I'm not
\<S01\>	[laughs]
\<S04\>	Just a strong colour. Just a nice . . .
\<S01\>	As long as it's not this blue. = =
\<S04\>	= = I painted my I painted my I painted my bedroom um bright yellow.
\<S01\>	Yes I like = =
\<S04\>	= = It's nice.
\<S03\>	I think there's, there's the colour I like is a sort of a buttery yellow. It's = = a
\<S04\>	= = Well I I my bedroom's quite smart.

(OZTALK)

3 The grammar of conversation

Introduction

There are at least two common misconceptions about the grammar of spoken language: it is assumed either that spoken grammar is simply written grammar realized as speech, or that spoken grammar is a less complex, even degenerate, form of its written counterpart. The first assumption seems to underlie the conventional pedagogic wisdom that the written grammar of the language is sufficient for the learning of both writing *and* speaking, as if the written grammar was the 'default' grammar, from which all language choices flowed. The following dialogue (from a textbook published in 1947) while extreme, exemplifies the way written language is often presented as if it were speech:

> The other day, on getting into the train, I found a Frenchman in my carriage, and the following conversation took place:
>
> Englishman: Good morning, sir. Isn't it lovely weather? Are you travelling far?
> Frenchman: No, sir, I get out at the first stop, the next station before Leeds.
> Englishman: Oh? Then I travel farther than you. I have to go as far as Glasgow. I get there early tomorrow morning. Do you know this line well? It is one of our best main lines.
> Frenchman: Oh no, not at all. It is the first time I have ever travelled on it; I have not been long in England . . . etc.
>
> (Hübscher and Frampton, 1947: 63–4)

The recognition that spoken language is characterized by, among other features, repetitions and simplifications – such as contractions, ellipsis and a lack of clausal complexity – began to emerge in teaching materials in the 1960s and 1970s. It may be no coincidence that, around the same time, dramatists and novelists were also attempting to capture the flavour of spoken language through the use of similar stylistic devices.

The grammar of conversation

This extract from a play by Pinter (1967, 1991: 49) shares some of the characteristics of the coursebook dialogue that follows it:

JOHN.	Cake, Granny?
MOTHER.	No, I've had one.
JOHN.	Have two.
FATHER.	I'll have one.
MOTHER.	He's had one.
FATHER.	I'll have two.
WENDY.	Here's a cup of tea, Mr Disson. Drink it. It's warm.
LOIS (*to* DIANA).	You're off to Spain quite soon, aren't you, Diana?
DIANA.	Yes, quite soon. (. . .)

A: What would you like to drink?
B: Beer, if you've got it.
A: I think so. Just a minute. Yes, here you are.
B: Thanks.
A: Cigarette?
B: No thanks, I don't. How's the family?
A: They're OK. Peter's gone to the States for a month.
B: Oh yes? Holiday? (. . .)

(Swan and Walter, 1984: 57)

Despite this acceptance of the distinctiveness of both written and spoken language, any differences were generally treated as being stylistic (i.e. a question of formality), or as resulting from the demands of performance factors, or simply as symptoms of laziness and lack of care. The distinction between what Saussure termed *langue* (that is to say, the underlying linguistic system) and *parole* (the actual utterances the speaker produces), was commonly invoked to describe – if not explain – the differences between written language and speech. Similarly, Chomsky distinguished between what he called *competence* and *performance*, and noted that 'a record of natural speech will show numerous false starts, deviations from rules, changes of plan in mid-course, and so on', but insisted that such performance phenomena 'cannot constitute the actual subject matter of linguistics' (1965: 4).

Thus spoken grammar continued to occupy an inferior position and seldom merited a footnote, let alone a full-blown description, in either descriptive or pedagogic grammars. Even the shift to a greater naturalism in coursebook dialogues only went so far. The following criticism by Crystal and Davy is just as applicable thirty years later:

74

People in textbooks, it seems, are not allowed to tell long and unfunny jokes, to get irritable or to lose their temper, to gossip (especially about other people), to speak with their mouths full, to talk nonsense, or swear (even mildly). They do not get all mixed up while they are speaking, forget what they wanted to say, hesitate, make grammatical mistakes, argue erratically or illogically, use words vaguely, get interrupted, talk at the same time, switch speech styles, manipulate the rules of the language to suit themselves, or fail to understand. In a word, they are not *real*.

(1975: 3)

More recently, the case for 'real English', including a recognition of the distinctive and systematic nature of spoken grammar, has been argued vigorously, particularly by researchers working with corpora of spoken language (such as the CANCODE corpus). Carter and McCarthy contend that 'written-based grammars exclude features that occur widely in the conversation of native speakers of English . . . and with a frequency and distribution that simply cannot be dismissed as aberration' (1995: 142). Biber *et al.* go further, and argue for the primacy of spoken grammar: 'Conversation is the most commonplace, everyday variety of language, from which, if anything, the written variety, acquired through painstaking and largely institutional processes of education, is to be regarded as a departure' (1999: 1038). Of course, this does not mean that the two grammars are so different as to deserve separate treatment. On the basis of their corpus data, Biber *et al.* conclude that so many language features are shared that 'the same "grammar of English" can be applied to both the spoken and the written language'. Nevertheless, as McCarthy points out, 'we should never *assume* that if a grammar has been constructed for written texts, it is equally valid for spoken texts. Some forms seem to occur much more frequently in one mode or the other, and some forms are used with different shades of meaning in the two modes' (1998: 76). In the rest of this chapter we shall be looking at those grammatical forms that occur more frequently, or are used differently, in casual conversation as compared to other registers.

3.1 Complexity

One issue that has attracted a good deal of attention is the apparent syntactic simplicity of casual conversation. This simplicity has been attributed both to its informal nature and to the constraints of real-time production. Halliday, however, takes issue with this view, arguing that 'the sentence structure [of speech] is highly complex, reaching degrees of complexity that are rarely attained in writing' (1985: xxiv). This is because, while the complexity of writing resides in the way lexical content is densely packed into fairly simple grammatical frames, 'the complexity of spoken language is more like that of a dance; it is not static and dense but mobile and intricate' (*ibid.*). This mobility and intricacy is in turn due to the fact that the context of spoken language is 'in a constant state of flux, and the language has to be equally mobile and alert'. He gives, as an example of the fluidity and intricacy of spoken language, the following:

> but you can't get the whole set done all at once because if you do you won't have any left to use at home, unless you just took the lids in and kept the boxes, in which case you wouldn't have to have had everything unpacked first; but then you couldn't be sure the designs would match so . . .

> (Halliday, 1985: xxiv)

Some evidence for this intricacy can be found in corpus data. Biber *et al.*, for example, note that 'speakers in conversation use a number of relatively complex and sophisticated grammatical constructions, contradicting the widely held belief that conversation is grammatically simple' (1999: 7). One example of this complexity that they identify is the use of complex relative clause constructions of the type *There's so many things that I want to learn*. . . . Nevertheless, they also note that the real-time production demands of conversation result, on the whole, in shorter and simpler clauses, less variation, and a reliance on certain more-or-less fixed sentence frames that are less grammatical than lexical in the way they are retrieved and deployed (1999: 964). McCarthy makes a similar observation: 'Anyone who looks at large amounts of informal spoken data . . . cannot fail to be struck by the absence of well-formed "sentences" with main and subordinate clauses. Instead, we often find turns that are just phrases, incomplete clauses, clauses that look like subordinate clauses but which seem not to be attached to any main clause, etc' (1998: 79–80).

In fact, the very terms *sentences, main clauses, subordinate clauses* etc. sit uncomfortably with spoken data. They belong to a 'text-on-the-page' view of language, where the constituents of sentences can be unpacked and analysed after the event, so to speak, producing what Brazil calls 'a hierarchical constituent-within-constituent account of how language is organised' (1995: 4). Such a product-derived account fails to capture the *processes* by which the grammar of speech is realized. Moreover, many features of spoken language – such as *heads* and *tails* (see below) – simply cannot be accounted for by 'sentence grammar'. Brazil, therefore, proposes a view of spoken grammar that is essentially dynamic, one in which we regard discourse as 'something that is now-happening, bit by bit, in time, with the language being assembled as the speaker goes along' (1995: 37). Such a view helps explain the seemingly fragmented, even inchoate, nature of transcribed talk. It may also put to rest the question of the relative complexity of written and spoken language: they are both complex, but in quite different ways.

To return to Halliday's example (quoted above), clearly the planning in advance of this utterance in its entirety, including the embedding within it of a number of subordinate clauses, would simply be beyond the capacity of most speakers' working memories, given that working memory has a span of only about seven items (whether single words or multi-word units). Moreover, the pause that would have been required in order to formulate such an utterance would have been unacceptably long for most conversational situations.

It is much more likely that the utterance was assembled in stages, each successive stage building on its predecessor, and each planned locally, so that the effect is something like the following (although in the absence of prosodic information – e.g. pausing and intonation – we can only guess):

but you can't get the whole set done all at once
+ because if you do
+ you won't have any left to use at home
+ unless you just took the lids in
+ and kept the boxes
+ in which case you wouldn't have to have had everything unpacked first
+ but then you couldn't be sure the designs would match
+ so . . .

The complexity is achieved not by embedding constituents within a predetermined sentence frame, but through the successive (and potentially limitless) accumulation of individual clause-like units. The logical connections between such units are indicated using discourse markers (*but, because, unless, in which case, so* . . .) to signal the incremental twists and turns of the speaker's train of thought. While the cumulative effect of these 'add-ons' appears syntactically complex, each segment is relatively simple – for example, every clause in the above text begins with *you*.

Nor is spoken language always conveniently packaged into clauses. In the following text, the segments in italics are non-clausal, that is they resist analysis in terms of combinations of subject and verb, or subject + verb + object, etc:

Chris: It's a nice area.
Doris: *Bardwell Park.*
Mark: Is it?
Gary: It's pretty dead. It's only a small shopping centre.
Chris: *Oh yeah, well* you don't really go to that shopping

centre. Where I live it's the worst shopping centre in
Sydney. They opened a new dress shop and I could see
the pink carpet going in and all and I thought *gee a nice
trendy dress shop. Thank goodness.* 'Cause there's
nothing there. You know what it is? *A middle-class
boutique for the middle-age set.*

Gary: *Yuck.* And everybody wears brown boots.
Doris: *Yeah?*
Chris: *Nothing worse. You know too, too dressy.*

(Authors' data)

Non-clausal material partly consists of a large class of items called *inserts*
(Biber *et al.*, 1999; see Chapter 2), which include response words (*Oh
yeah*), discourse markers (*well*), back-channel devices (*yeah?*), and interjections (*gee, thank goodness, yuck*). Inserts are stand-alone items – they
do not enter into syntactic relations with other structures. A second class
of non-clausal material consists of isolated phrases or clausal fragments
which *are* capable of forming elements of clause-and-sentence structures.
Hence they are called *syntactic non-clausal units* (Biber *et al.*, 1999).
Examples include answers to questions (*A middle-class boutique for
the middle-age set*), repetitions or elaborations of previous content
(*Bardwell Park*), and evaluative comments (*nothing worse*). In this short
exchange, syntactic non-clausal units are italicized, whereas inserts are
underlined:

Jessie: Can I borrow a biro <u>please</u>?
Di: <u>Pardon?</u>
Jessie: *A pen.*
Di: <u>Yeah.</u>
Judy: How are you *Jessie?*
Jessie: *Good.* How are you?
Judy: *Fine, not bad.*

(Authors' data)

A pen is syntactic as it is an ellipted re-phrasing of the question *Can
I borrow a biro?* while *good* is an ellipted form of the answer *I am
good.* (For more on ellipsis, see below.) Vocatives – where a speaker
addresses an interlocutor by name, such as *Jessie*, or by an endearment
(*sweetie*), or some other familiar term (*dad, mate*) – are considered to
be syntactic non-clausal units, in that they can be incorporated into
sentence structure (*My dad is a sweetie*). Inserts such as *please, pardon*
and *yeah*, on the other hand, operate 'outside' the domain of clausal
syntax.

Biber *et al.* (1999) use the term *C-units* as an umbrella term for both
clausal and non-clausal units, and consider such units to be the building

blocks of spoken grammar – what sentences are to written grammar. The following text (taken from Chapter 1) has been analysed into its component clausal (<Cl>) and non-clausal units (<NCl>):

Text 3.1: Hailstorm

(1) Odile:	. . . No <NCl>| I think I don't know many people who have been affected except you and I. <Cl>| That much.<NCl>|
(2) Rob:	|You don't know?<Cl>|
(3) Odile:	Well you know except for the neighbours.<NCl>|
(4) Rob:	|Oh a friend of ours in Paddington, they had to move out of the flat = =
(5) Grace:	|= = Mm.<NCl>|
(6) Rob:	because the whole = =
(7) Grace:	= = roof collapsed.<Cl>|
(8) Rob:	|The tiles fell through the ceiling = =
(9) Grace:	|= = Mm <NCl>|
(10) Rob:	into the room <Cl>| and they've actually had to move out completely. <Cl>|
(11) Odile:	|Oh really? <NCl>|
(12) Dan:	|And there was the little old lady over the road who . . . <Cl>|
(13) Rob:	|Oh yeah. <NCl>| [laughs] She was sitting in her living room <Cl>| and a hail stone fell through the skylight, <Cl>| |this old Italian woman. <NCl>| She had corrugated iron <Cl>|	but it fell through the skylight. <Cl>| It fell through the ceiling <Cl>| and landed in her lap when she was sitting = =
(14) Odile:	|= = Mm. <NCl>|
(15) Rob:	watching television. <Cl>|
(16) Dan:	|Watching *The X-files* probably. <NCl>|
(17) All:	[laugh]
(18) Odile:	|I'm so glad the kids were not there because you know that hole is just above Debbie's head. <Cl>|
(19) Rob:	|Yeah. <NCl>|
(20) Grace:	|Oh yeah. <NCl>|
(21) Rob:	|No, <NCl>| it is amazing more people weren't injured. <Cl>|
(22) Grace:	|Mm. <NCl>|
(23) Rob:	|So erm they go back to school tomorrow? <Cl>|
(24) Odile:	|Not tomorrow = = <NCl>|
(25) Rob:	|= = Monday. <NCl>|
(26) Odile:	|It's Sunday. <Cl>|
(27) Rob:	|Monday. <NCl>|
(28) Grace:	|Monday. <NCl>|

(29) Odile: |Monday. <NCl>|
(30) Rob: |Mm. <NCl>|
(31) Odile: |Yeah. <NCl>|
(32) Grace: |Is the school OK? <Cl>|
(33) Odile: |You mean, general damage? <NCl>|
(34) Grace: |Yeah. <NCl>|
(35) Odile: |I don't know. <Cl>|
(36) Rob: |The school's closed next to us, <Cl>| |yeah.
                <NCl>|
(37) Grace: |I was speaking to erm . . .<Cl>|
(38) Odile: |Oh my god <NCl>| I hadn't thought about that
                . . . <Cl>|

Note that, in this extract, there are 21 clausal units and 25 non-clausal units. This is unusual: corpus analysis suggests that the ratio of clausal to non-clausal units in conversation is roughly 2:1 (Biber *et al.*, 1999). The higher proportion of non-clausal units in the hailstorm extract may owe in part to the large amount of back-channelling that takes place, which in turn is an effect of the number of speakers.

3.2 Heads and tails

The complexity of spoken language, then, is achieved incrementally. One effect of this incremental construction – and one that the grammar of written language does not generally share – is that the body of the message is preceded and followed by optional slots into which matter (typically non-clausal) may be inserted, as in these italicized instances from the preceding extract:

> oh *a friend of ours in Paddington,* they had to move out of the flat

> she was sitting in her living room and a hailstone fell through the skylight, *this old Italian woman*

> I think I don't know many people who have been affected except you and I. *That much.*

These optional slots either before or after the body of the message are known, respectively, as *heads* and *tails*. The head slot typically consists of a noun phrase which serves to identify key information such as the topic and to establish a common frame of reference for what follows – whether a statement or a question:

> *Junket,* I mean you have junket and stewed rhubarb

> *Filing.* I'd love a whole day, one weekend, when there's nobody around to do it.

> *You know how kids* they always say if they can't get their own way they're going to kill themselves?

> *Good ground out there* is it? (cf: Is it a good ground out there?)

Where a narrative follows, the head slot can accommodate the *abstract* component of a story structure, according to Labov's (1972) model (see Chapter 5). The abstract is a short statement of what the story is going to be about:

> *Kedgeree,* I remember saying to my mum I've got to take a pound of fish next week we're making kedgeree

Note that noun phrase heads often result in such 'non-grammatical' constructions (by written grammar standards) as sentences with two subjects:

> [Where I live] [it]'s the worst shopping centre in Sydney.

> oh [a friend of ours in Paddington], [they] had to move out of the flat

> [The bloke behind], [he] can't see

> [His mate with him], [he] hit a tree.

Heads thus fulfil a discourse function, because one of their roles is to foreground the topical focus of what follows. Another discourse function of head-slot items is to flag the direction of the talk and its connection to preceding talk, and so it is common to find discourse markers and other interactional signals (see Chapter 2) in this position, as in the italicized examples in this short extract:

> Di: You cannot drink on the job
> Jessie: *Right yes* and if they did set him up what would they do? *I mean* how could you get him sacked?
> Judy: *Well* they just would-
> Di: *Really in a way* they don't really have to get anybody *I mean to say* if you are not doing the right thing and you feel there's this pressure on and they watch you like a hawk . . . in the end you're really going to crack

> (Authors' data)

While the head slot fulfils a largely prospective function, the tail slot is more retrospective in its use, serving to extend, reinforce, mitigate, clarify or otherwise comment on, what the speaker is saying or has just said. Typical tail-slot items are:

- *question tags*: Croatia's Yugoslav, *isn't it?* That Parramatta's a good side, *aren't they?*

- *interrogatives*: There's a nice big pub there, *no*? They started already *or*?;
- *reinforcement tags*: you're in trouble, *you are*;
- *noun phrase identifiers*: Yeah she's nice *Robyn*; They hate the Yugoslavs *the Croats*; Jeff's the other guy from Wollongong *that photo you saw*;
- *evaluative adjectives*: He drops them anywhere, *terrible*;
- *vague category identifiers* (see Chapter 2): you know high mass *and all the rest*; you trying to make me talk *or something*?;
- *comment clauses*: The things he does, *I don't know*; I was down there Sunday *I think*; That's a bit unfair *I reckon*.

Discourse markers and interactional signals can also occupy the tail slot, as in:

> Before we know it they've got Swiss bank accounts *you know*
> And, and as I said the language *you know I mean really*
> It's nice like that *though*
> Oh I shouldn't really do this *but*

Vocatives – such as *How are you, Jessie?*; *Good morning, brother* – are other common tail-slot items, and are more usually found in the tail slot than the head slot. If placed in the head slot, they tend to function as attention solicits, whereas tail-slot vocatives have the function 'of adjusting or reinforcing the social relationship between the speaker and the addressee' (Biber *et al.*, 1999: 1112). McCarthy and O'Keeffe (2003) use spoken corpus data to show that, in casual conversations, there is a fairly equal distribution of vocatives amongst speakers, and that this can be interpreted as a display of solidarity. This is consistent with Carter and McCarthy's contention that tails are 'an important part of what may be called *interpersonal grammar*, that is to say speaker choices which signal the relationships between participants and position the speaker in terms of his/her stance or attitude' (1995: 151).

In this fragment from a conversation between hospital clerical staff talking about paperwork (the 'sheets'), the tails are italicized:

Gary:	(. . .) Amongst the sheets, *you see*.
Pauline:	You doing the sheets, *are you*?
Gary:	Mmm. Which, which I don't know, they sort of grow overnight.
Pat:	It's exciting! *Sheets*. It's exciting.
Gary:	Mmm.
Bron:	We are going to have a lot of admissions to do this afternoon.
Pauline:	Is Jenny there, *by the way*? And what's she doing?

(Authors' data)

3.3 Grammatical incompletion

Because of the pressure of online planning, and the jointly constructed nature of conversation, spoken language is often ungrammatical, even by its own relatively 'relaxed' standards. For example, utterances are either left incomplete or non-standard usages arise through syntactic 'blending' – that is, where there is a grammatical mismatch between the start of an utterance and its completion. Here are some instances of typical incompletions and blends:

- *abandonment* (where the speaker abandons or re-starts an utterance):

  Odile: I'm so glad the kids were not there because you know that hole is just above Debbie's head . . .

- *interruption* (incompletion caused by the interruption of another speaker):

  Grace: I was speaking to erm . . .
  Odile: Oh my god I hadn't thought about that . . .

- *completion by other speaker:*

  Rob   . . . they had to move out of the flat because the whole . . .
  Grace: . . . roof collapsed

- *blending:*

  I think there's there's the colour I like is a sort of a buttery yellow.

The fact that such non-standard forms not only exist but are tolerated by native-speaker interlocutors suggests that to demand one hundred per cent accuracy in speaking activities in the classroom may not only be unrealistic but unwarranted.

3.4 Ellipsis

Unlike grammatical incompletion, ellipsis is the deliberate omission of items, such as subject pronouns and verb complements, that are redundant because they are recoverable from the immediate context, either the linguistic context or the situational one. We have already seen how a lot of non-clausal conversational material is elliptical, as in question-and-answer exchanges such as the following:

Chris: Is your wife working? She going back to work?
Gary: When she gets motivated I suppose
Chris: Good on her, stands her ground.
Chris: You going to stay in your mum's house?
Gary: Nah – moving . . . probably. Might move into a, Bardwell Park.

Here, the omitted elements have been re-instated between brackets:

Chris: Is your wife working? [Is] she going back to work?
Gary: [She's going back to work] when she gets motivated
I suppose
Chris: Good on her, [she] stands her ground.
Chris: [Are] you going to stay in your mum's house?
Gary: Nah [I'm] moving . . . probably. [I] might move into a,
Bardwell Park.

Note that omitted items can consist of single words and phrases (*is, she*) or whole clauses (*she's going back to work*). Commonly omitted items include sentence subjects (*[she]stands her ground, [I] might move . . .*), subjects and operators (*[I'm] moving*) and auxiliary verbs (*[Is] she going . . . , [are] you going*). Ellipses most frequently occur at the beginning of utterances rather than in their middle or at their end. This is because it is at the beginning of utterances that *given* (as opposed to *new*) information is usually incorporated – information that is more readily recoverable from the context, and hence redundant. Final ellipsis is common in replies to questions, or in comment questions (see below), where repetition is avoided by omitting any words following the operator (*do* in each of the following instances; omitted items in brackets):

Di S: Do you think women sw-swear as much here at each
other?
Judy: Oh they do [swear at each other] here.
Judy: I think they're awful.
Jess: Do you [think they're awful]?

'Ellipsis is pervasive in spoken discourse' (Carter and McCarthy, 1997: 14). This is particularly the case in language-in-action talk – that is, talk that accompanies the performance of some activity, where situational factors, plus the need for brevity and concision, render relatively elaborated language superfluous. In this highly elliptical extract, two girls (aged nine and twelve respectively), are making Christmas cards, with the occasional help of the father of one of them:

Father: So how's, how's it going?
Girl 1:   Going bad. Dad I want it to look like it's not really
added on. But how are we going = =
Father: = = Here. Roll of sticky tape.
Girl 1:   Clear sticky tape.
[Later:]
Girl 2:   Do you like that? Ah [2–3 inaudible words]
Girl 1:   Yeah.
Girl 2:   One in there.

Girl 1:   [sings to herself for 3 secs]
Girl 2:   Can I use the glue?
Girl 1:   Yep.
Girl 2:   Do you have a hole puncher?
Girl 1:   Ah yeah. Top drawer.

(OZTALK)

3.5 Deixis

Because conversation takes place in a shared temporal and spatial context (unless, of course, it is over the telephone), speakers frequently make direct reference to features of the immediate situation. They do this using *deictic* expressions. Deixis derives from the Greek term for 'finger' and is used to mean 'pointing with language'. In other words, using language devices such as personal pronouns, demonstratives (*this* and *that*), and adverbials (such as *here, there, now, then*), speakers can make reference to such features of the immediate context as themselves and the other people present (what is called *personal deixis*), the immediate space (*spatial deixis*), and the time (*temporal deixis*). Even on the telephone, speakers can 'point' to contextual features, using deictic expressions, as in **This** *is Dan. Is Louise* **there?** and *What's the weather like* **there now?** Deixis is mainly realized through lexical choices, but we have included it as part of the grammatical description of conversation since the bulk of the words that comprise deictic expressions are function words rather than content ones.

In a further extract from the Christmas card conversation (above), deictic references are italicized:

Father: Look *I* fixed *this*.
Girl 1:   *You* did?
Father: Okay.
Girl 1:   Thank *you*, Dad.
Father: No worries.
Girl 1:   Dad. Can *you* do *this* for *me*?
Father: *You*'ll have to press *this* extremely hard.
Girl 1:   Ah hm.
Girl 2:   And *you* don't have to use *that*.

(OZTALK)

The relatively high proportion of deictic expressions in casual conversation in comparison with other spoken genres, and the even higher proportion of deictic expressions in spoken language as compared to most written language, is one of the reasons why the reading of transcripts of conversation is so difficult. This is particularly so in the case of language-in-action talk (see above), as in the extract that was quoted in Chapter 2 (p. 44) where two boys are playing a computer game.

3.6 Questions

It goes without saying that conversation would be unsustainable without the use of questions. By definition interactive, dialogic and jointly constructed, conversation depends to a large part on questions to maintain its momentum and purpose. A coherent conversation that consisted solely of declarative statements is difficult to imagine. Indeed, the smallest unit of conversational exchange – the adjacency pair – frequently consists of some kind of question-and-answer exchange (see Chapter 4). This does not mean, however, that conversations have to start with questions. It is not uncommon for speakers to present facts or opinions in the form of declarative statements as a way of engineering a change of topic, as in this extract:

Chris:	I'm going to have a sleep in tomorrow, last day. Grand Final Day at Jubilee Oval tomorrow. Big day.
Gary:	Coliseum.
Chris:	Then they're going to have a drink for the parents, and a barbecue for the kids at Kingsgrove.
Gary:	In other words, it's going to be a piss-up for the parents.
Chris:	I don't think we'll go. I'll just take them to the barbecue and then we'll leave. I don't know anyone.

(Authors' data)

Nevertheless, it is unusual to find a lengthy sequence of turns without any form of question, even if it is only the speaker seeking confirmation that his or her listeners are still listening. Biber *et al.* have calculated that 'there is on average one question per every 40 words in conversation' (1999: 211). But they add that this figure is probably conservative since it is based purely on the number of question marks in transcribed data, and may not represent the full range of questions included.

Question types can be categorized in terms of either their form or their function. With regard to the latter, Tsui (1992) identifies three main functions: *to elicit information, to elicit confirmation* (of the speaker's assumption), and *to elicit agreement* (about something that the speaker believes is self-evidently true). Each of these functions is exemplified in this short extract:

<S01>	How many cats have you got? (= *eliciting information*)
<S02>	I don't have any but Philip's got two.

<S01>	Oh right.
<S02>	So and they sleep on my face basically. Or curled up which it doesn't matter which leg direction my legs are going they'll be here.
<S01>	It's very funny isn't it. (= *eliciting agreement*)
<S02>	Yeah.
<S01>	You don't like it? (= *eliciting confirmation*)
<S02>	Oh no I'm I'm fine with it.

(OZTALK)

In the following extract – in which two co-workers, John and Jo, are explaining to a third, Keith, the location of a football ground – questions are italicized and numbered for subsequent analysis:

Text 3.2: Football ground

John:	I estimate it took me, I was part down down the road from the time the game finished till the time I got home one hour. I couldn't get out. That's *you know how far it is from my place?* (1) About five miles, = = in the bush. Even dirt road, dirt road.
Keith:	= = Yeah. *It's a dirt road = = road through to your place.* (2)
John:	Yeah. No, where the ground was and that's where I had the car.
Keith:	*Whereabouts in Bonnyrigg is it?* (3)
John:	You know um where you keep going there, near the hostel.
Keith:	*Pass the drive in?* (4)
John:	Pass the drive-in, near the trots.
Jo:	Before you get to old Harry, *do you remember where old Harry used to live?* (5) *Have you been there lately?* (6)
Keith:	*Harry.* (7)
Jo:	*Have you?* (8)
John:	There's a nice big pub there, *no?* (9) On that road just on Anzac Drive.
Jo:	Yeah.
John:	Before you go to Elizabeth Drive, *right?* (10)
Keith:	*That's the turn that runs through like say from = = right through from Marylands*
Jo:	= = yeah
Keith:	*out through Smithfield and = =*
Jo:	= = That's it.
Keith:	*You've got the drive-in past the Shell place past the trots.* (11)
Jo:	Yeah as soon as you pass the drive-in, there's one, two . . . before one.

> Keith: On the right *is it?* (12) *Left or right* (13)?
> Jo: On the right.

With regard to syntactic form, questions can first be classified according to whether they take an interrogative or a declarative form. Notice that a number of Keith's questions in the above extract are syntactically indistinguishable from statements: (2) *It's a dirt road through to your place*; and the long question beginning *That's the turn that runs through . . .* (11). Likewise John's question (1) (*you know how far it is from my place*) is declarative in form. Context is the only clue that these are in fact questions. Even intonation is not a reliable guide (see below).

Declarative questions are relatively common in conversation compared to other registers – comprising roughly ten per cent of all question forms (Biber *et al.*, 1999). They function primarily as requests for confirmation: Keith's question (2) could be paraphrased as *Am I right in thinking that it's a dirt road through to your place?*

Questions with subject–object inversion – i.e. those that are interrogative rather than declarative in form – can be further subdivided into those that are fully independent clauses (such as (5) *Have you been there lately?*) and those that are elliptic (as in (8) *Have you?*, where *been there lately* has been omitted). Conversation tolerates a high degree of such fragmentation, since speakers normally share much more contextual – as well as co-textual – information than interactants in other registers. Another common type of truncated question is the question tag (e.g. *is it?* in *On the right is it?* (12)). Like declarative sentences, question tags function mainly to solicit confirmation and agreement and hence to facilitate and maintain involvement – they thus have a strong interpersonal function in conversation. This is clearly demonstrated in this sequence of a gossip exchange:

> Jess: Really.
> Judy: Yeah. I mean in this day and age! It's just
> Jess: Incredible *isn't it*?
> Di: But some people are really back in the Ark.
> All: Yeah

Holmes (1995) found that this facilitative use of question tags occurs more frequently in women's talk than in men's, lending support to the view that women tend to adopt a more supportive role in conversation – an issue that we will return to in Chapter 4. But, even discounting gender differences, question tags are extremely common: according to Biber *et al.* 'about every fourth question in conversation is a question tag; the most common type of question tag is negative' (1999: 211). Alternative question words that can substitute for question tags are words like *right?* and *no?* (as in John's questions 9 and 10 above), *yeah? innit?* and *don't you think?*

Elliptic questions and question tags comprise nearly half of all questions in conversational data (Biber *et al.*, 1999). As it happens, in the above extract (Text 3.2) seven of the thirteen questions are fragmented in some way, while three others are declarative in form. That leaves only three that are fully realized as independent interrogative clauses:

> Whereabouts in Bonnyrigg is it? (3)
> do you remember where old Harry used to live? (5)
> Have you been there lately? (6)

These can in turn be divided into yes/no (or polarity) questions (5 and 6) and *wh-* (or information) questions (3). Stenström (1994) calls the latter 'identification questions' since they ask for an answer that identifies the *wh* word (e.g. *whereabouts*). Yes/no questions, on the other hand, function to negotiate the status of shared knowledge. While both types are common in conversation, yes/no questions outnumber *wh* ones, a fact that to Biber *et al.* 'indicates that questions in conversation are used less to seek information than to maintain and reinforce the common ground among participants' (1999: 212). Eggins and Slade (1997) found that polarity questions and *wh*-questions can be distributed unequally amongst participants in conversations, reflecting a lack of reciprocity between interactants, in turn a function of power differentials. Again, there is an implication that a preference for certain question types might be gender-influenced.

Elliptic yes/no questions are common in conversation and serve less to elicit information than to maintain the conversational flow through demonstrating interest and involvement, i.e. as a form of back-channel device. They are sometimes known as *comment questions*:

> Gary: She's doing a BA on the side as well.
> Pauline: *Is she?* Well, that is no reason to be so arrogant.

Less common question types include *alternative* questions, of which Keith's *Left or right?* (13) is an elliptic example. Echo questions, where the *wh*-word is not fronted – as in *You did what?* – are used to express surprise and disbelief. *Rhetorical* and *self-answered* questions (as in John's: *you know how far it is from my place? About five miles*) are also common in conversation. Again these may sometimes be a symptom of the demands placed on speakers by the need to marshal their propositions in real time, as in this example:

> He was coming down this track in fact, I think it was *was it Perisher? No it wasn't*, uh I forget where it was

It is important to note that, as Stenström puts it: 'It should neither be taken for granted that all interrogative utterances can be interpreted as questions, nor that questions cannot take other than interrogative form' (1994: 97). Thus *Can you____?*, while interrogative in form, functions as a request. (*Can you lend me your pen?*), or even as an order (*Can you be quiet please?*). And a declarative sentence might, in context, be a question, even if uttered with falling intonation, as in this example from Coulthard and Brazil:

> A: So the meeting's on Friday.
> B: Thanks.
> A: No I'm asking you.
>
> (1981: 84)

Stenström concludes: 'What finally decides the function of an utterance is the actual speech situation, including the speakers' shared knowledge' (*ibid.*), an observation that applies, of course, not only to questions, but to all spoken language.

3.7 Tense and aspect

The way tense and aspect are used in conversation generally parallels their uses in other registers. That is, tense is used as a grammatical marker of time, while aspect serves to distinguish between verbal situations that are seen as in progress (or not) or complete (or not). However, there are important differences in the frequency and distribution of these verb forms – differences that reflect both the 'here-and-now' nature of conversation, as well as its largely interpersonal function.

The present tense is by far the most common tense in casual conversation, outnumbering past tense forms by roughly four to one (Biber *et al.*), a fact that 'reflects speakers' general focus on the immediate context' (1999: 457). It is used primarily to refer to current states or to current habitual behaviour, as in this extract in which a group of women are looking at holiday photos (present tense forms – including present perfect, but excluding modal verbs – are italicized):

Text 3.3: Beaches

> Judy: What *are* their beaches like? *Are* they pebbles?
> Di: You *get* sand, you *get* pebbles, you *get* yuck. This was a sandy beach, but as you can see it*'s* not really golden.
> Judy: You*'re* not riding on sand *are* = = you?
> Di: = = No . . .
> Judy: You *know* what you *look* like? You should be here?

	You should be in an Omo ad, you *know*, really you *got** the smile and then the bright lights.
Di:	There*'s* there*'s* sand.
Deidre:	And there*'s* rock.
Di:	Yeah well, further up the coast *is* all this rock. Imagine lying on that in your bikinis!
All:	[laugh]
Di:	They *go* down there with their little deck chairs . . .
Deidre:	And their shelves = =
Judy:	= = You can always tell English people at the beach
Deidre:	You can . . .
Judy:	They always *wear* their short socks and their sandals. *Have* you ever seen them?
All:	[laugh]

* in this instance *got* is considered an elliptical form of *have got*

(Authors' data)

Present tenses with past reference (also called the *historic present*) are sometimes used in narratives in order to create immediacy, either in setting the scene, or in order to signal the *complicating event* (Labov, 1972), as in this example (analysed in more detail in Chapter 5):

Text 3.4: Russell Stouffer mints

Irene:	I*'m* on a diet and my mother *buys* . . .
Zelda:	You're not!
Irene:	My mother *buys* these mints . . .
Zelda:	Oh yeh.
Irene:	The Russell Stouffer mints. I said, 'I don't want any Mum'. 'Well, I don't wanna eat the whole thing.' She *gives* me a little tiny piece, I *eat* it. Then she *gives* me another = =
Henry:	= = Was
Irene:	= = so I threw it out the window.

(after Schiffrin, 1987: 80–81)

Jokes in particular lend themselves to the use of the historic present (*There're these two goldfish in a tank. One of them says to the other, 'How do you drive this thing?'*). On the whole, however, tellers of narratives and personal anecdotes favour past tense forms over present tense ones, with only occasional shifts into the present. The majority of past forms in casual conversation occur in narratives. In the following short extract, the speaker constructs her narrative by weaving together past simple, past continuous, past perfect and present simple forms with all the skill of a film-maker varying between wide-angle shots,

91

flashbacks and close-ups (past tense forms underlined; present tense forms in italics):

> I <u>came</u> out I <u>was filing</u> the sheets and I'<u>d done</u> up to the 50s and I <u>was</u> coming out for a cigarette and I *sit* down, and the minute I <u>sat</u> down, <u>lit</u> up a cigarette, she <u>looked</u> out of the window and she *can* see me so I just sort of <u>slid</u> behind the boxes where all our papers *are*

(Authors' data)

Progressive aspect is found in past narrative (as in the above extract: *was filing, was coming*) to provide the narrative 'frame' for the key events in a narrative, as well as being frequently used for reporting verbs (see below). But on the whole progressive verb forms are relatively uncommon in conversation, being outnumbered by simple forms by roughly twenty to one (Biber *et al.*, 1999). Of these progressive forms the majority (70 per cent) are in the present (*ibid.*). Curiously, progressive aspect is more common in American conversational data than in British data (*ibid.*).

Perfect aspect is also far less frequent than simple forms in conversation, even taking into account *have got*, the single most common present perfect in British English. The present perfect is often used to comment on changes, such as when reporting news, or commenting on situations whose effects are evident at the time of speaking, as in these two extracts:

Extract (1)
Keith: *He's changed.*
Jim: *I have changed.*
Steve: *He's shaved* his mo' off.
Gary: You ought to see it. It's unbelievable.

Extract (2)
Pauline: What'*ve they done* to the seats?
Bron: They're all re-covered, yeah.
Pauline: With what?
Gary: Yeah, all the floors *have been redone.*
Bron: It was, it was velvet where I was.
Pauline: Mmm.
Bron: Which was up in the circle.
Pauline: Mmm.
Bron: Don't know what it was downstairs, but all the *paintings have been restored.*
Pauline: Oh good.
Bron: And all the gilt'*s been done* and the chandeliers *have been* . . .

In contrast to the progressive, perfect aspect is less frequent in American English than in British English (Biber *et al.*, 1999). Combinations of perfect and progressive aspect, as in the present perfect progressive, are even rarer, across all dialects. (This fact suggests that the amount of time devoted to these verb forms in conventional teaching materials may be somewhat disproportionate, a point that will be taken up at the end of this chapter).

Perfect aspect is most commonly found in its present form (*have been, have done* etc). The relatively rare past perfect (*had been, had done* etc.) has a 'backgrounding' function – typically referring back to a time prior to the main focus of a narrative:

> Jessie: And what was it like when you first saw him? Were you really = = nervous?
> Di: = = Well I was hanging out of a window watching him in his car, and I thought 'oh God what about this!'
> Jessie: [laughter]
> Di: And *he'd combed* his hair and shaved his eyebrows = = and
> Jessie: *Had you seen* a photo of him?
> Di: Oh yeah, I had photos of him, photos . . . and *I'd spoken* to him on the phone.
> Jessie: Did you get on well straight away?

(Author's, data)

McCarthy points out that the past perfect is often used in indirect speech reports (. . . *And then when I finally went they said I'd chipped this bone*; 1998: 74) and to provide background information of an explanatory or justificatory type:

> . . . Cooksie drove cos *he'd been driving all night* and he drove the minibus down

(McCarthy, 1998: 74)

The use of the past perfect to background information in this way suggests to McCarthy that the verb form has a discoursal macrofunction at a level beyond the sentence, allowing speakers to organize their message in terms of the relative importance of its propositions. The same may be said for the use of continuous aspect in narratives, which, as we have seen, is commonly used to frame events:

> I remember *we were sitting* for our analytical chemistry exam and I *was sitting* there, and I thought 'Geez I can feel something on my foot'. And *I am trying* to think, but there's something on my foot . . .

(Authors' data)

Such pragmatic uses of different combinations of tense and aspect are not always easily captured by traditional pedagogical rules, suggesting to

McCarthy that '[spoken] grammar is often most adequately explained by referring to contextual features and, above all, by taking into account interpersonal aspects of face-to-face interaction' (1998: 86). A case in point is the use of the passive voice, also very rare in talk. According to Biber *et al.*, only two per cent of finite verbs in conversational data are in the passive form, which they attribute to the fact that 'conversation, having a human-centred concern with people's actions, thoughts and stances, usually does not demote the subject, who is often the speaker' (1999: 477). However, to maintain topic consistency – and where the agent is either not known or can be taken for granted – the passive is sometimes employed, as in this extract (passive clauses are italicized):

Text 3.5: Richard

> Jessie: Mmm, what's happened about Richard?
> Judy: Ah about Richard. Ah nothing [laughs]. *He's been spoken to.* It'll be a a sort of a watch and wait = = something.
> Jessie: = = Yeah, what do you reckon is going to happen?
> Judy: Not a thing.
> Jessie: What could they do to him?
> Di: Richard's not a very nice person anyway. He just doesn't fit into the system in general. It's not nice what's happening to him, but the thing is he is em creating the situation just as much as what they . . . because *he's been caught drinking on the job* [whispers] which is no good you know and he hasn't been really doing his job properly anyway . . .

(Authors' data)

3.8 Modality

Modality is another area of grammar that is best understood by taking into account the interpersonal features of its contexts of use. Modality, very broadly, has to do with the way speakers indicate their attitudes or judgements with regard to the message in hand, as in utterances like *X probably happens* or *X should happen* or *I think X might've happened*, in contrast to bald assertions of fact of the type *X happens* or *X does not happen* or *X didn't happen*. Modality is signalled principally by the use of modal verbs (*must, may, will, could* etc.), along with the marginal modals (*need to* and *ought to*), and the so-called semi-modals such as *have to, be supposed to, be going to, had better*. However, as McCarthy points out 'large numbers of "lexical" words (nouns, adjectives, verbs and adverbs) carry the same or similar meanings to the modal verbs' (1991: 84–5).

Within a systemic functional framework, moreover, modality is a dimension of the *mood* system of a language, which can be broadly defined as that grammatical system that is centrally concerned with the expression of interpersonal meaning. Later in this section we will look briefly at how choices within this larger system are distributed in conversation.

Analysis of corpus data (e.g. Biber *et al.*, 1999) suggests that the use of fully modal, marginal modal, and, especially, semi-modal verbs is more common in conversation than in other registers (such as news reports, fiction or academic prose). This is hardly surprising, given conversation's largely interpersonal function and the fact that modality is strongly associated with the expression of interpersonal meaning. Eggins, for example, notes that 'the systems of Mood and Modality are the keys to understanding the interpersonal relationships between interactants' (1994: 196). This is particularly salient where an imbalance in terms of power – whether due to social distance, gender, or other contextual factors – requires some speakers to defer to others. Such deference is frequently realized by means of modality. In fact, wherever any threat to face is felt to be imminent, modal systems are employed to defuse such a threat. In this short exchange between clerical staff, the participants are discussing work schedules, a potential source of friction. Expressions of modality are italicized (King George is the name of a hospital):

Text 3.6: Work schedules

Bron: We are *going to* have a lot of admissions to do this afternoon.

Pauline: Is Jenny there, by the way? And what's she doing?

Bron: Well, Jenny and I'*ll* finish the admissions now, but Sue's going at half past three and she's half done King George.

Pauline: Oh is she? Why is she going early?

Bron: She *needs to* go to the post office, so *apparently* she asked if she *could* go early and make up the time.

Pauline: Oh well. Jenny *better* stay and help me with those then.

Bron: Yeah. 'Cause we haven't started on them yet.

Pauline: Mmm.

Bron: And of course she's pulled all the EASY King George.

Pauline: Oh well, I don't suppose she's any idea of what *could* happen. And I said on Monday she *can* do PA because it's different to King George.

(Authors' data)

In the above extract a number of common modal meanings are realized, and can be divided into those that express a speaker's judgement as to the likelihood of an event (whether past, present or future) – what is called *extrinsic modality* – and those that express the speaker's judgement of the desirability, necessity or permissability of an event occurring – that is, *intrinsic modality*. Likelihood (whose shades of meaning include predictability, certainty and theoretical possibility) is represented by these examples:

> We are *going to* have a lot of admissions to do this afternoon. [prediction]
> I don't suppose she's any idea of what *could* happen. [possibility]

Intrinsic modal meanings in the extract include:

> Jenny and I*'ll* finish the admissions now. [volition]
> She *needs to* go to the post office. [obligation]
> Jenny *better* stay and help me. [desirability]
> And I said on Monday she *can* do PA. [permission]

Note that *I don't suppose* (as in *I don't suppose she has any idea of what could happen*) can also be classed as a form of modality, in that it indicates the speaker's assessment of the situation as being uncertain.

Other conversational contexts that have been identified as favouring a high incidence of modality include speculating and the exchange of opinions. In the following extract the speaker – a member of the hospital clerical staff – is speculating on the implications of the fact that many of the hospital staff are related. She moves from a statement of how things *are* to a discussion of what this *might* mean (exponents of probability are italicized):

Text 3.7: Hospital staff

> Di: We have a lot of staff here that are either, if they're not related they're by natural family, they're related through marriage or they went to school together. But erm so you really, so you've got to be careful (if) you make an off-hand comment about somebody. They *may* not have been doing their job properly, but if you say something in the wrong area, you know, when you're not watching to see who's standing around you *can* find yourself in a, you know, er and wonder why people aren't doing things because they'd say, 'oh well she said this about my mother you know?' And it *might* just be something you said, meaning, *maybe* just for yourself before another supervisor in anger and *probably* if you'd cooled down a bit you *mightn't* even have said it, but if somebody heard it, they*'ll* just transfer it right back. And you can't understand why, but you know that there's something wrong.

> (Authors' data)

Note that in the above extract the lexical items *maybe* and *probably* are included as instances of modality. The frequency of conditional clauses (beginning *if . . .*) in this highly 'modalized' extract is also to be expected. Given that both conditionality and modality encode non-assertive meanings, it is not surprising that where you find one you find the other. (Biber *et al.*, 1999, found that conditional clauses are much more common in conversation than in other registers.)

Among other findings that researchers have observed in corpus data we note the following:

- The modal verbs *can, will* and *would* are extremely common in conversation, as are the semi-modals *have to, used to* and *going to* – this last being used much more frequently in conversation than in written language; the fact that the semi-modals are relatively recent introductions to the language may account for their high rate of occurrence in conversation relative to more formal and/or written registers (Biber *et al.*, 1999).
- On the other hand, the modals *may, shall* and *must* are relatively infrequently found in the data; and *must* is used more to mark logical necessity, especially with regard to the past (*that must've been awful*) than the more face-threatening function of obligation.
- McCarthy (1998) notes the frequency of the semi-modal *tend to* in spoken language data, occurring nine times more often in spoken than in written English, and making it more common than some of the more 'canonical' modals, such as *ought to*, for example. McCarthy and Carter suggest that 'its use allows speakers to express points of view or describe habitual actions with a certain degree of tentativeness, where bald and direct statements may appear too assertive in an interpersonal context' (1995: 212) – a conclusion that might well apply to the use of modal verbs in conversation in general.

Within a systemic functional framework, modality is just one way of nuancing the *mood* structure of the clause. Mood is the way different configurations of clause elements enable speakers to encode such speech functions as offering, commanding, making statements and asking questions, thereby making interaction possible. Through the use of modality, these speech functions can be adjusted to take into account certain interpersonal dimensions – that is to say, the *tenor* – of the interaction. Eggins (1994) argues that these different configurations of mood structure are not always equally distributed in talk. For example, a lack of assertion in language – e.g. a tendency to modalize statements and questions – may by symptomatic of non-symmetrical power relationships. Even in casual conversation between friends, where one would least expect to find evidence of power differentials, analysis of mood structure can reveal an unequal distribution of assertiveness. Eggins presents evidence to support her claim that 'in the selection of speech roles, and their corresponding realization in the Mood structures, we see the linguistic realization of gender expectations of our culture: that women are conversationally "supportive", while men just sit back and perform' (1994: 194). (Issues of gender and talk are further discussed in Chapter 4.)

3.9 Reporting

Another aspect of the grammar of conversation that has attracted attention is the way speech is reported. McCarthy notes that, while corpus data 'confirm the common-sense intuition that speech reporting is exceedingly common in everyday language . . . spoken data . . . exhibit choices which are rarely, if ever, found in written speech reports' (1998: 151). For example, while reporting verbs are not usually marked for aspect in written registers (*he said, she told me*), it is very common in conversational data to find such verbs in their continuous form – an extension of the 'framing' function of the continuous aspect at the orientation stage of narratives, perhaps. Thus:

> (1) Mary: *I was telling* Gary last night about orchiopexy. *I was saying* to Eric = what I told you about orchiopexy. It was Gary and Bronwyn at the front desk.

> (2) Judy: I had this friend, and she came to me and *she's saying, she was talking* about, you know, she understood sort of problems of mixed marriage

Biber *et al.* note that the use of the continuous carries no implication that the speech event took place at a specific time, but rather refers 'somewhat vaguely to a recent time in the past, and may also give the general gist of what was said, rather than a word-by-word account' (1999: 1121).

A sequence of exchanges are usually reported in simple aspect, however, and often through a succession of *and she said . . . and I said . . .* moves, as in this gossip extract:

Text 3.8: The files

> Mary: She gets really pushy. I'm looking for a file for Adam. Kerry gave me three others and I was in the middle of finding the third one for her.
> Adam: Kerry gave you three did she?
> Mary: Yeah, you know they have to be done and Joanne came up *and she said*, 'oh, can you do this?' *and I said*, 'well you're at the end of a very long line if you're prepared

to wait' *and she said*, 'well, she's at the Oncology clinic right now' *and I said*, 'but these have to be done as well'. A*nd* sort of smiling all the way through it *I said*, 'look, you know it's three minutes to three. Liz should be down in a minute if you want to wait till then.' *And she went* ahhh [huffing sound] then she went away and I thought, 'oh yeah, end of the = = story.'

Adam: = = she gets very worried

Mary: And then she came back in again *and um she said*, 'are those files there? Did Kerry give you those files there?' and I knew what she was going to say next. *And I said*, 'oh, among others' *and she went*, 'oh it's just that they can wait until after this one 'cause they're needed today.'

(Authors' data)

This extract displays some other characteristic features of speech reporting in conversation, including the predominance of direct reporting over indirect reporting. Indirect speech reports seem to be reserved for very short narratives of a non-humorous type, as in this example:

> Well he he told me the day before that he was going going on jury service and when I heard on radio (iv) that the jury had been discharged, I thought it might have been him, but he said it wasn't.

(Authors' data)

Note the use of tense 'backshift' in indirect speech reporting: '*I am going on jury service*' → *he was going on jury service*; '*the jury has been discharged*' → *the jury had been discharged*. Apart from anything else, the use of direct speech saves the speaker the necessity of making these somewhat complex syntactic adjustments.

Another feature of speech reporting in Text 3.8 (The files) is the use of discourse markers to launch direct speech quotations (and, in the absence of verbal 'speech marks', perhaps to make it clear that what follows is direct speech): <u>oh</u>, *can you do this?*; <u>well</u> *you're at the end of a very long line*; <u>look</u>, *you know it's three minutes to three*; <u>oh</u> *it's just that they can wait . . .*

Text 3.8 includes the use of the verb *to go* as a reporting verb (or *quotative*): *and* <u>she went</u> *ahhh [huffing sound]*; *and* <u>she went</u> '*oh it's just that they can wait . . .* Another common quotative (not represented in this extract) is *be like* which, as Yule (1998) notes, is particularly common for introducing direct speech that conveys a person's attitude:

S: I know a lot of people who just gas their animals, because they're inconvenient.

> T: Well that's why Wendy – that's why Wendy did it. She was
> just like, *she was like*, 'I can't take care of this dog. I can't
> take it with me. It's, you know, it was a bad choice. I think
> I'm gonna put it to sleep.' And *I'm like*, 'Well, it's your dog
> you know. It's your choice.'
>
> (Yule, 1998: 283)

Text 3.8 includes the use of 'dramatic' devices to enhance the narrative,
such as imitating exclamations ([*huffing sound*]) and parenthetical comments on paralinguistic features of the exchange: *and sort of smiling all
the way through it I said*. . . . Here is another example (also from the same
source):

> The other day I said, just to be friendly, 'Anna, you look really nice
> today'. And she said, *in a really kind of arrogant voice*, 'well, I do
> like to make an effort at work as well'.

Finally, text 3.8 demonstrates the way that thoughts are also reported in
their direct form: *I thought 'oh yeah, end of the story.'* Yule notes that
'on many occasions [speakers] also report thoughts or attitudes (that
they and others may have had) in a form which looks as if they had given
voice, in direct speech, to those thoughts and attitudes during the
reported interaction' (1998: 283). The following is an example of this
'thinking-as-if-talking': 'Eh, I went down there once. I froze all the time.
I said *never again*' (Authors' data).

3.10 What do learners need to know?

What is it, then, that learners need to know about grammar in order to
achieve conversational competence? First of all, what they probably
don't need to know is a lot of the formal grammar that is typically presented in EFL materials. Pedagogical grammar is essentially *written*
grammar – that is, it is a grammar derived from an analysis of the
written language. It is the grammar which, by virtue of being more
thoroughly researched as well as more prestigious, is the grammar that
is customarily taught to EFL learners. As was pointed out earlier, it is
this grammar which determines the content of much of the coursebook
'conversations' students are exposed to in the course of their studies.
Yet many of the grammar items that are ingeniously incorporated into
such conversations – and whose presentation and practice can take up
a good deal of classroom time – only rarely feature in authentic conversational data.

The second point that needs to be made is that conversation places fewer demands on learners in terms of grammar – in its conventional sense – than do other registers such as academic prose or more formal spoken genres. Indeed, spoken grammar shares a number of the features of interlanguage grammar. Ochs (1979), for example, in comparing planned and (relatively) unplanned discourse, notes that in the latter there is greater use of grammatical features that are associated with the early stages of language acquisition. These features include less frequent use of definite articles and a preference, instead, for demonstratives (as in '*this* place where I go'); greater use of active rather than passive constructions; and more frequent use of the present as opposed to past or future verb forms. According to Givón (1979), these features are typical of what is called a *pragmatic* language mode, as opposed to a *syntactic* one. Other features of a pragmatic mode include short verbal clauses with a low proportion of noun phrases per verb, and reduction and simplification of grammatical morphology.

In a sense, this is good news for the language learner, and it is a view that flatly contradicts the position taken by some writers (see Chapter 8), who claim that conversational competence depends on a high level of linguistic competence, and is therefore late-acquired. Moreover, since *interlanguage* (i.e. learner language) is characterized by a number of pragmatic mode features, including greater reliance on lexis than on syntax, it could be argued that conversation is the 'natural' medium for learners to operate in, even those who are at a very elementary level. Thus Nattinger suggests that 'one way to promote fluency is by encouraging "pidginization", urging students to put language together the best they can and avoid the self-monitoring that would inhibit its use' (1988: 70). Other writers, such as Skehan (1998), however, caution against such a laissez-faire approach since they see this as likely to lead to an over-reliance on a lexicalized system at the expense of a syntacticalized system, with the associated risk of fossilization (i.e. the premature stabilization of the learner's interlanguage).

There is a further danger, however, that, as more and more features of spoken grammar are identified and described, they become a focus of instruction in their own right. Thus, valuable time may be wasted teaching learners about syntactic noun-clausal units or ellipsis or heads and tails when their natural tendency, in the interests of simplification, is to use these features anyway. An extreme statement of the scepticism is Prodromou's: 'The status of spoken English may be a subject of debate in Applied Linguistics but I do not think it is for language teachers' (1997: 20). Prodromou argues, instead, for a methodology that 'takes the students' interlanguage as a starting point and seeks to build on that rather than on language imposed from the outside'.

It is this thinking that underlies the so-called *lexical approach* to course design, including the design of materials that foreground the lexical needs of learners, e.g. Willis (1990) and Lewis (1993). It is also the view that informed the research undertaken by Gairns and Redman in the preparation of an intermediate-level general English course (2002a). They were interested in comparing the output of intermediate-level learners with that of more advanced learners (rather than with native speakers, on the grounds that a 'native speaker model represented a target that was unattainable for intermediate learners of English' (2002a: 2)). They therefore recorded and transcribed learners at these two different levels performing a variety of speaking tasks. Among their findings, they noted that:

- *Modal verbs* appeared frequently in the higher-level output, but were notably scarce in the intermediate data, especially *will, would, might, could, should.*
- *Tenses* were still generally problematic at intermediate level, but backshift in reported speech seemed largely superfluous.
- Learners at the intermediate level seemed to shy away from adverbs. *Very* appeared everywhere, but not some of the high-frequency adverbs found in the more advanced-level data, such as *extremely, slightly, occasionally, fortunately* etc.

What they found most significant was the fact that 'learners lacked a wide range of frequently occurring lexical items, many of them lexical chunks, which are an important part of sounding natural, either in your own or another language' (Gairns and Redman, 2002b: 6). Again, this is a finding consistent with the view that spoken language consists, to a large extent, of prefabricated lexical 'chunks', as argued by Pawley and Syder (1983) and Nattinger and DeCarrico (1992), among others (see Chapter 2).

Nevertheless, based on the findings reviewed in this chapter, there seem to be good grounds for arguing for the acquisition of a 'core grammar' as a basis for developing conversational competence, and that this grammar would include the following features:

- some basic conjunctions (*and, so, but*) in order to string together sequences of clausal and non-clausal units;
- the use of deictic devices (*here/there; now/then, this/that,* etc.) to anchor utterances in the immediate context, and to refer to other contexts;
- a command of simple verb tense forms, both present and past, and the ability to use the latter to sequence narratives;
- familiarity with the use of aspect both to frame and to background information in narratives, as in *it was snowing . . . I'd been working . . .*
- a knowledge of the most frequently occurring modal and semi-modal

verbs (i.e. *can, will, would, have to, going to, used to*) and the ability to use these to express both intrinsic and extrinsic meanings;

* the ability to formulate questions, especially *yes/no-* but also *wh-* questions (but not perhaps question tags and comment questions which – although frequent – are syntactically complex, and can readily be replaced by lexical items such as *no?* and *really?*):
* a repertoire of head- and tail-slot fillers – principally discourse markers – items which perhaps belong to the lexicon rather than the grammar (see Chapter 2); and
* one or two all-purpose quotatives, of the *he said . . . and then I said . . .* type.

Clearly this is a very short list, and bears little relation to the fairly elaborate grammar syllabuses of standard ELT materials. This is not to say that such syllabuses are ineffective nor that this core grammar guarantees conversational competence. For a start, it assumes that learners have sufficient communicative strategies to compensate for any deficiencies in their linguistic competence. It is also difficult to avoid the conclusion that a significant proportion of what we have identified as core grammar is reducible to formulaic language of a lexical, rather than strictly grammatical, nature. In other words, a repertoire of sentence starters, discourse markers, back-channel devices and so on, may provide the learner with a more effective bridgehead into conversation than any number of traditional syllabus items such as *tenses* or *conditionals* and so on. This 'lexical approach' to conversational competence will be revisited in Chapter 9, when we look at the implications of our analysis in terms of a pedagogy for conversation.

Task

A. In the following extract four adults are discussing the best way of arranging a garden for a wedding ceremony. The speakers are:

Claudia: Female, aged 30. Erik's partner. Chris's and Ana's friend.
Erik: Male, aged 40. Claudia's partner.
Chris: Female, aged 35. Ana's partner, Claudia's friend.
Ana: Female, aged 33. Chris's partner, Claudia's friend.

Read the transcript and:

1. find an example of a clausal and of a non-clausal unit, and, of the latter, a syntactic non-clausal unit and an insert (see page 78 for examples of these);
2. identify any heads and any tails;

3. identify any instances of deictic language;
4. categorize the different questions in terms of form and of function;
5. identify and classify any examples of modality.

1.	Claudia:	We have to maybe dismantle the sauna.
2.	Erik:	I don't know about that!
3.	Claudia:	Well. But how, sort of if we don't calculate the kids, you're probably looking at roughly thirty people having dinner.
4.	Chris:	You could still do it though. I think you could still do it. But because where is that going to be moved to would be your problem.
5.	Erik:	I was just planning just to put it = = on its side.
6.	Claudia:	= = No the sauna you can just dismantle and put the the individual pieces somewhere in the back of the house.
7.	Chris:	But the spa, you might want = = to use it you know.
8.	Erik:	= = But see, but see, you see it's only a section sticking out the side there = =
9.	Claudia:	= = Yeah that's true = =
10.	Erik:	= = 'cause you've got to move the spa then as well.
11.	Ana:	What . . . yeah I mean, what are you using as tables? Are you going to hire like a type of . . .
12.	Claudia:	The the the caterers are coming this week and they and they are going to do everything.
13.	Chris:	Oh and they sort of bring the tables?
14.	Ana:	Oh good.
15.	Erik:	They're going to do it and so it's – you don't have to worry too much
16.	Chris:	Yeah there's an idea.
17.	Claudia:	So um we've even thought about things like that. Have something in the middle for people here, but that could be a bit cramped. Like a horseshoe.
18.	Erik:	A horseshoe type thing.
19.	Chris:	Oh yeah.
20.	Claudia:	I think that will = =
21.	Erik:	= = There's two separate, two tables coming down there. Just in case we need = = some more room or whatever.
22.	Ana:	= = Yeah.

23.	Chris:	You thought having people on opposite sides then might be a bit much?
24.	Claudia:	Yeah it's not very nice is it? But here at least everyone can see everyone else.
25.	Chris:	Mmm.
26.	Ana:	Mmm.
27.	Claudia:	You know. And the kids, I think the kids need to be, the kids have have to = = go inside
28.	Erik:	= = Chuck them inside.
29.	Claudia:	there. And I think that's probably = =
30.	Chris :	= = Mmm
31.	Ana:	They'll probably like it.
32.	Chris:	Yeah.
33.	Erik:	Yes.
34.	Claudia:	Plus they won't sit there very long, because the kids just want to get out.
35.	Ana:	Yeah.
36.	Erik:	Mmm
37.	Claudia:	And with the speeches – it's not for the kids not very interesting.

(OZTALK)

B: In the following narrative, identify the ways the speaker uses tense and aspect to relate the different events to one another.

We were burgled the first time when we were at home in our beds, remember? We were at home in our beds and they came to, in between the, I was breastfeeding at 1.30 and again at 5.30. In between 1.30 and 5.30 when I was getting up to breastfeed, the burglars came in, went to every single room in the house, helped themselves to anything, left lights on, took off on Rod's bike with his backpack and everything inside, our whole CD collection and Christmas presents and everything and I got up at 5.30 to find the lights on in the living room, knowing that I hadn't left them on and that we'd been burgled and we hadn't heard a thing. And then we knew we were going up to Cairns at Christmas and we'd be away, so we, we deadlocked everything and we told people we were going away, we told the neighbours, we got mum to go and check the place while we were away and on Christmas night they came back and they took all our music equipment which [inaudible]. Well I think it's the same people.

(OZTALK)

105

C: In the following two extracts, identify characteristic features of the reporting of speech and thought.

(1) But when I went to uni and ermm did a course which meant that I had to go to France for a year, it was a French exchange programme, all the students got together and said 'before you go to France you've got to learn these steps because that's what they're all doing in France. So, they call this rock 'n' roll'. The ones, the group of students who'd been there the year before came back and said 'okay, we'll teach you these steps'. And so we got to know these steps and off we went to France and okay, right I'm ready, I can do rock 'n' roll now, and nobody, 'cause they're all dancing to disco. [laughs].

(2) I rang the Children's Book Council today and and she said – I said, 'I'd like to join' and she said, 'well how will we join you under?' And she said, 'have you got anything published?' And I said, 'well yes. I have got two books coming out this year.' She said, 'well, we'll join you as an author.'

(OZTALK)

4 The discourse features of conversation

Introduction

In Chapter 1 we described a number of approaches to the study of conversation. Common to each of these approaches is the concern to interpret language within a socio-cultural context, and by doing so to relate the language features to social factors. It is precisely because of this interest in the relationship between language and social factors that conversation is seen as crucial. Depending on the theoretical underpinnings, conversation is seen either as the key to understanding social life (as in the socio-linguistic approaches, for example), or as a way of shedding light on the nature of language itself (as in the linguistic approaches). What they share is the belief in the social nature of language: that conversation builds social contexts at the same time as these contexts guide and shape conversation. Such an interest, departing from formal linguistics, leads to an interest in discourse. Formal grammars focus on the lexical and grammatical properties of sentences, whereas socially oriented, functional approaches focus not only on the grammar and lexis but also on the analysis of the surrounding discourse – that is, on the analysis of texts in social contexts. Chapters 2 and 3 described the vocabulary and grammar of conversational English and in this chapter we will continue to build up this picture of spoken language by focusing on linguistic features of extended text as well the links between text and its social context.

Discourse is language functioning in its context of use. It is what we engage in throughout the course of our daily lives – from talking at breakfast, to reading a newspaper, to chatting on the bus, to teaching a class. Discourse analysis is the study of these texts, whether spoken or written, and the relationship between the texts and the contexts in which they occur. Discourse analysts are interested in the analysis of real texts – and in this they differ significantly from formal grammarians, whose data for analysis is as often as not derived from their intuitions as from attested examples. In addition, discourse analysts typically study extended stretches of language, with the utterance rather than the sentence as their primary unit of analysis. McCarthy,

Matthiessen and Slade describe the questions that discourse analysts focus on:

> (1) Who are the participants in the discourse, i.e. the writer and reader(s), the speaker(s) and listener(s)? What is their relationship? Is it one between equals? Are there differences in power or knowledge between the participants? What are their goals? (A formal grammarian does not usually take any of these factors into account when working with out-of-context sentences.)
>
> (2) How do we know what writers and speakers mean? More specifically, discourse analysts ask 'What does this piece of language *mean in this context?*', and 'What does the speaker/writer *mean by* this piece of language?' What factors enable us to interpret the text? What do we need to know about the context? What clues are there in the surrounding text which will enable us to apprehend the meaning? (In contrast, a formal grammarian can ask the question 'What does this sentence *mean?*', and a lexicologist can ask 'What does this word *mean?*', independently of context.)
>
> (2002: 56)

The extent to which a stretch of discourse 'means', or 'makes sense', is a measure of its coherence, i.e. its capacity to achieve its communicative purpose. The above quotation reminds us that the sense of a text is recoverable by reference to at least two levels of context: the context of the 'surrounding text' (what, for convenience, is often called *co-text*), and the context of the situation in which the interaction takes place. In other words, a stretch of language achieves coherence to the extent that it 'fits' into both of these levels of context. The use of language in order to achieve this fit is called *cohesion*. Before we look at the discourse structure of conversation from an interactive perspective, then, we will briefly review the features that contribute to its cohesion.

4.1   Cohesion in conversation

A cohesive relation is one in which the interpretation of one element in the discourse presupposes, and is dependent upon, another. The connection that is created is integrated into the fabric (or 'texture') of the discourse. For example, in the hailstorm conversation that we looked at in Chapter 1, the following exchange occurs:

> Dan: And there was the little old lady over the road who . . .
> Rob: Oh yeah [laughs] *she* was sitting in her living room

The pronoun *she* in Ron's turn is interpretable only by reference to Dan's preceding utterance and his mention of *the little old lady*. In their classification of different ways in which cohesion is achieved in English, Halliday and Hasan (1985) distinguish between *grammatical* and *lexical* cohesive devices. Among the former are the various ways of *referring*, principally through the use of demonstratives and pronouns, as in the above example. Other examples from the same conversation (with the referring pronouns italicized) are:

> a friend of ours in Paddington, *they* had to move out of the flat
> [. . .] *they*'ve actually had to move out completely
> a hailstone fell through the skylight, this old Italian woman
> [. . .] *it* fell through the skylight *it* fell through the ceiling

Sometimes the referent (i.e. the entity that is referred to) may not be a specific person or thing, but a proposition that has been previously introduced, as when Odile responds to the suggestion that the school might be closed:

> Oh my god I hadn't thought about *that* . . .

Odile's use of *that* to refer to the proposition expressed by another speaker also demonstrates the fact that, in spoken language, cohesion is achieved *across* speaker turns as well as within them.

So far, all the examples of reference we have looked at have referred *back* in the discourse. In other words, their reference has been *anaphoric*. But the reference can be forward (i.e. *cataphoric*) as in this example:

> My idea is *this*. We all go to the airport we all meet them we bring them back to Trafalgar Street everyone stays there the night and the next morning Carl goes on the train you take the girls and Fuzz up in the car and we go back to MacMasters Beach.

> (OZTALK)

In each of the above examples the referent is recoverable by reference to what has just been said, or what is about to be said. The reference is said to be internal to the text (or *endophoric*). But some references can only be interpreted by reference 'outside' the co-text, that is, to the context of situation – including the knowledge that is shared by the speakers. An example of this *exophoric* type of reference is Odile's mention of *that hole*:

> I'm so glad the kids were not there because you know *that* hole is just above Debbie's head

It is a characteristic of spoken language that many of the references are exophoric, that is, their interpretation is context dependent. This quality – called *implicitness* by Hasan (1996) – distinguishes spoken text from written text, which is typically more *explicit*. The production and interpretation of spoken discourse is facilitated by reference both to the 'here-and-now' of the immediate context, and to the speakers' shared knowledge. In conversation among friends, the amount of shared knowledge is likely to be high, allowing a proportionally high degree of implicitness. This is evidenced in the frequency of the use of the definite article *the*, the most common word in spoken English. *The* is commonly used as a form of exophoric reference, as in *the kids* (above) and *the school*, in Grace's question:

> Is *the* school OK?

Here, the intended reference goes beyond the immediate context, and assumes knowledge that is mutually shared, which, as Hasan puts it, 'argues for the existence of interaction in the past, and for a consequent rapport between the speaker and the addressee' (1996: 204).

Other grammatical means of achieving cohesion include the use of *substitution* and *ellipsis*. An example of the former is the use of *does* in the following exchange, where *does* substitutes for the verbal element *come*:

> Speaker 1: He has to leave Helen in Britain because she's she doesn't want to come.
> Speaker 2: But I thought she said she'd come for . . .
> Speaker 1: Well if she *does* she's got to give up her job

(OZTALK)

In the following extract, Speaker 3 uses *did* to substitute for the italicized clausal element in the previous speakers' utterances:

> Speaker 1: I believe you *bought a lovely Dawn Allen lamp at the school fete.*
> Speaker 2: *At a bargain price.*
> Speaker 3: We did!

(OZTALK)

Ellipsis is a form of substitution whereby a previously mentioned element is replaced by 'zero', as in this utterance, where the ellipted element is in square brackets:

> You know he feels he should be able to provide for his family and he can't [*provide for his family*].

As we saw in Chapter 3, ellipsis is used frequently in conversation, and, extended across speaker turns, it contributes to the contingency of much spoken language, i.e. the effect that talk is jointly constructed through the successive borrowings from, and additions to, other speakers' previous utterances. For example, in this short exchange from the hailstorm conversation, the content of the square brackets represents ellipted material:

> Odile: No I think I don't know many people who have been affected except you and I. That much.
> Rob: You don't know [*many people who have been affected*]?
> Odile: Well you know [*I don't know many people who have been affected*] except for the neighbours.

Both substitution and ellipsis are used to align successive speakers' utterances in order to indicate agreement, sympathy and such, and their use therefore serves an important interpersonal function:

> Speaker 1:   Hmm I love this eggplant.
> Speaker 2:   So do I.
>
> Speaker 1:   Wouldn't it be funny if they were on the same flight?
> Speaker 2:   Oh wouldn't it!

Another class of grammatical cohesive devices are those that signal the logical relation between elements, and are called *conjunctions*, or, less formally, *linkers* or *linking devices*. The most frequently used linkers in conversation are *and*, *but* and *so*. Because they not only link utterances but indicate the direction that the discourse is taking, linkers are a kind of *discourse marker* (see Chapter 2). In the following extract, four speakers are discussing a current affairs programme in which the prime minister and his wife were interviewed. The underlined linkers connect utterances across speaker turns, while the linkers in italics connect linkers within the turn:

Text 4.1: Howard

> <S 01>   And it was very interesting the way that they responded to the questions. Howard was very stiff *and* even his wife, basically refused to answer questions.
> <S 02>   Yeah when she was asked for her opinion she said 'Oh well you know um Johnny's got the answers.' [laugh]
> <S 01>   Yeah.
> <S 02>   'Don't come to me'.
> <S 01>   And they asked they asked her just about what is it about your husband that you like? Just something, what is it about John that you admire. *And* she just wouldn't answer the question.
> <S 03>   Oooh.
> <S 04>   So there was nothing to admire.
> <S 02>   Because she didn't have an answer though. She didn't have an opinion on it you know.

111

<S 01> She had no opinion. *And yet* when the following week when they interviewed . . .
<S 03> Yeah *but* she only does the washing at home.
<S 01> Oh *but* apparently behind closed doors she has a very very strong opinion.
<S 02> Yeah she looks like it.
<S 03> She looks like that kind of woman.

(OZTALK)

Lexical means by which links are made across stretches of discourse include the use of repetition, synonyms and lexical chains of topically related items. Perhaps more than any other factor, the use of lexical cohesion is an indicator of topic consistency, and hence contributes significantly to the sense that speakers are 'talking to topic', and that the talk is therefore coherent. In this extract from the hailstorm conversation (Text 1.3), the different ways that cohesion is achieved lexically are identified:

(4) Rob: Oh a friend of ours in Paddington, they had to move out of the flat = =
(5) Grace: = = Mm.
(6) Rob: because the whole = =
(7) Grace: = = roof[1] collapsed.
(8) Rob: The tiles[2] fell through the ceiling[3] = =
(9) Grace: = = Mm
(10) Rob: into the room[4] and they've actually had to move out[5] completely.
(11) Odile: Oh really?
(12) Dan: And there was the little old lady over the road who . . .
(13) Rob: Oh yeah. [laughs] She was sitting in her living room[6] and a hailstone fell through the skylight[7], this old[8] Italian woman[9]. She had corrugated iron[10] but it fell through the skylight[11], it fell through[12] the ceiling[13] and landed in her lap when she was sitting[14] = =
(14) Odile: = = Mm.
(15) Rob: watching television.
(16) Dan: Watching[15] *The X-files* probably.

1. *roof*: topically related to *flat*. (A roof is *a part of* a flat: the relationship is one of *meronymy*)
2. *tiles*: topically related to *roof*
3. *ceiling*: topically related to both *flat* and *roof*
4. *room*: as 1
5. *move out*: repetition
6. *living room*: as 1
7. *skylight*: as 2
8. *old*: repetition
9. *woman*: synonym for *lady*
10. *corrugated iron*: as 2

11. *skylight*: repetition
12. *fell through*: repetition
13. *ceiling*: repetition
14. *sitting*: repetition
15. *watching*: repetition

Note that the extract also includes instances of *parallelism,* that is, the repetition of syntactic units larger than individual words, as in:

> *it fell through the skylight*
> *it fell through the ceiling*
>
> *watching television*
> *watching* The X-files

As we saw in Chapter 2, repetition serves a number of important functions in conversation, both textual and interpersonal. In the following extract, both lexical repetition and rhyme are used for creative effect, serving not only to bind the talk together but to reinforce the social ties between the speakers. It is cohesive in every sense.

Text 4.2: Iced coffee

Speaker 1: Now who can I make an iced coffee for?
Speaker 2: Oh I think you could make one for my fat stomach.
Speaker 1: And Gavin?
Speaker 3: Iced coffee or a nice coffee?
Speaker 1: Iced coffee.
Speaker 3: Um.
Speaker 4: A nice iced coffee.
Speaker 1: A nice iced coffee = = you can have it with
Speaker 2: = = Or you can have an unpleasant iced coffee.
Speaker 1: you can have it with milk and ice-cream.
Speaker 3: Could I have just like a hot coffee?
Speaker 4: No reason why not.

(OZTALK)

4.2   Interaction in conversation

In the analysis of spoken discourse we are interested not just in how utterances are made cohesive, nor in how cohesion is achieved across turns. We are also interested in how *interactivity* is achieved: that is, what roles speakers take on, how they position other interactants into particular roles, how turntaking and topic change occurs in contexts where one person is not in control (as, for example in an interview), and the different kinds of feedback strategies that participants use. As the primary motivation of conversation is interpersonal, in this next section

113

we will be focusing on how these interpersonal goals are realized at the discourse level. We will be describing how conversation unfolds and the patterns of coherence both across and within speaker turns.

Conversation is co-constructed by two or more participants, unfolding dynamically in real time. One of the major interests for spoken discourse analysts is how to describe the to-and-fro micro patterns of conversational interaction. As we explained in Chapter 1, ethnomethodology (in particular Conversation Analysis), the Birmingham School and Systemic Functional Linguistics (SFL) all developed conceptual frameworks to describe the basic pattern of interaction in spoken English. The ethnomethodologists used the concept of the adjacency pair to describe the relationship between two adjacent utterances, and the Birmingham School used the concept of the exchange. SFL uses the concept of speech function to describe the adjacency pair structure of dialogue, and each utterance within this is called a move.

4.2.1 Adjacency pairs

In Conversation Analysis (CA) the basic unit of interaction is the adjacency pair. In this section we will describe CA's concept of adjacency pairs and in Section 4.2.3 below we will look at CA's research on turn-taking in conversation.

Conversation Analysis was strongly influenced by the sociologists Garfinkel (1967) and Goffman (1981) and developed into a distinctive field of enquiry by Sacks (1972a, 1972b, 1992). In their analysis and description of naturally occurring conversations, conversation analysts' primary concern is to explain how it is that everyday talk makes sense. The questions they pose all have relevance to the description and teaching of conversation and include:

- Why does only one person speak at a time?
- How do speakers know when to change turns?
- How do speakers know when to initiate new topics?
- How do speakers know when it is appropriate to interrupt?
- How can one speaker complete another speaker's utterance?
- How do interactants recognize when a speaker wants to close a conversation?

In pursuing these questions, Conversation Analysis has focused on the micro-interactional features of conversation:

- the adjacency pair structure of conversation (Schegloff and Sacks, 1973/1974);
- the turntaking mechanisms in conversation (Sacks, Schegloff and Jefferson, 1974);

- how speakers initiate, shift and close topics, referred to as *topic management* (Sacks, 1992);
- how conversations can keep going indefinitely and continue to make sense.

One of the most significant contributions of CA is the concept of the adjacency pair. An adjacency pair is composed of two turns produced by different speakers which are placed adjacently and where the second utterance is identified as related to the first. Adjacency pairs include such exchanges as question/answer; complaint/denial; offer/accept; request/grant; compliment/rejection; challenge/rejection, and instruct/receipt. Adjacency pairs typically have three characteristics:

- they consist of two utterances;
- the utterances are adjacent, that is the first immediately follows the second; and
- different speakers produce each utterance.

Here are some examples, taken from authentic conversational data:

Question/answer:

A: You don't like the fish?
B: No, it's not that I don't like it, it's the way it is done.

Offer/accept:

A: Now who can I make an iced coffee for?
B: Oh I think you could make one for my fat stomach.

Request/grant:

A: Jerry hi, where's our cake?
B: It's coming, it's coming. [laugh]

Compliment/response:

A: Great haircut.
B: Do you think? The hair colour burnt my scalp!

Challenge/rejection:

A: Mmm, don't speak with your mouth half full, pull the bloody thing out.
B: I will do what I bloody well like.

Instruct/receipt:

A: Hand me the knife from the bench, will you.
B: Here you go.

(Authors' data)

Where there is a choice of responses – as in an invitation or a request, for example – one of these choices typically requires less elaboration than the other. Accepting an invitation, or granting a request, require less 'face work', that is to say, they are less face-threatening – than refusing either an invitation or a request. The less face-threatening response is referred to as the preferred sequence, as in:

> A: Would you like to try my Armenian dessert George?
> B: I'll taste it yes, thank you.

whereas a sequence such as:

> A: Why don't we go to see it tonight?
> B: No-way! I just want to collapse in front of tele.

is a dispreferred sequence. It is often the case that mitigating strategies – such as giving the reason for the refusal or apologizing – are used with dispreferred sequences to ensure conversational co-operativeness.

The initial identification of a two-part structural unit – the adjacency pair – led to the recognition of sequences that are longer than two units and of more complex sequential organizations than strict adjacency. A sequence is an adjacency pair and any expansions of that adjacency. There are three types of expansions: *pre-sequences, insertion sequences* and *post-sequences,* where the sequence is the base adjacency pair and its expansions. For example:

1.	pre-sequence	first pair part	A:	What are you doing tonight?
2.	pre-sequence	second pair part	B:	Nothing
3.	base adjacency pair	first pair part	A:	Do you want to have a drink?
4.	insertion sequence	first pair part	B:	Where?
5.	insertion sequence	second pair part	A:	Down the pub
6.	base adjacency pair	second pair part	B:	Great

In this example turns 3 and 6 constitute a question/answer pair. However, turns 1–6 are all related semantically – there is a sense of their belonging together. It is instances such as these that CA refers to as sequences.

The concept of the adjacency pair has been extremely significant as it provides a way of capturing the local organization of talk. In fact Taylor and Cameron (1987) argue:

> The concept of the adjacency pair is, arguably, the linchpin of the ethnomethodological model of conversational structure.

Not only . . . does the operation of the turn-taking system rely
upon it, but . . . without the concept of the adjacency pair there
would be no ethnomethodological model of conversation.

(1987: 109)

The concept of the adjacency pair, however, is limited as it can only
describe the relationship between the base adjacent utterance and its
expansions. It cannot so easily account for the structure of extended
stretches of conversation, including the relationship that exists between the
different moves made by the same speaker in longer turns of talk. In short,
it cannot account on its own for the discourse structure of conversation. In
the next section we will expand the notion of the adjacency pair to describe
the structure of the related semantic units of the move and the exchange.

4.2.2   Moves and exchanges in conversation

Adjacency-pair structure is one way of describing some basic elements
of discourse interactivity. In this next section we will explore the
unfolding of conversational exchanges, describing how one speaker's
move leads to another, and then to another. The concern in this analysis is to demonstrate how it is that conversation keeps going – how the
conversation unfolds. To account for the interactivity of conversation,
we need to go beyond an analysis of the vocabulary and grammar of
spoken English and give functional labels to the different roles speakers can assume, and to the roles they assign to others. To do this we will
outline a functional interpretation of interaction. Both the Birmingham
School and Systemic Functional Linguistics (outlined in Chapter 1)
describe the pattern of interaction in conversation functionally – that
is, by describing what function each speaker's move achieves in that
context.

Each utterance in a conversation (described above as one pair part of
an adjacency pair) can be referred to as a *move* (see Martin, 1992). A
move is, therefore, the basic semantic unit in interactive talk – it is the
smallest unit of potential interaction (see Slade, 1996; Eggins and Slade,
1997). It indicates a point of possible turn-transfer, and therefore
carries with it the idea of 'it could stop here'. (This is what the ethnomethodologists call a 'turn-constructional unit': see below.) By describing the different types of moves that can occur in English conversation
we can begin to describe the patterns of conversational structure, that
is, the way interactants negotiate the exchange of meanings in dialogue.
According to Halliday's functional description (1994: 69), the basic initiating moves in conversation are the four primary speech functions of
command, *statement*, *offer* and *question*.

The discourse features of conversation

A command is typically realized by an imperative, a statement by a declarative, and a question by an interrogative:

Speech function	Grammatical structure that typically realizes it (mood of the clause)	Example
command	imperative	*'Eat your vegetables'*
statement	declarative	*'I love vegetables'*
offer	no corresponding congruent form	*'Would you like some vegetables?'*
question	interrogative	*'What kind of vegetables do you like?'*

(adapted from Halliday, 1994: 69)

With each speech function there is an expected response and a discretionary alternative, with each of these examples constituting an interactive move in conversation:

Initiating speech function	Expected response	Discretionary alternative
offer	acceptance*	rejection
Do you want to get married?	*Absolutely.*	*Certainly not!*
command	compliance*	refusal
Get married first.	*Okay.*	*Under no condition.*
statement	acknowledgment	contradiction
I am getting married.	*Wonderful news!*	*Over my dead body.*
question	answer	disclaimer
Are you getting married?	*Yes.*	*What do you mean?*

these responses are frequently non-verbal

(adapted from Halliday, 1994: 69)

Every move in dialogue can be assigned a *speech function*. So the definition of a move can now be refined as being the basic semantic unit in interactive talk that selects for speech function. Speech function then describes the adjacency pair structure of dialogue.

Both expected and discretionary responses engage with the initiating move. However, the difference is that the expected responses tend to finish the exchange as there has been a resolution (for example, an offer followed by an acceptance; or a question followed by an answer). Discretionary responses, on the other hand, tend to open out the exchange because, for example, if an offer is rejected or a statement contradicted, further

118

negotiation is needed – such as a reason, an excuse or an apology. Expected responses support the proposition of the speaker and thereby serve to create alignments and solidarity. By contrast, the discretionary responses are either disengaging and non-committal or openly confronting.

Ironically, discretionary moves occur more frequently in casual conversation than do expected responses. This is because of the social role of conversation, which is not only to affirm likenesses and similarities but also to explore differences. Many conversations between close friends involve as much probing of difference as they do confirming of similarities.

Due to the frequency of discretionary moves in conversational English, Martin (1992) and Eggins and Slade (1997) have extended the analysis of the different types of discretionary moves that can occur. There are two categories of discretionary moves: *tracking* and *challenging* moves (see Martin, 1992: 70, and Eggins and Slade, 1997: 207).

Tracking moves monitor, check or clarify the content of prior moves. For example:

> A: I'm just going to the shop.
> B: Where did you say?

where the content of what was said is being clarified. Or:

> A: I'm just going to the shop.
> B: To the shop?

where speaker B seeks confirmation of what she heard.

Challenging moves challenge the speaker's initiating move in some way. For example, in the case of one speaker trying to terminate the interaction:

> A: I'm leaving tomorrow.
> B: I don't want to hear about it.

Or where the proposition is countered in some way. For example:

> A: I'm leaving tomorrow.
> B: I thought you said next week.

The tracking and challenging moves tend to trigger sequences of talk that interrupt, postpone, abort or suspend the initial speech function sequence. In many ways tracking and challenging moves are characteristic features of conversational English – they occur much less frequently in formal spoken English. As Eggins and Slade point out (1997: 212), this is because formal interactions, such as job interviews or interactions in the bank, aim at closure and completion. On the other hand, casual conversations are aimed at sustaining and maintaining social relationships, a goal which is never completely achieved, hence the need for linguistic strategies that open out, rather than foreclose, the conversation.

We can now list the major types of moves that can occur in conversation in English (examples of each of these are above):

Initiating moves (I)
statement: I:S
question: I:Q
rhetorical question: Q:R
offer: I:O
command: I:C

Expected responding moves (R)
answer: R:A
acknowledge: R:K
response acknowledge offer: R:O
response to command: R:C

Discretionary moves
tracking: tr (confirming, checking and clarifying)
response to tracking: rtr
challenging: ch (disengaging, challenging, countering)
response to challenge: rch

When we focus on the interactional structuring of exchanges, we find that a single move will often make a distinct contribution to the development of the exchange. It may serve to initiate a new exchange; it may serve to respond to an exchange that has been initiated; or it may serve to complete an exchange after a response has been supplied.

However, at other times, these functions in an exchange will be achieved not by a single move but by a group of moves. We will refer to this as a *move complex* (Slade, 1996). For example, in this extract from a coffee-break conversation between a group of women supervisors in a hospital, Jessie asks a question that elicits gossip about Richard:

Exchange structure	Move	Speaker	Transcript
I:Q	1	Jessie:	Mmm, what's happened about Richard?
tr	2a	Judy	Ah about Richard.
R:A	2b		Ah nothing [laughs].
	2c		He's been spoken to,
	2d		it'll be a sort of a watch and wait == something
			. . .
I:Q	3	Jessie:	== Yeah, what do you reckon is going to happen?

(Authors' data)

Judy's response in the exchange is not a single move but three grammatically related moves that form her answer to the question. This then is followed by a new exchange, initiated by Jessie asking another question. For this reason, functional linguists refer to this basic interactive pattern as an *exchange* (rather than the similar concept of an adjacency pair). An exchange then can be defined as 'the sequence of moves concerned with negotiating a proposition stated or implied in an initiating move. An exchange can be identified as beginning with an opening move, and continuing until another opening move occurs' (Eggins and Slade, 1997: 222).

We will now analyse an authentic conversational extract in terms of its exchange structure. In the extract a group of supervisors at a hospital are chatting during their morning tea-break. There are three participants in the conversation – Mary, Fran and Adam – and they are gossiping about Joanne, a work colleague.

Text 4.3: Joanne

Exchange structure	Speaker	Transcript (divided into moves)
I:S	Bron:	I'm about to throw Joanne out the window
tr	Pat:	Joanne who
rtr	Bron:	Peterson
I:Q	Pat:	Why?
R:A	Bron:	She gets really pushy.
I:S		I'm looking for a file for Gary.
		Kerry gave me three others and I was in the middle of finding the third one for her.
I:Q	Gary:	Kerry gave you three did she?
R:A	Bron:	Yeah, you know they have to be done
		and Joanne came up
		and she said 'oh, can you do this?'
		and I said . . . and she went 'oh it's just that they can wait until after this one 'cause they're needed today'. Oh I was about ready to strangle her =she gets
R:K	Gary:	Joanne's too busy
R:K	Bron:	I know
		and I appreciate that she's busy
		but she gets really pushy
R:K	Pat:	Yeah,
		I don't like pushy people either

(Authors' data)

The first column of the transcript details the interactive structure, that is the relationships between moves produced by different speakers. Bron's first initiating statement, *I'm about to throw Joanne out the window*, immediately establishes Joanne as the topic. This is followed by a tracking move to clarify who Bron is talking about. After Bron responds to the tracking move, Pat asks why she is annoyed with Joanne and this then is followed by a detailed response, clearly stating her negative evaluation. Bron then initiates another statement, providing evidence or justification for her negative evaluation of Joanne. In the rest of the text Bron develops the 'case' that Joanne is really pushy. Adam and Fran contribute to the construction of the gossip sequence by means of a few simple moves where they ask for further information from Bron. She then responds in turn, using a series of move complexes in each case. Initially, Pat and Gary are reluctant to gossip about Joanne, but Pat's final 'response: acknowledgement' provides tacit approval of the gossip, with her comment: *I don't like pushy people either.*

In most gossip sequences, unless there is agreement, the speaker is likely to back down. If the participants in these contexts (colleagues chatting at work) do not agree with the gossip, they are more likely to be non-committal to enable the gossip to continue. Gary, for example, was non-committal with his comment, *'Joanne's too busy'*. (Note that gossip sequences, including this one, will be the subject of further analysis in Chapter 5.)

The conversational structure analysis has demonstrated that the exchange is jointly constructed by the two roles of gossip provider and gossip seeker/participant, where the gossip provider then launches into longer move complexes in order to build up a case against 'the absent other'. The analysis has also demonstrated who the dominant and incidental participants are, which participants produced the most moves and move complexes, and the kind of speech functional selections speakers made.

The purpose of this analysis is to focus on the micro-interaction of conversation: analysing the exchanges in terms of speech function and categorizing each move according to what it is doing in that context. Interactants develop conversation locally move by move. For each move, the current speaker will make a particular set of speech-function selections. By analysing each move we get a clearer picture of how the interactants propel the conversation forward – initiating, responding, challenging etc. Exchange structure analysis is, therefore, a way of capturing the semantic coherence across moves by different speakers.

In Chapter 5 we will be describing the same extract from the perspective of genre – outlining the text structure of gossip, and detailing the different stages the text moves through to reach its goal. Each of these different accounts provide complementary perspectives and begin to build up a comprehensive picture of how conversation is structured to achieve its goals.

In the next section we will continue our description of the interactivity of conversation by describing one key aspect of interaction: how interactants know when it is their turn to talk, at what points in the conversation another interactant can self-select to take the turn or what linguistic strategies the speaker uses to select the next speaker.

4.2.3 Turntaking in conversation

Perhaps the most significant studies on turntaking have come from CA, from within sociology rather than linguistics. In Section 4.2.1 above we described CA's concept of adjacency pairs and in this section we will describe CA's research on turntaking.

Sacks (1974), who developed CA into a distinctive field of enquiry, transcribed and analysed many hours of naturally occurring conversations. He describes how turntaking works in English: the current speaker can either select the next speaker, by for example, naming them, looking at them, directing a question to them, or the next speaker can self-select, with many possible strategies, such as *that reminds me of* or *have you heard what Mary did yesterday?*

In conversations, although there are many overlaps and interruptions, the way people take or allocate turns is not random. It is systematic and the signals, which may not be explicit, are clearly understood by speakers familiar with the cultural context. This is evidenced by the fact that conversations can flow coherently for extended periods of time, and without prolonged silences or breakdowns in communication. CA is interested in uncovering how it is that conversation keeps making sense and how people know when and how to make a contribution.

So, in trying to explain how it is that speakers keep taking turns, Sacks (1974) argued that it is because interactants in the conversation recognize points of potential speaker change, these being indicated by linguistic units which he calls *turn-constructional units*. A turn-constructional unit (TCU) is the minimal semantic unit that can constitute one complete turn of talk. In this example each of these turns is a TCU:

A: Do you want to have a drink?
B: Great idea

However in the following example each utterance could constitute a complete turn in its own right. Hence there are two turn-constructional units within the one speaker turn:

A: Do you want a drink? We could go somewhere after work.

The turn-constructional unit is a central concept in the CA explanation of how it is that in conversation

i) only one speaker speaks at a time; and
ii) speaker change recurs (Sacks, Schegloff and Jefferson, 1974: 700).

It is at the end of the turn-constructional unit that interactants in conversation recognize points of potential speaker change. One of the problems, however, with using the TCU as the basic descriptive unit of conversational interaction is that it is not clear how to identify the boundaries of a TCU.

A related issue of interest for CA researchers is how interactants determine, at the end of the turn-constructional unit, who the next speaker will be. There are two possibilities: the first is that the current speaker selects the person who is to be the next speaker, and the second possibility is that the next speaker self-selects. Sacks, Schegloff and Jefferson (1974/1978) argue that speaker change needs to be negotiated at every turn. This is partly motivated by the need to avoid the possibility of a lapse, i.e. of no one speaking. Thus central to CA's modelling of conversation is the existence of a turntaking mechanism, having the function of assigning turns to interactants in conversation.

In formal spoken English contexts, such as a doctor's appointment or a job interview, the turntaking is more ordered. The person with the higher status (e.g. doctor or interviewer) assigns the turns. In an interview the interviewer initiates the exchange and then, through a series of questions, assigns the turn. For example, the following extract is from an authentic interview with a prospective student who wishes to apply to do an English honours degree.

A= interviewer; B= prospective student

A	Come in. Come in. Ah good morning.
B	Good morning.
A	You're Mrs Finney?
B	Yes.
A	I am, *((syll))* How are you? My name's Hart and this is Mr Mortlake.
B	How are you?
A	How do you do? Won't you sit down?
B	Thank you.
A	Well you are proposing taking on a, quite something Mrs Finney, aren't you?
B	Yes.

(from London – Lund Corpus of Spoken English, Svartrik and Quirk, 1980)

Note that the turntaking is ordered and assigned by a series of questions by the interviewer. Essentially the talk consists of a series of exchanges, or adjacency pairs. From this it can be seen how the concept of the adjacency pair is closely linked to the formulation of turntaking 'rules'. It is a strategy for assigning turns, since a question seeks an answer, a statement, a response, etc.

By contrast the turntaking in casual conversations is not assigned by any particular person, and so it is much more intricate than a series of exchanges or adjacency pairs. As can be seen in the extract that follows, overlapping, interruptions and back-channelling are very common. They are all aspects of successful conversations and demonstrate that the speakers are collaborating and actively participating in the conversations.

The transcript is from an authentic conversation between two cooks and two kitchen hands in a hospital on their break. There are four participants: Gary, Mark, Chris and Doris. They first talk about food and then the conversation abruptly shifts to the discussion of a programme ('Willesee') on the previous night's television about delinquent children.

Text 4.4: Willesee

Gary:	Oh I've forgotten about lunch.
Mark:	Have you? You don't like the fish?
Gary:	No it's not that I don't, I LIKE it, it's the way it's done.
Mark:	Every time it's the same there's fish on every day.
Gary:	Yeah, called fish of the day.
Doris:	Yeah I mean some of the patients have got to have it for dietary reasons.
Chris:	Yeah. I love fish, = = I like
Gary:	= = That's stylish.
Chris:	I like Jewfish cutlets grilled or = = barbecued.
Gary:	= = See Willesee last night?
Mark:	Yeah that was good eh? Kids at the Cross.[1]
Gary:	Kids at the Cross.
Chris:	The young ones? The babies?
Gary:	Fourteen, fifteen.
Chris:	They start at nine.
Mark:	And the language.
Chris:	Mmm it's not their fault.
Gary:	The hooker brings back the
Mark:	I blame their parents.
Chris:	That's right.
Mark:	At fourteen they ended up the Cross doing it themselves.

---

[1] Cross refers to a suburb of Sydney called King's Cross which is well known for its brothels and nightclubs.

Chris: But mm, the thing is Mark until you have children you
don't understand. To me, you just don't understand.
The, you can have the best of parents
Mark: Oh true. Things can still go wrong.
Chris: You just guide them and hope that they = =
'cause I've got
Mark: = = Yeah sure because
Chris: I've got a nephew that his mother just raised three kids
by herself and they get everything. She works hard you
know. They've got a nice = = home, they've got
everything and now he is twelve and and he's an animal.

(Authors' data)

When Gary says *Oh I've forgotten about lunch*, this is a turn – constructional unit (TCU), where speaker change can occur. Mark's response *Have you? You don't like the fish?* is two TCU's within one turn of talk. The conversation proceeds with the participants self-selecting to talk, ensuring that there are no long lapses or awkward pauses – and the change of speaker occurs either at the end of a TCU, or a person interrupts and takes the turn. The more informal the conversation the more overlapping and interruptions occur. As you can see from this conversation, overlaps are very common, and speakers interrupt or complete each other's turn. For example:

Chris: Yeah. I love fish. = = I like
Gary: = = That's stylish

This extract also demonstrates how, amongst participants who are familiar, conversation tolerates – indeed thrives upon – disagreement and difference, whereas the talk between people less familiar to one another is characterized more by the exploration of similarity.

The conventions for turntaking in a language can be culturally specific and can therefore cause misunderstandings in cross-cultural contexts where these conventions are not shared. Moreover, Slade's (1996) research on workplace conversations (see below) has shown that there are significant differences in the way men and women take turns: the men interrupted each other much more frequently, while the women asked many more questions to indicate interest.

Because CA was one of the first approaches to demonstrate that conversation is systematically structured, it has had an important influence on the teaching of conversation. Structures lend themselves to instruction, and it is easy to see how such features as adjacency pairs, turn-taking strategies, conversational gambits and different feedback mechanisms, might inform the content of conversation classes. (For a more detailed discussion on teaching conversation see Chapter 9.)

4.3 Topic management: Topic development, topic change and topic choice

The way speakers introduce, develop and change topics is an important dimension of conversational structure. If, for example, a topic starts to flag, the participants may either change topic or reintroduce (or *recycle*) a topic from earlier in the conversation. If a new topic is introduced, then some link is usually made with the previous topic, the link being indicated by such initiating moves as *this reminds me of*, or *that is what happened to me*. The following gossip sequence illustrates at least two clearly signalled topic shifts.

Jenny:	I haven't decided what day I want to go on holidays = = because
All:	= = ( )
Jenny:	I don't know French and I don't know = =
Brenda:	= = But this reminds me of Tamara. She comes back from two months away, organises an extra month the following year and how she accumulates so many holidays is beyond me.

(The conversation then continues on the subject of Tamara, including a description of a fancy-dress costume she wore to a party.)

Jenny:	And then she had . . . I can't think what else, I know . . . eye shadow and the whole bit and then she had this old stick with a star on it. Um, and she had this stick thing . . . this stick thing that had a star on it and then she had a cape around her shoulders or something, and went 'poof' or something to people and then started = = laughing.
Brenda:	= = Yeah, here's something. You'd just go and break off a tree and stick a star on it.
Judy:	Reminds me of my Mum with a Christmas tree every year. We've got pine trees along the back fence. Mum gets up the barbie or whatever she can stand on, she just yanks off a branch and there's the tree.

(Authors' data)

However, it is not always the case that such strategies are used to introduce a new topic. In Text 4.4 (Willesee), a new topic is introduced without any overt signposting:

Chris:	Yeah. I love fish. = = I like
Gary:	= = That's stylish.
Chris:	I like Jewfish cutlets grilled or = = barbecued.
Gary:	= = See Willesee last night?

Mark: Yeah that was good eh? Kids at the Cross.
Gary: Kids at the Cross.

(Authors' data)

Expectations of what are appropriate and acceptable topics for conversation differ from context to context as well as from culture to culture. Differing perceptions of what is acceptable are one of the contributing factors to cross-cultural misunderstandings. As an example of how topics can be culturally and contextually specific, research into conversations between work colleagues at coffee time in Australian workplaces (see Slade, 1996), has shown how the topics of conversation differed according to the gender make-up of the group, class, age and ethnicity as well as degree of familiarity or distance between the participants. The conversations of three groups in workplaces were collected and analysed – an all-male group of supervisors in a car factory (group 1, between the ages of 40 and 60 and of different nationalities but all speaking English fluently), an all-female group of supervisors of a hospital kitchen (group 2; all in their late 20s and 30s, mainly Anglo-Australian) and a group of men and women, clerical staff in a hospital (group 3; all in their 20s). As work colleagues the participants see each other frequently but are not close friends, and the kind of language used reflected this. The topics of conversation with each group were:

Group 1 (all men)

- Joking or teasing each other – friendly ridicule at a personal level. This can sound offensive to those not familiar with the culture but in fact indicated solidarity and friendship. Teasing each other was the dominant type of talk that occurred in the all-male group and occurred very rarely in the other two groups.
- Telling stories (personal narratives). Particularly stories involving danger, violence, heroic deeds etc.
- Leisure and entertainment – football, rugby, soccer. Unlike Groups 2 and 3, this group rarely discussed what they did on the weekend, that is, past activities and future plans were only occasionally mentioned.

Group 2 (all women)

- Gossiping or chatting about others – this was the dominant text-type with the all-female group in this context. In Chapter 5 we present examples of these gossip texts.
- Personal information – for example, about boyfriends, weddings, families, future plans, etc.
- Exchanging opinions.
- Leisure and entertainment (cinema, TV. etc.).

- Telling stories of personal experiences (anecdotes – particularly amusing stories that involved embarrassing, humiliating or worrying situations). Examples of these are in Chapter 5.

Group 3 (men and women)

- Telling narratives and anecdotes – especially amusing ones.
- Joking or teasing was less explicit and direct than in Groups 1 and 2.
- Employment.
- Leisure and entertainment – especially what they did on the weekend. Unlike the other two groups, this group had detailed discussions on restaurants, food, clothes, discos, pubs, parties, plays, cinemas, etc.
- Personal information – work, study, family, future plans (e.g. travel).
- Chatting about others.
- Future plans.
- Illness and death.

The most frequently occurring stretch of talk in the all-male group was teasing or sending up (friendly ridicule). Gossip did not occur at all and there were fewer story-telling texts. The interesting contrast with the all-female group is that there was no teasing at all; the two most frequent genres were gossip and the story-telling genres (see Chapter 5 for a description of these). In the chat segments women discussed quite personal details including boyfriends, weddings, marriages, children and relatives. They also discussed their future plans and past activities in detail, such as weekends, holidays etc. Instances of voicing opinions occurred more frequently than with the men and there were more instances of story-telling.

In the mixed group amusing or surprising stories dominated the conversation and so there were many more story-telling texts including anecdotes, narratives, recounts and exempla (see Chapter 5 for a detailed discussion of the different types of stories told in conversation). Joke-telling was more frequent than in the all-female group. There was some teasing but not nearly as much as in the all-male group.

This analysis of what topics are appropriate in particular cultural contexts has important implications for both the description and teaching of conversation. For a start, it reveals the social role and purpose of the conversations in these contexts. The primary motivation behind casual conversations between work colleagues (who see each other frequently but are not good friends) is to share opinions and attitudes about the world, to explore similarities and likenesses. So, for example, in the gossip texts, by criticizing an absent third person, the women are explicitly or implicitly saying what the appropriate way to behave is. Similarly, the men teasing each other about physical or behavioural differences are establishing what they consider to be the appropriate way to behave or to appear. It is this exploration of similarity, therefore, that is the motivation behind these conversations. As a consequence of this functional motivation, disagreement rarely occurs within the talk at coffee time at work, whether it be telling a story, recounting or gossiping. This contrasts with conversations between close friends at dinner parties, for example, where there is likely to be much more debate and disagreement about issues – where they are motivated by not only exploring similarities but also exploring differences. By exploring how and what topics are initiated and developed we can see the powerful social work achieved by conversations.

It is important to stress that the topic differences and characteristics described apply to these particular cultural contexts. We would not claim, on the basis of these findings alone, that men do not gossip, or that women do not send each other up. But it does seem to be case that, in these particular sub-cultures, men will send each other up when they are getting to know each other and gossip only when they are close friends. Conversely, for women in these contexts, we believe that gossip is a way of showing their group affiliation, and their willingness to get to know each other. Women, in these cultural contexts, are only likely to send each other up when they are close friends.

In language-teaching contexts it is obviously important to be aware of what topics and genres the learners will need when speaking English. Most EFL/ESL textbooks cover a limited range of topics and genres, some of which may not be relevant to the learners' needs. A knowledge of the learners' likely conversational needs and the contexts in which they will need English allows the possibility of making comparisons between the way gossiping, teasing and telling stories, for example, are achieved in the learners' own culture and in the target culture.

4.4 Discourse strategies

4.4.1 Openings and closings

As with topic choice, the ways speakers open and close conversations are culturally and contextually dependent. Compare these two opening exchanges: one in a formal interview (cited above) and one between friends at work :

(1)	A	Come in. Come in. Ah good morning.
	B	Good morning.
	A	You're Mrs Finney?
	B	Yes.

(2)	Jim:	Good morning brother.
	Keith:	Sit down take a seat.
	John:	Good morning brother. How the hell are you?
	Keith:	Good morning brother. Oh come in. Sit yourself down and shut up.

(Authors' data)

In formal spoken contexts such as the first example above, there is a specified setting with formal turn assignment where openings are more likely to be in a simple adjacency pair, such as *Come in, good morning, Good morning.*

In contrast, openings and closings in casual conversation are rarely achieved through a simple adjacency-pair structure, such as *hi*, followed by *how are you?* or *bye* followed by *See you later*. Much more frequently the opening or closing is achieved through an exchange of three or more moves, as in the conversation with Keith and John above. Closings are often preceded by pre-closings such as *Anyway, I have to go now* or *look at the time, I have to rush*, or as in the following authentic example:

Harry:	Yeah time to go. Well enjoy your male volunteers group.
Jim:	I'll talk to her on Monday.
Harry:	Yeah talk to us all.
Jim:	See you later.

Pre-closings, however, do not always lead to closing the conversation as they can also be a marker of a change of topic, providing the way for a new topic to be introduced. It is only when no participant initiates a new topic that the final closings are said and the conversation ends.

So conversations tend to be closed in such a way that 'one speaker's completion will not occasion another speaker's talk, and that will not be heard as some speaker's silence' (Schegloff and Sacks, 1973: 294). Speakers tend not to finish a conversation abruptly. Rather, they set the scene for a final closing.

Language learners often encounter difficulties with conversational openings and closings, partly because of the cultural specificity of the strategies that are used, and also because of lack of familiarity with standard formulaic expressions.

4.4.2   Feedback in conversation

Feedback (or *back-channelling*) refers to ways in which listeners show that they are following the conversation and ways that speakers check on the attention of their listeners. Feedback conveys agreement, disagreement, interest and attention, and is essential for maintaining coherent and

131

smooth conversation. The form and rate of feedback is culturally specific: inappropriate or apparently absent feedback can contribute to the breakdown of conversation.

Gardner (1994) outlines seven different types of listener contributions that are common in casual conversation in English. These are:

1. *continuers*: these signal the present speaker's right to continue holding the floor, e.g. *mmhm, uh, huh*;
2. *acknowledgments*: these claim agreement or understanding of the previous turn e.g. *mm, yeah*;
3. *assessments*: these are appreciative in some way of what has just been said e.g. *how awful, shit, wonderful*;
4. *news markers*: these mark the speaker's turn as news e.g. *really, is it!*;
5. *questions*: these indicate interest by asking for further details, or they may be asked in order to repair some misunderstanding;
6. *collaborative completions*: one participant finishes or repeats another's utterance; and
7. *non-verbal vocalizations*: e.g. laughter, sighs etc.

McCarthy (2003) also describes the role of non-minimal responses and argues that tokens, such as *really* and *fine* show 'engaged listenership' and thereby communicate a greater degree of interpersonal information than the more minimal back-channels.

As with many other discourse strategies, feedback is not only culturally specific but also changes from context to context, depending on the level of formality, the gender make-up and the level of contact between the participants. The following two transcripts demonstrate these differences. The first transcript is from a conversation between a group of women and the second transcript is from an all-male group. The group of women are supervisors of the kitchen staff at a hospital, and are all between the ages of 28 and 37. They are all Anglo-Australian. The all-male group are shop floor supervisors at a car factory, between the ages of 40 and 60, and of different nationalities, but all speak English fluently.

Text 4.5: First meeting

Jessie: Right. Right and so when did you == actually meet him?
Brenda: == So we didn't actually meet until that night.
Jessie: Until that night.
Judy: Oh hysterical! [laughs]
Brenda: Well, I met him that night. We were all, we all went out to dinner. So I had champagne and strawberries at the airport.
Jessie: And what was it like the when you first saw him? Were you really == nervous?

Brenda:	==Well I was hanging out of a window watching him in his car, and I thought 'oh God what about this!'
Jessie:	[laughs]
Brenda:	And he'd combed his hair and shaved his eyebrows == and
Jessie:	== Had you seen a photo of him?
Brenda:	Oh yeah, I had photos of him, photos . . . and I'd spoken to him on the phone.
Jessie:	Did you get on well straight away?
Brenda:	Uh, well we sort of. I'm a sort of nervy person when I first meet people, so it was sort of . . . you know . . . == just nice to him.
Jessie:	== [laughs]

(Authors' data)

In this conversation Jessie and Judy are asking Brenda about her husband and how they first met. Her feedback is consistently supportive – asking questions to indicate interest and probing the conversation forward by positive assessments, such as *Oh hysterical* and laughter. There are no pauses – in fact there are many overlaps (transcribed as ==) indicating a supportive, collaborative conversational style.

The feedback is quite different in the all-male conversation below. Keith's initial feedback does not encourage John to continue; it is a negative evaluation of the topic John has raised. However, John continues, but at the end of his turn about soccer there is a three-second pause. Although there is no feedback at all from the other participants, John tries to continue on the topic but it fades out without encouragement from Keith. Keith's *yeah* is a continuer that does not really indicate involvement.

Text 4.6: Soccer

John:	I never miss a game. The only time I don't go and watch them is, when they play Queanbeyan against Monaro. It's too far away. And that time there was um the England soccer team.
Keith:	It's only a game.
John:	I soccer mad. The police yesterday they turned the radio on to have a look to score the goals, firstly in the morning they have a look who won the game in English soccer then in the afternoon they my brothers, they're glued to the ABC, because here they tell who scored the goals but in the morning once on the radio they say, 'oh Liverpool won one nil or two nil' or but in the afternoon he always say, 'I hate to see who score'. [pause three seconds]
John:	I thought there's going to be a big fight yesterday you know.
Keith:	Yeah.

(Authors' data)

4.4.3 Cross-cultural variation in the use of discourse strategies

In Chapter 1, we briefly described the orientation to discourse coming from interactional sociolinguistics, a branch of sociolinguistics that blends anthropology, sociology and linguistics. Interactional sociolinguistics is concerned with the relationship between language, society and culture and as such it has made a significant contribution to our understanding of cross-cultural variation in the use of discourse strategies. In this section we will look in particular at Gumperz's research into cross-cultural communication.

Gumperz's studies focus on variation in the use of language, such as the different ways speakers pronounce words, structure arguments, take turns or give feedback. He is interested in examining the variation in language use, and correlates the linguistic differences with non-linguistic differences, such as ethnicity, gender and class. His (1982) central tenet is that the actual ability to communicate depends on much more than a knowledge of the grammatical and lexical features of English. His studies have shown that misunderstandings and breakdowns in communication that so often occur between members of minority groups who have English as a second language and English native speakers are not so much due to a lack of syntactic or semantic knowledge but arise because of a lack of knowledge concerning the procedures and strategies used in conversation and the conventions underlying language in use.

Through detailed analyses of grammatical, lexical, prosodic and discourse features of conversations involving interracial and interethnic groups, Gumperz has demonstrated that misunderstandings and miscommunication which occur are due not to grammatical problems but to different ways of speaking (prosodically and phonologically) and different ways of structuring discourse. Gumperz's studies show that cross-cultural communication can be riddled with misinterpretation of intent and mutually negative reactions which can result in increasing alienation and frustration felt by members of minority groups. Many native speakers are unlikely to recognize that these are communication problems caused by linguistic differences. Systematic linguistic and cultural differences in the use of English can result in damaging group stereotypes which in turn increase the chance of miscommunication.

Gumperz, Jupp and Roberts (1979: 5), working on cross-cultural communication with the National Council of Industrial Language training in the United Kingdom, identified three main causes of misunderstanding which can arise in conversation. These are:

- misunderstandings which arise from the different cultural assumptions about the situation and about appropriate behaviour and intentions within it;

- misunderstandings which arise from different ways of structuring discourse;
- misunderstandings which occur as a result of the use of a different set of unconscious linguistic conventions such as prosodic features, intonation, stress, etc.

Gumperz, Jupp and Roberts point out, for example, that there are linguistic skills involved in sounding polite, in maintaining conversational continuity, and in building up what sounds like a reasonable and polite argument. These skills are learned as a child acquires a language but become so unconscious and automatic that we forget that they are language skills that might need to be taught to learners of English as a second language. The following is an example of a misunderstanding that occurred, purportedly because of culturally different ways of structuring discourse:

(An employee, a speaker of Indian English, is asking for two extra days holiday):

Kulwant:	Dave, I want two more extra days = =
Dave:	= = Hang on a minute. What are you talking about, two more = =
Kulwant:	= = I want two more extra days off.
Dave:	Why? For what? What are you talking about?
Kulwant:	Well, my sister is going to be married on 2nd August. I have to go there so I want two extra days off.
Dave:	So you want two days off, not two extra days. You meant two days off.
Kulwant:	Not two days. You know, I'm going on holidays at the end of this month for two weeks, I want two more extra days in that.

(Gumperz and Roberts, 1980: Unit 3: 11)

The employee plunges straight into his request for more leave without first establishing the reason for the request or that he has already booked his holiday. So (from the perspective of his interlocutor, a speaker of British English) he presents the information in the 'wrong' order and with the 'wrong' focus. These kinds of linguistic difficulties at the level of discourse result in miscommunication and often misleading inferences being drawn about the person, for example that he is rude, boring or not talking sense.

Gumperz, Jupp and Roberts' research led to the development of materials to be used in language teaching as well as in cross-cultural training programmes in industry. The aim of the training programmes, involving both English native speakers as well as employees with English as a second language, was to develop awareness skills for inter-ethnic communication and to develop an understanding of the causes of cross-cultural miscommunication. These materials have also been effectively used for teaching discourse skills to ESL learners.

135

4.4.4 Gender differences in the use of discourse strategies

Mention has already been made about gender preferences in topic choice amongst work colleagues. Recent research on gender and language has shown that there are also systematic and generalizable differences in the ways men and women structure discourse. All the discourse features we have discussed in this chapter – the interactional structure (moves and exchanges), turntaking, topic development, feedback strategies – display variation according to the gender of the participants.

Coates' research on women's talk (1995, 1996) in the UK has shown that in these cultural contexts women tell stories that are significantly different from stories told by men. Her research has shown that women often tell stories against themselves – where they find themselves in impossible, humiliating or embarrassing situations, where the stories are not only told to amuse or entertain but by doing so they create new worlds or new ways of seeing the existing order:

> Story-telling functions to bind these women together, through creating a shared world . . . through our story-telling we create and re-create our identities and experiment with possible selves, in a context of mutuality and trust.
>
> (Coates, 1996: 115)

Men's stories by contrast in similar contexts tend to be about danger, violence, heroic deeds, etc.

Fishman (1980), in a seminal article based on an analysis of conversations collected in the USA, argues that the feedback strategies used by women are significantly different from those used by men and that this is a result of the 'necessary work involved in producing successful interactions' (1980: 1270). She argues that women ask a lot more questions than men and that their greater use of questions 'is an attempt to solve the conversational problem of gaining a response to their utterances' (1980: 129). Fishman's other findings included:

- women are more likely than men in those particular contexts to make utterances that demand or encourage responses from their fellow speakers;
- women in those particular contexts showed a greater tendency to make use of positive minimal responses (such as *mm*, *hmm*);
- women in those particular contexts showed a greater tendency to use the pronouns *you* and *we* which explicitly acknowledge the existence of the other speaker;
- men, in those particular contexts, were more likely to challenge or dispute the speaker's statements and;

- men, in those particular contexts, used more mechanisms for controlling the topic of conversation, including both topic development and the introduction of new topics, than did women.

It is important to stress that these findings may be indicative of other English conversational contexts but not necessarily so. Nevertheless, there is a body of research (such as Coates, 1996, 2003; Tannen, 1990) that suggests that there is consistent and describable variation according to a range of factors such as gender and culture.

Summary

In this chapter we have described the discourse structure of conversation, focusing primarily on those features which are distinctive of spoken English. We first described how cohesion is achieved, both within and across speaker turns. While not necessarily guaranteeing the overall coherence of talk, cohesion contributes to the sense that talk is jointly constructed, contingent, and on topic. We next looked at how interactivity is achieved, identifying the basic move-and-exchange structure of conversation and the turn-taking mechanisms used in casual speech. Other discourse features of conversation were then described – how topics are initiated, developed and exchanged, and the different kinds of feedback strategies listeners use to ensure the flow of conversational discourse.

Throughout the chapter we referred to many of the different theoretical approaches we briefly described in Chapter 1. Each of the approaches discussed in this chapter share a functional orientation to the analysis and description of conversation in English. What they have in common is the view that conversation cannot be described purely in terms of grammatical units. Each of these approaches therefore recognizes the need to posit as the basic unit of analysis a semantic unit rather than a grammatical unit. Conversational discourse cannot be envisaged as a 'super-sentence', since the point is not that it is larger than a sentence but that it is different in kind. To put it another way, conversational discourse is not a collection of decontextualized units of language structure. Rather it is a semantic entity consisting, at least in part, of interactional units, such as moves, turns, exchanges etc. Depending on their theoretical orientation, researchers have come up with supra-grammatical units to explicate the structure of extended discourse. The units we described in this chapter – adjacency pair, move, exchange, speech function, turn-constructional unit – are all semantic units, useful for analysing the micro-interactions of conversation. The micro-analysis can show how conversation can keep

The discourse features of conversation

going and continue to be coherent, but what is also needed is a macro-global picture: a top-down picture that can capture how participants in conversations weave in and out of telling stories, gossiping, exchanging opinions, joking etc. To account for the global structure of extended conversation we will use the concept of *genre* – and this is the focus of the next chapter. It is in the complementarity of each of these descriptions – from vocabulary, to grammar, to discourse, to genre – that we begin to be able to describe how language is organized to enable conversation to work and to have the social power it does.

Tasks

1. In the following extract, in which four women are talking about interior decorating, identify the ways in which cohesion is achieved. For example, can you find instances of:

   - grammatical cohesion: e.g. reference (both internal and external), conjunctions;
   - lexical cohesion: e.g. repetition, synonyms, and lexical chains.

Extract 1

<S01>	I think it's a nice blue.
<S04>	I quite like it.
<S03>	I think I find it too too.
<S01>	Mother's = =
<S04>	= = I'm going to paint my new room, like I wanted. I'm going to paint the side wall a colour.
<S01>	Well I think, 'cause I I'm, it's lovely this terrific bold bright. Lesley's, Lesley's = = got that.
<S04>	= = Lesley's, oh Lesley's house is gorgeous.
<S01>	That um you know
<S04>	Pink and = = yellow and
<S01>	= = She's got this you know this terrific one wall which is just hot pink and it looks = =
<S04>	= = And it's great.
<S01>	And then she's got a beautiful royal blue couch right in front of it. It's the most uncomfortable couch in the world but it's, it looks = = terrific.
<S02>	= = Gorgeous.
<S01>	[laughs]. But um
<S04>	Well that's what I thought I'd do in that room. I thought I'd just paint = =
<S01>	= = something bold yeah.

> <S04>   know something fairly bold along that middle
> wall that's you know that's
> <S03>   Back to the fifties.
> <S04>   What do you mean, 'back to the fifties'?
> <S03>   That's what you used to do in the fifties. Feature
> walls.= =
> <S02>   = = Feature wall yes.

(OZTALK)

2. Here is the transcript from a family dinner table conversation. Read the transcript and then:

   i) Identify the different kinds of adjacency pairs and the different types of expansions used.
   ii) Reclassify these adjacency pairs and their expansions in terms of exchange structure and classify the different move types within this structure.
   iii) Describe the different types of feedback in the transcript and the role that these perform in this conversation.
   iv) Describe the ways the speakers introduce, develop and change topics in this conversation.
   v) Outline some of the cultural assumptions embedded in the talk, and comment on how the participants' familiarity, age and gender are both constructed and reflected in the talk.

Extract 2

There are five participants:

Kate	female, aged 41, Anglo-Australian
Craig	male, aged 47, Anglo-Australian
Jane	female, aged 47, Anglo-Australian, sister of Kate
Mother	female, aged 74, Anglo-Australian, mother of Kate and Jane
Father	male, aged 70, Anglo-Australian, father of Kate and Jane
Context:	The dinner is at a holiday house in Bandon Grove, in the Hunter Region of New South Wales, where the five participants are staying for a long weekend. The house is owned by Craig and the others are his guests. Craig is a criminal laywer, Jane is a corporate lawyer, Father is a retired defamation lawyer and journalist, Mother is a retired arts administrator and Kate is a transcriber (formerly journalist and restaurateur).

Text 6: 'Bandon Grove'

CRAIG:	Kate I must say this fish is cooked beautifully.
MOTHER:	It's lovely darling.
KATE:	Thanks. Thank you Craig so much for saying so. Jane, Jane's not happy.
JANE:	Mine's cold and [general laughter]
MOTHER:	You're having me on. [inaudible overlap]
KATE:	Well Jane think of smoked salmon.
CRAIG:	Grab the pan.
JANE:	Oh no I'll grab the pan I think.
KATE:	Oh.
JANE:	Oh no no. It's, I'm sorry.
CRAIG:	Mmm. Mine is sensational. Sensational.
JANE:	It's alright Kate. Oh the pan's been washed has it.
CRAIG:	It hasn't has it. God mine's terrific. Do you know how to turn the stove on? Look everybody. Watch. This is the, this is the stove turning on demo. Stand back so you can see. Turn it to the right. Turn it on like . . . that . . . press the button. Very easy.
FATHER:	Oh automatic.
CRAIG:	You don't even need a match.
KATE:	Mmm.
FATHER:	Is that electricity is it?
CRAIG:	It's gas.
KATE:	Mum, you're not enjoying your dinner are you?
MOTHER:	I am.
CRAIG:	She is. Her fish. Look at these chefs. They're so sensitive, aren't they?
MOTHER:	But you know that I have a very small appetite.
KATE:	Si.
MOTHER:	Si. [. . .]
JANE:	Oh dear. I'm very . . . [whispers] I absolutely hate the smell of fish cooking.
MOTHER:	What?
JANE:	Turn it down.
CRAIG:	She says she prefers cigarettes to fish.
JANE:	Oh shut up. I didn't say = = that.
MOTHER:	= = Well that's a fair comment.
CRAIG:	Oh so.
KATE:	Just leave her alone.
CRAIG:	Oh.

KATE:	Nothing worse than bloody . . .
CRAIG:	Vigilantes.
KATE:	Non smokers.
JANE:	Oh look will you all shut up.
CRAIG:	[laughs]
JANE:	I really do hate the smell of fish.
CRAIG:	Well we'll stop cooking it now.
MOTHER:	Well we won't do it again.

(OZTALK)

5 Genres in conversation: Storytelling and gossiping

Introduction

In Chapter 1 we described the significance of conversation, arguing that it is a critical site for the maintenance and modification of our social identities. We argued that it both creates and reflects our social worlds and that it is the primary location for the enactment of social values and relationships. And because of its centrality in our daily lives we argued that it ought to be given more prominence in ELT classes. In Chapters 2 to 4, by providing an account of conversational structure at the level of vocabulary, grammar and discourse, we demonstrated that conversation is a highly structured, functionally motivated, semantic activity. In this chapter we will be building on the description outlined in previous chapters, describing conversation at the level of *genre*. The focus therefore has moved in this chapter from the micro-structure (i.e. the vocabulary and grammar) to the macro-structure (i.e. the overall organization) of casual talk, building up a cumulative description of conversation in the process. We will first describe the different genres that commonly occur in English conversation and then we will describe in detail two of the most frequently occurring genres: storytelling and gossip.

5.1 Chat and Chunks in conversation

Here is a segment of naturally occurring conversation. It takes place in the coffee room of a hospital at morning break time. There are four participants: Gary, Pauline, Bron and Pat. They are all clerical staff in the hospital and have worked together for over two years. They are in their mid- to late twenties. (A short segment of this conversation, turns 26–37, was presented in Chapter 4, detailing a move-by-move analysis.)

Text 5.1 State theatre

1	Gary:	Well, I got the pictures tomorrow night. Boy! I I love that, that State Theatre.
2	Pauline:	Oh isn't it beautiful!
3	Gary:	Yeah.

4	Bron:	Yeah.
5	Gary:	Yeah.
6	Pauline:	I really love, it's my favourite.
7	Pat:	I've never been there.
8	Bron:	Oh, it's beautiful! Oh it's beautiful! It's got chandeliers and things.
9	Gary:	I usually just wear jeans and sand shoes to go to the pictures but if, if I go to the State, I usually put on something just a little bit better.
10	All:	[laugh]
11	Gary:	You can't outdo the place.
12	Pauline:	No.
13	Bron:	Exactly.
14	Pat:	I remember once I went to a film and ah I'd just bought this new outfit and it was long silky black pants that came up all in one.
15	Pauline:	Mmm.
16	Pat:	And then it was an overlay with splits right up to here, and that was in silk, and then it had a black sash. And I didn't think anything of it till I had to go to the toilet. I had to take the whole lot off and pull the whole lot down. [laughs]
17	All:	[laugh]
18	Pat:	So I missed half the film.
19	All:	[laugh]
20	Pauline:	Have you been to the State since? Oh, you wouldn't have. It's been renovated, 'cause it looks really nice.= = See I I, I last time I went to see
21	Bron:	= = Yeah.
22	Pauline:	Now, what'd I see? Can't remember what it was, but I keep saying gosh, it's you know it's lovely but it smelled dusty. Even the seats = = smelled dusty.
23	Bron:	= = yeah. No it's absolutely beautiful.
24	Gary:	[coughs] [inaudible]
25	Pat:	I'm not going to last out the day. I've had to pull I had to pull about twenty files and about eleven ops = =
26	Bron:	= = I'm about to throw Joanne out the window.
27	Pat:	Joanne who?
28	Bron:	Peterson.
29	Pat:	Why?
30	Bron:	She gets really pushy. I'm looking for a file for Gary. Kerry gave me three others and I was in the middle of finding the third one for her.
31	Gary:	Kerry gave you three did she?
32	Bron:	Yeah. You know they have to be done and Joanne came up and she said, 'Oh, can you do this?' and

I said, 'Well you're at the end of a very long line
if you're prepared to wait' and she said, 'Well,
she's at the Oncology clinic right now' and I said,
'But these have to be done as well' and sort of
smiling all the way through it I said, 'Look, you
know it's three minutes to three. Liz should be
down in a minute if you want to wait till then.'
and she went ahhh [huffing sound] then she went
away and I thought, 'Oh yeah, end of the = =
story.'

33 Gary: = = she gets very worried.

34 Bron: and then she came back again and um she said,
'Are those files there? Did Kerry give you those files
there?' and I knew what she was going to say next.
And I said, 'Oh, among other things' and she went
'Oh it's just that they can wait until after this one
'cause they're needed today'. Oh I was about ready
to strangle her = = she gets

35 Gary: Joanne's too busy.

36 Bron: I know and I appreciate that she's busy but she gets
really pushy.

37 Pat: Yeah, I don't like pushy people either.

(Authors' data)

The extract displays a number of features typically associated with the
interactional, spontaneous and interpersonal nature of casual conversation – features which were dealt with in the preceding chapters. For
example, from the interactional perspective, the interactants take turns,
they interrupt and they use back-channel devices; there are topics (at least
two) and instances of topic shift (at least one). There is a high incidence
of discourse markers characteristic of informal speech (*well, oh, so, and,*
etc). The text also contains various spontaneity phenomena, such as hesitations, incompletions, false starts, fillers and repetitions. Utterances are
lexically sparse, and the vocabulary is of a fairly high frequency. The
interpersonal nature of the conversation is encoded in the number of
instances of appraisal language (Martin, 2000), such as *absolutely beautiful, really pushy, appreciate, don't like*, and of vague language, for
example *sort of smiling*.

Notice, also, that the extract consists of segments of highly interactive, multi-party talk (such as turns 1 to 13) and longer, more structured
and more monologic segments such as the story Pat tells (turns 14 and
16) and the gossip sequence (turns 26–37), with Bron's relatively long
turns (30, 32 and 34) where she provides evidence for why Joanne is
annoying her. This feature – what we will call *chat and chunk* – is
typical of much casual conversation. That is to say, conversation

consists of different kinds of talk – *chat* sequences interpersed with larger *chunks*. The chat segments are those where structure is managed 'locally' – that is, turn-by-turn. The chunks are those stretches of conversation that have a global (or macro-) structure, that is, they appear to move through predictable stages where the structure beyond the exchange is predictable.

Chat segments are amenable to the kind of analysis outlined in the previous chapters, i.e. analysis that models conversation in terms of the micro-interaction, the move-by-move unfolding of talk. The chunk segments, on the other hand, require an analysis which can capture the predictable macro-structure. For example, as soon as we hear Pat say *I remember once . . .* (turn 14) we have the expectation that not only is Pat going to hold the floor (or at least make a bid to do so) but that she is going to embark on some kind of story. This in turn sets up an expectation that the story will unfold through various stages, including some kind of complication (*I had to go to the toilet*) and its outcome (*So I missed half the film*). We will attempt to show how not only do stories in conversation have a predictable schematic structure (see Chapter 1), but that, within the the general category of *story* there are different subtypes, each with its characteristic structure. We shall also show how gossip texts, too, have a predictable structure. The focus of the rest of this chapter, then, is on describing these macro-structures of casual conversation.

5.2 Genre theory

We will use the concept of *genre* to describe the structure of these longer turns of talk. There are many different approaches from different disciplines to the analysis of genre (see Chapter 1). What all the approaches have in common is the recognition that there are, in both spoken and written language, different text-types or genres with their own different internal structures, which accord with different social goals. Each approach is interested in the analysis of linguistic variation. Where they vary is in their particular orientation, in their formulation of relevant issues, and their adoption of different methodologies.

The term 'genre' is used in an everyday, non-technical sense simply to refer to a distinctive category of discourse, whether it be spoken or written. For example it is not uncommon to hear or read such comments as *it's a new rock and roll genre* and *his genre-breaking crime novel*. It is also a term that is now widely used by theoreticians and practitioners across a number of different disciplines – the central issue being what features are criterial in distinguishing different genres.

In sociolinguistics, as described in Chapter 1, the term genre is used in the ethnography of communication to refer to such textual categories as jokes, stories, lectures or sermons. In variation theory, although the term genre is not used, the notion of the overall text structure, corresponding to the notion of generic structure, has been central to much of Labov's (1972) work on discourse. In linguistics, the term is used in Critical Discourse Analysis (CDA) and in Systemic Functional Linguistics (SFL). In the former a genre is defined as 'a socially ratified way of using language in connection with a particular type of social activity (e.g. interview, narrative exposition)' (Fairclough, 1995: 14). In Systemic Functional Linguistics the term has been used to describe how people use language to achieve culturally recognized goals.

Within an SFL framework, Martin defines genre as 'a staged, goal-oriented, social process in which speakers engage as members of a culture' (1984: 25). His definition can be elaborated as follows:

- *staged*: a genre is referred to as staged as its meanings are made in steps; it usually takes more than one step for participants to achieve their goals;
- *goal-oriented*: it is goal-oriented in that genres typically move through stages to a point of closure, and are considered incomplete if the culmination is not reached; and
- *social processes*: genres are negotiated interactively and are a realization of a social purpose.

As genres are enacted in texts (either spoken or written), and as texts have different purposes in the culture; they will unfold in different ways, working through different stages. Martin (1984) refers to this patterned staging of texts as the genre's *schematic structure*. Each stage of the structure contributes a part of the overall meaning that is necessary to ensure the successful achievement of the goal of the genre. Schematic structures typically consist both of obligatory and of optional elements (Halliday and Hasan, 1985). Thus, a shopping encounter in western cultures may or may not begin with a salutation (*good morning*) and an offer of service (*how can I help you?*), but will always include a request for service (called a *sale request* in Halliday and Hasan, 1985) and some form of sale compliance, which in turn is followed by the obligatory sequence: sale, purchase and purchase closure:

> *A bag of crisps, please.* [sale request]
> *Here you are.* [sale compliance]
> *That'll be a dollar fifty.* [sale]
> *There you go.* [purchase]
> *Thanks.* [purchase closure]

Again, a parting salutation (*have a nice day*) is optional although in some cultural contexts it may be considered obligatory. Halliday and Hasan argue that it is the obligatory elements of the schematic structure that define the genre and that

> the appearance of all these elements in a specific order corresponds to our perception of whether the text is complete or incomplete.
>
> (1985: 62)

Central to genre theory is the notion that genres are culturally embedded, and that, within a particular culture, there tend to be regularly patterned and socially sanctioned ways in which genres unfold. So, in contrast to the western pattern of a service encounter outlined above, Mitchell (1957) found that market transactions in Tunisia tended to follow this pattern: *salutation → enquiry as to object of sale → investigation→ bargaining→ conclusion.* Neither pattern is arbitrary: each reflects the way, in its particular cultural context, that the function of obtaining service is most efficiently *and* most effectively achieved. That is, the need for prompt service has also to be balanced against the need to maintain a degree of social harmony – hence the salutations.

Familiarity with generic structures is a characteristic of members of the same speech community; ignorance of genres can therefore exclude people from effective social participation. Thus, there is a strong argument for a pedagogical role for genre analysis, a view that underlies approaches to the teaching of writing that foreground the explicit teaching of generic structures. As we shall show, this view also supports a genre-based approach to the teaching of spoken language. First, though, we shall take a closer look at the genres of casual conversation. This in turn will involve describing in more detail the analytic tools involved in genre analysis.

The analysis of a spoken genre involves a number of steps:

- identifying a 'chunk' of talk that is amenable to a generic description;
- defining the social purpose of the genre;
- differentiating the different stages (the macro-structure), including specifying obligatory and optional stages; and
- analysing the linguistic features of each stage.

The first stage in genre analysis is the identification of chunks of text that have internal consistency, and seem to move through predictable stages. This is where one participant holds the floor for a period, for example to tell a story, to gossip etc. When reporting conversations, people will often say things like *Chris told us this amazing* story *about when he was hitchhiking in Italy*, or *We had a good* gossip *about work while Jack was in the men's room*. These conversational chunks are often monologic, as is the case of stories, and once initiated, constrain the other interactants to yield the floor until all the stages of the sequence have been realized. In the example quoted at the beginning of the chapter (Text 5.1), Pat's turns in this segment have this 'chunk-like' quality:

14	Pat:	I remember once I went to a film and ah I'd just bought this new outfit and it was long silky black pants that came up all in one.
15	Pauline:	Mmm.
16	Pat:	And then it was an overlay with splits right up to here, and that was in silk, and then it had a black sash. And I didn't think anything of it till I had to go to the toilet. I had to take the whole lot off and pull the whole lot down. [laugh]
17	All:	[laugh]
18	Pat:	So I missed half the film.
19	All:	[laugh]

It is not, enough, of course to identify a single chunk in a single text; for a chunk to be considered *generic*, it must occur with sufficient regularity and consistency across a range of texts distributed among a representative sample of members of the same discourse community. This means that the analysis must draw on a representative corpus of texts, identifying those chunks that seem to share similar features.

Having identified a chunk, the second stage in genre analysis is to define its social purpose in terms of its typical contexts of use, and, at the same time, to supply it with a functional label that reflects this purpose. Is the text's function to inform, to amuse, to criticize, to warn, for example? Simply 'telling a story' is too broad a description of the genre's purpose, and does not necessarily capture the way that social reality is constructed by means of telling and being told stories. Speaker–hearer conceptions of the kind of social activity taking place and its social purpose determine the way that the discourse is structured. As we will see, stories are told for different purposes, and the functional label needs to reflect each purpose accurately.

The third stage in genre analysis is the identification and differentiation of the genre's constituent stages. These are best labelled in terms of their function, too. A widely accepted model of the narrative structure of personal anecdotes is that described by Labov and Waletzky (1967):

(Abstract) ^ Orientation ^ Complication ^ Evaluation ^ Resolution ^ Coda

where ^ = is followed by.

The stages are written in a linear sequence and the symbol ^ is placed between them to indicate how they are ordered with respect to one another.

The abstract stage announces the onset of a narrative, often in a way that encapsulates the point or theme of the story (*speaking of X . . .*), and/or by attributing it: *A friend of mine told me this amazing story the other day . . .* (Brazil, 1995). The purpose of the orientation is to provide circumstantial information, as in:

> I went to a film, and ah, I'd just bought this new outfit and it was long silky, black pants that came up all in one ...

The purpose of the complication is to introduce, into a sequence of events, a problem:

> And I didn't think anything of it till I had to go to the toilet.

The evaluation signals the speaker's attitude to the events: this may in fact be spread throughout the text, and it may take a paralinguistic form, such as laughter. The resolution shows how the actions of the protagonist or of another character resolve the problem, while the coda serves to connect the story to the conversational context in which it takes place – providing a bridge from the past (event time) to the present (utterance time). Labov and Waletzky (1967) explains that the two stages – *abstract* and *coda* – are optional stages, that is, they occur in many, but not all, instances of narratives. The other stages of *orientation – complication, evaluation* and *resolution* – are obligatory and are therefore defining stages of the genre. The optional stages of a genre can be captured using this notation:

(Abstract) ^ Orientation ^ Complication ^ Evaluation ^ Resolution ^ (Coda)

The stages within the brackets ( ) are optional, occurring only in some instances of the genre.

The final stage in the analysis of a genre is a description of the micro-features of the genre, specifically the lexico-grammatical features that characterize the genre, and which serve both to differentiate the genre from other genres, and to differentiate the stages within the genre from each other. For example, it is apparent that the following four orientation stages of four different conversational stories share features in common:

1. I remember once I went to a film, and ah, I'd just bought this new outfit and it was long silky, black pants that came up all in one.

(Authors' data)

2. I remember we were sitting for our analytical chemistry exam and it was the final exams, and they have sort of like bench desks

(Authors' data)

149

> 3. I remember that journey, we went from Yarmouth, when we had the car [Yeah] and we went into Norwich and there's a ring road . . .
>
> (McCarthy, 1991)

> 4. I still remember going to one of those meetings they brought out the sandwiches, at one of those meetings they brought out the sandwiches – in London when they had meetings at lunchtime or something . . .
>
> (Authors' data)

Apart from the use of the discourse marker *I (still) remember* . . ., other linguistic features shared by these texts are the use of:

- past tenses;
- first person pronouns;
- time references (*once, the final exams, when we had the car, at lunchtime*);
- references to place (*went to a film, bench desks, from Yarmouth . . . into Norwich, in London*);
- parataxis (i.e. the linking of clauses using co-ordinating conjunctions such as *and*); and
- the parenthetical embedding of background information (*I'd just bought this new outfit, it was the final exams, when he had the car, when they had meetings at lunchtime*).

Note also that texts (1), (3) and (4) include instances of deixis using demonstrative pronouns: *this new outfit, that journey, those meetings*.

However, it would be misleading to assume, on this limited basis, that all orientations exhibit all these features. Compare the use of tenses in this narrative, for example:

> Irene: I'm on a diet and my mother buys my mother buys these mints. The Russell Stoufer mints. I said I don't want any Mom . . .
>
> (after Schiffrin, 1994: 80)

The micro-analysis stage needs to take account of typical features as well as variants within generic models. As in the case of the macro-structure, a micro-analysis should try to identify obligatory and optional elements at each stage. But identification alone is not enough: according to genre theory, the analysis should also explain the effect of these lexico-grammatical choices and relate these effects to the overall function of the text. Thus, as we shall see below, the effect of choosing a present tense rather than a past tense to introduce the narrative is to give it greater immediacy and hence intensify the dramatic effect.

5.3 Storytelling genres

Cheepen (1988), in an analysis of 20 conversations (12 telephone and eight face-to-face) finds not only that stories occur with great frequency but that they are often the most likely element to occur in the second slot in interactions, i.e. after the conversational opening. Admittedly, Cheepen's definition of *story* is quite broad: she classifies any stretch of speech as story if it includes these four factors:

- a coherent sequence of state–event–state
- specification of participants
- temporal location
- evaluation

(Cheepen, 1988: 53)

By a state–event–state sequence she means any sequence in which at least one event arises out of a particular state and which results in a different state. Thus, in Cheepen's data, the following comprises a story:

> she [the cat] bit Dave yesterday no she didn't she scratched him he said she got rabies

(1988: 73)

The event that changes the state of things is the cat's scratching Dave; the participants are the cat and Dave; the time *yesterday*; and the evaluation of the event is Dave's comment with its pejorative implication through the use of the word *rabies*. (A speaker's responding *How awful!* would also constitute an evaluation. Cheepen makes the point that stories are very often jointly constructed, i.e. they are dialogic, not monologic.) While Cheepen's definition of conversational story is parsimonious, from a genre-theory perspective it lacks sufficient delicacy to capture the range of different story types that occur.

We have already mentioned Labov and Waletzky's (1967) slightly more elaborated story structure:

(Abstract) ^ Orientation ^ Complication ^ Evaluation ^ Resolution ^ (Coda)

However, there are a number of problems with this structure, too, one being the fact that the evaluation component does not fit neatly into the sequence but tends to be distributed throughout it. Another problem is that, like with Cheepen's model, the structure is not sensitive enough to capture different types of story – such as those narratives where there is no clear resolution (as in Pat's story in Text 5.1). Further typification is needed in order to capture the fact that conversational narratives vary in terms of their function and structure.

151

By contrast, Slade (1996) analysed hours of casual conversations collected during coffee breaks in three different workplaces, and found that the story-telling segments differed in significant ways. While all shared such features as being temporally sequenced, and incorporating some kind of evaluative comment, there were marked differences, particularly in their middle sections. Some stories involved reactions and not resolutions, others were concerned more with the moral interpretation of the events, and others simply recounted events where nothing significantly went wrong. Following Plum (1988), Slade categorized these stories into four generic types: narratives, anecdotes, exemplums and recounts:

Table 5.1.   Generic structure of storytelling genres (adapted from Eggins and Slade, 1997: 236)

	Beginning	Middle	End
Narrative	(Abstract) ^ Orientation	^ Complication ^ Evaluation ^ Resolution ^	(Coda)
Anecdote	(Abstract) ^ Orientation	^ Remarkable Event ^ Reaction ^	(Coda)
Exemplum	(Abstract) ^ Orientation	^ Incident ^ Interpretation ^	(Coda)
Recount	(Abstract) ^ Orientation	^ Record of Events ^ (Reorientation)	(Coda)

We will now look at each of these storytelling genres in turn.

5.3.1   Narratives

The narrative genre follows the macro-structure outlined by Labov and Waletzky: a situation is established and a complication is introduced and then resolved (although the resolution does not necessarily involve the agency of the protagonist). The events are given their significance through evaluative comment. The narrative may or may not be introduced by some kind of indication that signals what is to follow (the abstract), and may or may not be 're-attached' to the surrounding chat by means of a bridging coda. Protagonists in narratives may be represented as powerful or powerless, as acting alone or with others. The story that is told often involves some loss of face, either to the speaker or to the protagonist of the story (not necessarily the same person). Depending on how the loss of face is resolved, and on the speaker's evaluative comment, the function of the narrative will differ. In casual talk among friends, the function of a narrative is typically to entertain and amuse, but it may also be told in order to solicit expressions of mutual shock, outrage or dismay. Narratives are assumed to be true, thereby distinguishing them from jokes.

The following is an example of a narrative, or, rather, of two narratives, since the telling of one narrative sets the scene for the telling of a second one:

Text 5.2 Bag in turkey

(1)	Jean:	We were laughing the other uh day at work. We were talking about making turkeys and stuff. And um Chris Jankowski said, well, one of her girlfriends one time made a turkey. First time. And she said, 'oh' she was so proud of herself, she made the turkey. The only thing, she left the bag in. She said, and then I said 'Well nobody saw it, right?' She said, '*Everybody* saw it.' I said 'Oh *that was terrible*. How would anybody keep a bag in there.' Mary, Mary kept watching and she said, 'I did it. Nobody saw it. And I didn't tell anybody.' She said, 'first of all, I thought ='
(2)	Lynn:	= She left the bag *in?*
(3)	All:	It's the giblets the turkey has all =
(4)	Jean:	= With the giblets in it and stuff. You know there's a bag inside, yeah?
(5)	Lynn:	*I've* never made a turkey. *I've* never made a turkey.
(6)	Jean:	So I said, to Mary, I said, 'Mary,' I said, 'Didn't you know? Didn't you . . .' she says, 'I saw the thing.' She said, 'It said "Ready to Cook" so I,' she said, 'Who, nobody told me I had to *clean* it.' She said, 'So I put it in the oven.'
(7)	Annie:	Who?
(8)	Jean:	This girl at work.
(9)	Annie:	Oh.
(10)	Jean:	She put it in with all the guts and everything. With the bag inside and everything.
(11)	All:	[laugh]
(12)	Jean:	She said, 'But nobody knew it.' But, she said, 'They ate it. It was good.'

(Norrick, 2000)

Jean's recounting of Chris Jankowski's turkey story provides the background (or orientation) to the second, which is Mary's 'confession' that she also *did it*. Both stories are preceded by a brief abstract, or summary of what the story is about: *We were talking about making turkeys and stuff.* The first story (Chris's, as recalled by Jean) includes its own orientation and complicating event, as well as Jean's evaluation of the story:

Orientation	Chris Jankowski said, well, one of her girlfriends one time made a turkey. First time. And she said, 'oh' she was so proud of herself, she made the turkey.
Complication	The only thing, she left the bag in. She said, and then I said 'Well nobody saw it, right?' She said, '*Everybody* saw it.'
Evaluation	I said 'Oh *that was terrible*. How would anybody keep a bag in there.'

In this story there is no real resolution, since *everybody saw it*. In this sense, this story has the structure of an *anecdote* (see below). The second story (Mary's) does have a resolution however, in Jean's turn 12: *They ate it. It was good.*

Abstract	'I did it. Nobody saw it. And I didn't tell anybody.'
Orientation	'I saw the thing.' She said, 'It said "Ready to Cook" so I,' she said, 'Who, nobody told me I had to *clean* it.' She said, 'So I put it in the oven.'
Complication	She put it in with all the guts and everything. With the bag inside and everything.
Resolution	She said, 'But nobody knew it.' But, she said, 'They ate it. It was good.'

Jean's evaluation of the story is implied by the repeated use of *and everything*, and the audience's laughter (turn 11) suggests that the point of the story has not been lost.

The orientation, complication and resolution are the defining characteristics of the genre: these are obligatory elements whereas the abstract and coda are optional. The obligatory evaluation typically occurs after the complication and serves to index the speaker's attitude to the event.

5.3.2 Anecdotes

Unlike narratives, anecdotes lack a 'sense of an ending': a situation is created in which something out of the ordinary occurs, whether amusing, surprising or shocking, and this is presented, along with the speaker's reaction, to be shared with other speakers. No resolution is necessarily expected – it is assumed that it is obvious from the cultural context how the story unfolds. Jean's account of Chris's story (Text 5.2) is an anecdote, as is the story of the huge hailstone (in Chapter 1):

> (12) Dan: And there was the little old lady over the road who . . .
>
> (13) Rob: Oh yeah. [laughs] She was sitting in her living room and a hailstone fell through the skylight, this old Italian woman. She had corrugated iron but it fell through the skylight. It fell through the ceiling and landed in her lap when she was sitting = =
>
> (14) Odile: = = Mm.
>
> (15) Rob: watching television.
>
> (16) Dan: Watching *The X-files* probably.
>
> (17) All: [laugh]

In the following extract the conversation has been about smoking and prohibitions against smoking in the workplace. One of the speakers tells an anecdote:

Text 5.3 Sandwiches

Orientation	Nigel: (1)	I still remember going to one of those meetings. They brought out the sandwiches, at one of those meetings they brought out the sandwiches – in London when they had meetings at lunchtime or something and the trays of sandwiches =
	Pat: (2)	= That's right yeah =
Remarkable event	Nigel: (3)	= and then there was this little voice: 'What about the non, what about, [laughs] what about,' the smoke I think it was. What was it? 'What about the non-vegetarian smokers?'
Reaction		[laughs] Sandwiches with like lettuce, carrot. Non smoking. One little voice.
Coda		I think it was Murray Parker or someone like that. (0.5) Is he still a smoker?

(Authors' data)

155

As with narratives, the orientation situates the event and includes the virtually obligatory place and time references, as well as appealing to shared knowledge (*one of those meetings*). The remarkable event is, in this case, something that someone said. The speaker's reaction to the event is first expressed non-verbally, through laughter, and then by re-iterating and elaborating on crucial circumstantial details in order to 'explain the joke'. The coda re-connects the anecdote to the theme of the conversation, i.e. smoking, and the speaker demonstrates his readiness to surrender the floor by asking a question.

5.3.3 Exemplums

Exemplums are stories told in order to make a moral point. Like gossip (see below), exemplums fulfil the function of prescribing what is considered to be acceptable behaviour in the cultural context in which they are told. The difference in text structure between exemplums and other narrative texts is that the narrative stage serves as exemplary evidence for the moral that the speaker draws: the events are not necessarily problematized (as in narratives) or remarkable (as in anecdotes), but they are told in order to illustrate the speaker's judgement of what constitutes socially acceptable or unacceptable behaviour. The generic structure of an exemplum, then (as described by Plum, 1988), includes the optional elements (abstract) followed by (orientation) and then the obligatory sequence incident ^ interpretation, after which an optional coda leads the way for the story to finish and for the conversation to return to chat.

Here, for example, is an exemplum told to illustrate the speaker's approval of the conviviality of village life (after Myers, 1999):

Text 5.4: Village life

	I like it very much up here actually [yeah]
Abstract	what I was impressed with really was the first day we moved in.
Orientation	and whilst the removal people were still. unloading the van [uh-huh]. uhh my wife said to me will you ((laughs)) pop up the village. hadn't a clue where I was going ((laughter)) and get some boiled ham or something to make some sandwiches.
Incident	and I called in the village there's a butcher's on the main road there [yeah] and he uh had just shut the shop for lunchtime [yeah] and I had a look in his window and he said do you want anything [oh: right]. and I said well you're closed. and he said I'll open. so he opened the shop

156

Interpretation	[oh that's nice] which I thought was very *good* really yeah.
Coda	but apart from that the area I know very little about it yet you know. I'm finding my way round it [okay]

(Myers, 1999: 383)

5.3.4 Recounts

Whereas narratives and anecdotes typically function to entertain, and exemplums have a didactic function, recounts have an expository function – they tell the listener that something happened:

> Roger: I did a helluva lot of work last Saturday. I put three different engines 'n three different cars plus a brake job.

(Sacks, 1992: 124)

Recounts simply narrate a sequence of events – as when reporting recent activities, narrating a shopping excursion or a sports event, recalling the events of a holiday, or reminiscing about the start of a relationship, for example. In this sense, recounts are the least elaborated form of story: the core ingredient of a recount is simply a record of events. There is no complication that is resolved, no remarkable event as such, nor any moral to be drawn. Borrowing Forster's distinction between story and plot, recounts have more in common with the former than the latter:

> *The king died and then the queen died* is a story. *The king died, and then the queen died of grief* is a plot. The time sequence is preserved but the sense of causality overshadows it . . . Consider the death of the queen. If it is in a story we say: 'And then?' If it is in a plot we ask 'Why?'

(1990: 87)

The listener's response to a recount is much the same: *What happened then?*

Here, for example, is a recount of a wedding (Slade, 1996):

Text 5.6 Small wedding

Abstract	Jess:	What about you Judy? How did you, did you have a big wedding?
Orientation	Judy:	No no, because my husband didn't know very many people like we we really, I just invited really close friends of his he knew and he was

157

		really shy so he didn't want many people so we had about, no == actually about
	Jess:	== It's nice like that though.
Record of events	Judy:	Yeah, well it was up it was in Mum and, well we were married in the church and we and then we just went to Mum and Dad's house which is what I'd always wanted. I can't stand these big formal things. And I just wore a really simple dress.
Coda:		I can't stand these big you know . . . weddings. I think it's awful.

The record of events in this instance comes as a response for a request for information. Interwoven into this story, however, are a number of evaluative, self-justificatory comments (*I can't stand these big formal things*). The use of evaluative language is an obligatory feature of all the storytelling genres. However, in recounts the evaluative comments tend to be spread throughout the story, and are not realized as a discrete stage, as with the other three kinds of stories. It is these interwoven evaluative comments that give recounts their purpose. It is also this feature of adult conversational recounts that distinguishes them from recounts told by young children – children only learn how to intersperse the evaluative comments as they get older.

In the following recount, in which (in a continuation of the wedding conversation above) another speaker describes an unorthodox wedding she attended, the evaluative comments are italicized:

> . . . and they'd picked out a poem between the pair of them and he recited that. And then he made them face the rest of the people standing sort of like around and there was oh some little conversation that they had, you know. And em then they took their vows and it was all over. *It was really, it was really lovely*, because she got married, married em, the house they were renting at the time was right on the shores of Lake Macquarie. And so, when it was all over, which it was a long week, Australia Day weekend. Most people came from either Sydney or interstate, from Queensland or wherever and we had a picnic the next day, a barbecue down on the shores and everyone went swimming and they hired a boat and went around the lake. *It was really nice.*

(Authors' data)

5.4 Lexico-grammatical features of storytelling genres

Having identified the generic stages of four sub-classes of conversational story-telling, the next stage is to identify specific lexico-grammatical features that typically occur within these genres. Since a number of stages are shared across these genres (such as abstracts, orientations and evaluation), there is considerable overlap in discrete features, even though their use may be directed towards different ends. In order to avoid repetition, therefore, we have divided this description into (1) abstracts and orientations; (2) events (including complications, resolutions, remarkable events, incidents and records of events); and (3) evaluations, reactions, interpretations and codas.

5.4.1 Abstracts and orientations

Abstracts, minimally, signal the onset of a story, and may make explicit reference to the genre, as in this introduction to a narrative:

> Yes I remember there was a terrible *story*, horrifying *story* that was told by a colleague of mine when I used to teach years ago

> (Crystal and Davy, 1975)

As in the above example, abstracts also encode some evaluative comment, in the form, for example, of adjectives: *terrible, horrifying.* Not knowing the speaker's attitude to a story is unsettling for listeners, since they cannot anticipate appropriate reponses, in the form, for example, of back-channel devices (*how awful*! *how lovely*!). The attribution of a story is often mentioned (*that was told by a colleague of mine*), giving the story more authority while at the same time disowning any personal involvement. Topic information is also often embedded in abstracts:

> what I was impressed with really was *the first day we moved in.*

> (Myers, 1999)

Such information helps activate a 'moving in' script: removal men, furniture, unfamiliarity, meeting the neighbours etc. Compare:

> Well, I'll always remember *that time we were struck by lightning* coming back from Hong Kong, well landing in Bahrain actually . . .

> (McCarthy and Carter, 1994: 143)

In this sense, abstracts act as schemata activators, triggering appropriate expectations about the text-type, topic, and tone of what follows. Compare the difference between:

159

> Yes I remember there was a terrible story about an accident . . .
> Yes I remember there was a hilarious story about an accident . . .
> Yes I remember there was a hilarious joke about a nun . . .
> Yes I remember there was a sick joke about a baby . . .
> (etc).

Moreover, as Coulthard points out, the abstract 'gives the listener some idea of what is required for the story to be complete' (1985: 83). A joke is not over until the punchline; an anecdote requires more than an orientation. By providing the story in miniature in the form of an abstract, the speaker cues the listener to adopt the appropriate listening strategies.

As we have seen, orientations typically encode circumstantial information, including the setting in time and place, the protagonist and other characters, and a situation or activity. The time and place setting may simply be hinted at. In Text 5.2 (Bag in turkey) all we know is that *Chris Jankowski said, well, one of her girlfriends one time made a turkey.* Compare this with the much more detailed and explicit information that is provided in the narrative 'A driving incident', where the speaker cannnot rely on shared knowledge, and where the story's effect depends on a fairly detailed understanding of the physical location, including the observer's perspective on the events:

> This chap lived in erm a semi deta- detached house and next door there was a man who'd just bought a new car and he [the colleague of the story-teller's] was telling me that one morning he was looking through the window and this man allowed his wife to drive the car very unwisely and she was having a first go in it [m] . . .
>
> (Crystal and Davy, 1975: 44)

Typically, the orientation includes verb phrases marked for progressive aspect: *one morning he* was looking *through the window,* or present participles as in *I still remember* going *to one of those meetings* . . . The pragmatic effect of progressive aspect is to provide a temporal frame around an event or series of events: circumstantial information is backgrounded in order that events expressed in simple tenses are foregrounded:

> I remember *we were sitting* for our analytical chemistry exam and it was the final exams . . . and *I was sitting* there and I thought 'geez I can feel something on my foot'. . .
>
> (Authors' data)

> I remember one day *going* for a um walk along the harbour – one
> of those harbour routes that had been opened up. And um he
> started kicking up from about five o'clock . . .

> (Eggins, 1994: 6)

Hutchby and Wooffitt (1998) analysed a corpus of personal accounts of
paranormal experiences and identified a characteristic pattern that they
call the *X then Y format*: as in *I was just doing X, when Y happened*:

> and I was just looking at the coffin (= X)
> and there was David standing there (= Y)

> (1998: 188)

The first element (X) is described as a *state formulation*, and describes,
usually in the past progressive, 'a particular state of activity or state of
mind that the speaker was engaged in immediately prior to the onset
of the paranormal experience . . . A common characteristic of state
formulations is that they seem to report very mundane or ordinary
activities' (1998: 191). This contrasts with the Y event, which introduces the paranormal 'complication'.

Orienting the listener to the setting of a story may also require providing a retrospective viewpoint on the situation, where relevant events that
occurred previous to the narrative event time need to be mentioned. In a
past tense narrative this typically requires the use of past perfect forms:

> I remember once I went to a film, and ah, *I'd just bought* this new
> outfit . . .

In this instance it is the going to the film that is the situation that the
speaker wants to evoke, not the buying of the outfit, although this has
relevance that will soon become obvious. Sometimes processing constraints mean that the speaker omits relevant information and so has to
interrupt and repair the narrative sequence, a break in the chain of events
that typically requires the past perfect:

> and he backed it out of the garage so that it was standing on the
> driveway and *he'd closed* the garage doors [yeah] and she came
> out of the house . . .

> (Crystal and Davy, 1975: 44)

5.4.2   Events

The middle stage of a story is the obligatory detailing of events, whether
they form the complication and resolution of a narrative, the remarkable
event of an anecdote, the incident of an exemplum, or the record of
events of a recount.

Both in the orientation stage and in the subsequent middle stages the activity in which the characters are situated is typically realized through *material process verbs*, that is verbs that encode actions carried out by agents, as in this continuation of the driving incident story (material process verbs are italicized):

> . . . and he *backed* it out of the garage so that it was standing on the driveway and he'd *closed* the garage doors [yeah] and she *came* out of the house to *take* the car out and *go* shopping for the first time, so she *came* out very gingerly and *opened* the door and *sat* in the car and er began to *go* back, very very gently, *taking* great care, you see that she didn't *do* anything to this to this new car . . .

> (Crystal and Davy, 1975: 44)

It is not unusual to have narrative sequences that consist largely of verbal processes, as in this example (from Text 5.1; verbal process verbs are italicized):

> . . . Joanne came up and she *said* 'oh, can you do this?' and I *said* 'Well, you're at the end of a very long line if you're prepared to wait' and she *said* 'well, she's at the Oncology clinic right now' and I *said* 'but these have to be done as well' and sort of smiling all the way through it I *said* 'look, you know it's three minutes to three Liz should be down in a minute if you want to wait till then.' and she *went* ahhhh [huffing sound] then she went away and I thought 'oh yeah, end of the == story'

> (Authors' data)

All of the examples of narrative verb phrases that we have looked at so far have been encoded in the past tense: stories are notionally set in the past and are typically told in the past, often in conjunction with adverbal markers of non-specific past time, such as *once, one day, that time, the other day*. The use of the past also has a pragmatic function, as Schiffrin explains: 'shifts in reference time often help to initiate a story world, separating it from an ongoing conversational world' (1994: 81). But, as we saw earlier, the use of the past is not an obligatory feature of narratives. Speakers may choose present forms to create a greater sense of immediacy, especially at climactic points in a narrative:

> . . . and I thought 'Geez I can feel something on my foot.' [Uuhh] And I thought 'No, no, don't worry about it,' you know 'what on earth is this chemical equation?' and I *am trying* to think but *there's* something on my foot! . . .

> (Authors' data)

However, present tense may occasionally be used in the orientation stage, in order to orientate the listener to the 'drama' of the situation, analogous to the way the present is used in stage directions: *RAY opens the door. He is dressed in pyjamas*. (Orton, 1976: 172). Thus:

> Irene: I'm on a diet and my mother buys my mother buys these mints.

(Schiffrin, 1994: 80)

Schiffrin herself admits that Irene's initiating utterance is ambiguous: does it refer to a repeated, habitual action, or to a past event? (One of the other speakers – Zelda – seems to make the former interpretation.) As the story develops, it exhibits several further examples of tense shift (italicized):

Text 5.8 Russell Stouffer mints

> Irene: I'm on a diet and my mother buys = =
> Zelda: = = You're not!
> Irene: My mother buys these mints,
> Zelda: Oh yeah.
> Irene: the Russell Stouffer mints. I *said*, 'I don't want any Mum'. 'Well I don't wanna eat the whole thing.' She *gives* me a little tiny piece, I eat it. Then she gives me another = =
> Henry: = = Was . . .
> Irene: so I *threw* it out the window = =
> Henry: = = there a lot of people?
> Irene: I didn't tell her.
> Henry: Was there = =
> Irene: = = She'd kill me.

(after Schiffrin, 1994: 80–81)

The previous story exhibits another feature of spoken narratives: the use of direct speech in reporting what was said. Tannen (1989) argues that reported dialogue is in fact *constructed* dialogue, constructed in order to create listener involvement, and bears only a notional relationship to what was actually said: 'By giving voice to characters, dialogue makes story into drama and listeners into an interpreting audience to the drama' (1989: 133). This dramatic effect is often heightened by marked changes in voice quality and/or accent, as in this instance (from Text 5.1):

and she went ahhhh [huffing sound] then she went away

Myers (1999), on the other hand, argues that reporting what people say has less of a poetic function than an indexical one. Following Goffman (1986/1974), he argues that the reporting of speech indexes a frame shift 'from the primary frame that we take to be immediate reality, to another frame shared for the purposes of the interaction' (1999: 379). Reporting what was said can provide the listener with 'direct experience' of the original talk, while allowing the speaker some detachment from it. The frame shift is typically accompanied by shifts in tense, pronouns and deictic devices, as in this example (from Myers, direct speech italicized):

Text 5.9: Mobile phones

Peter: I've got me mobile ((laughter)) everywhere I go [yeah] I'll give you an example

I was by a pool in Majorca last year and daughter rings me up [yeah] all right I was sitting by the pool she thought I was by the van ((laughter))

and she is talking away for about 5 minutes and I am nattering away to her it's clear as a bell [yeah] and she says *uh. are you in the van?* I said *no I am in Majorca. oh my God* she says *I'm on me boyfriend's phone* slammed the phone down – ((laughter))

you know I mean. it was so – all right we were thousands of miles away whatever [yeah] but it was so close isn't it

(Myers, 1999: 384)

Notice that in this example, and in the Russell Stouffer mints story (Text 5.8), present and past tend to alternate according to the degree of foregrounding and of agency associated with the events. Circumstantial information is set in the past; events that intrude on those circumstances are expressed in the present. Similarly, initiating actions (like questions) are framed in the present; responding actions are framed in the past:

Foreground/initiation (present tense)	Background/response (past tense)
	I was sitting by the pool
daughter rings me up	
she says uh . are you in the van?	I said no I am in Majorca
she says I'm on me boyfriend's phone	slammed the phone down
My mother buys me these mints	I said 'I don't want any'
She gives me a little tiny piece.	
I eat it.	
Then she gives me another.	So I threw it out the window.

Reporting of thoughts is also a characteristic of spoken narratives, and lends support to the view that direct rather than indirect reporting both heightens the drama and indexes a frame shift. Compare the difference between (a) and (b):

> (a) and I thought 'Geez I can feel something on my foot.' [Uuhh] And I thought 'No, no, don't worry about it,' you know 'what on earth is this chemical equation?'

> (b) and I thought I could feel something on my foot. And I told myself not to worry about it and tried to think of the answer to the exam question

Another feature of quoted talk is the use of *discourse markers* (such as *oh, look, well*) to frame the onset of direct speech. This is very clear in the example quoted earlier:

> . . . Joanne came up and she said '*oh*, can you do this?' and I said '*Well*, you're at the end of a very long line if you're prepared to wait' and she said '*well*, she's at the Oncology clinic right now' and I said 'but these have to be done as well' and sort of smiling all the way through it I said '*look*, you know it's three minutes to three . . .

> (Authors' data)

Since the middle stage of a narrative involves a *sequence* of events, it is not unusual to find sequencing devices in the form of conjunctions or adverbials:

> they'd picked out a poem between the pair of them and he recited that. *And then* he made them face the rest of the people . . . *And em then* they took their vows and it was all over . . . And so, *when it was all over* . . . we had a picnic *the next day* . . .

> (Authors' data)

However, since the default interpretation of any two past events in sequence is that the first preceded the latter, the use of explicit sequencing devices is generally redundant, with *and* serving to do the job of *then, when* etc.:

> I'm on a diet *and* my mother buys my mother buys these mints

Schiffrin notes that *and* is 'the most frequently used mode of connection at a local level of idea structure' (1987: 128), being used not only for additive purposes but for contrastive ones as well, i.e. where *but* would be predicted in written discourse, as in this sequence, where the first *and* is additive, and the second contrastive:

> *and* I called in the village there's a butcher's on the main . road there [yeah] *and* he uh had just shut the shop for lunchtime

More frequent than temporal relations, however, is the explicit signalling of causality, particularly the resultative use of *so*:

> Nobody told me I had to clean it.' She said, '*So* I put it in the oven
>
> I said well you're closed . and he said I'll open . *so* he opened the shop

Because *so* signals the consequence of an event, it often indexes the resolution stage of a narrative:

> Pat: I had to take the whole lot off and pull the whole lot down. [laugh]
> All: [laugh]
> Pat: *So* I missed half the film.

So is also used as a means of returning to the events of the story after a temporary diversion:

> and she came out of the house to take the car out and go shopping for the first time, *so* she came out very gingerly and opened the door and sat in the car
>
> (Crystal and Davy, 1975: 44)

5.4.3 Evaluations, reactions, interpretations and codas

As we have seen, the evaluation component is, of all the generic stages, the most diffuse, being distributed across texts from abstract to coda. The function of evaluative language is to signal the speaker's attitude to the events being related. In Labov's words:

> Evaluation devices say to us: this was terrifying, dangerous, weird, wild, crazy; or amusing, hilarious, wonderful; more generally, that it was strange, uncommon, or unusual – that is, worth reporting. It was not ordinary, plain, humdrum, everyday or run of the mill.
>
> (1972: 371)

Evaluation can take the form of explicit comment, either by the narrator to his/her listeners in the course of telling the story (i.e. in utterance time), or through the reported words (or thoughts) of protagonists in the story in event time. An example of the former is in the recount of the unorthodox wedding, cited earlier:

> And em then they took their vows and it was all over. *It was really, it was really lovely*

An example of an event-time evaluation comes from the story about the village butcher (Myers, 1999):

and he said I'll open . so he opened the shop [oh that's nice] which
I thought was very good *really* [yeah]

In this story (about a baby) the feelings, rather than the thoughts of the
protagonists, are reported, and these contribute to the evaluation of the
events:

> I remember one day going for a um walk along the harbour – one
> of those harbour routes that had been opened up. And um he
> started kicking up from about five o'clock and *we were getting
> panic stricken.*

(Eggins, 1994: 6)

In the above examples, evaluative comment is largely encoded in lexical
choices, particularly adjectives, and often in the pattern:

> subject + *thought* + *it/this* etc. *was* + AdjP
> *I thought [it] was very good*
> *they thought this was wonderful*

Or:

> subject + copula + AdjP
> *it was really lovely*
> *I was really delighted*

In this anecdote about a dead pig the use of evaluative adjectives is particularly marked (Crystal and Davy, 1975: 40):

Text 5.10 Pigs

> A: Oh and one pig died because it ate too much. Oh it was
> *revolting*. Oh they were *terrible* the pigs. They made a
> *dreadful* row in the morning when it was feeding time and
> one pig it was erm a young pig about that size you know –
> middling – and erm it was dead and it was lying there. I'd
> never seen a dead pig before – *absolutely stiff.*
> B: Did the children saw it did they?
> A: Oh they were *engrossed* you know – it was *marvellous* erm
> they thought this was *wonderful*

(Note how the protagonist's reaction to the event contrasts with the children's.) The use of highly coloured and exaggerated language in the previous example is typical of conversation generally, and is used in the
following anecdote to magnify the drama of the situation: a schoolgirl is
caught with cigarettes by her parents while her schoolfriends are waiting
for her:

> I still remember all waiting outside the garden gate and coming
> across the garden was a voice and the mother said [imperious
> voice] 'Charles! This girl smokes!' And there was – just waiting
> there *for hours* and we could hear this *huge – it was such a
> drama* – she'd been caught on the stairs leaving for school with a
> pack of cigarettes. She was *so radical* and then *they just couldn't
> believe it.*

(Authors' data)

Finally, the coda is typically used to recapitulate the speaker's stance on
the story just told: in this sense, it often echoes the sentiment of the
abstract. However, there seem to be no consistently used linguistic features of codas, apart perhaps from evaluatory language, as for example
in the coda to the story about the girl caught smoking:

> . . . She was so radical and then they just couldn't believe it. She
> used to take orange juice in a tupperware to school with vodka,
> can you believe it [laughter] For school tea. *She had every vice,
> boy.*

And, in the story of the dead pig (Text 5.10), the coda is supplied by the
listener:

> . . . so they went to burn the pig and all the kids hanging over the
> gate watching this pig and they were very er very taken that the
> pig had died because it had eaten too much
>
> D. *What a marvellous death!*

5.5 Storytelling genres: Summary

The telling of stories is a universal human activity, with a wide range of
social, religious, artistic, didactic, cultural and even therapeutic functions. It is through the exchange of stories that social life is both represented and shaped, and by means of which identity is instantiated, as
Oliver Sacks observes:

> If we wish to know about a man [sic], we ask 'What is his story? –
> his real, his inmost story?' – for each of us *is* a biography, a story.
> Each of us *is* a singular narrative, which is constructed continually,
> unconsciously by, through, and in us – through our perceptions,
> our feelings, our thoughts, our actions; and, not least, our
> discourse, our spoken narrations. Biologically, we are not so
> different from each other; historically, as narratives – we are each
> of us unique.

(1985: 105)

Despite their universality, the way that stories are told, and what makes them relevant, funny or shocking, will differ significantly from culture to culture, and from context to context within a particular culture. This chapter has been looking at stories told in conversational English, of which there are different types. The common thread is that they '*depict a temporal transition from one state of affairs to another*' (Ochs, 1997: 189, original emphasis). The four storytelling genres of casual conversation that we have identified have this common core: a series of notionally past events, removed from the moment of telling, involving characters who are assumed to be real, i.e. not mythical, imaginary or fictional. While they share this common narrative core, they differ in terms of their function, and this difference is reflected in their overall text structure as well as in the way they are realized at the lexico-grammatical level.

If (as we have argued) it is by means of conversation that much of the work of building and maintaining social relations is done, then the telling of stories plays a crucial role. Tannen (1989) notes that speakers whose conversational style she characterizes as 'high involvement' tell more stories than those with a less involving style. Moreover, 'their stories [are] more often about their personal experiences; and their stories more often [include] accounts of their feelings in response to events recounted' (1989: 28), a characteristic we have labelled as the *evaluative* component of stories.

As we have seen, all the four story-telling genres that we have looked at incorporate evaluative language. This is hardly surprising in the case of anecdotes and narratives, whose purpose it is to elicit an emotional response. Nor is it surprising in exemplums, which are told in order to make a moral point. But even recounts, whose function would appear to be – on the surface – more referential than interpersonal, are interwoven with evaluative comment. (As noted, this is what distinguishes adult recounts from many recounts told by children). Indeed, it would be hard to imagine a conversational story where the teller's attitude could not be inferred at all.

In Slade's (1996) study of workplace conversations, she found that the frequency of any particular storytelling genre seemed to depend on the degree of familiarity and contact between participants. Thus, sharing an emotional reaction to an event by telling an anecdote seems to happen most when participants are more familiar with one another. Often such anecdotes are told at the expense of the teller: this seems to be the case particularly with women, who, according to Coates (1996), frequently cast themselves in awkward or embarrassing situations. Men, by contrast, more generally portray themselves as overcoming adversity, solving problems, being in control (see Eggins and Slade, 1997).

Eggins and Slade found that narratives and exemplums are more likely than recounts to occur in situations where participants are less familiar or have less contact with each other. By contrast, recounts seem to occur with greater frequency among people who are in regular contact or quite familiar with one another, possibly because familiarity can tolerate the often rather mundane detailing of events typical of this genre. The frequent banality of recounts has often been the object of satire, as in this extract from the British comedy series *The Royle Family*, where a wife is telling her husband about an incident at the bakery where she works:

Mam:	Do you know him from the flats?
Dad:	Who? There's loads of people in the flats.
Mam:	You know which one . . . he used to have a string for a belt. [. . .] He came in the baker's today.
Dad:	And?
Mam:	He bought a sliced loaf.
Dad:	What did you tell me that for?
Mam:	You can't say anything in this house without having your head bitten off . . .

(Cash, *et al.*, 2002: 47–48)

5.6 Gossip

We shall now return to part of the extract that started this chapter (Text 5.1. State Theatre):

26	Bron:	= = I'm about to throw Joanne out the window.
27	Pat:	Joanne who?
28	Bron:	Peterson.
29	Pat:	Why?
30	Bron:	She gets really pushy. I'm looking for a file for Gary. Kerry gave me three others and I was in the middle of finding the third one for her.
31	Gary:	Kerry gave you three did she?
32	Bron:	Yeah. You know they have to be done and Joanne came up and she said, 'Oh, can you do this?' and I said, 'Well you're at the end of a very long line if you're prepared to wait' and she said, 'Well, she's at the Oncology clinic right now' and I said, 'But these have to be done as well'. And sort of smiling all the way through it I said, 'Look, you know it's three minutes to three. Liz should be down in a minute if you want to wait till then.' And she went ahhh [huffing sound] then she went away and I thought, 'Oh yeah, end of the = = story.'
33	Gary:	= = she gets very worried.

34 Bron: and then she came back again and um she said, 'Are those files there? Did Kerry give you those files there?' and I knew what she was going to say next. And I said, 'Oh, among other things' and she went 'Oh it's just that they can wait until after this one 'cause they're needed today'. Oh I was about ready to strangle her = she gets

35 Gary: Joanne's too busy.

36 Bron: I know and I appreciate that she's busy but she gets really pushy.

37 Pat: Yeah, I don't like pushy people either.

Applying a genre analysis to conversational chunks (as in the previous section), it might appear that Bron's turns 30, 32, and 34 constitute a kind of recount: there is an orientation (turn 30), a section that looks like a record of events (turns 32 and 34) into which evaluative comment is interwoven (*Oh I was about ready to strangle her*), and a jointly constructed coda in turns 36 and 37. However, the function of this chunk is more than simply expository: there is clearly a critical agenda to Bron's story, and it is signalled both at the outset (*I'm about to throw Joanne out the window . . . she gets really pushy*) and at the close (*she gets really pushy*). In fact the whole story is framed by the two negative evaluations of the absent Joanne, an evaluation to which the other participants contribute, either attempting to mitigate it by making excuses for it (Gary) or to show solidarity by invoking some shared moral code (Pat). The evaluation in this case is about another person; it is not, as with stories, concerned to evaluate the events being discussed but rather to share opinions and judgements about an absent person. In this way the function is quite different from that of a story – it is the evaluation of Joanne that motivates the conversation. This pejorative evaluation of an absent other is recognizably gossip, the function of which is to share 'opinions and judgements about a person's behaviour or physical attributes, and by doing so implicitly asserting appropriate behaviour or defining a physical norm. In this way gossip reinforces and maintains the values of the social group' (Eggins and Slade, 1997: 276).

Slade (1996) defines gossip broadly as talk which involves pejorative judgement of an absent other. It is talk that has a confidential air about it – and where the person being gossiped about is known to at least one of the participants. Gossip texts feature prominently in our conversational data, unsurprisingly since gossip performs a powerful social regulating role – it reinforces, enacts and modifies social attitudes and values. By sharing and negotiating opinions about other people, members of a group demarcate the bounds of acceptable behaviour and implicitly situate themselves within these bounds. Through this mutual construction of shared values, gossip maintains and reinforces group unity and solidarity (Slade, 1996).

Cheepen (1998) points out that gossip has an interactional function as well: it serves to repair conversational 'trouble'. Where the conversation gives rise to actual or potential loss of face to a participant, conversationalists can co-operate to repair this lapse by gossiping about an absent 'scapegoat', thereby deflecting the damage on to someone who, not being present, suffers no face threat.

Gossip is a highly interactive genre: it requires participant complicity and is typically co-constructed. It is therefore inherently dialogic (or multilogic) rather than monologic, participants frequently ask questions and provide feedback to indicate explicit or tacit agreement for the gossip to proceed. There are highly interactive sections in the gossip that are more like 'chat' segments of conversation. Yet, despite the chat-like nature of much of the above segment there is a clearly discernible generic structure, described by Slade (1996) and Eggins and Slade (1997). A gossip text typically begins with a *third-person focus*, followed by one or more alternating sequences of *pejorative evaluation* and *substantiating behaviour*. Thus:

Third-person focus	Bron:	I'm about to throw Joanne out the window
	Pat:	Joanne who?
	Bron:	Peterson.
	Pat:	Why?
Pejorative evaluation Substantiating behaviour	Bron:	She gets really pushy. I'm looking for a file for Gary. [. . .] and Joanne came up and she said, 'Oh, can you do this?' and I said . . . [etc] . . . and she went 'Oh it's just that they can't wait until after this one 'cause they're needed today'. Oh I was about ready to strangle her = she gets
	Gary:	Joanne's too busy
	Bron:	I know and I appreciate that she's busy but she
Pejorative evaluation		gets really pushy
	Pat:	Yeah, I don't like pushy people either

172

Gossip

The third-person focus indicates the speaker's intention to gossip and introduces the subject of the gossip sequence, whose behaviour is disapproved. A pejorative evaluation can either precede or follow the description of the disapproved behaviour: in this text, it does both. Substantiating behaviour, where the speaker or another participant provides evidence for the negative judgement, then follows. It is here that the participants establish and reinforce their shared values by criticizing an outsider for failing to conform to the group's values. The cycle of behaviour and evaluation is often prompted by another speaker requesting further details, what Eggins and Slade (1997: 286) call a *probe*. For example, in this sequence, Donna itemizes substantiating behaviours to reinforce a pejorative evaluation about Richard, and is prompted by Sue to add further behaviours and evaluations:

Text 5.11 Caught drinking

Pejorative evaluation	Donna:	Richard's not a very nice person anyway. He just doesn't fit into the system in general. It's not nice what's happening to him
Substantiating behaviour		but the thing is he is creating the situation just as much as what they are . . . [whispers] because he's been caught drinking on the job [whisper]
Pejorative evaluation		which is no good you know
Substantiating behaviour		and he hasn't really been doing his job properly = = anyway
Probe	Sue:	= Do the girls like him?
Pejorative evaluation	Donna:	No
Substantiating behaviour		because he's got this attitude 'I am superior' you know. He talks down to people
Pejorative evaluation		which automatically puts people's backs up.
	Sue:	Right

(Authors' data)

173

While probes have the effect of prolonging the gossip sequences, other speaker moves can curtail gossip, as when participants show reluctance to 'play the game'. Except in the context of very close friends (where there is often disagreement) gossip depends on consensus, so any move that counters the pejorative evaluation usually brings the sequence to a close. This can happen when speakers defend or excuse the behaviour of the targeted person, or when they withhold pejorative evaluation. In this sequence both daughter (Bea) and husband (John) seem reluctant to pursue a gossip sequence initiated by the mother (Sarah):

Text 5.12 Two chicks

Sarah:	Those two chicks are obsessed with their children, eh? In that party, Jesus!
Sam:	Who? Which?
John:	Can you pass me a little bit of that bread?
Sam:	Have the lot.
Sarah:	Maybe I was like that, I can't remember. I hope = =
John:	= = Thanks.
Sarah:	I didn't talk about Bea like that at parties. Did I stand at parties and talk about Bea the whole night?
John:	I don't think we even went to parties.
Bea:	They're probably very proud of their children.

(Authors' data)

Like the narrative coda, in gossip there is also a final optional stage, labelled *wrap up*, which typically provides a closing summary of the behaviours and judgements that have formed the body of the text.

The following extract (collected by Slade as part of a database of conversations amongst adolescents) displays each of the stages of a typical gossip sequence. It comes from a telephone conversation between Susie and a girlfriend, both aged 14. Susie is travelling back from a skiing holiday with her family; she rings her friend who then phones her back. Susie is gossiping about Stephen; only Susie's turns are recorded.

Text 5.13 Stephen

Third-person focus	[Laughs] Oh, oh it was so funny we got like into the . . . okay we were down at the snow, like me, Sarah and Ann and Josie and he was like he was like oh 'I want to go skiing with you', blah blah but okay.

174

Substantiating behaviour	So we arranged to go skiing with him on Tuesday afternoon, we bumped into him on Monday and so like we went on like one run with him and then he had to go. And then he had to go but um, and then he came, 'cause it, every afternoon we met in the village with like lots of people and stuff and had a hot chocolate and stuff and he came on, he came on Monday night and um we got – everyone else left but me, Sarah and Ann. We got into this fight with him because did I tell you about what happened at Isabella's house? I mean yeah-yeah. Well like, I don't know how it got raised, but it got raised,
Pejorative evaluation	and we started like, Stephen why are you doing this, it's disgusting. And he was like, we're not standing up for Isabella, Isabella like she wanted you to do it to her, it is disgusting, we don't even like Isabella but the fact that you did it, it's disgusting and he was like rah-rah. And then he, then he went on about how drunk he was, and we're like, what the hell? You don't drink when you're 14 you lamo!
Substantiating behaviour	And then we're like attacking him like full big. And he got like and then he was like, 'Oh fuuck you!' And then he sent me a message, saying, it was the most abusive message and then um, he was like- (pause: 6 secs) oh horrific and um, and then yeah um, he was really abusive text and he rang me that next night and said, 'Look I'm sorry I sent you the abusive text message, I was drunk!'. I'm like, 'You are the biggest alcoholic in the history of alcoholics!' And he was like,
Pejorative evaluation	he's such a – I'm mean drinking at 14 is so sad you drink when you're 18 not when you're 14 rah-rah-rah.

175

Wrap-up	And then it ended up and I'm like just say sorry Stephen and I'll forgive you. So he said, 'I'm sorry' but I didn't see him for the rest of the week. So it was fine.

(Authors' data)

This text demonstrates the recursive nature of gossip. First, evidence is provided for why the person is being criticized. This is followed by a pejorative evaluation, after which either the initiating speaker (as in Text 5.13), or another participant, provides further evidence. This cycle of substantiating behaviour followed by pejorative evaluation is often prompted by someone asking for more details. The third person focus then concludes the gossip. It often does this by making a final moral point: *just say sorry Stephen and I'll forgive you. So he said, "I'm sorry"*, or by referring back to the behaviour referred to in the third person focus.

To summarize, then, the generic stages of gossip we have looked at so far are:

(Third-person focus) ^ Substantiating behaviour * (Probe) * Pejorative evaluation ^ (Wrap-up)

where ^ = is followed by; * = occur in either sequence; and ( ) = optional.

5.7 Lexico-grammatical features of gossip

The social purpose of gossip, i.e. the creating and maintaining of group solidarity, is reflected in the choice of language used, particularly in the way that group membership is indexed by invoking a *them* vs. *us* polarity. The use of third-person pronouns and distancing demonstratives (as in *Those two chicks . . .*) is a feature not only of the introduction but throughout gossip sequences. Once the subject of a gossip sequence has been identified by name, most subsequent referents are pronominal, hence the high frequency of *he/him/his* and *she/her* forms, especially in conjunction with the verb *said*: Biber *et al.* (1999) note that the lexical bundles *he/she said to me, and she said oh*, and *I said to him/her* are very frequent in spoken language. A projection of the inclusivity–exclusivity axis is realized by grammatical and lexical oppositions that are set up, as in this segment where positive and negative adjectives and adverbials are used to establish a contrast between acceptable behaviour (as manifested by the speaker, i.e. one of *us*) and unacceptable behaviour (as manifested by *her*, one of *them*):

> Well, that is no reason to be so *arrogant*. *She* is so *up herself*. The other day *I* said, just to be *friendly*, 'Anna, you look really *nice* today'. And *she* said, in a really kind of *arrogant* voice 'well, I do like to make an effort at work as well'. And *she* looked at *me*, you know, as if to say '*I* wish *you* made an effort too.'

(Authors' data)

The substantiating behaviour stage of gossip sequences provides evidence of how the third person acts or acted uncharacteristically, excessively or unacceptably. It is typically realized either by means of a narrative, or by reference to characteristic – but disapproved – behaviour. In the former case, a storytelling genre is often nested within the gossip sequence, as we saw in the anecdote cited earlier:

> Pat: I find her really snooty == too.
> Pauline: == The other day, I ran into her and she had videotapes with her and I said 'what are they for' and she said 'oh, just sick and dying people and how to treat them.'
> All: (laughs)

(Authors' data)

Stories are told to vindicate negative judgements, so they often take the form of exemplums, but with a primarily third-person focus. Gossip narratives include the typical lexico-grammatical features of narrative texts identified earlier, such as the use of material-process and reporting verbs, simple co-ordination using *and*, tense deixis, and direct speech. They are also rich in evaluative language, as we will see below.

Substantiation of pejorative evaluations may also take the form of critically reporting habitual behaviour, either in the present or in the past. Present habitual behaviour is typically reported in the present simple:

> Can't find him anywhere he just *saunters* in . . . as though nothing's happened, about say for tea on Sunday night. He *comes* in always in different he *goes* out and he's nicely dressed, he *comes* home he's got someone else's big top on and someone else's pants. He's just one of these kids that *thinks* he's eighteen and can do as he *likes* now.

(Authors' data)

Other verb forms associated with habitual behaviour are *will* (as in *he'll saunter in* . . .) and the present progressive (*he's forever sauntering in* . . .). Past habitual behaviour is expressed using the past tenses of these forms (past simple, *would*, past progressive), as well as *used to*:

177

She'*d be ringing* up on the weekend as if you know . . . and we *could* hear her voice on the phone, all through the week, and then on the weekend she'*d pretend* she *didn't know* you she *was* someone different

. . . when he was working in Gloucester House he *used to* lock himself in the office, pull down the blinds, put his feet on the desk, turn on the radio, listen to the races, and drink and smoke

(Authors' data)

Adverbials such as *forever, always, repeatedly*, etc. are frequently associated with habitual verb forms and connote speaker disapproval:

I don't think either of them enjoy drinking but they get drunk *every day*.

(Eggins and Slade, 1997: 294)

Did I stand at parties and talk about Bea *the whole night*?

(Authors' data)

As we have seen, evaluation occurs throughout gossip texts, and is encoded in lexical and grammatical choices, but at each pejorative evaluation stage there is a peak of evaluative prominence. This is typically realized by means of attributive adjectives, often intensified:

Stephen did something that I find *particularly weird*.

(Eggins and Slade, 1997: 293)

He's *so inefficient* . . .

(Cheepen, 1988)

I find her *really snooty*.

(Authors' data)

That is no reason to be *so arrogant*.

(Authors' data)

These evaluations often have a repetitive refrain-like quality, with other participants echoing speaker disapproval or disbelief:

Emma: She made [erm] . . . Heather a birthday cake the other day and, I, I've got to say actually this cake was pretty good but like she had to take it to school! I mean, *the girl is sad*! If you're going to take a birthday cake to school, I mean, *that is sad*, isn't it?
Kelly: *My brain's just died*!
Emma: But *that is very, very sad*!

(British National Corpus)

The use of *I mean* in the previous extract exemplifies the way pejorative evaluations are typically introduced with verbs of cognition which serve both to modalize the proposition, and to mitigate the force of it, while inviting concurrence:

> *I mean*, it was the laughing stock of the whole hospital . . .
> *I think* she's atrocious . . .
> *I mean*, I *think* she's made an absolute fool of herself . . .
> *I find her* real snooty . . .

(Authors' data)

Invitations to concur with the negative evaluation are typically encoded in question tags: *I mean, that is sad, isn't it?* Note, also, the use of tails (see Chapter 3):

> She's pretty insecure, *that girl.*

(Authors' data)

Tails, as Carter and McCarthy note, 'often serve to express, on the part of the speaker, some kind of affective response, personal attitude or evaluative stance towards the proposition or topic of the clause' (1997: 18).

The speaker's and listener's evaluations are typically expressed in terms of disapproval, disbelief or disassociation. These are often encoded idiomatically, as in *She's made an absolute fool of herself* (disapproval); *My brain's just died!* (disbelief); and *I wouldn't have been seen dead . . .* (disassociation).

5.8 Gossip texts: Summary

Gossip, we have argued, has an essentially interpersonal function: through gossip social bonds are formed and cemented. It achieves this in two ways: by establishing a *them* and *us* polarity, gossip confers group membership on the gossipers – anyone not participating is reneging on their 'duty to gossip' and one way of excluding a member of a group is to gossip about someone that that person doesn't know. Moreover, gossip, by labelling behaviours acceptable or non-acceptable, asserts collective values and thereby exerts a subtle form of social control.

Since conversation, as a whole, is also essentially interpersonal, it could be argued that gossip is the very essence of casual conversation – and even its origin – despite the negative associations it has accrued. Certainly, its pervasiveness suggests that it merits close study and analysis, and genre theory offers a useful tool for this purpose, since not only does genre analysis help display the structures of conversational gossip – both at the macro- and at the micro-levels, but it also relates these structures to gossip's social function.

The above analysis suggests that gossip shares a number of features with the storytelling genres analysed previously. Both stories and gossip share a primary conversational purpose, that of providing a site for inter-actants to construct solidarity through the exploration of shared values. As Oscar Wilde put it: 'Talk is a sort of spiritualised action'. It is through talk that important social work is done.

5.9 Classroom implications

The pervasiveness both of spoken stories and of gossip suggests that learners would benefit if they had at least a basic command of these conversational genres. This in turn reinforces the arguments made in Chapters 2 and 3 with regard to the importance of achieving control of the following lexical and grammatical features of conversation:

- *appraisal language*: both stories and gossip rely heavily on ways of indexing speakers' evaluation of the events or behaviours they are describing;
- *narrative tenses*, especially the past simple: the use of past tense verb forms is a defining feature of storytelling and, given the importance of narrative, these are arguably of greater utility than present or future verb forms in achieving a degree of overall conversational competence;
- *quotatives*: both stories and gossip involve reporting one's own or others' speech and thoughts; and
- *discourse markers*: speakers need to provide clear indicators as to the direction their stories or their gossiping is taking, and need to be able to link events in sequence.

At the macro level, that is, at the level of the overall schematic structure of stories and gossip, a knowledge of how these genres are staged is useful both to teachers and to learners. Apart from anything else, these structures provide a coherent framework on to which to map the teaching of the discrete lexico-grammatical features that are itemized above. Moreover, providing learners with the terminology for describing the structure of conversational genres – such as *orientation, complication, resolution* – makes the job of teaching their specific realizations arguably more efficient. This does not, of course, assume that learners may not have similar generic structures in their first language (an issue that will be addressed in Chapter 7). The claim is simply that teaching is considerably enhanced by the discretionary use of models and meta-language. Indeed, proponents of genre-based teaching argue that to withhold linguistic information of this type is to deprive learners of the means by which they may become members of the target discourse community – effectively it is to disempower them. On this point, Martin states: 'Conscious knowledge of language and the way it functions in social contexts . . . enables us to make choices, to exercise control. As long as we are ignorant of language, it and the ideological systems it embraces control us' (1989: 62–3). To this end, a genre-based pedagogy, such as that outlined by Cope and Kalantzis (1993), typically proposes a teaching cycle that begins with explicit modelling of the features of the target text type, while, at the same time, relating these features to the text's purposes in its cultural context. This might be followed by supervised practice of such features, followed by a stage of independent text construction.

Burns, Joyce and Gollin advocate a similarly staged approach to the teaching of spoken language in general, based on the notion of 'shifting levels of support and responsibility' (1996: 88), in which learners will initially depend on explicit instruction before becoming autonomous skill-users in their own right. The explicit instruction might take the form of:

- providing and discussing relevant cultural, social and contextual information associated with the text or topic;
- linking cultural, social and contextual information with student experiences;
- using typical and/or predictable models of natural spoken discourse related to the topic or field;
- focusing on and guiding students on various aspects of the discourse (e.g. the overall structure, specific discourse strategies, particular lexical items, grammatical structures);
- providing native-speaker models of spoken discourse;
- giving explicit explanation and modelling of the tasks to be undertaken; and
- setting up tasks for guided practice on various components of the text.

(1996: 89)

It is not difficult to see how the generic structure of spoken narratives, in particular, could be incorporated into this model. Studying transcripts of authentic stories can be an effective means of highlighting narrative structure, bearing in mind the difficulties that can arise when

181

reading transcribed talk. Simplified transcriptions, or transcripts used in conjunction with an audio recording (as in Carter and McCarthy, 1997), offer alternative sources for raising awareness about spoken discourse.

The same applies to the use of gossip texts, although here the difficulties of using transcripts are exacerbated by the fact that gossip texts tend to be distributed among several speakers and therefore less monologic than narratives. Moreover, gossip is less easily elicited or practised in the classroom, since it depends on a high degree of in-group familiarity *and* the absence of at least one member of the group (the target of the gossip). As an alternative, the activities and characteristic behaviours of public figures, such as film stars or sports personalities, can be used as the butt of classroom gossip sequences, as can the fictitious goings-on of soap opera characters.

Summary

It has been the argument of this chapter that a distinction needs to be made between conversational 'chat' – the highly interactive sections of talk – and conversational 'chunks' – those sections, where one or more participant holds the floor for an extended period and tells a story, gossips etc., and that allow an analysis using tools derived from genre theory. These tools help display the architecture of such chunks – their macro-structure – and to relate this architecture to the overall social function of the genre. Such an analysis also describes the lexico-grammatical features of the genre, and relates these to the larger purpose of the genre as a whole.

Tasks

1: Here is the transcript of a conversational anecdote. Match its schematic structure to the generic types listed in Table 5.1 (p. 152). What 'micro-features' of a conversational anecdote does it display (e.g. at the level of grammar and vocabulary)?

Extract 1

Richard:	I'll tell you one thing. When we moved to London and we'd been here for about a month and we were just driving around looking at the sights and we were driving past Buckingham Palace right and Chloe's in the back of the car right, this is so funny, um and she said, 'There it is! There's Buckingham Palace woah woah. Oh we should open the window. Oh and the Queen lives there. Oh look the flag's up the Queen's in there now.' and she said, 'Is that the Queen's house then?' and we said, 'Yeah!' she said, 'Oh fancy building a palace next to the main road.'
Raj, R & J:	[laughter]
Judy:	On the main road [laughs] which is logical = =
Richard:	= = which is very observant absolutely. 'Why did they do that?' she said and actually I couldn't think, because the road was probably there when they built it although there wouldn't have been cars on it.
Raj:	I hope you praised her for making a good point.
Richard:	Well we fell apart.

(Pridham, 2001: 14)

2: Read the following transcript and identify features of the schematic structure of gossip. The schematic structure of gossip is:

(Third-person focus) ^ Substantiating behaviour • (Probe) • Pejorative Evaluation^ (Wrap-up)]

where ^ = is followed by; • = occur in either sequence and ( ) = optional

Extract 2

Setting:

Participants:	Debbie, aged 13, Australian; Francesca, aged 13, Australian; Christina, mother of Olivia.
Context:	The conversation takes place at Olivia's home in Sydney. The two girls attend school together and have been close friends all their lives. They are discussing two other girls who go to the same school.

Speaker	Transcript
Francesca:	You know, okay you know at lunch-time today when Susan says like, "Oh! DP likes you Liv" and I'm like, "Oh sure, Susan!" and she's like, "No no no seriously!" He likes a girl who had her hair up at um at == the play
Debbie:	==Yeah Annie's like, "but yeah but I had my hair up half way through"==
Francesca:	== And we're like, "Well no you didn't Annie!" and she's like, "Yes I did". Well and Susan's like, and Katelan's like, "No you didn't!" And then, then she, anyway you know, Su- and then no, she'll say, and then all of us says, "No you didn't Annie!" And she's like, "Yeah I did, I put it up in the middle of the play no one just saw!" OK? Oh it's so sad.
Christina:	Was this the SCEGGS concert?
Francesca:	It was then – do you know then, you know, she was like, "He's not even hot!" and oh my god "He's so ugly!" And I'm just like, "Oh okay."
Debbie:	She's so weird. Like, I don't get her sometimes.

Francesca: I kind of like her but then, then she's just being, she's not – but she seems really upset at school lately have you noticed that? Like not as in like. She's really strange.

(Authors' data)

6 Acquiring L1 conversational competence

Introduction

In the chapters so far, we have been concerned – from various points of view – with *describing* conversation: how is it structured? what is its purpose? how does it differ from other ways of using language? The purpose of the description is to help inform the teaching of conversation. But a description is not a pedagogy (i.e. a way of teaching). Simply describing the rudiments of conversation to learners is likely to be about as effective as describing the rudiments of grammar – ultimately a fairly unproductive and even frustrating exercise. A pedagogy, to be fully effective, must take into account the way that conversational skills develop in a first language and the way that they respond to instruction in a second. It is the purpose of this chapter and the next, therefore, to review current theory and recent research into the acquisition of conversational competence. First, though, it is necessary to explain what we mean by conversational competence.

6.1 Conversational competence

The notion of conversational competence derives from Chomsky's (1965) distinction between *competence* and *performance*. According to Chomsky, competence is the idealized and internalized knowledge of the rules of grammar that native speakers possess, and which allows them to distinguish well-formed from ill-formed sentences. Competence contrasts with performance, which is the way that this idealized knowledge is realized, with all its 'imperfections', in actual speech. The concept of competence was subsequently extended by Hymes to include not just knowledge of the rules of grammar, but knowledge of 'when to speak, when not, and . . . what to talk about with whom, when, where, in what manner' (1972b: 277). This formulation recognizes that competence in a language involves not just linguistic but social and cultural dimensions. These dimensions are elaborated in the model of communicative competence proposed by Canale (1983, following Canale and Swain, 1980), which distinguishes between:

- *grammatical competence*: this encompasses Chomsky's 'linguistic competence', i.e. knowledge of the rules of grammar and lexis;
- *sociolinguistic competence*: this refers to knowledge of how contextual and cultural factors are realized through language;
- *discourse competence*: this refers to knowing how meaning is represented through connected text; and
- *strategic competence*: this refers to the coping strategies that learners employ to compensate for limitations in their other competences, and includes the use of *communication strategies* (see Chapter 7).

In a further development, Bachman (1990) defined language ability as involving two components, the combination of which provides users with the ability to create and interpret discourse. These two components are *language competence* and *strategic competence*. Language competence (also called *language knowledge* (Bachman and Palmer, 1996)) consists of a hierarchy of knowledge systems, one of which is *textual knowledge*, which in turn includes *knowledge of rhetorical or conversational organization*. This is the knowledge required to produce and understand the organizational development of written texts and conversations. Language knowledge also subsumes *pragmatic knowledge* (*pragmatic competence*), defined in Bachman and Palmer in these terms:

> Pragmatic knowledge enables us to create or interpret discourse by relating utterances or sentences and texts to their meanings, to the intentions of language users, and to relevant characteristics of the language use setting. There are two areas of pragmatic knowledge: functional knowledge and sociolinguistic knowledge.
>
> **Functional knowledge** . . . enables us to interpret relationships between utterances or sentences and texts and the intentions of language users [. . .]
>
> **Sociolinguistic knowledge** enables us to create or interpret language that is appropriate to a particular language use setting. This includes knowledge of the conventions that determine the appropriate use of dialects or varieties, registers, natural or idiomatic expressions, cultural references, and figures of speech.
>
> (1996: 69–70)

Finally, the other major component of language ability, *strategic competence*, is defined as 'a set of metacognitive components, or strategies, which can be thought of as higher order executive processes that provide a cognitive management function in language use' (1996: 70). It is their strategic competence that enables language users to mobilize their language knowledge effectively for communicative purposes, through

187

goal-setting, planning, and on-line monitoring of the communication. Strategic competence, then, is not simply a coping strategy used by learners, but – according to Bachman's model – has a central executive function for all language users.

It should be obvious that conversation draws on all these different competences, especially textual knowledge, including the knowledge of conversational organization, as well as pragmatic knowledge, including both functional and sociolinguistic knowledge. Moreover, in conversation strategic knowledge is crucial in enabling the deployment of these different competences in real-time interaction. We can thus define *conversational competence* as that subset of linguistic and strategic competences that are implicated in conversation (as opposed to writing, or other non-conversational spoken registers), according to the definition of conversation outlined in Chapter 1.

In what follows we address the issue of how conversational competence is acquired. We start by attempting to answer the question: How do children learn to 'do conversation' in their first language? For example, to what extent are conversational skills modelled for them, and in what order? What is the role of input, of practice, and of feedback? Is the acquisition of conversational competence an entirely unconscious process? At what stage – if ever – is it completed? Another note of caution is in order here: by addressing these issues we are not implying that first-language acquisition offers a blueprint for second-language teaching. The conditions under which the two processes occur are vastly different. Nevertheless, there are features of first-language acquisition – including the linguistic and psychological support offered by caregivers – that are suggestive. The picture would not be complete, though, without a review of what the research has to tell us about how conversational skills emerge in a *second* language. That will be the focus of the chapter that follows.

6.2 Turntaking

As we have said repeatedly, conversation is by definition dialogic (or, better, multilogic): it involves multiple partners, and is necessarily interactive. Conversational interaction is jointly managed through a shared understanding of the 'rules' of turntaking (see Chapter 4). When and how does the capacity to manage conversational interaction develop? Basic turntaking conventions, involving reciprocating activity patterns of eye contact, movement and vocalization, appear to establish themselves at a very early age – much earlier than the advent of language itself. Even children as young as two weeks are able to participate in very rudimentary exchanges with their caregivers. These follow a pattern whereby one of the 'conversational' partners moves or vocalizes while the other partner remains still, and then the roles are reversed. This is particularly apparent in such ritualized routines as feeding, dressing and bathing. The parent will typically comment on an object of shared attention and then respond to the child's own vocalizations by expanding and elaborating on them, as if the child were intentionally communicating. The following typical example is an exchange between a mother and her three-month-old daughter:

Ann:	(smiles)
Mother:	Oh what a nice little smile!
	Yes, isn't that nice?
	There.
	There's a nice little smile.
Ann:	(burps)
Mother:	What a nice little wind as well.
	Yes, that's better isn't it?
	Yes.
	Yes.
Ann:	(vocalizes)
Mother:	There's a nice noise.

(Snow, 1977: 12)

Simply responding to smiles and burps, though, would be an insufficient basis for turntaking routines to develop. Snow (1977) found that mothers spend a lot of time trying to elicit responses – such as smiles – from their babies, which in turn accounts for the repetitiveness of 'motherese', as well as the high frequency of questions, especially tag-questions, it displays.

Around about the age of seven months, babies start to become more active conversational partners, producing cries or babble that seem designed to elicit a response. By the age of 12 months, these noises are being replaced by rudimentary words. The child uses these words to initiate 'proto-conversations' by, for example, reaching for, or looking at, an object and vocalizing at the same time. Such conversations are typically very brief, as in this description where the child is 15 months old:

> Kate is having her morning drink. Suddenly she looks off to the corner of the room and says /gæ/. Her mother says, 'What can you see?' Kate repeats /gæ/. Her mother says, 'The ball? Where's the ball?' Kate points to it. 'Yes, over there', says her mother. Then Kate resumes her drinking and the 'ball topic' is over.

(Foster, 1990: 65)

189

This rudimentary six-turn exchange contains a number of the basic interactional features of adult talk, including a topic initiation, a clarification
request, a repetition, a question–answer adjacency pair, and a follow-up
move. Onto such interactive frameworks the child's first words, and ultimately whole conversational routines, will be mapped. Reciprocal games,
such as 'peekaboo', which infants learn to play from the age of five
months or so, have similar clearly defined turntaking structures. It is
through participation in these playful collaborative routines that 'the
child gradually learns the reversability of the roles of actor and recipient-
of-action and maps these on to the somewhat parallel roles of sender and
receiver of verbal communication. In this way the concept of dialogue is
established' (Wells, 1981: 101).

The following exchange between a mother and her two-year-old child
incorporates the same interactional ingredients as in Kate's 'conversation' above, but in a more fully verbalized and extended form:

Text 6.1: Popped on

[The central heating boiler has just reignited]
Mark: oh popped on
Mother: pardon?
Mark: it popped on
Mother: it popped on?
Mark: yeh
Mother: what did?
Mark: er – fire on
Mother: the fire?
Mark: yeh pop the. fire. Popped it fire
Mother: oh yes. the fire popped on didn't it?
Mark: yeh

(Wells, 1981: 105)

6.3 Child-directed speech

Parent-to-child talk is typically structured so as to maximize opportunities for reciprocal interaction, and the previous extract (Text 6.1)
demonstrates a number of ways that this is achieved. For example,
child-directed speech is characterized by a large number of questions
(*pardon? it popped on? what did? the fire? didn't it?*) which elicit either
a repeat (*it popped on*), a confirmation (*yeh*) or an elaboration (*the
fire*). The mother also uses what are called 'continuing moves', i.e.
turns which respond to what the child has just said or done and which,
at the same time, serve to initiate a new exchange:

```
Mark:        pop the. fire popped it fire
→Mother:     oh yes. the fire popped on didn't it?
Mark:        yeh.
```

Notice how the mother maintains topic continuity by repeating elements of the child's utterance (*fire popped*), but recasts them in a more fully grammaticized form (*the fire popped on*), as well as commenting (*oh yes*) and elaborating on the child's contribution (*didn't it?*). Moreover, in the absence of a response from the child, parents will answer for them, and continue with a follow-up utterance, as if the child had in fact responded, for example:

```
Child:     Daddy?
Father:    What?
Child:     Daddy?
Father:    What've you done?
           Broken a toy?
           Eh?
           Little scamp.
Child:     [laughs]
```

(MacLure, 1981: 120, cited in McTear, 1985: 68)

In this way, adults compensate for the child's conversational immaturity and 'ensure that conversational exchanges with their infants have the appearance of being well-formed' (McTear, 1985: 68). These compensatory strategies, along with the use of questions, continuing moves, repetitions, comments and elaborations, all support – or *scaffold* (see below) – the child's emerging conversational and linguistic competence. They provide a secure linguistic and interactional environment within which the child can take the initiative while the parent, as it were, 'leads from behind' (Wells, 1981).

Other features of child-directed speech that may contribute, directly or indirectly, to the development of conversational competence include such adjustments as slowing of pace, higher pitch, syntactic simplicity, and the use of a restricted vocabulary. These features serve to make parent-to-child talk more intelligible, and hence increase the likelihood of the child's responding. Moreover, by choosing familiar topics, especially those related to the immediate situation (the here-and-now), and by avoiding topics that are displaced in time and space, parents optimize the communicative potential of the talk. And because parents and caregivers are primarily motivated by the need to communicate with their children, they tend to ignore the grammatical accuracy of child speech, concentrating instead on the content. It is in this message-driven and highly supportive linguistic environment that the child's conversational competence develops apace.

6.4 Formulaic language

The language that the child incorporates into the turntaking routines it has acquired consists, initially, of single words. The one-word stage appears around the age of 12 months and typically lasts for about six months, whereupon two-word sentences, exhibiting basic syntax, start to emerge. However, the terms 'one-word' and 'two-word' are misleading, as both stages see the emergence, not only of individual words, but of word-like chunks, such as *allgone, all-all-down*, or *see you later*. Like words, these formulaic items (also called *holophrases*) are used consistently with a particular meaning. And, although they appear, superficially to 'have grammar', they are unanalysed. That is, they are not generated by internalized grammatical rules, but are instead learned, stored, retrieved, and used as if they were single lexical items and without regard for their internal grammar, as these short extracts demonstrate:

> Mother: We're all very mucky.
> Child: I all very mucky too.
>
> Mother: That's upside down. (child is putting on his coat the wrong way round)
> Child: No, I want to upside down.
>
> (Clark, 1974: 3–4, cited in Wray, 1999: 220)

Even when child language becomes more fully grammaticized, it still retains formulaic elements. Because children are restricted both by their immature knowledge of the linguistic system and also by the limitation on the number of items they can combine in one utterance, using borrowed chunks of language allows them to communicate beyond their present level of grammatical competence, and without any sacrifice of fluency. By using memorized chunks, or by incorporating chunks from their interlocutor's previous turn (as in the two examples above), children learn to avoid the pause that would ensue if they were to construct an utterance entirely from scratch. They therefore have an important function in the development of conversational competence.

Wray (1999), in a review of the research, identifies at least four classes of formulaic language used by children. They are:

1. under-analysed forms, such as *allgone* and *wanna*, that 'display grammatical and/or lexical knowledge beyond the child's current generative capacities' (p. 220);
2. fixed formulae, such as lines from songs and nursery rhymes (*Twinkle twinkle little star*), as well as institutionalized ways of saying things (*May I leave the table?*);

3. fused utterances, i.e. original creations of the child's, rather than 'bor-rowings', which are found to be pragmatically useful, so become 'fused' into a fixed expression, and are used frequently; and
4. 'gestalt' utterances: these are typically long, often phonologically imprecise, but appropriately used utterances, picked up from peer or adult talk, and which give the impression of precocity, given the child's more characteristically telegraphic output.

As we have noted, formulaic language enables the child to have chunks of language available for immediate use to 'plug conversational gaps' and thereby save processing time, but it may also have a developmen-tal function. Peters (1983) suggests that these gestalt items provide at least some children with data to hold in reserve for subsequent analysis. That is, these memorized chunks are available as raw mater-ial for subsequent segmentation into, and storage as, smaller units, from which regular syntactic rules are then generalizable. Other researchers dispute this claim, insisting that formulaic sequences are simply communicational fillers. Rather than assisting development, they may, if the child learns to depend on them, actually inhibit ana-lytical processes: a view that has implications on second-language learning (see below).

Whether or not formulaic language performs a developmental func-tion, it is now generally accepted that the acquisition of a bank of mem-orized, fixed (or semi-fixed) expressions is of enormous utility in the development of conversational fluency. And it is not a capacity that is peculiar to the child. As noted in Chapter 2, Pawley and Syder (1983) suggest that adult native speakers have literally thousands of these routines at their disposal, without which the ability to maintain a con-versation under real-time conditions would be impossible. Among the examples they give are:

> Can I help you?
> Need a hand?
> It's on the tip of my tongue.
> There's no pleasing some people.
> You can't be too careful.
> Would you like some more?
> Watch your step.
> It's easy to talk.

(1983: 206–7)

In this short extract, a number of these formulaic chunks are in evidence:

<S 02>   They were awake at five-thirty Stefan.
<S 01>   Yeah.
<S 02>   It's way too early after a night like they had last night.

<S 01> Yeah *that's right*. . . . yeah. *You live and learn.*
<S 02> And sometimes you don't live and learn. Sometimes you live and repeat and repeat and repeat.
<S 01> [chuckles] *Would you like a cup of tea?* = =
<S 02> = = I . . . *no thanks.* I'm sick of that alarm going off *all the time.*
<S 01> Yeah.
<S 02> *Don't you?*
<S 01> Yeah. *What can you do?*

(OZ TALK)

To put it bluntly, then, a lot of conversation is second-hand. Or, in Schmidt and Frota's words: 'Most sentences that one produces and hears during the day are really not creative or novel in any interesting sense . . . When we actually produce language in ordinary conversation . . . it seems much more reasonable to assume as the psychological basis for fluency that we alternate between two modes of production, one creative and hesitant, the other rehearsed, formulaic to varying degrees, and fluent' (1986: 310). This 'dual-mode' processing capacity (Skehan, 1998) seems finely balanced in native speakers, allowing them to cope effectively with the processing demands of online communication in real time, so that conversation is neither totally formulaic nor totally original. As we shall see, though, in second-language learning the balance is achieved only with difficulty, if at all.

6.5 Repetition

The use of formulaic language is one instance of a phenomenon which is crucial to the development of conversational competence, and that is repetition. In fact, as Tannen notes, 'formulaic language (or fixed expressions) is language repeated by multiple speakers over time' (1989: 54). Tannen lists several different criteria for identifying instances of conversational repetition:

> First, one may distinguish self-repetition and allo-repetition (repetition of others). Second, instances of repetition may be placed along a scale of fixity in form, ranging from exact repetition (the same words uttered in the same rhythmic pattern) to paraphrase (similar ideas in different words) . . . There is also a temporal scale ranging from immediate to delayed repetition, where 'delayed' can refer to delay within a discourse or delay across days, weeks, months, and years.

(1989: 54)

As instance of other-repetition, we have already seen how chunks are borrowed from previous utterances and incorporated into the child's responses, using what is called an *incorporation strategy*:

> Mother: We're *all very mucky*
> Child: I *all very mucky* too.

Itoh and Hatch (1978) observed a similar strategy being used by a two-and-a-half-year-old Japanese child learning English, whose first coherent utterances involved the repetition of the final part of the utterances addressed to him:

> Y: Make it one at a time.
> T: One at a time.

Like adults, children also buy processing time by repeating their own utterances, either whole or in part. This is a common device for the staged construction of a proposition where they lack the linguistic means to construct it in one uninterrupted run – what Peters (1983) calls 'repetition and build-up':

> Child: Me want house for Kate. Me want make house for Kate. You, you help. You make house for Kate.

(Peccei, 1999: 96)

In the following example, a question is repeated that the child initially had to struggle to formulate. It is just possible that the self-repetition is – or acts as – a form of review and reinforcement, and could be the first step in the eventual storage of the whole utterance as a ready-made chunk for future retrieval:

> Child: Why – why do – me – why didn't me get flu ever?
> Mother: I don't know. you didn't get it. did you that time?
> Child: Why didn't me get flu?

(Peccei, 1999: 96)

On the other hand, the child may be repeating the question simply in order to maintain the conversational flow, a strategy that is reinforced by the insistent use of *why*-questions:

> Child: Why did you give her – to her when been flu?
> Mother: To cheer her up.
> Child: What did her have wrong with her?
> Mother: Flu.
> Child: Why – why do – me – why didn't me get flu ever?
> Mother: I don't know. You didn't get it, did you that time?
> Child: Why didn't me get flu?
> Mother: Because you're so healthy.

> Child: Why are me so health – healthy?
> Mother: You're such a fatty

(1999: 96)

Children are also on record as using self-repetition as a form of solitary creative verbal play, as they rehearse and manipulate words and chunks that they have picked up in talk. Itoh and Hatch observed, of the Japanese child acquiring English, that, 'as he became proficient in repetition, he was no longer satisfied with repeating just what was said to him. He began to expand on his own spontaneous repetitions by recalling other possible similar patterns:

> This is my fork. Fork. This is my fork.
> The sun. Sun. This. This sun. This is a sun.
> Don't know. I don't know. I don't know, dummy.'

(1978: 83)

Interactive verbal play, relying on repetition to create the effect of a cohesive exchange – even when the content of the exchange is nonsensical – has also been observed in children's conversations with one another, as in this instance of the private talk between twins aged two years and nine months:

> Toby: You silly. You silly.
> David: No Toby's silly.
> Toby: You silly.
> David: No. You silly. No not you silly.
> Toby: You silly.
> David: No. Not. No silly.
> Toby: No silly.
> etc.

(Ochs, 1983: 22)

Thus, repetition, whether exact or approximate, serves a variety of functions in the development of conversational ability. It allows the child to connect his or her turn to the preceding turn and thereby maintain the conversational flow; it acts as a stalling device in order to 'buy' processing time; and it seems to serve a developmental function, helping recycle and consolidate what has been learned. As we shall see, repetition serves the same or similar functions in the development of second-language conversational competence.

6.6   Scaffolding

Child-directed talk, as we have seen, provides a supportive 'climbing frame', or verbal *scaffold*, within which the child can achieve a degree of communicative success, and success, moreover, that he or she would not have been able to achieve unaided. By asking questions, and by repeating, recasting and extending the child's utterances, the parent 'draws the child out', such that it almost seems to be the child who is doing all the conversational work. The metaphor of scaffolding captures the supportive yet temporary nature of this kind of facilitative talk: as the child's ability to handle the skills of conversation increases, the adult's support and control is gradually withdrawn. But until it is, the scaffold enables the child to participate in verbal interaction that is beyond his or her actual developmental level, as in this example of narrative telling:

It is mealtime, and Ross (2; 6) and his mother are gazing at the food they are eating.

Child:	Sometimes.
Mother:	(she looks at him).
Child:	Ross come out bed bed come out my.
Mother:	What are you talking about? What about the bed at night?
Child:	Mm.
Mother:	What did you say?
Child:	In a dark.
Mother:	In the dark?
Child:	Ross em Ross runs in a dark.
Mother:	Run in the dark?
Child:	Ross runs.
Mother:	You get out of the . . . you got out the bed in the night, did you, and ran round in the dark?

(Foster, 1990: 128)

The mother's last turn summarizes the account that Ross is able to tell only with her assistance. Through her questions and recasts, she prompts Ross at an utterance-by-utterance level, while at the same time, at the level of the discourse, they co-construct the framework of a mini-narrative: notice how the mother recasts Ross's account in the past tense.

6.7 Syntax: Vertical constructions

Apart from providing on-the-spot conversational support, scaffolding may play an important role in the development of language itself, especially of its syntax. The co-construction of a proposition over a number of turns (called a *vertical construction* (Scollon, 1976)), may prepare the child for subsequent production of *horizontal constructions*, that is, syntactic sequences of propositions embedded in a single turn. This increase in complexity may represent a developmental stage in the emergence of the child's grammar.

In the conversation between Mark and his mother (Text 6.1), the child produces a horizontal construction (*fire popped*) combining both subject and verb, accumulating elements that had first been proposed separately (*popped on . . . fire on*):

Mark:	oh popped on
Mother:	pardon?
Mark:	it popped on
Mother:	it popped on?
Mark:	yeh
Mother:	what did?
Mark:	er–fire on
Mother:	the fire?
Mark:	yeh . . . pop the. fire popped it fire

Hatch (1978), arguing from the basis of discourse analysis, was one of the first researchers to put the case for the pivotal role of conversation in early language development: 'Our basic premise has long been that the child learns some basic set of syntactic structures, moving from a one-word phase to a two-word phase, to more complex structures, and that eventually the child is able to put these structures together in order to carry on conversations with others. The premise, if we use discourse analysis, is the converse. That is, language learning evolves *out of* learning how to carry on conversations' (1978: 403–4, emphasis in original). Hatch extends this theory to the acquisition of a second language, a view that, as Ellis notes, 'informs all interactionist theories [of SLA]' (2003: 79). Wells (1987, 1999) goes even further and argues that conversation can provide the matrix for *all* learning. These are views that we shall return to later in the chapter.

6.8 Cohesion

As we have seen in the discussion on repetition, the child learns to initiate and sustain talk independent of adult support, by incorporating elements from preceding turns in order to create the effect of a cohesive exchange. At the early stages, cohesion from one turn to the next is achieved by exact repetition, but by the age of three this gives way to modifications of the original utterance:

Adult:	You do that one.
Child:	Now I do that one.

(Bloom *et al.* 1976, quoted in Foster 1990: 114)

Other cohesive devices, such as (in this order) the use of ellipsis, pronominal forms and discourse markers (*well*, *right*, *now* . . .), also emerge at an early age, as in these examples (from Foster, 1990: 115):

Mother:	What's George doing?
Child (aged 2):	[*George is*] doing cars
Mother:	Let's have some vegetables.
Child (aged 2 years 8 months):	Oh, I'll get *some*.
Siobhan:	I want to play with all the Lego.
Heather (aged 4):	*Well*, you can't have that.

In fact, if conversational competence is narrowly defined as the ability to take turns, and to connect successive utterances, then most of the features of adult conversational competence are already in place by the age of four. In this short extract between a mother and her three-and-a-half-year-old daughter, the cohesive devices the child uses are identified:

Child:	Why d'you never buy me a guitar?
Mother:	Well, I don't know. Would you like one?
Child:	Yes[1.]
Mother:	A little guitar.
Child:	No.[2] A big[3] one[4]. A big one.[5]
Mother:	You wouldn't be able to play a big one.
Child:	I would.[6] I would[7]. I would be able to.[8]

(Fletcher, 1988, cited in Peccei, 1999: 95)

Key:

1. adjacency pair (question – answer)
2. adjacency pair (suggestion – refusal)
3. lexical – antonym
4. substitution
5. repetition
6. ellipsis
7. repetition
8. ellipsis

6.9 Coherence

But conversation is not simply cohesive – it is also coherent. That is to say, it is *about* something, and successive utterances need to be made relevant both to each other and to the topic of the conversation as a whole. As we saw in the exchange between Toby and David, utterance-to-utterance relevancy is achieved, initially, through repetition:

| Toby: | You silly. You silly. |
| David: | No Toby's silly. |

as well as by using several utterances to convey a single piece of information:

flower broken/ flower/ its flower broken/ eh/ oh/ end/ – many many flowers broken/

(Ochs, 1983: 20)

At a later stage, coherence is achieved through 'contingency' – i.e. by maintaining the topic of the preceding utterance but adding or substituting information into it. For example, in the following the information *sharp* builds on the adult's utterance:

Adult: Put this on with a pin.
Child: Sharp.

(Bloom *et al.*, 1976, quoted in Foster, 1990: 118)

Achieving topical relevance, both across turns and in relation to the overall topic, requires that speakers have some idea of what the hearer knows, a capacity that starts to emerge in the third year. It has been observed, for example, that three- and four-year-old children demonstrate respect for Grice's Cooperative Principle (see Chapter 1) in that they take extra care when introducing topics unfamiliar to their conversational partners.

6.10   Functions, genres and speech acts

As well as being interactive and coherent, conversation is also functional and goal-directed. That is to say, it fulfils certain *purposes*, both personal and social. Through talk 'the child is learning to be and to do, to act and interact in meaningful ways' (Halliday, 1975: 15). Halliday categorizes the functions of early child language as being:

- instrumental: the *I want* function
- regulatory: the *do as I tell you* function
- interactional: the child's equivalents of *hello, pleased to see you*
- personal: what Halliday calls the *here I come* function, i.e. language of personal feelings and of involvement, expressing the child's sense of its own uniqueness
- heuristic: the *tell me why* function – the language the child uses as a tool for learning
- imaginative: the *let's pretend* function

Wells (1981) notes that 'the emphasis in Halliday's account is on language as "meaning potential" – a cultural resource for social interaction – which has its beginnings in the, often idiosyncratic, interchanges between the child and his immediate caregivers' (1981: 89). Out of these interchanges develops the capacity to engage in dialogue, which in turn assumes the ability to adopt different social roles and to assign these roles to others.

Instrumental purposes – specifically requests for objects – develop

200

soonest, at around eight months. At the early stage requests are always accompanied by reaching gestures, but by the end of the second year gestures are an optional extra, and requesting exchanges such as the following are handled mainly verbally:

C: Me want that.
M: What is it?
C: Seen.
M: Plasticine?
C: Mmm.

(after Peccei, 1999: 95)

At a later stage, between 12 and 16 months, a representational – or 'proposition-oriented' – use of language develops, whereby the child learns to refer to, and name, objects and activities in the immediate context. At first, this referential function is very much focused on the 'here-and-now', involving look-and-comment exchanges which evolve into more fully verbalized exchanges such as the following (Mark is 23 months):

Mark: Jubs (= birds).
Mother: What are they doing?
Mark: Jubs bread.
Mother: Oh look. They're eating the berries aren't they?
Mark: Yeh.
Mother: That's their food. They have berries for dinner.
Mark: Oh.

(Wells, 1981: 102)

Eventually, at around the age of two, the child learns how to communicate information and experiences that his or her interlocutors are not privy to, such as events recalled or imagined, a function Halliday calls the informative (or, the *I've got something to tell you*) function: 'This is a highly complex function, since it is one that is solely defined by language itself' (1975: 58). This in turn releases the child from the constraints of the here-and-now, permitting what Bruner (1974) calls 'operations in the absence of what is represented' – a 'transformative' function of language.

Telling your conversational partners about events removed from the here-and-now requires the use of narrative, which in turn calls on the ability to construct discourse. In this extract Nigel, aged 20 months, reviews an incident that occurred that day at the zoo, where a zookeeper intervened to prevent a goat eating a plastic lid:

Text 6.2: The goat

Nigel: Try eat lid.
Father: What tried to eat the lid?

Nigel: Try eat lid.
Father: What tried to eat the lid?
Nigel: Goat. Man said no. Goat try eat lid. Man said no.

Then, after a further interval, while being put to bed:

Nigel: Goat try eat lid. Man said no.
Mother: Why did the man say no?
Nigel: Goat shouldn't eat lid. [shaking head] Good for it.
Mother: The goat shouldn't eat the lid. It's not good for it.
Nigel: Goat try eat lid. Man said no. Goat shouldn't eat lid.
          [shaking head] Good for it.

The story is then repeated as a whole, verbatim, at frequent
intervals over the next few months.

(Halliday, 1975: 112)

As Halliday comments 'an interesting feature of such sequences is how
they are built up through dialogue' (1975: 111). The adults scaffold the
emergent story, by asking leading questions and recasting the child's
utterances, until the child is ready to 'go it alone'. Note that the adults'
questions help orient and develop the story, providing 'textuality', so
that, in its finished form, it contains what might be considered certain
obligatory elements of narrative genres (see Chapter 5):

goat try eat lid → complication
man said no → resolution
goat shouldn't eat lid . . . (shaking head) good for it → coda

The story, then, is collaboratively constructed, and the scaffolding serves
both as a temporary frame on which to 'hang' the story, as well as a generative model (or *schema*) for other narratives of this type.

By the age of four or five, as Wells observes, children are usually able
to tell their stories unaided, 'although the causal relationships are frequently left implicit in the ubiquitous use of "and" or "and then"'
(1987: 198). At around the same time, children's stories move beyond
the simple recount, and enter the realm of the imaginative and dramatic,
as they co-construct fantasy worlds in which to situate their play. Wells
provides an example:

Lee (age 5) and Robert (age 6) are playing cops and robbers.
Robert: Right. I'm Starsky. You're Hutch.
Lee: Hello. I'm Hutch.
Robert: You don't need to go in there [imaginary building].
Lee: I'm going in.
Robert: Come out.
[*Lee makes car noises.*]
          I drive. Starsky drives. [*He pretends to drive.*]

Lee: No. I've got to take my car.
Robert: No. They have, have only got one car.

(1987: 198)

6.11   Pragmatics

As we have seen, children's capacity to regulate their environment, through the use of instrumental language such as commands, develops early. Very young children are able to make requests, and to provide responses to requests. But a more fully functioning pragmatic competence, including the capacity to modify talk to take account of situational factors, and to use context to infer the pragmatic force of speech acts, develops relatively late. Children of two and three, for example, often fail to respond to questions, or they respond inappropriately. Even five- and six-year-olds have difficulty distinguishing between yes/no-questions that are simply requests for information (*can you read?*) and directives (*can you read it to me?*). The following telephone exchange, where the six-year-old child has answered the phone but does not recognize (or acknowledge?) the pragmatic force of the adult's question, is typical:

Adult: Is your dad there?
Child: Yes.
         [pause]
Adult: Well, can you go and get him for me?

The more formulaic aspects of pragmatic and sociolinguistic competence – such as the correct use of forms of address and of politeness markers – start to appear around the age of three. Some polite forms, such as the use of *please* and *thank you* are taught explicitly, as in 'Say "please"!' or 'What's the magic word?' Others may be inferred from observation of, and interaction with, adults. One researcher showed, for example, that when four-year-olds were asked to play roles such as doctor and patient, or teacher and student, they were able to adjust their speech according to their role, suggesting that they had internalized knowledge about certain sociolinguistic conventions (Andersen 1978, cited in Foster, 1990).

Children also learn how to pre-empt points of potential breakdown, and to make the appropriate conversational repairs when breakdowns occur. And they learn how to use talk in order to get their own way, including the use of negotiating and bargaining skills, as in this example:

A: Say yes.
B: No.
A: I'll be your best friend if you say yes.

(McTear, 1985: 109)

Such skills may be best learned, McTear argues, when interacting with peers. 'In peer situations children have to learn the principles of negotiation. A common situation, which is less likely to arise in families, is where a child attempts to gain access to an ongoing activity in a nursery where rules of access are negotiated by peers rather than imposed by adults. Such a situation gives considerable scope for the development of the child's communicative competence' (McTear, 1985: 72). The negotiation of conversational turntaking 'rights' is attested, for example, in data collected by Blum-Kulka (1997), during dinner table conversations. Here Marvin (age 8) and Daniel (age 6) engage in 'metapragmatic' discourse – that is, they talk *about* pragmatics – as they battle for the right to speak:

Marvin:	Can I say something? Is it my turn?
Mother:	I don't know.
Daniel:	No! You have to wait until I finish!
Marvin:	[whining] You had a long turn. So there.
Daniel:	You had a longer one!
Marvin:	No, I didn't.
Daniel:	Yes, you did.
Father:	Daniel, are you finished saying what you were going to say?

(Blum-Kulka, 1997: 184)

Nevertheless, sociocultural theory (see below) suggests that interactions with, if not an adult, at least a 'more capable other' are essential for the continuing development of communicative – including pragmatic – competence. Wells (1981) insists that 'becoming a communicator' requires that 'the child should have a conversational partner who is oriented to his needs as a language learner' (1981: 109). It is only through engagement in interaction with such partners that children get feedback on, and are able to evaluate, the effect of their communicative acts, of the matching of form with function, and of matching language with context. Language socialization, in other words, occurs largely through participation in recurrent communicative practices.

6.12 Educated discourse: Talk at school

However, some studies of the communicative competence of children, including their ability to process and transact information co-operatively for a shared purpose, suggest that the mere fact of having conversational skills does not automatically translate into *communicative* competence. Anderson *et al.* (1994) set groups of children aged between seven and thirteen a collaborative map-reading task, and found that the deployment of such interactive skills as asking and answering questions, volunteering information, and responding sensitively to their partners' contributions, varied greatly, irrespective of age, and despite their overall fluency. They concluded that 'children apparently do not all automatically acquire comparable skills as communicators as they do fluency in their native language or skill as conversationalists' (1994: 461).

As Wells has noted, the failure of some children to become effective collaborative partners may be exacerbated by the mismatch of styles between talk at home and talk at school: 'Compared with parents, it is only half as often that [teachers] incorporate the meanings offered in the children's utterances, either by extending those meanings or by inviting the children to extend them themselves. By contrast, teachers are twice as likely as parents to develop the meanings that they themselves have introduced into the conversation. Small wonder that some children have little to say or even appear to be lacking in conversational skills altogether' (1987: 87).

Talk at school has been the subject of many studies, notably the Bristol Study of Language Development (Wells, 1981), which followed the language development of a group of children from pre-school to primary school, and from which the following short segment is taken. The teacher and class are talking about seasons; Betty is five and a half:

Teacher: Now when winter is over a new season will start. Do you know the name of that season?
Betty: January
Teacher: No, that's the name of the month. What season will it be? After winter will be s——?
Betty: Spring
Teacher: Good girl springtime

(MacLure and French, 1981: 218)

Even in this short extract a number of typical features of teacher talk are represented. The teacher's questions are all *display questions*, that is questions designed to elicit knowledge from the learners (as opposed to *referential questions*, where the asker does not know the answer). They are also *closed* in that they elicit short – characteristically one-word – answers. Because of this, the teacher contributes a greater quantity of talk to the interaction than the learner. The questions are all initiated by the teacher (there are no learner-initiated exchanges), a reflection of the unequal distribution of speaking rights. Each question forms the opening move in an IRF sequence (I = *initiate*, R = *response*, F = *follow up*, or *feedback*). The feedback is evaluative, commenting on the correctness or not of the response (*No . . . good girl*), rather than on its meaning (compare this to continuing moves, mentioned earlier in this chapter). IRF sequences are often chained together to form large chunks of lesson time. Although there is no information about the pause lengths in the extract, it is likely that the teacher didn't allow a great deal of *wait time* between the initiating move and the response. In classrooms, there is typically little or no time for learners to formulate longer, more complex, more reflective responses, or to initiate their own topics (Rowe, 1986).

None of these features of teacher talk are alien to caretaker talk: parents, too, ask display questions, give evaluative feedback, and tend to initiate exchanges. But children also participate in conversations with their caregivers where they play a far less passive role, and where there is a greater symmetry in the distribution and initiation of turns. On the other hand, the demands of the classroom situation, including the large number of learners that the teacher has to deal with, and the pedagogic motivation of classroom discourse, often mean that learners are exposed to very little other than the kind of interaction exemplified above. Wells summarizes the problem:

> [. . .] not only do the children speak less with an adult at school. In those conversations they do have, they get fewer turns, express a narrower range of meanings, and, in general, use grammatically less complex utterances. They also ask fewer questions, make fewer requests, and initiate a much smaller proportion of conversations . . . The result is that, at school, children are reduced for a much greater part of the time to the more passive role of respondent, trying to answer the teacher's many questions and carrying out his or her requests.

(1987: 87)

In itself, this might not seem to be a problem, especially if children are getting plentiful opportunities to participate more reciprocally and more actively in conversations outside the classroom. However, there are strong arguments to suggest that conversation 'when engaged in collaboratively, . . . can be an effective medium for learning and teaching' (Wells, 1987: 218). By extension, a learning environment in which there are few or no conversational opportunities will be an impoverished one. The theory underpinning such a view will be the subject of the next section.

6.13 Sociocultural theory and 'instructional conversation'

We have seen how the conversational scaffolding provided by a caregiver creates a secure language environment, within which the child can function better than he or she would be able to unassisted. We have also seen how such scaffolding may provide material for language development, in the form, for example, of vertical constructions. Interactionist theory argues that language learning may emerge *out of* conversation, rather than simply being a pre-condition *for* conversation. An even stronger claim for conversation is that it provides the matrix not just for the learning of language, but of learning in general. As Wells puts it: 'One of the central claims put forward in the language-based theory of learning . . . is that the very same conversations that provide the opportunity for the child to learn language also provide the opportunity to learn *through* language' (1999: 51, emphasis in original).

A language-based theory of learning is fundamental to a sociocultural view of learning, as first propounded by Vygotsky (1978), a view that focuses primarily on the social and cultural processes that contribute to the development of higher order cognitive functions. Sociocultural theory rejects both a behaviourist view of learning, i.e. that behaviours are externally modelled and 'conditioned', and an information-processing view, which argues that the mind is a limited-capacity input processing system. Rather, according to the sociocultural view, knowledge – including knowledge of language – arises from activities in particular contexts of use, and learning is essentially a social, rather than an individual, process. The child (or learner) achieves the capacity to function autonomously in a skill by first sharing responsibility for the achievement of tasks with a more competent adult or peer – a process of joint problem-solving, or *other-regulation*. Gradually the child-learner appropriates the regulatory means to perform the task him- or herself, and is able to function independently and without mediation – achieving what is called *self-regulation*.

Mediation by a more competent 'other' is optimal when it takes place in what Vygotsky called 'the zone of proximal development' (ZPD), that is 'the distance between the actual developmental level as determined by independent problem solving and the level of potential development as determined through problem solving under adult guidance or in collaboration with more capable peers' (Vygotsky, 1978: 86). The notion of 'assisted performance' as a prerequisite for unassisted performance is fundamental to a sociocultural view of learning. Verbal scaffolding is one of the ways in which such assistance is provided and by means of which cognitive structures are inferred. As the structures become internalized, the scaffolds are gradually removed.

Because conversation is a natural context for verbal scaffolding (witness the talk between parents and children), it has been argued that instructional talk that is modelled on conversation – that incorporates, for example, such features of conversation as reciprocal turn-taking, referential questions, elaborations and continuing moves – is likely to be more effective than sequences of teacher-initiated display questioning. In arguing for this view, van Lier (1996) highlights the *contingency* of conversation – specifically the way it links what is already known to what is new – as being central to its pedagogical effectiveness. Since learning takes place 'when the new is embedded in the familiar' and since 'conversational interaction naturally links the known to the new' (1996: 171), it is ideally suited as a vehicle for instruction.

Thus, conversation, by being jointly constructed, interactive and contingent, is not just a metaphor for learning, but it is its medium. In fact, Mercer characterizes successful teaching as being a 'long conversation', in which 'talk is used to construct knowledge . . . so that the knowledge that is created carries with it echoes of the conversations in which it was generated' (1995: 84).

This is not to say that teaching should simply be free-ranging, informal chat. As Mercer notes: 'Conversations in which people are self-consciously trying to teach and to learn will have special characteristics. These characteristics reflect not only the functional pursuit of teaching and learning, but also the cultural histories of schools as social institutions and the accountabilities of teachers and students within them' (1995: 84). To capture the pedagogical nature of such talk, Tharp and Gallimore (1988) coined the term *instructional conversations*. They comment:

> The task of schooling can be seen as one of creating and
> supporting instructional conversations. . . . The concept itself
> contains a paradox: 'Instruction' and 'conversation' appear
> contrary, the one implying authority and planning, the other
> equality and responsiveness. The task of teaching is to resolve this
> paradox. To most truly teach, one must converse; to truly converse
> is to teach.
>
> (1988: 111)

What characterizes such 'conversations'? One feature that Wells (1999) identifies is the use of continuing moves, as the 'F' stage of IRF exchanges. That is, rather than – or as well as – providing evaluative feedback on learners' responses, it is crucial that the teacher sustains the conversation by confirming, clarifying, elaborating on, or otherwise extending what the learner has just said. Always evaluating what learners say, whether 'right' or 'wrong', creates a context not unlike a quiz show, where being correct is prioritized. 'By contrast, frequently to choose the "extend" option creates a different context – one which emphasizes the collaborative construction of meaning, both in the setting of goals to be aimed for and in the construction of "common know-ledge" ' (1999: 264).

As an example Wells cites this short extract, in which the teacher is soliciting ideas on how to deal with the topic of the weather:

Teacher:	Other ideas about how we can go about this?
Salina:	We can look in newspapers and stuff [inaudible] = =
Teacher:	= = OK.
Salina:	See if we can find articles or something like magazines or something
Teacher:	Great. So I'd like you to start looking in the newspaper and when you find articles about weather you could cut them out and bring them in. Ask first to make sure whoever at home reads the paper is finished with it. But that's a great idea, Salina.

(Wells, 1999: 254–5)

Wells comments: 'In response to the teacher's request, Salina offers a rele-vant suggestion and the teacher extends that suggestion by proposing practical ways in which it could be put into effect' (1999: 246). The capacity to extend the child's utterance presupposes a degree of attention on the part of the teacher, as well as an intuition as to the child's inter-pretive ability with regard to how best the extension should be formu-lated. In an earlier work, Wells suggests four principles that might guide adults in order to facilitate their children's language development, and these principles would seem to apply equally well to the management of instructional conversations. Adults are urged:

• to treat what the child has to say as worthy of careful attention;
• to do one's best to understand what he or she means;
• to take the child's meaning as the basis for what one says next;
• in selecting and encoding one's message, to take account of the child's ability to understand – that is, to construct an appropriate interpreta-tion.

(1987: 218)

Wells adds, somewhat warily: 'Conversation may not be perfect as a means of information exchange . . . but when engaged in collaboratively, it can be an effective medium for learning and teaching. In any case, since there is no better alternative, we must do the best we can.'

In Chapter 9 we will look at how sociocultural theory, and the notion of instructional conversation, might apply to the learning of a second language. Meanwhile, it is time to address the way second language con-versational competence is acquired.

Tasks

A:

1. Study the following two extracts of child–parent talk (Wells, 1987), recorded a few months apart. Use this data to identify ways in which Mark's conversational competence has developed over this period.
2. Identify features of his mother's talk that are characteristic of child-directed speech.

Extract 1

Mark is looking out of the window and sees a man digging in his garden.

Mark: A man. A man er dig down there.
Mother: A man walked down there?
Mark: Yeah.
Mother: Oh yes.
Mark: Oh, yes. A man's fire, Mummy
Mother: Mm?
Mark: A man's fire.
Mother: Mummy's flower?
Mark: No.
Mother: What?
Mark [*emphasizing each word*]: Mummy. The man. Fire.
Mother: Man's fire?
Mark: Yeah.
Mother: Oh yes, the bonfire.
Mark: Bonfire.
Mother: Mm.
Mark: Bonfire. Oh, bonfire. Bonfire. Bon a fire bo bonfire. Oh, hot Mummy. Oh, hot. It hot. It hot.
Mother: Mm. It will burn, won't it?
Mark: Yeah. Burn. It burn.

Extract 2

Mark is doing a jigsaw puzzle with his mother.

Mother: There. Now you've got two Camberwick Green pictures.
Mark: Yeah.
Mother: One you made, mm? And one on the box.
Mark: Mm.
Mother: Look, these Camberwick Green men are the same as the dominoes in Camberwick Green.
Mark: Mm.
Mother: Look!
Mark: Can I see which is like that one?

Mother:	There's the policeman.
Mark:	Yeah.
Mother:	[*comparing the puzzle with the dominoes*] I don't think there is a man with a yellow hat.
Mark:	I made this puzzle, didn't I?
Mother:	Mm.
Mark:	Shall we do the puzzle again?
Mother:	Yes. Break it up, then.
Mark:	Break it up. And I got to start the words of it, haven't I?
Mother:	Go on, then.
Mark:	I got to start the word. You got to do. Now what does it say now? [*pretending to read instructions*] Make the lorry. You make the lorry, mummy.
Mother:	Mm.
Mark:	And make the cars, please. Have I got to, um, do the most of it?
Mother:	Well, it would help.

B: Here are two transcripts of classroom interaction. Compare them, using criteria mentioned in the discussion on sociocultural theory and instructional conversation.

Extract 1

This comes from a science class in a secondary school, where the class has been working with the teacher for a couple of terms.

Teacher:	Right, so we've just read through the actual, Gary – just read through the actual instructions for the experiment. We want to talk a little about the equipment, now that we're going to be using a fireproof mat. Um. Debbie, what about the fireproof mat, why's that important? Put it on the table, don't we. Why?
Debbie:	'Cos it might burn the table.
Teacher:	Yes. Because something in our experiment might burn the table. OK. So we need to have a fireproof mat. It is made of asbestos which doesn't burn in actual fact, which is quite, you know, useful to use. We're going to be using a tripod as well. Sarah, why do we use the tripod? Hannah?
Hannah:	To fit the, er, so you can fit the um, the bunsen underneath and have something for things to actually rest on.
Teacher:	To actually stand on, OK. What do you need to do to a bunsen when you are not using it?

John: Turn it to a yellow flame.
Teacher: Need to turn it to the yellow flame. Why is that
           important, Oliver?
Oliver: So that nobody'll put their arms through it.
Teacher: So that nobody'll put their arms through it, OK.

(Mercer, 1995: 37)

Extract 2
This extract comes from a science class, and takes place when a visiting teacher joins three students who are investigating the metamorphosis of caterpillars.

Ian: How do they eat?
Nir: Well they can go out through their [inaudible word]
Teacher: Well, when you say 'how do they eat' you're
           making an assumption that they DO eat.
Ian: I know they eat when they're not in the chrysalis.
Teacher: HOW do you know?
Ian: Well, [inaudible word] food.
Teacher: What did you see that makes you think they eat
           when they're in the chrysalis?
Ian: [1–2 inaudible words]
Teacher: Pardon? Sorry, I didn't hear. Say it again.
Ian: Do they eat?
Teacher: Do they?
Ian: Yeah, like is there food for them in the chrysalis?
Teacher: Well, wait a minute, there are two ways you
           can think about this: Does the chrysalis go to
           its – the chrysalis make contact with food outside
           itself?
Ian: No.
Teacher: Okay. So, so if the chrysalis feeds inside the
           chrysalis, what would the food be? Where does it
           come from?
Ian: [inaudible word]
Nir: I think that they like ate, they ate a lot to get energy
           to change inside the chrysalis. So I think they were
           eating the, like [inaudible word] for seven days and
           they almost ate the food. You see there's almost
           none left = =.
Teacher: = = Uhhuh.
Nir: and, and now it's got like a lot of energy to change
           and it's changing inside. That's what I think.
Teacher: So you're – you think it doesn't need food during
           THIS stage because – it's already stored a lot?
Nir: Yeah.

212

Teacher:	Yeah.
Nir:	What do YOU think?
Teacher:	What do I think? I think I agree with you.
Ian:	I think I agree with you too.

(Wells, 1999: 255–7)

7 Acquiring L2 conversational competence

Introduction

In the previous chapter we defined conversational competence and reviewed the way it develops in the mother tongue. The relevance of L1 development in terms of L2 teaching depends very much on whether we view L2 language development as being similar to L1 development, or different. Opinion is still divided on this issue, but one thing we can say with a degree of confidence is that, similar or not, the way conversational skills develop in an L2 is not the *same* as the way they develop in the L1. This is because, unlike first-language learners, second-language learners (unless they are very young children) already have a well developed conversational competence on which to draw. They know how to open and close conversations, take turns, change topic, interrupt, yield the floor, fill pauses, indicate discourse direction, back-channel, tell stories and be co-operative – in their *first* language. At issue, then, is not how second-language conversationalists acquire such skills from scratch, but how and to what extent these skills are transferred from their L1 to their L2. Related questions are: what factors – including instruction and exposure – might facilitate (or impede) the transfer of these skills into the second language? And, what is the relation between conversational competence and the learner's overall language proficiency? These questions will be addressed in this chapter.

7.1 Fluency

'The ability to carry on conversations is not just a reflection of grammatical competence . . .' (Schmidt and Frota, 1986: 262). Generations of disappointed learners – and teachers – can verify this fact. Grammatical competence does not predict conversational ability. Conversely, conversational ability is not necessarily a sign of a sophisticated grammar. In a landmark study (Schmidt, 1983), Wes, an adult Japanese immigrant in Hawaii, was at first an awkward conversationalist but after three years' living in Hawaii, he was able to carry on sustained conversation in English 'without running out of discussable topics or limiting interlocutors to his

214

topics, and without losing the thread of conversation from one topic to the next' (1983: 144). However, in the same three-year period 'Wes's grammatical control of English [had] hardly improved at all'. Here, for example, is an extract of spontaneous conversation in which Wes recounts an anecdote to a native-speaker friend:

> Wes: listen/today so funny story
> NS: yes/what happened?
> Wes: you know everyday I'm go to McDonald for lunch
> NS: yeah
> Wes: and today I saw so beautiful woman/so beautiful clothes/make-up/everything/but/so crazy!
> NS: how?/what do you mean?
> Wes: talking to herself/then she's listen to some person/everybody watch/but no one there/then/somebody/local woman I think say 'are you OK?'/'can I help?'/but beautiful woman she doesn't want talk to local woman/she's so snobbish!/so funny!
> NS: Jesus

(Schmidt, 1983: 159)

Note the complete lack of articles, the overgeneralized use of auxiliaries (*I'm go*, *she's listen*), the lack of verbs in some clauses (*today so funny story*), and the redundant subject pronouns (*beautiful woman she doesn't want talk*) – all features of a fairly unsophisticated interlanguage grammar. Yet, as Schmidt points out, 'the story is not only well formed but cleverly formed and funny, and on those grounds it compares well with good stories told by native speakers'. Moreover, Schmidt reports that 'friends and acquaintances who are not in the language . . . teaching business generally evaluate Wes's English favourably, pointing out, for example, that "I understand him a lot better than X, who's been here over twenty years"' (1983: 159). Wes succeeds as a conversationalist, despite his poor command of grammar. Even when communication breakdowns occur 'Wes is almost always able to repair these breakdowns, and it seems that his confidence, his willingness to communicate, and especially his *persistence* in communicating what he has in his mind and understanding what his interlocutors have in their minds go a long way towards compensating for his grammatical inaccuracies' (1983: 161). Clearly, the ability to carry on conversations is not just a reflection of grammatical competence.

In an attempt to identify exactly what the ability to carry on conversations *does* reflect, Schmidt and Frota charted the progress of one learner (R) over an extended period of time. They analysed R's conversational behaviour in (Brazilian) Portuguese over the five-month period from soon after his arrival in Brazil to just before he left. Unsurprisingly, his first conversations were halting and barely coherent, as he struggled to communicate his intended message. But, by the end of his stay in Brazil, R was able to express relatively complex notions 'in a smoother and communicatively more effective manner' (1986: 263). Specifically, in the later conversations there was evidence of:

- fewer comprehension checks and requests for help, reflecting improved comprehension;
- a higher proportion of questions to statements, resulting in increased topic control and a more assertive conversational style;
- fewer repetitions, especially self-repetitions, reflecting improved processing control;
- longer turns, as measured by the number of words per turn; and
- a faster speech rate, as measured by the number of words per minute.

The fewer repetitions, longer turns and faster speech rate are all indicators of an increase in *fluency* (or what Schmidt (1992) prefers to call *automatic procedural skill*). To anyone talking with R, it was apparent that he had become more *fluent*. But what does fluency involve?

Fluency phenomena are of two basic kinds: *temporal variables*, such as speech rate, pause length and length of run (i.e. the mean number of syllables between pauses); and *hesitation phenomena*, such as filled pauses (e.g. *erm*), repetitions and self-corrections (Ellis, 1994). Of these, the ability to produce lengthy runs seems to be a defining characteristic of oral fluency. Towell *et al.* (1996), for example, studied a group of learners of French over a four-year period, which included six months spent in a French-speaking country. The researchers found a marked increase in fluency, less the result of an increase in speed or a reduction in pausing, than 'an increase in the length and complexity of the linguistic units which are uttered between pauses' (1996: 112). Chambers summarizes the research into the temporal features of fluency as follows:

> Speech rate alone cannot be what contributes to the feeling that, as a listener, we are interacting with a foreigner. What appears significant from research in this area is:
>
> 1. the frequency of pauses rather than the length,
> 2. the length of run (the number of syllables between pauses),
> 3. the place of pauses in an utterance,
> 4. the transfer (or not) of pausing pattern from L1 to L2.
>
> (1997: 541)

One simple way of filling pauses is by means of repetition. Schmidt and Frota noted that 'R used repetitions (both self- and other-) to hold the floor and gain planning time and, often, to say a second time more completely or more smoothly what he said first incompletely or hesitantly' (1986: 270). Initially, many of these repetitions were self-corrections:

> R: todos os alunos adultos, são adultos
>   (all the students adults, are adults)

Others were simply a means of 'buying' planning time:

> R: agora
>   agora comendo
>   estamos
>   estamos comendo
>   estamos comendo ao restaurante italiano,
>   toda noite
>
> (R: now
>   now eating
>   we are
>   we are eating
>   we are eating at the Italian restaurant
>   every night)

(1986: 270)

Increasingly, R began to use repetition not merely as a time-saving device, but as a way of connecting his immediate utterance to the one that preceded it:

> S: Já surfou alguma vez no Havai:
> R: Surfou? Não, body surf só.
>
> (S: Have you ever surfed in Hawaii?
> R: [You] surfed? No, only body surf.)

(1986: 268)

Note that R repeats the verb form exactly, failing to inflect it for the first person (*surfei* ['I surfed']). This is evidence of an *incorporation strategy* at work, that is, the strategy of borrowing a chunk verbatim from the preceding discourse and then extending it in some way. While the strategy may result in non-standard forms, it nevertheless seems to be a productive one. In this example (Wagner-Gough, 1975, cited in Ellis, 1994: 284), Homer, an Iranian boy, repeats and extends his English-speaking interlocutor's turns:

> Mark: Come here.
> Homer: No come here.
>
> Judy: Where's Mark?
> Homer: Where's Mark is school.

(Ellis, 1994: 284)

7.2 Formulaic language

Repetition avoids the expenditure of valuable processing time that would otherwise be spent on generating original utterances from scratch. But it is a fairly primitive means of maintaining conversational fluency. Another way that learners fill pauses, while at the same time increasing the length and complexity of their between-pause units, is to rely on the use of 'ready-made' or – pre-fabricated – units. According to Pawley and Syder (1983), native-like fluency is possible only because speakers have memorized literally thousands of lexicalized multi-word units and pre-assembled, formulaic patterns (see Chapter 2). In real-time speech processing, where planning time is at a premium, these memorized 'chunks' offer speakers 'islands of reliability' (Dechert, 1983) where they can settle momentarily while they monitor input and plan subsequent output. We have already seen how, in first-language development, such chunks play an important role, both in the development of fluency, and in the acquisition of syntax. We have also noted how, in the conversation of native-speaking adults, formulaic language is used to achieve specific interactional goals (such as greetings) as well as to sustain interaction. To what extent, if at all, are these uses of formulaic language replicated in second-language acquisition?

Here we need to distinguish between 'naturalistic' learners and classroom learners. In an overview of the research, Wray (1999) notes that the use of formulaic language varies considerably in the former group. Some research subjects display little use of formulaic language. The Portuguese learner, R, in Schmidt and Frota's study, showed some evidence of increased idiomaticity, but there were fewer instances of formulaic language than might have been expected, given his frequent contact with native speakers. Wes (see above), however, was much more 'holistic' in his approach. Despite his rudimentary grammatical competence, he achieved considerable communicative success simply through the use of formulaic language: 'Wes has a rather rich repertoire of formulaic utterances, memorized sentences and phrases . . . which increase the appearance of fluency in English' (Schmidt, 1983: 150). Schmidt observed that Wes was skilful at identifying fixed phrases – such as *So, what's new?*, *Whaddya want?* and *I dunno why* – in the input he was exposed to, and he would practise these consciously, incorporating them into his talk and making great gains in communicability thereby. Likewise, in a study by Raupach (1984) of a German learner of French, the subject's use of formulaic language – including discourse markers, sentence starters and fillers – greatly increased after a period of residence in a French-speaking environment, contributing to a marked improvement in fluency.

How are such chunks acquired? Johnson (1996) argues that some language items can be acquired procedurally, that is they are 'imported' without conscious knowledge or attention, and constitute what Johnson calls 'acquired output'. Acquired output typically takes the form of fixed phrases, formulaic chunks and routines – these are either imported directly from the L1 (such as when learners use L1 hesitation devices when speaking their L2) or from exposure to authentic L2 input. Such output is especially useful in tasks requiring 'high automaticity', that is, where speed of processing disallows the use of rule-based systems. 'One would predict . . . that there would be more acquired output in fluent conversation than in writing. This prediction seems to fit what researchers like Tarone (1983) have found. Her "casual" style is the one associated with fluent conversation, and it is in this that the most "acquired output" occurs' (Johnson, 1996: 99).

Because of their limited exposure to authentic input, and hence, fewer opportunities for acquiring output, classroom learners tend to under-use formulaic language, relying instead on their grammatical knowledge to generate well-formed but essentially unidiomatic language. In a comparative study between native-speaker and non-native-speaker corpora, de Cock *et al.* (1998) found that advanced speakers were using prefabricated language with less frequency than native speakers and for different pragmatic purposes. For example, the evidence suggested that non-native speakers were underusing the formulaic chunks that expressed vagueness (e.g. *stuff like that, that sort of thing . . .*). In a similar vein, Prodromou (forthcoming) found that, while the frequency of two-word chunks such as *I mean* and *you know* were evenly matched in native-speaker and advanced non-native-speaker corpora, the vagueness chunks *sort of* and *a bit* were used significantly less frequently by non-native speakers. In a classroom study of two children learning English, Ellis (1992) tracked the development of requesting formulae (such as *Can I have . . . Have you got a . . . ?*), and found that, although both learners improved in this respect, they still used only a limited range of request forms by the end of the study, and were unable to adapt the few they did have to different situations and registers. Ellis also noted that the formulae that were learned were those that had occurred frequently in the course of organizing classroom activities, suggesting a relation between acquisition and frequency of use in communicative contexts. If this is the case, there are important implications in terms of the classroom development of conversational fluency (see Chapter 9).

7.3 Communication strategies

Another well-documented and highly useful resource in the development of fluency is the use of *communication strategies*. Communication strategies are deployed in order to overcome difficulties, specifically 'to compensate for some deficiency in the linguistic system, and [to] focus on exploring alternate ways of using what one does know for the transmission of a message' (Tarone, 1981: 287). Typically, these involve either avoiding the potential problem altogether by, for example, abandoning the message, or achieving communication through some kind of compensatory strategy. A compensatory strategy might be the use of paraphrase to convey a meaning for which the exact word is not known. Such strategies involve an ability to monitor the state of the communicative situation and to respond accordingly. And, theoretically at least, as the learner's interlanguage develops, the need to rely on these strategies decreases.

Communication strategies are often distinguished from *production strategies*. A production strategy is defined as consisting of 'an attempt to use one's linguistic system efficiently and clearly, with a minimum of effort' (Tarone, 1980: 419), or what Skehan (1998) has described as 'coping with one of the greatest problems of all: how to keep speaking at normal rates in real time' (1998: 3). Thus, production strategies include such devices as:

Facilitation:

- simplifying structure
- ellipsis
- using formulaic expressions
- the use of fillers and hesitation devices

Compensation:

- repairs
- false starts
- repetitions
- rephrasing

(Bygate, 1987: 15)

Production strategies help ease processing demands, as distinct from communication strategies, which are designed to make up for deficiencies in the speaker's linguistic system. However, there is clearly a degree of overlap and it is often difficult to determine what motivates strategy use. Not being able to access the right word in a conversation may owe just as much to real-time processing demands as it does to a gap in the learner's lexicon. There is a tendency, moreover, to equate production strategies with native-speaker language production (on the assumption that the native-speaker has no linguistic gaps) and communication strategies with non-native-speaker production. Again, this distinction is probably somewhat simplistic. A typology of communication strategies can be found in the table below.

Table 7.1. *Typology of communication strategies (Dörnyei, 1995)*

Avoidance or reduction strategies

1. Message abandonment – leaving a message unfinished because of language difficulties.
2. Topic avoidance – avoiding topic areas or concepts which pose language difficulties.

Achievement or compensatory strategies

3. Circumlocution – describing or exemplifying the target object or action (e.g. *the thing you open bottles with* for *corkscrew*).
4. Approximation – using an alternative term which expresses the meaning of the target lexical item as closely as possible (e.g. *ship* for *sail boat*).
5. Use of all-purpose words – extending a general, empty lexical item to contexts where specific words are lacking (e.g. the overuse of *thing, stuff, make, do*, as well as using words like *thingie, what-do-you-call-it*).
6. Word-coinage – creating a non-existing L2 word based on a supposed rule (e.g. *vegetarianist* for *vegetarian*).
7. Use of non-linguistic means – mime, gesture, facial expression or sound imitation.
8. Literal translation – translating literally a lexical item, an idiom, a compound word or structure from L1 to L2.
9. Foreignizing – using an L1 word by adjusting it to L2 phonologically (i.e. with an L2 pronunciation) and/or morphologically (e.g. adding it to an L2 suffix).
10. Code switching – using an L1 word with L1 pronunciation or an L3 word with L3 pronunciation in L2.
11. Appeal for help – turning to the conversation partner for help either directly (e.g. *What do you call . . . ?*) or indirectly (e.g. rising intonation, pause, eye contact, puzzled expression).

Stalling or time-gaining strategies

12. Use of fillers/hesitation devices – using filling words or gambits to fill pauses and to gain time to think (e.g. *well, now let me see, as a matter of fact*).

Note that, in Dörnyei's typology, most communication strategies target vocabulary problems. That is, they compensate for gaps in the speaker's lexicon. They are also aimed at resolving production difficulties, rather than problems of understanding. But it makes equal sense to consider receptive strategies, such as clarification requests (*Can you explain what you mean exactly?*), as forms of communication strategy, since they may also be attempts to compensate for interlanguage deficiencies. It is also worth pointing out that many communication strategies, such as types 3, 11 and 12 in Table 7.1, are realized through formulaic expressions, such as (type 3) *It's the sort of thing you . . .*; *It's when you . . .*; (type 11) *How do you say . . .? What's it called when . . .?* and (type 12) *Hang on a mo, just a second . . .* In this short extract in which a non-native speaker is describing a picture (Bygate, 1987) the communication strategies are italicized:

> S1: They are carrying a man, in ahm, erm in a *portable bed, the one that hospitals use to carry people that got an accident* and they're taking him, ah from the, from the road. He was on the road. OK. But they have just come because a man has called the police – I mean *the the people in charge of looking for these people that have had accidents.* Right.

The speaker uses the approximation *portable bed* for 'stretcher', and then goes on to use a circumlocution to clarify the meaning further. Later the speaker uses another circumlocution in place of the (presumably) unknown expression 'emergency services'.

In terms of the development of these strategies, Ellis conjectures that 'we might expect . . . that the choice of communication strategies will reflect the learners' stage of development. For example, learners might be expected to switch from L1-based strategies to L2-based strategies as their knowledge of the L2 develops' (1997: 61). However, there is as yet little or no research to support this hypothesis. Nor is it clear to what extent a reliance on communication strategies in the short term might be counterproductive in terms of the learner's long-term language development. In Schmidt's (1983) case study of Wes, it was found that Wes made spectacular progress in terms of communicability through his use of communication strategies, but at apparent cost to the development of his linguistic competence. Skehan comments: 'Reliance on communication strategies . . . seemed to be harmful to his linguistic health, a point that evidently did not disturb Wes, since he had achieved the goals he had set for himself as far as communication was concerned' (1998: 23). Given these possible negative long-term consequences, the advisability of encouraging the development of communication strategies – e.g. through explicit instruction – needs to be tempered with some caution. This is an issue that we will return to in Chapter 9.

7.4 Pragmatic competence

In referring to Bachman's (1990) model of communicative competence in the previous chapter, we noted that *pragmatic competence (pragmatic knowledge)* is that aspect of linguistic competence that constitutes the ability to relate language to its contexts of use. This ability varies considerably across learners. Some achieve a high degree of competence both in understanding their interlocutors' communicative purposes, and in producing socially and culturally acceptable responses. Others are less successful. In fact, even advanced non-native speakers seldom achieve the same degree of success as native speakers do on tasks 'where contextualized reaction data are available (as in the case of authentic conversations and institutional talk)' (Bardovi-Harlig, 2001: 14). The absence of certain high-frequency, often idiomatic routines, or 'typical expressions', is frequently cited as characteristic of non-native pragmatics. Bardovi-Harlig observes that 'routines such as *Could you give me a ride/a lift*, as part of a request, or *How clumsy of me*, as part of an apology, make the speech act . . . immediately recognizable to the hearer, and are used more often by NSs [native speakers] than NNSs [non-native speakers]' (2001: 19).

The relation between pragmatic competence and overall language proficiency, particularly in the area of grammar, is unclear. In the case of Wes (Schmidt, 1983), his pragmatic competence, as evidenced by his ability to make requests, relied initially on a limited number of memorized formulae (e.g. *'Shall we go?'*). Over time, and despite the lack of real development in his interlanguage grammar, these became more elaborated, e.g. *'Shall we maybe go out for coffee now, or you want later?'* Matsumuru (2003) has shown that improvement in a group of Japanese learners' command of appropriacy in advice-giving situations was due more to the amount of exposure they had had, rather than to their proficiency in English.

In summarizing the research evidence, Ellis notes that 'pragmalinguistic failure by learners is widely reported in the literature' (1994: 166) and lists such problems as learners using a very limited range of forms for realizing specific speech acts; choosing inappropriate forms; translating directly from their L1; overusing certain politeness markers (such as *'please'*); and erring on the side of verbosity (when making requests, for example).

Following, and building on, Blum-Kulka (1991), Ellis (1997) charts three broad phases in the development of pragmatic competence:

1. a message-orientated stage, in which learners rely on context clues to interpret speaker intentions, and use any means, including gesture

and an over-reliance on a few simple formulae, to convey their own meanings;

2. an interlanguage-orientated stage, where a range of strategies are used with varying degrees of success, but still showing evidence of transfer from L1, and also a tendency to verboseness; and
3. an interculturally orientated stage, in which learners approximate closely to native speakers with regard to the use of politeness strategies, although they may still retain certain 'deep' cultural habits, such as the importance attached to status.

Ellis adds that the evidence suggests that very few learners achieve stage 3, even after years of exposure. There is also some doubt as to whether classrooms provide a sufficiently varied social context in which to acquire certain speech acts, a point which we will address shortly.

Apart from the amount and type of instruction available, factors that seem to influence the development of pragmatic competence include the amount of exposure (the more the better, on the whole), and the influence of the learner's first language and culture, an issue which we will now address.

7.5 Transfer

Unlike first-language learners, second-language learners (unless they are very young children) already have a well-developed conversational competence on which to draw. As Kasper and Rose (2001) put it: 'Adult learners get a considerable amount of L2 pragmatic knowledge for free' (2001: 4). Conversation, after all, is a language universal: it is a form of behaviour common to all languages and to all cultures. It is 'the most fundamental and pervasive means of conducting human affairs' (Crystal, 1987: 116). Unsurprisingly, therefore, and irrespective of the language they are conducted in, conversations share a great many features. The following items, taken more or less at random from the index of a book on verbal interaction (Coulthard, 1985), are all arguably conversation universals: adjacency pairs, back-channels, closings, face-threatening acts, greetings, hesitations, interruptions, jokes, moves, overlaps, politeness, questions, responses, silences, speech acts, stories, style, topic changes, and turntaking. This is confirmed by a glance at recent back-issues of the *Journal of Pragmatics*: in the last few years there have been articles on such subjects as Jordanian college students' responses to compliments; opening moves in informal Chinese telephone conversations; expressions of disagreement by Venezuelans in conversation; stories in Turkish preschool conversations; conversational turntaking in a Caribbean English Creole;

repetitions as self-repair strategies in English and German conversations, and discourse markers in Modern Greek.

Claiming universality for these features of conversation does not, of course, preclude the fact that there is variation in the way they are realized from one language to another, and from one culture to another, and even from one speaker to another. The very fact that there are journal articles that analyse conversational features with respect to specific languages suggests that there is variability across languages. In that sense, *variability* is a language universal too. But while variability is local, the basic framework on to which this variability is mapped is, arguably, global.

As an example of how one conversational genre is realized in a different language, here is a narrative that occurred in a conversation between a number of Spanish speakers (from Soriano, 2000), along with its free translation.

Text 7.1: The taxi driver

PIL: yo una vez: / me metí en un taxi con: con una amiga y cuando estábamos a medio camino nos dimos cuenta de que ni ella llevaba un duro ni yo llevaba un duro [risas]

PIL: Once I got in a taxi with a friend and when we were half way there we realised that neither of us had a bean [laughter].

SAN: ¡hala!

SAN: Oh no!

PIL: y las dos así // *ostia que hacemos* y eran las do- las tres de la mañana o así y: *perdone mmm tenemos un problema* y el hombre se quedó así dice *¿qué pasa? mmm es que NO tenemos dinero* dice / [cambia a una entonación muy chillona imitando la del señor] *¡ah bueno! pensaba que era un problema de verdad* [risas] y yo [. . .] *tío que t'estoy diciendo que no tengo un duro* dice *bueno, no*

PIL: And the two of us are like *oh shit what are we going to do?* and it was three in the morning or so and we are *Excuse me but we have a problem* and the guy is like this and says *What's the matter? Erm we don't have any money* and he says [shrill voice to imitate the taxi driver] *Ah well, I thought it was a real problem* [laughter] and I'm like *Listen mate, I'm telling you I don't have a penny* and he says *well, it's*

225

pasa nada eso me pasa	nothing, this happens to me
a mí cada noche no te	every night, don't worry
preocupes digo *bueno si me*	about it and I say *well if you*
llevas a una: – *al lao de*	can drop me off at a . . . near
mi casa hay una: caja y tal si	my house there's one . . . a cash
quieres vam- a sacar dinero	point or something, if you want,
y él ah! sí sí sí no te preocupes y	we can . . . to get some money
además yo sé que vosotras sois	out and he's *ah yes yes yes,*
((unas buenas)) chicas y que me	don't worry, and what's more
vais a dar- dice *porque eso se ve*	I know you're good girls and
a mí me pasa muchas veces	you'll pay me and he says
	because this happens to me all
	the time . . .
¿?: Síi: [risas]	¡?: Yes [laughter]
PIL: = *a mí cuando alguien me*	PIL: . . . *when someone says to*
dice 'oiga que no tengo dinero'	me 'listen I don't have any
ya sé si me va a pagar luego o	money' and I know if they're
no ¿sabes? porque con la pinta	going to pay me later or not,
que tienen ya lo sé pero ehh me	you know what I mean?
da lo mismo yo le digo yo te	because depending on how they
llevo y si me pagas bien y si no	look I know, and it's all the
pues no pasa nada [risas] *pero*	same to me and I tell them I'll
	take you and if you pay me,
	OK, and if not, no matter
	[laughter] but
NV: no, hay gente maja	NV: no, there are some really
	good people round
SAN: hmmm	SAN: hmmm

It should be obvious from the description of conversational narratives (in Chapter 5) that the above story shares a number of features – both macro and micro – with its English-language equivalents. For a start it includes an orientation (*Once I got in a taxi with a friend . . .*), an X–Y sequence (Hutchby and Wooffitt, 1998) where the imperfective tense frames a preterite tense: *cuando* estábamos *a medio camino nos* dimos *cuenta . . .* , similar to the use of the past progressive and past simple contrast in English; a complicating event (*we realised that neither of us had a bean*); and a resolution (the taxi driver's generous attitude). There is also a coda in the form of the 'moral' of the story: *there are some really good people round.* The speaker's evaluation of the complication (at event time) is captured in her question: *oh shit what are we going to do?* and the subsequent use of the word *problem.* Various dramatic devices are used to highlight both the gravity of the problem and the unexpectedness of the taxi driver's response. These devices include the extended use of direct speech, with or without quotatives, the adoption of the taxi driver's voice quality, and the marked use of a colloquial style when adopting the different 'characters'. These are all features of conversational style that have been identified in narratives in English.

Support for the case for *positive* transfer comes from studies of bilingualism, principally in children, which demonstrate that, as Cummins and Swain point out, 'developing full proficiency in the first language promotes the same in the second language' (1986: 103). They use as their example the development of literacy-related skills. 'The difficult task is learning to read. Once reading, as a skill and as a knowledge source, has been learned, then it is a relatively simple matter to transfer the skill and knowledge to a second language context. In other words, one does not relearn to read every time a new language is learned' (1986: 103). Accordingly, Cummins and Swain posit what they call a 'common underlying proficiency' (CUP) model of bilingualism. It follows that learners who can already converse in their L1 have a common underlying proficiency in conversation on which they can draw when conversing in their L2.

Nevertheless, there is an extensive literature on the potential for misunderstandings due to *negative* transfer, specially of discoursal and sociolinguistic features of the learners' L1. These are forms of transfer that, as Richards and Schmidt point out, 'may have much more serious consequences than errors at the level of syntax or pronunciation, because conversational competence is closely related to the presentation of self, that is, communicating an image of ourselves to others' (1983: 150). Whereas learners are generally aware that direct transfer of lexical and grammatical features of their L1 may not always result in communicative success, they are often unaware that patterns of interaction may be differently structured in other cultures, and find it harder to accept, therefore, that transfer of their L1 norms can be the source of communication failure. 'They are justifiably sensitive about having their social (or even political, religious or moral) judgement called into question' (Thomas, 1983: 104).

Accordingly, researchers have identified a number of features of conversational competence which, when transferred indiscriminately from the learner's L1, may have negative outcomes. These can be broadly categorized as *sociolinguistic* factors and *sociocultural* factors. Sociolinguistic factors refer to the speaker's ability to choose the appropriate linguistic forms in order to achieve their conversational objectives, whether they be to open a conversation, to close it, to take a turn, or to tell an anecdote. Sociocultural factors, on the other hand, refer to the speaker's understanding of when such conversational moves (as closing, turntaking, story-telling etc.) are appropriate. It is one thing to know, for example, that *by the way* and *that reminds me* . . . are two ways that a change of topic is typically signalled. It is another thing altogether to know when a change of topic would be considered acceptable. Likewise, it is a sociolinguistic error to greet someone by saying *good night* instead of *good evening*, but a sociocultural one to individually greet all the occupants of a lift.

Negative sociolinguistic transfer can occur when learners directly 'translate' into their L2 the way that, in their L1, they would perform a specific speech act. For example, in Russian the equivalent of *I think* . . . (*Po moemu* . . .) translates as *in my opinion* . . . (Thomas, 1983). Russian speakers who use *in my opinion* . . . to preface a considered judgement – such as *In my opinion, St Sophia's is the finest example of Byzantine architecture in Russia* – would sound perfectly appropriate. But to preface a more trivial remark with *in my opinion*, such as *In my opinion, there is someone at the door*, might seem odd. Similarly, Borkin and Reinhart (1978) point out that *excuse me* and *I'm sorry* are often used inappropriately by Thai and Japanese learners because these forms only approximately match analogous forms in the students' native languages. They cite the following example:

| American tutor: | I have so much homework to do. |
| Japanese student: | I'm sorry. |

where *That's too bad* might be more appropriate, given the relative lack of severity of the complaint.

Problems can also result when the speaker chooses a degree of formality or informality which, while appropriate in their L1, would be inappropriate in their L2. Thus, where in English a speech act such as making a request might be made less assertive by the use of modal verbs and interrogatives (e.g. *Excuse me, could you tell me the way to* . . . ?) in other languages, such as Russian, the equivalent request would be realized more directly: *Tell me (please) how to get to* . . . Obviously, 'transferred into English, such direct imperatives seem brusque and discourteous' (Thomas, 1983: 102).

Socio*cultural* factors that are transferred indiscriminately may lead to communication failure (sometimes called *sociopragmatic failure*). Such factors include what are called very generally 'the rules for speaking' (Hymes, 1972b). These rules include, for example, 'knowing when and how it is appropriate to open a conversation, what topics are appropriate to particular speech events, which forms of address are to be used to whom and in which situations, and how such speech acts as greetings, compliments, apologies, invitations and complaints are to be given, interpreted and responded to' (Wolfson, 1983: 61). These are what Goffman called (1976) the *ritual constraints* affecting interaction. All cultures have ritual constraints on the way social interaction is mediated, but the ways these constraints operate vary from culture to culture. Thus, knowing how to respond appropriately to certain speech acts – such as requests, apologies, compliments etc. – requires knowledge of the L2 rules of speaking, since the relevant L1 rules may not be transferable. For example, a comparative study of Israeli and American responses to compliments (reported in Cohen, 1996) found that Americans were more likely to accept the compliment (by saying *Thank you*) while the Israelis tended to apologize, to justify the compliment, or to be surprised. Odlin (1989), in discussing the issue of transfer, identifies other areas of cultural mismatch that have the potential, at least, of creating misunderstanding. These include:

- greetings, e.g. the extent to which greeting sequences are variable or fixed;
- turntaking conventions, e.g. the extent to which interruptions are tolerated;
- formality, e.g. when and with whom a formal conversational style, rather than an informal one, is considered appropriate;
- silence, the extent to which this is tolerated in conversation; and
- narratives, the way stories are structured in different cultures.

However, the fact that there are differences between ways of doing things in different cultures does not in itself predict negative transfer. Richards and Sukwiwat (1983), for example, itemize a host of differences between Thai and American conversational styles, but (despite the title of their paper) produce no evidence that these differences cause negative-transfer problems. Most anecdotes about cross-cultural social faux pas – such as accepting food with the wrong hand, or not taking off one's shoes – are in fact non-linguistic in origin (although they may often be resolved by linguistic means).

Odlin acknowledges the problem: 'The extent of discourse transfer is not clear. Some studies of contrastive discourse have found little or no evidence for transfer [which] suggests that the discourse influences from the native language may be weaker than, for example, phonological influences' (1989: 67). This applies as much to positive transfer as it does to negative transfer. Kasper and Rose (2001) note, for example, that 'learners frequently underuse politeness marking in L2 even though they regularly mark their utterances for politeness in L1' (2001: 6). They argue, therefore, that 'there is . . . a clear role for pedagogical intervention, not with the purpose of providing learners with new information but to make them aware of what they know already and encourage them to use their universal or transferable L1 pragmatic knowledge in L2 contexts' (2001: 6–7).

Moreover, many of the differences that have been identified in, for example, the way speech act strategies operate in different languages, may simply be exceptions to the fact that such strategies seem to be more often the same across languages than they are different. Discussing the universality of speech acts, Schmidt and Richards (1980) cite research by Fraser (1978) that suggests that request strategies, for example, are essentially the same in the 14 languages studied. (In a more recent study Nelson *et al.*, the researchers, concluded: 'Findings from this study indicate many more similarities than differences among Americans and Egyptians in making refusals' (2002: 182).) Schmidt and Richards also mention the argument put forward by Brown and Levinson (see, for example, 1987) with regard to the universality of politeness strategies, which claims that the concepts of negative and positive politeness are shared across cultures. It may in fact be the case, as Schmidt and Richards observe, 'that acquiring social competence in a new language does not involve substantially new concepts concerning how language is organized and what types of devices serve what social functions, but only new (social) attitudes about which strategies can be used appropriately in a given context' (1980: 139). We will return to the subject of crosscultural communication in Chapter 9.

7.6 Acquisition vs learning

'Can conversation be taught or is it something that can be acquired simply by doing it?' asks Richards (1990: 67). Richards' use of the term *acquired* covertly acknowledges Krashen's (1982) distinction between *learning* and *acquisition*. According to Krashen, language *learning* is the development of language knowledge through formal study. Language *acquisition*, on the other hand, refers to the process whereby language knowledge is internalized incidentally through experiencing natural language use. Krashen attributes language proficiency (including conversational competence) entirely to acquisitional processes. It is clear that – given the right conditions – a satisfactory standard of conversational competence can be achieved 'simply by doing it': the Japanese learner Wes (Schmidt, 1983), who had no formal instruction, is a case in point. But it is also clear that many learners do not have the kind of exposure and practice opportunities that were available to Wes. What evidence is there that classroom instruction can compensate for these factors? And is there evidence that classroom instruction could speed up the process, even when natural exposure is available?

It is also clear that, however communicative he was, Wes was not a completely proficient speaker. Schmidt for example, reports that 'there are clear limits to Wes's communicative ability . . . both receptive and productive. All legal discussions . . . are extremely frustrating for him, and he considers himself lucky to grasp the main points through the verbiage' (1983: 144). So, would some formal instruction have helped? Perhaps, therefore, Richards' question needs to be elaborated slightly:

- Are there features of second-language conversational competence that can *only* be learned, i.e. that *cannot* be acquired 'simply by doing it'?
- Are there features of second-language conversational competence that are more quickly (or easily, or durably) learned than acquired?
- Are there features of second-language conversational competence that can *only* be acquired, i.e. that cannot be learned, and therefore cannot be taught?
- Are there features of second-language conversational competence that do not *need* to be either acquired or taught (e.g. because they are already in place)?

The answer to the first two questions is a tentative *yes*. In other words, some features of conversation seem to respond only, or better, to instruction. Most of the evidence relates to the understanding, or accurate and appropriate production, of formulaic routines.

For example, House (1996) set out to investigate the effects of explicit instruction in the use of conversational routines and gambits, such as openings and closings, and 'clarifiers' (*I mean, you know* . . .) and 'starters' (*well (now)*). She compared two groups – one that was given exposure to a rich repertoire of these conversational features, as well as opportunities to practise them, but who received no explicit instruction (in the form of 'metapragmatic information') about these features. The other group had the same input and practice opportunities, but, as well, received explicit instruction. Both groups seemed to have benefited from the treatment, but the 'explicit group' 'was superior in realizing a more richly varied, more interpersonally active repertoire of gambit and strategy types and tokens' (1996: 245). Both groups, however, showed no improvement in what were called *responding moves*, tending to overuse the all-purpose *yes* when turntaking, and reciprocating inappropriately in conversational openings, as in this example (the utterances marked with an arrow were judged to be instances of lack of appropriate reciprocation):

	NNS1:	Hi Bettina
	NNS2:	How, how are you?
	NNS1:	Quite fine thank you and you?
	NNS2:	I'm fine too.
→	NNS1:	Oh.
	NNS2:	So how's life?
→	NNS1:	Yes [laughs] I've got a big problem
→	NNS2:	Ah you do?
→	NNS1:	Yes I have.

(1996: 241)

The researcher attributes this failure to the difficulty of 'managing both discourse comprehension and discourse production tasks in the fast give-and-take of ongoing spontaneous talk' (1996: 249). Simply giving learners metapragmatic information doesn't seem to make up for a lack of control over the processing of incoming input. Nevertheless, on balance, House concludes that explicit instruction helps, especially in countering the effects of negative transfer from the learner's L1, and adds that 'with respect to developing pragmatic fluency, it is better to know what one is doing than simply to be doing what one is doing' (1996: 250).

There is also evidence that without direct instruction, the learner is unlikely to acquire certain sociocultural rules necessary if conversation is to be sociolinguistically appropriate. We have already noted, for example, that some learners fail to transfer politeness strategies from their L1 to their L2, a failure that might be obviated by explicit instruction. Cohen (1996) reports a study that investigated the learning of speech acts such as apologies, and which found that explicit instruction in speech act strategies and the use of intensifiers and downgraders had positive effects: after instruction learners were more likely to select apology strategies similar to those used by native speakers. Likewise, Dunham (1992) investigated complimenting strategies and what he terms 'connecting' – that is, maintaining or continuing the conversation based on the response of the addressee. After instruction in these features, students claimed an improvement as well as experiencing increased confidence in initiating and maintaining conversations with native speakers.

With regard to other areas of pragmatic competence, Bouton (1999) investigated the learning of conversational implicature, such as learners' ability to interpret irony in exchanges of the type:

Celia:	So, do you think Mr. Stinguy will give me a raise?
Ron:	Do cows fly?

or their ability to recognize understated criticism:

George:	So, what did you think of the house?
Sheila:	Well, it had a nice mailbox.

His findings show that conversational implicature of these types presents varying degrees of difficulty for learners, that length of exposure to English gradually reduces these difficulties, but that explicit instruction can significantly speed up learners' ability to interpret the implied meanings, especially of formulaic-type utterances, such as *Do cows fly?* or *Is the Pope a Catholic?*

Summarizing the results of research into the role of instruction in learning second-language pragmatics, Kasper and Rose conclude that 'the results of these studies strongly suggest that most aspects of L2 pragmatics are indeed teachable . . . and that for the most part explicit instruction combined with ample practice opportunities results in the greatest gains' (2002: 273).

Explicit instruction *without* such practice opportunities seems to be fairly ineffective however, judging by case study of an adult learner of Japanese in Hawaii (Cohen, 1997). Cohen monitored his own pragmatic development over an accelerated four-month period of instruction, in which 'the teacher provided numerous pragmatic facts, as did the textbook' (1997: 152). However, although he succeeded in learning a lot of linguistic information about Japanese, he was unsure as to how to engage Japanese tourists in conversation, principally because he felt that little of the language he had learned had become automatized. He attributes this partly to the limited practice opportunities provided in class: 'I found the focus on the transmission of short segments primarily in order to practice structures did not give me much practice communicating information in full. Without this practice, I was not comfortable enough in communicative situations to be motivated to try out my language knowledge in such contexts' (1997: 155).

But simply interacting with other learners is probably insufficient too. In a contrastive study of learner–learner and learner–native speaker interaction, Porter (1986) investigated whether the language produced by learners was appropriate for use in settings outside the language classroom, and specifically, whether learners could learn various features of sociolinguistic competence from each other. On the basis of a comparison between the learners' language with native-speakers' language, Porter concluded that they couldn't: 'The finding was that learners did not provide socioculturally accurate models for expressing opinions, agreements, and especially disagreements' (1986: 220). However, Porter adds that 'this finding does not mean . . . that learners should stop interacting with each other; it suggests the need for contact with native speakers or the need for explicit classroom presentation of the forms and strategies necessary to develop sociolinguistic competence'.

In the area of communication strategy training there is also evidence for the positive effects of instruction. Dörnyei (1995), for example, investigated the effects of instruction on three communication strategies (CSs): topic avoidance and replacement; circumlocution; and using fillers and hesitation devices. The instruction involved six interrelated procedures:

1. raising learner awareness about the nature and communicative potential of CSs;
2. encouraging students to be willing to take risks and use CSs;
3. providing L2 models of the use of certain CSs;
4. highlighting cross-cultural differences in CS use;
5. teaching CSs directly; and
6. providing opportunities for practice in strategy use.

(1995: 63–4)

While the results of the study were 'far from conclusive' (1995: 79), there did appear to be some increase in the number of fillers used by students who had had explicit instruction in this feature. There was also an associated gain in fluency, evidenced by increased speech rate.

Fillers are typically realized by lexical phrases, or 'chunks'. In fact, all the research studies we have cited in support of direct teaching have dealt, at least in part, with language at the level of lexical phrases and formulaic routines, whether opening and closing routines, clarifiers, and starters (House, 1996), ways of expressing opinions, agreements and disagreements (Porter, 1986), apologies (Cohen, 1996), compliments (Dunham, 1992), or fillers and hesitation devices (Dörnyei, 1995). Even Bouton's (1999) study of implicature found that the understanding of formulaic implicatures (such as *Is the Pope a Catholic?*), improved dramatically with explicit focused instruction.

We have seen already how important it is for conversational fluency that learners have command of an extensive repertoire of such chunks. Some learners (such as Wes) seem able to acquire them easily. This may be because of a natural aptitude – they are what Skehan (1998) calls 'high memory learners' as opposed to 'high analysis learners'. High memory learners are good at storing and retrieving a wide range of lexicalized exemplars, or what Johnson (1996) refers to as 'acquired output'. Learners who are not so disposed, however, may need more assistance.

In their study of lexical phrases, Nattinger and DeCarrico (1992) recommend the use of pattern practice drills as a means of 'gaining fluency with certain basic fixed routines' (1992: 116). Lewis (1993) claims (but without offering concrete evidence) that such fluency is best achieved through exposure to large amounts of comprehensible input in combination with awareness-raising activities such as the identification of frequently occurring word strings and collocations in association with their communicative function. N. Ellis (1998, 2005) offers some support to this view by suggesting that the acquisition of pre-fabricated chunks involves the same psycholinguistic processes as the acquisition of single-word units, and that, while the form of these chunks can be acquired implicitly, given enough exposures, the mapping of these forms onto their meanings depends largely upon conscious, explicit learning processes – such as deducing meaning from context. This suggests a role for acquisition through massive exposure, plus a role for explicit instruction in the form of, for example, training in learning strategies.

We will now return to the third of the questions that we posed at the beginning of this section: Are there features of second-language conversational competence that can *only* be acquired, i.e. that cannot be learned, and therefore cannot be taught?

It does seem the case that some aspects of conversational competence are resistant to direct intervention on the part of the teacher. We have already mentioned, for example, House's (1996) finding that learners were unable to process incoming input sufficiently well to be able to respond appropriately, however much metapragmatic information they had been provided with. We also noted Ellis's (1994) observation that few learners ever approximate closely to native speakers with regard to the use of politeness strategies, whether instructed or not. And, as Wennerstrom (2001) notes, 'prosody tends to be acquired unconsciously without any "monitoring" with learned rules' (2001: 249).

In the development of R's conversational competence in Portuguese, referred to above (Schmidt and Frota, 1986), one feature that showed little or no improvement was the way R realized the pragmatic function of answering questions affirmatively. In Brazilian Portuguese affirmative answers are typically realized by repeating the verb of the question, or the auxiliary if there is one, while the word for 'yes' (*sim*) is restricted to emphatic agreement. However, R continued to use *sim* (*yes*) or even *uh-huh*, throughout his stay, even though he knew these forms to be inappropriate, and despite having been drilled in the correct forms during the month of formal instruction that he had undergone.

It may be that the difficulties and inherent risks involved in mastering the subtleties of many of the pragmatic features of conversation may simply elude both direct explanation and conscious control in real-time conditions. Prodromou (1997), for example, identifies at least eight indicators of the kind of micro-cultural and macro-cultural knowledge that the learner would need in order to avoid pragmatic failure when using the expression *Bottoms up*! He wonders 'whether the socio-pragmatic-cultural competence necessary to acquire the more idiomatic syntactic and lexical features thrown up by [language] corpora is achievable or necessary for most EFL learners' (1997: 20).

Whether or not acquisition is possible, some critics would argue that a reliance solely on acquisitional processes may be ill-advised, on the grounds that there is a risk that, if learners are too quickly allowed to experience unmonitored communicative fluency, their developing interlanguage system will 'close down' prematurely, or *fossilize*. Taylor and Wolfson are emphatic on this point:

> We take the position that free and unstructured conversation classes designed to get students simply to 'talk' are incompatible with the belief that students should learn through goal-oriented activities. At best, all that students can learn from this class is fluency, and, more often than not, it is the students who are already fluent who dominate the class. At worst, students spend their class time listening to each other's ungrammatical utterances.
>
> (1978: 33)

Instead, Taylor and Wolfson advocate explicit instruction in the rules of speaking, including what they call 'linguistic etiquette', for example 'which kinds of questions are considered appropriate in which situations and which are considered rude' (1978: 37).

Higgs and Clifford (1982) provide some evidence to vindicate the view that unstructured conversation may have negative consequences, concluding that 'the premature immersion of a student into an unstructured or "free" conversational setting before certain fundamental linguistic structures are more or less in place is not done without cost' (cited in Richards, 1990: 74). The cost is over-reliance on a limited set of communication strategies, and on lexis rather than syntax, so that the linguistic system fails to restructure itself, resulting in the kind of fossilization (or premature stabilization) that characterized Wes's interlanguage (Schmidt, 1983, referred to earlier). But this may only be a problem if grammatical accuracy is prioritized over conversational fluency. In fact, as Wes demonstrated, his conversational competence made great strides, even if at the cost of his grammar, which he himself seems to have considered a small price to pay: 'I know I'm speaking funny English/because I'm never learning/I'm only just listen/then talk/but people understand' (1983: 168). Schmidt himself makes the point that 'if language is seen as a means of initiating, maintaining, and regulating relationships and carrying on the business of living, then perhaps Wes is a good learner. If one views language as a system of elements and rules, with syntax playing a major role, then Wes is clearly a very poor learner' (1983: 159).

Wes's case is perhaps less relevant to our purposes, in that he had no classroom instruction. In fact he tended to resist help of any kind.

236

A learner who *only* had classroom instruction was Cohen (1997), whose failure to achieve conversational competence in Japanese we have mentioned. Wes and Cohen represent opposing poles in the acquisition-learning spectrum. Somewhere in the middle, perhaps, is R, the student of Portuguese in Schmidt and Frota's (1986) study, who combined both classroom instruction with natural exposure, and did, in fact, achieve a degree of conversational fluency that was not compromised by a complete lack of accuracy. The accuracy was not simply a direct result of the instruction ('Instruction was helpful but did not guarantee grammaticality' (1986: 281)). Nor did real-life interaction guarantee fluency. It seemed, however, that the initial instruction 'primed' R to notice features of the grammar in naturally occurring conversation, and that he used the conversations to practise such features. This is nicely captured in this edited journal entry:

> This week we were introduced to and drilled on the imperfect. Very useful! . . . Wednesday night A came over to play cards . . . I noticed his speech was full of the imperfect, which I never heard (or understood) before, and during the evening I managed to produce quite a few myself, without hesitating much. Very satisfying!
>
> (1986: 279)

At other times the strategy of noticing-and-then-using was less successful:

> I noticed that N always orders from X using *a gente*, for example *café prá gente*, 'coffee for the person,' but meaning 'coffee for *me*.' Seems odd, but I've used it a few times.
>
> (1986: 286)

In fact, R later discovered that he had misunderstood the form, and was subsequently misusing it, and adds 'this is a case where direct explanation might have been very useful' (1986: 286).

It seems that the combination of instruction, exposure and authentic practice opportunities (although not necessarily in that order) ensured that R was able to develop conversational fluency but not at the expense of his emergent interlanguage grammar. In R's case the instruction dealt solely with the language systems of grammar and vocabulary and was not targeted at features of conversation, such as discourse markers, communication strategies, or the realization of specific speech acts. Had it targeted such features, it is safe to assume – on the basis of the evidence for direct instruction in these areas – that his conversational fluency may have developed even more rapidly. Likewise, it is a fair assumption that, had Cohen had more opportunities for authentic conversation practice in the

237

classroom, he may have been less inhibited when meeting Japanese tourists. And, finally, if Wes had not avoided opportunities for classroom instruction from the outset, his interlanguage may have stabilized less rapidly or less durably.

This suggests that, in order to provide the optimal conditions for the development of conversational fluency (but not at the expense of long-term accuracy), learners need exposure *and* instruction *and* opportunities for meaningful practice. We will elaborate on this claim more fully in Chapter 9.

7.7 Classroom talk

If learners need exposure and practice, as well as instruction, are classrooms the best place for this? It would seem, on the face of it, that they are not. Talk in second-language classrooms shares many of the characteristics of talk in first-language classrooms, as outlined in the previous chapter. In traditional, teacher-driven lessons, there seems to be little opportunity for exposure to, or practice of, conversational interaction of the type we have been describing in this book. Just as first-language classrooms are dominated by long sequences of display questions, and IRF (initiate – respond – follow up) exchanges (see Chapter 6), so too are second-language classrooms similarly structured. In their pioneering study of teacher–learner interaction, Sinclair and Brazil (1982) concluded that learners 'have only very restricted opportunities to participate in the language of the classroom'. In similar vein, Nunan claimed that 'there is growing evidence that, in communicative classes, interactions may, in fact, not be very communicative after all' (1987: 144). The growing evidence Nunan adduces includes studies that characterize teacher–learner interaction as being almost entirely teacher-led and dominated, and as consisting largely of IRF sequences, of which the initiating element is almost always a display question (as opposed to a referential one). Long and Sato (1983) analysed teacher–learner interaction in elementary ESL classes, and found that on average only one in every seven questions was referential as opposed to display, while feedback was limited to acceptance or rejection of the learners' responses. Slimani (2001), researching an EFL classroom in Algeria, found that the vast majority (nearly 80 per cent) of topicalizations (i.e. introductions of new topics) in the lessons she observed were initiated by the teacher, who also did 45 per cent of the talking.

In the light of such findings, the following extract (from Nunan, 1990) would seem to be fairly representative – and about as far from 'real' conversation as could be imagined:

Classroom talk

Text 7.2: Clothes

T: Anything else? Hair. Height. What about this? [Gestures to clothing]
S: Clothes.
T: Clothes. Clothes.
S: (Inaudible)
T: What's the question? (Inaudible) Not colour. What's the question for clothes? You ask the question for clothes? What . . . The question. Come on! We did this last week. Can you remember? The question?
S: What clothes do you like?
S: What kind of clothes do you like?
T: Not like.
S: Wear.
T: Wear, yeah. What's the question? Wear.
S: What kind of a
S: ==What . . .
S: ==Where do you buy . . .
T: Wear. No, not where do you buy. Clothes.
S: What clothes do you usually wear?
T: Good question. What clothes do you usually wear? What about now. What? What's the question now? What . . . ?
S: What do you wear?
T: What do you wear? No. What . . . ? Question. Now. Me. What.
S: Clothes. What.
T: What's the question? Wear. What. Not do. Not do. What . . . ? OK, let's think of the answer. What're these?
S: Pants. Clothes.
T: Trousers. Trousers.
S: Trousers. Trousers.
T: Colour?
S: Green.
T: Green, green, OK. Green trousers. Sentence!
S: What colour are you==
T: ==Not question, sentence!
S: You, you wear wear, you are wearing . . .
T: Joe.
S: You are wearing the green trousers.
T: Ok, I'm wearing, I'm wearing . . . green trousers. I'm wearing green trousers. What's the question? What==
Ss: ==are you wearing.
T: What're you wearing? What're you wearing? What're you wearing? Everyone.
Ss: What are you wearing?

(Nunan, 1990: 18–19)

239

Conspicuous in this extract is the fact that the teacher controls both the content and management of the talk, asking all the questions, asking only display questions, at times nominating individual speakers, overtly correcting students' responses, and all but putting words into the students' mouths. Moreover, it is entirely structured around IRF exchanges, as in this example:

T:	... What about this? (Gestures to clothing)	Initiate
S:	Clothes.	Respond
T:	Clothes. Clothes	Follow-up

Table 7.2 summarizes and contrasts some of the more obvious characteristics of classroom discourse (in its traditional mode, at least) and of casual conversation, and draws largely on van Lier (1996).

Table 7.2. Ways in which classroom talk contrasts with conversation

Classroom talk	Conversation
product-oriented	process-oriented
transactional	interactional
asymmetrical	symmetrical
teacher-led	jointly constructed
topicalization by teacher	topicalization shared
display questions	referential questions
IRF sequences predominate	adjacency pairs; 'chat-and-chunk'
turns nominated	turns self-selected
other repair	self-repair
low contingency	high contingency

In describing classroom talk as *product-oriented*, we mean that it is motivated by the need to achieve a pre-selected pedagogical goal. In the case of Text 7.2 (Clothes), for example, the immediate goal is the linguistic form *What are you wearing?* Conversation, on the other hand, is more *process-oriented*. For a start it is motivated less by the need to achieve a specified objective than to construct and maintain interpersonal relationships. This is not to say that conversation is aimless (although sometimes it may seem so), but rather to reiterate that the success of a conversation is evaluated less on its outcome than on the quality of the conversational process itself. By the same token, classroom talk, even in second-language classrooms, is typically *transactional*, in that the goal is the transmission of subject-matter knowledge from teacher to learners. Syllabus specifications and examinations are the physical embodiments of the twin ends of this transactional conduit. The transactional, as opposed to interactional, style in turn accounts for the asymmetrical relationship between participants: that is to say, the speakers' rights are unevenly distributed, with the teacher asking the majority of the questions, initiating topics, nominating speakers and providing evaluative feedback. This contrasts with conversation, where speakers' rights are more evenly distributed, so that the talk is collaborative, with speakers free to take turns and to introduce topics of their own choice, and where talk typically follows a 'chat-and-chunk' development (see Chapter 5) rather than being a sequence of IRF exchanges. And, unlike conversation where, if something goes wrong, such as a breakdown in communication, speakers usually take the initiative for repairing their own utterances, in classrooms it is typically the teacher who initiates repair, as in this example from Text 7.2:

> S: What colour are you . . .
> T: Not question, sentence!

Finally, classroom talk is low on contingency, that is to say it is 'not anchored within the experiential world (including the here-and-now context) of all participants, nor does it set up expectancies for what is to happen next' (van Lier, 1996: 183). Conversation, on the other hand, is typically highly contingent, such that 'turns are tightly interwoven, each one firmly anchored to the preceding one and holding out expectations (creating possibilities, raising exciting options) for the next one' (van Lier, 1996: 177).

In short, there is very little that classroom talk of the Clothes type has in common with casual conversation, apart from the fact that it is real-time, spoken interaction. It is unlikely, therefore, that exposure to talk that is mainly of this type can prepare learners for the kinds of interactions that will occur outside the classroom. For a start, the limited opportunities they have to ask questions, to initiate topics, or to repair breakdowns do not match the frequency of these conversational moves in real talk. Nor – in the absence of any real communication – are there likely to be many opportunities to develop strategic competence through the use of communication strategies. Kasper and Rose note that 'one recurrent outcome of . . . observational studies is the limited opportunities that teacher-fronted instruction offers for the acquisition of target-language pragmatics' (2001: 11). Kasper (2001) reviews studies that compare teacher-fronted classroom interaction with discourse practices outside the classroom. She finds that these comparisons 'demonstrated that teacher-fronted interaction is substantially more restricted in providing pragmatic input and occasion for productive language use' (2001: 36) and she adds that 'the simplification of discourse organization and management is an immediate consequence of the IRF structure'.

Moreover, as van Lier (2001) observes: 'Students' opportunities to exercise initiative . . . or to develop a sense of control and self-regulation (a sense of ownership of the discourse, a sense of being empowered) are extremely restricted in the IRF format'. He adds that 'prolonged use of the IRF format may have a negative effect on intrinsic motivation and cause a decrease in levels of attention and involvement' (2001: 96–97). Even in classrooms where conversation is tolerated, it is often peripheral to the main body of the lesson, as this extract (from Cadorath and Harris, 1998) tellingly demonstrates:

> [After taking the register the teacher starts chatting to students]
>
> T: Well then, Jorge. Did you have a good weekend?
> S: Yes.
> T: What did you do?
> S: I got married.
> T: You got married! You certainly had a good weekend then.
> [laughter and buzz of conversation]
> T: Now turn to page 56 in your books. You remember last time we were talking about biographies . . .
> [T checks book and lesson plan while other students talk to Jorge in Spanish about his nuptials.]
>
> (1998: 188)

In short, the research evidence suggests that elicitation routines of the type in Text 7.2 tend to dominate in many classroom contexts, and often at the expense of more conversational talk. But, as some commentators argue (e.g. Seedhouse, 1996, and Cullen, 1997), there may be good reasons for this. As Cullen points out, 'defining communicative teacher talk purely in terms of the norms of communication outside the classroom ignores the context of the classroom itself, and what is communicative within that context' (1998: 182). Cullen goes on to argue that the non-conversational features of teacher talk – such as display questions and evaluative feedback – are entirely consistent with its pedagogical function, and this is precisely what distinguishes classroom talk from other, non-pedagogical, spoken genres. In a similar vein, Seedhouse argues that, unlike conversation, classroom talk is a form of institutional discourse. From a sociolinguistic perspective, it is 'an institutional variety of discourse produced by a speech community or communities convened for the institutional purpose of learning English, working within particular speech exchange systems suited to that purpose. The discourse displays certain distinctive and characteristic features which are related to the institutional purpose' (1996: 23). In fact, the very idea of conversation having a pedagogical function is – in Seedhouse's opinion – a contradiction in terms:

> The stated purpose of ELT institutions is to teach English to foreigners. As soon as the teacher instructs the learners to 'have a conversation in English', the institutional purpose will be invoked, and the interaction could not be conversation as defined here. To replicate conversation, the lesson would therefore have to cease to be a lesson in any understood sense of the term and become a conversation which did not have any underlying pedagogical purpose, which was not about English or even, in many situations, in English. All this is not to suggest that it is impossible for conversation to take place in the classroom, simply that it cannot occur as part of a lesson.
>
> (1996: 18–19)

One wonders, given such strictures, how classroom learners ever achieve conversational competence at all. The fact that many don't achieve it may owe to the continued allegiance, on the part of many teachers, institutions and materials writers, to a narrow interpretation of 'the stated purpose of ELT'. When this purpose is construed as being nothing more than imparting knowledge of English grammar, and to a lesser extent, of vocabulary and pronunciation, then, clearly, conversation has no obvious role.

Of course, it would be misleading to characterize *all* classroom talk as being of the kind illustrated in Text 7.2 (Clothes). Van Lier (1988) identifies at least five different classroom discourse types, of which *elicitation* (as in Text 7.2) is only one. Others include *telling*, where the teacher imparts knowledge directly; *ritualized* classroom activities, such as drilling; *group work*; and even *conversation* itself, as in the form of the chat that often precedes the lesson proper, or more, formally, when the teacher introduces a topic for classroom discussion.

In a study of what she calls the 'talking circle', that is, a whole-class chat phase at the beginning of a conversation class, Ernst (1994) found that learners did indeed engage in 'meaningful conversation': they selected topics, took turns, interrupted, and listened actively. The teacher's role varied between being simply another participant in the conversation, and 'supporting students' conversations by encouraging, acknowledging, and extending their contributions' (1994: 301). Here is an extract from one of these initial phases, in which a Korean student, Ji-Hae, aided by her brother, Hyun-Tae, recounts an anecdote:

Teacher: Ji-Hae.
Ji-Hae: You know I'm I swi I umm in Korea
Teacher: um-huh

243

Ji-Hae:	I'm going to the swimming pool. They have many people, but maybe may be we
Hyun-Tae:	Not the pool.
Teacher:	Yeah.
Hyun-tae:	We don't go pool we went beach.
Teacher:	To the beach.
Ji-Hae:	um-huh. Too too
Teacher:	shallow
Ji-Hae:	Too higher. [hands one on top of the other within a one feet distance]
Teacher:	Um-huh.
Hyun-Tae:	Too deep.
Teacher:	Yes.
Ji-Hae:	And I can go to the too higher. It's too higher augh brother brother help me.
Borui:	[ ]
Ji-Hae:	My brother is going to swim and my brother is going to push me like that. [moves hands as if she were pulling a rope]
Teacher:	Ohh.
Students:	[laugh]
Teacher:	and it
Ji-Hae:	You know what I did?
Teacher:	Yes?

(Ernst, 1994: 302)

Ernst also noted that this free-flowing, learner-led chat occurred principally during those lesson phases where the students were free to nominate and change topics themselves. There was a marked contrast, however, between these phases and a subsequent phase where the teacher took over control of the topic agenda: 'Although many factors remained the same . . . (i.e. participants, activity, physical arrangement, medium), the opportunities to participate and to try out a variety of linguistic skills changed dramatically' (1994: 314). Ernst concludes that, in order to develop conversational competence, learners 'need to be in classroom environments where conversation and negotiation are not only encouraged but carefully orchestrated, supported, and monitored by the teacher' (1994: 315). Ernst's study is one of a few that suggests that classrooms *can* provide exactly these conditions, at least some of the time.

In a similar study, Bannink (2002) recognizes the paradox inherent in creating opportunities for spontaneous talk in classroom contexts: 'It seems that traditional classroom environments do not lend themselves very well to conversation: by definition the classroom is a formal, institutional, and asymmetric setting. And, paradoxically, in this setting the informal, unpredictable, spontaneous 'conversational' interactions which should lead to communicative competence have to be accommodated' (2002: 267). Bannink believes that these spontaneous conversational interactions cannot be planned for, but that they tend to occur in the 'cracks and seams' of lessons, and that, in order to optimize these opportunities, teachers need 'to play multiple roles at the same time (teacher, conversational partner, stage director, etc.)' (2002: 272). Far from conceding that classrooms are 'conversation-unfriendly', Bannink concludes that 'the classroom may be viewed as an ecological environment in which "lesson" and "conversation" are relational to each other, needing one another for ecological balance' (2002: 285).

We take the view that this ecological balance is certainly achievable. Not only is it possible to incorporate conversation into language lessons as a part of the curriculum (in the form, for example of 'talking circles'), but it is possible to structure the classroom talk along more conversational lines, in keeping with the notion of 'instructional conversation' (Tharp and Gallimore, 1988). In fact, it is not only possible, but desirable – a view we will develop in Chapter 9. But before that, a 'brief history of conversation teaching' is in order.

Task

In the following transcript of learner–learner talk, evaluate the state of the learners' conversational competence, such as:

- fluency, as indicated by:
  - number of comprehension checks and requests for help
  - proportion of questions to statements
  - topic control
  - amount of hesitation and repetition, especially self-repetitions, and incompletions
  - length of turns
  - use of communication strategies

- idiomaticity, including indications of the use of formulaic language and vagueness expressions
- pragmatic competence, with regard to
  - turntaking conventions
  - responding moves and back-channelling
  - use of discourse markers
  - sociolinguistic appropriacy
  - contingency

The extract has been taken from a small-group classroom interaction in which a number of students are discussing the topic 'bad habits'.

Bad habits

S1   My next door neighbour . . . he makes eh very noisy, very noisy. I can't tell him, because he's very good people.

S2   You can't say.

S1   He's very good neighbour.

S2   You can't say, because if you say, maybe will feel different.

S3   Yes, you don't like it = =

S1   = = I don't like.

S3   Independence . . . those people probably very protective.

S2   Yes, I think so.

S1   In my time, when I go to sleep = =

S2   = = go to bed [*yes*]

S1   These people is very good.

S2   You don't want to say anything because you might get upset, of course. Me do the same thing because I've got neighbours in my place and always you know do something I don't like it but I don't like to say bad because I think maybe you know make him upset or = =

S4   = = I've got bad neighbour but I feel embarrass = =

S2   = = to say something of course, like everyone = =

S4   = = They always come in and see what I'm doing – who's coming.

S2   No good. Yeah, that's no good.

S4   They want to check everything. If they see I buy something from the market they expect me to give them some.

S2   Oh yeah. Oh that's not nice.

S4   But I . . . it's difficult.

S2   It's a difficult, yeah, but sometimes it's difficult.

S4   They can't understand. I bought them and I gave money . . .

[*laughter and general assent*]

S4   You know sometime difficult to the people because sometime I can't speak the proper, the language, and little bit hard to give to understand . . . and that's sometime feel embarrass then, I can't say it, you know?

S1   Sarah, you tell.

S5   My, er, for example, my sister in law she all the time snores in her sleep. And my brother say, 'Oh, I'm sorry, we must sleep separate.

[*laughter*]

S5   They did. A good idea because she couldn't sleep.

(Nunan, 1989: 42)

8 Teaching conversation: A history

Introduction

In Chapters 1 to 5 we looked at the way conversation is structured, and at its characteristic features, and in Chapters 6 and 7 we discussed how these structures and features develop both in a first and a second (or other) language. It is time now to address the pedagogical implications of the issues raised, and look at ways that the development of second-language conversational competence might best be served by classroom instruction (assuming, of course, that there is a role for instruction at all). This chapter provides an historical overview, which aims to situate and contextualize a number of the key issues involved in the teaching of conversation – not the least of which is: what does it mean when we talk about a conversation class, a conversation lesson, or of teaching or learning conversation? These and other key themes will be explored in the next – and final – chapter.

8.1 Pre-reform and reform

Barbara:	Peter, where layde you your nightcap?
Peter:	I left it vpon the bedde.
Barbara:	Are you ready?
Peter:	How should I be ready? You brought me a smock insteade of my shirt.
Barbara:	I forgat myselfe. Holde, here is your shirt.
Peter:	Now you are a good wenche . . .

The above dialogue, in which Barbara, a domestic servant, is helping Peter get ready to go to school, is an example of what was a staple of the earliest extant manuals for teaching English. It comes from Bellot's *Familiar Dialogues* (1586; quoted in Howatt, 2004), which used such 'conversations' as the principal medium for contextualizing language content. As Howatt (2004) notes, 'there is nothing self consciously "literary" about the exchanges, and they make a curiously "modern" impression, almost as though Bellot were illustrating a situational language syllabus' (2004: 24). Because the 16th-century equivalent of the modern coursebook functioned primarily as a phrasebook for new arrivals in Britain, it consisted for the most part of 'familiar dialogues' of the Barbara-and-Peter type, padded out with some grammatical description. This was a tradition that persisted through the 17th and 18th centuries. However, the introduction of foreign languages into school curricula during the 19th century shifted the focus off the functional and on to the more academic aspects of language learning. Instead of dialogues to be learned by heart, language courses, borrowing from a classical tradition, consisted largely of isolated sentences – typically highly contrived – for translation.

Doubts as to the capacity of this 'grammar–translation' approach to deliver what would now be called communicative competence triggered a reaction in the form of the Reform Movement, whose philosophy is embodied in the six Articles of the International Phonetic Association (founded in 1886). The core tenet of Reform Movement philosophy is simply stated, but still resonates over a century later: 'Foreign language study should begin with the spoken language of everyday life' (IPA Article 1, quoted in Stern (1983: 89). For the early reformers, an important implication of this founding principle was the prioritizing of larger stretches of text, including dialogues, over the study of isolated sentences. In the words of the Association: 'Pupils should study consecutive texts – dialogues, descriptions, and narratives – which should be as easy, natural, and interesting as possible' (IPA Article 3).

In the absence, however, of adequate descriptions of 'the spoken language of everyday life' these worthy aims were often only sketchily translated into practice. Here, for example, is an extract from a conversation in Berlitz's *First Book for Teaching Modern Languages* (1906):

The invitation
A. Will you go to London with me?
B. With the greatest pleasure. I have never been there and as I have always wished to see the great Metropolis, I shall be glad to go with you.
A. Very well. We can start to-morrow, if you have no objection.
B. Oh, not the slightest. We can stay there a week and then go to Paris. Crossing the Channel in fine weather is not at all disagreeable . . .

(1906: 70)

Unlike Bellot's dialogues of three centuries earlier, such conversations sound stilted and contrived. By adhering to the conventions of formal written language, they seem ill-suited as models for spoken interaction.

8.2 Direct method: Learning-through-conversation

A parallel development, and a pillar of Reform Movement philosophy and of the Direct Method that later emerged from it, was the use of oral methods of instruction. Typically, 'oral communication skills were built up in a carefully graded progression organized around question-and-answer exchanges between teachers and students' (Richards and Rodgers, 1986: 10). For want of a better word, such exchanges were termed 'conversations'. So, in Berlitz's direct method course 'the entire stock of words used in the book is given principally in the form of conversation between the teacher and the student' (1906: 6). Thus, spoken language was not only the goal of language instruction, but the means by which this goal was to be achieved.

'Learning-through-conversation' was not an entirely new concept. Individual educational reformers had promoted this idea off and on over the preceding two centuries. For example, Locke had written in *Some Thoughts Concerning Education* (1693): 'Men learn languages for the ordinary intercourse of Society and Communication of thoughts in common Life without any further design in their use of them. And for this purpose, the Original way of Learning a language by Conversation, not only serves well enough, but is to be prefer'd as the most Expedite, Proper, and Natural' (quoted in Howatt, 2004: 211). Even earlier, Joseph Webbe (c.1560–1633) 'was proposing a form of "direct method" of language teaching, without the use of reference grammars, which would depend heavily on spoken interaction' (Howatt, 2004: 41).

But it was not until the second half of the 19th century that interactional approaches became both systematized and widely applied. Such approaches were loosely grouped together in what came to be known as the 'Direct Method'. One of the prototypical Direct Method courses (in French) was called *Causeries avec mes élèves* (*Conversations with my students,* Sauveur, 1874). Its author, Lambert Sauveur, describes the first lesson: 'It is a conversation during two hours *in the French language* with twenty persons who know nothing of this language. After five minutes only, I am carrying on a dialogue with them, and this dialogue does not cease' (1874: 8, cited in Howatt, 2004: 219).

Sauveur's 'conversations' were structured according to two basic principles: the first being that the teacher should ask only *real* questions (what Sauveur called '*earnest* questions'), as opposed to the display questions that characterize much teacher–student interaction (see Chapters 6 and 7), and, secondly, that the conversation should be *coherent,* that is, that the questions should be connected 'in such a manner that one may give rise to another' (Howatt, 2004: 220). Howatt comments: 'This principle probably explains his success in communicating with his students better than

249

anything else. They understood what he was talking about because they were able to predict the course of the conversation'. Of course, the teaching 'conversations' promoted by Sauveur and his imitators were entirely one-sided, the right to initiate questions being the exclusive prerogative of the teacher. In this sense, to call such interactions 'conversations' is a misnomer. Nevertheless, Sauveur's intuition – that spoken interaction, if not authentic conversation, offers a more 'natural' site for language acquisition than do grammar explanations and translation exercises – predates by a century the notions of *instructional conversation* (Tharp and Gallimore, 1988) and *contingency* (van Lier, 1996).

The need to formalize Sauveur's conversational teaching style ('or, as it might be called today, "discourse-model" of teaching-through-talking' (Howatt, 1984: 295)) so that novice teachers could be trained in it, challenged a number of enterprising (but perhaps less inspirational) 19th century reformers. Manuals were produced that scripted teacher– student exchanges in exhaustive detail. Thus, in Berlitz's *First Book* a typical 'conversational' sequence goes like this:

> I am opening the door. Am I opening the door? (You are.) Are you
> opening the door? (I am not.) Who is opening the door, you or I?
> (You are.) Carry the chair towards the door. Are you carrying
> the chair towards the door? Is Mr. B. carrying the chair towards
> the door?
>
> (Berlitz, 1906: 17)

If nothing else, such sequences demonstrate how loosely construed the concept of 'conversation' had become, and how rapidly the notion of instructional conversation had parted company from Sauveur's recommendation that the questions should be both real and coherent. In fact, as Howatt points out, 'When Berlitz and others systematized Sauveur's conversational methods, they simplified the language used in the lessons and pared it down to a few utterances which were easy to demonstrate in class . . . Instead of talking to the students in a simple way so that they would understand (Sauveur's principle), the Direct Method taught the language system by using simple sentences (which is not at all the same thing)' (2004: 272).

Thus, the notion that participation in *real* conversation – Locke's 'Original way of Learning a language' – might provide the means for language acquisition was effectively jettisoned. Sweet (1899), for example, was dismissive of such 'natural methods': 'Most good linguists will confess that they learnt nearly everything from books, especially in the beginning of their study of the foreign language, and but little from conversation. There are, indeed, many obstacles to learning from conversation. In the hurry of talk we are apt to mishear and forget, so that what

250

we pick up in that way is never reliable. Conversation is really not a means of learning new words and expressions, but only of practice in hearing and reproducing what we have already learnt' (1899: 75). This view – that talk (or *parole*) was in some way degenerate, and therefore not a useful resource for language learning – pervaded for nearly a century.

8.3 Audiolingualism: Drills, dialogues and the conversation class

Systematization of the Direct Method was taken several steps further by Palmer, who described 'various techniques of teaching through conversation' (1940: 9) in a number of teachers' guides, including *English Through Questions and Answers* (1930) and *The Teaching of Oral English* (1940). But for Palmer, like Berlitz before him, conversation seems to have meant nothing more than a series of display questions. His question–answer sequences were tightly controlled, 'comparable to the commands and movements of military drill' (1940: 21):

1. Is this *my* head?　Yes, it *is*.
2. Is this your *head*?　No, it *isn't*.
3. Whose head is it?　It's *your* head . . . etc.

(Palmer, 1940: 52)

The similarities to audiolingual pattern practice drilling are evident, and although audiolingualism was largely an American phenomenon, it shared many features with Direct Method teaching, not least the prioritizing of the speaking skill. Nevertheless, with its primary focus on intensive oral drilling of basic sentence patterns, audiolingualism, like Palmer's Oral Approach, and grammar translation before it, was little concerned with language beyond the sentence level. Conversation, if it existed at all in the audiolingual lesson, was simply a way of dressing up pattern practice drills. Thus, in the teacher's guide to a typical course of its time, the following appears as 'Conversation Practice':

(S₁) Are you a lawyer?　(S₂) No, I'm not a lawyer. I'm a student.
(S₂) Is that a window?　(S₁) No, it's not a window. It's a blackboard.

Continue round the class. This practice should be as natural as possible. Questions are to be restricted only in that they must have been covered previously in class. *An authentic conversation atmosphere is what is desired.*

(Ramsey, 1967: 7 (emphasis added))

Thus, conversation was accommodated into audiolingual programmes solely on the grounds that conversation consists, at least in part, of questions and answers, and that, in the words of another such course (*First Book in American English*): 'Memorization of conversation patterns often helps to form correct speech habits' (Alesi & Pantell, 1962).

Real conversation – as opposed to scripted dialogues – was considered too risky for anything but the most advanced student, for whom the specially constituted 'conversation class' was (and still is) a common option. The teacher's role in such classes was to introduce topics for discussion, for which some vocabulary preparation was recommended, and to intervene where necessary to maintain the flow: 'The course the conversation takes is spontaneous and not guided by the teacher, who does, however, redirect it or inject it with new interest when it appears to be flagging' (Rivers, 1968: 203). Correction was recommended only where it could be done without inhibiting the flow; otherwise it would be withheld until a post-conversation stage at the end of the session. Explicit teaching of conversational strategies or skills was not considered necessary, since it was assumed that the capacity to engage in 'spontaneous expression' was simply a case of calling into play 'a multiplicity of structures and lexical items that have been learned over a period of years' (Rivers, 1968: 200).

8.4 Situational English: Conversation in context

Contemporary with the spread of audiolingualism in the United States, an alternative, *situational approach*, was emerging on the other side of the Atlantic and in Australia, and was represented by such courses as Alexander's *First Things First* (1967a). Situational teaching derived from the *audiovisual* method, developed in the 1950s to teach French. Characteristically, an audiovisual lesson began with a film strip shown in conjunction with a taped dialogue. By these means the context-dependent and interactional nature of language was established, in the belief that 'le langage est avant tout un moyen de communication entre les êtres ou les groupes sociaux . . .' ('language is above all a means of communication between people or between social groups . . .' (CREDIF 1961: viii; cited in Stern, 1983: 468), a view that pre-figured the advent of a more communicative methodology. In the same year, Billows captured this paradigm shift eloquently: 'The material of the language lesson is not language, but life itself; the language is the instrument we use to deal with the material, slices of experience' (1961: 17).

By extension, *situational* came to mean any approach in which contextual factors were foregrounded and in which connected texts (almost always spoken) were the main means of presentation. The emphasis on spoken language was axiomatic: 'If we decide that language must be taught situationally, there is no alternative to teaching it through speech' (Billows, 1961: 18). More narrowly, situational English became associated with phrasebook-type English, consisting largely of transactional exchanges such as service encounters. Such exchanges quickly found their way into general coursebooks, often incorporated under the heading of 'Everyday Conversation', so as to distinguish them from more structurally oriented dialogues. Transactional exchanges were also a common feature of ESP (English for Special Purposes) courses, whose rise to prominence in the 1970s reflected the needs of more specialized markets, such as businessmen, scientists and academics. Such courses were often situationally organized (*Making an appointment*; *Meeting a client*; *Negotiating a deal*), and included models of spoken interaction designed to sensitize learners to different *registers* of spoken English.

The use of the term *situation* in conjunction with the notion of *register* echoes the functional trend in British linguistics that had emerged in the 1930s with the work of Firth, and which had been developed and refined by his student Halliday. The Hallidayan concept of most relevance at this point is the one of *register*. Halliday identified three aspects of any *context of situation* that have linguistic consequences: *field, tenor* and *mode* (see Chapter 1). A register description identifies each of these variables and thereby aims to offer a coherent account of how situational factors influence the linguistic choices in any verbal interaction. The implications for course design were spelled out in Halliday, McIntosh and Strevens (1964), in which an attempt was made to integrate contextual factors into a hierarchy of levels of analysis: 'The emphasis now is on the description of language activity as part of the whole complex of events which, together with the participants and relevant objects, make up actual situations' (Halliday, *et al.*, 1964: 38). Since conversation is a 'language activity' it follows that it is best described – and taught – by reference to the register variables of the situations in which it occurs.

It is doubtful, however, that the concepts of *context of situation* and of *register* were even indirectly responsible for the widespread use of contexualized dialogues in language-teaching materials in the pre-communicative era, such as Alexander's *First Things First* (1967a) or O'Neill's *English in Situations* (1970). The situational – and, by extension, dialogic – focus may have had more to do with the common sense recognition of the fact that, in the absence of translation, a situation provides useful contextual clues to help the learner induce the meaning of targeted language forms. The prominence of the *dialogue* cannot, therefore, be read as evidence of an awareness either that conversation was systematic in a generic sense, or that it was worth practising for its own sake. For a start these dialogues, like those of the Direct Method and

Audiolingualism, had only the slenderest relation to the 'spoken language of everyday life'; they were, rather, 'a rehearsed, theatrical substitute for the real world of improvization' (Howatt, 1984: 296). As models for natural conversation, therefore, they were of little use. Moreover, the ongoing obsession with grammatical accuracy effectively ruled out conversation practice until the most advanced stages. Alexander (1967b) was adamant that 'the traditional "conversation lesson" is of no value at all if the student is not ready for it . . . The student must first be trained to use patterns in carefully graded aural/oral drills. Only in this way will he finally learn to speak' (1967b: viii). The 'chat' stage of the lesson, if it occurred, was simply there as a curtain raiser to the main event – the controlled practice of sentence patterns. Indeed, one London language school that subscribes to a rigorous Direct Method philosophy, until recently was still advising its students that 'the teacher and the student must not chat during the lesson. They must only ask and answer the questions in the book. Chatting is a waste of time.'

8.5 Oral English: Conversation as speaking practice

Nevertheless, and even before the advent of a communicative methodology, the tightly controlled *presentation–practice* (PP) paradigm exemplified in courses such as Alexander's and O'Neill's had begun to yield in the face of the crying need for freer speaking practice. Fluency could not be deferred indefinitely. As Byrne wrote in *Teaching Oral English*, such an approach sets students 'on a seemingly never ending path towards an ever receding horizon' (1976: 4). Accordingly, a *production* stage was added on to the presentation–practice sequence (PPP). The aim of the production phase is, according to Byrne, 'to provide the learners with opportunities to use the language for themselves: to say what *they* want to say rather than what they are *directed* to say' (1976: 78). Typical activity types include such relatively formal and structured ones as *discussions* and *role plays*. Once again, casual conversation, if treated at all, tends to be treated as if it happened only incidentally, and somewhat apart from the main vector of the lesson. Thus, Byrne, writing on group work, points out that in this kind of organization students 'can *talk to one another* and therefore, in discussing an activity . . . real conversation is one of the side products' (1976: 82, original emphasis). Similarly, Haycraft (1978) treats conversation as a pleasant but somewhat peripheral option – something for Friday afternoons, perhaps: 'Most classes are designed to practise specific speaking or listening skills. However, there should be times when students can express themselves without any aim in mind except general conversation' (1978: 86).

Nevertheless, as the PPP paradigm took hold, materials targeted at fostering conversation, and not just of the transactional kind, became more conspicuous, even if the conversations they attempted to foster were still window-dressing for an essentially grammatical agenda. For example, in *Picture it! Sequences for Conversation* (1981), learners are first presented with a set of sentence patterns followed by pictures 'and finally a CONVERSATION section with lead-in questions' (n.p.). Thus:

Describe the last party you went to.

> What time did you get there?
> What did you eat? drink?
> Who was the host?
> Did you meet anyone?
> When did you leave?

(1981: 95)

The instructions to the teacher suggest that 'when you have completed all the Practices, introduce the Conversation section . . . Encourage students to talk freely about the topic and to make connections with their own lives' (n.p.). Despite the fact that the structural tail may still be wagging the conversational dog, the invitation to 'talk freely' and to make connections with their own lives is a far cry from the belief that 'chatting is a waste of time'.

8.6 CLT: Conversation as communication

Despite the promotion of oral fluency, there was still a sense that, within the PPP paradigm, 'talking freely' was an add-on: a pedagogical option rather than a core element of language learning. And there was the suspicion that this apparent 'freedom' was tightly, if covertly, constrained. For a start, in the absence of an accurate description, the IPA objective of 'the spoken language of everyday life' continued to be as elusive as ever. By default, the standards of written English still prevailed: learners were judged on the extent to which their spoken language conformed to literate norms.

In a landmark attempt to remedy this lack of an accurate description, Crystal and Davy (1975) assembled, transcribed and analysed a collection of naturally occurring conversations, whose purpose was 'both to provide language practice material and to guide the teacher and advanced learner to be aware of the communicative signals present in actual speech' (according to the blurb of the 1981 edition). Here, for example, is the opening turn of the first extract in the book (*Talking about football*) with the original orthography preserved:

Teaching conversation: A history

A   well I what's the · Iwhat's the 'failure with the ↑ FÒOTBALL
     I I mean Ithis · I this I don't 'really ↑SÈEI I mean it · I cos the
     ↑MÒNEY I · I how 'much does it 'cost to get ÌN I Idown the
     ↑RÒAD I I NÒW I

As Candlin notes, in his preface to the 1975 edition, the book 'supports a
growing concern that learning materials which have communication as
their aim should themselves be based on accurately reported models with
essential features distinctively highlighted' (1975: vi). The use of the terms
'communicative' (in the blurb) and 'communication' (in the preface) is significant, coinciding as it does with the advent of what is now known as
the *communicative approach* or *communicative language teaching* (CLT).

   Essentially, three major – and related – developments fed into the emergence of CLT, all three of which were also to provide a new impetus to the
design and methodology of the teaching of conversation. The first was
functionalism – the realization that language is used not simply to *represent* the world, but that it functions to *do things* in the world. The second
was a shift in the focus of language analysis to the level of *discourse* and
text, and hence the development of both *discourse* and *genre analysis*.
And the third was the emergence of the notion of *communicative competence* (Hymes, 1972b), the view that that being able to *do things* with the
language requires more than a knowledge of the grammar and vocabulary
of the language (or *usage*) but also the ability to know how to put this
knowledge to communicative *use* (Widdowson, 1978). All three developments contributed to the theoretical underpinnings of CLT, and each had
an impact, directly or indirectly, on the teaching of conversation.

8.6.1 Functionalism

The implications of a functional view of language were not realized until
the early 1970s, when a number of scholars, notably Wilkins (1976),
argued the case for adopting a communicative orientation to syllabus
design. Wilkins proposed the use of *notional functional syllabuses*. These
comprised three parts: (i) semantico-grammatical categories (e.g. past,
future, location); (ii) modality (e.g. possibility, necessity, obligation); and
(iii) communicative functions (e.g. asking questions, making requests,
agreeing). It was this third section that generated the greatest interest
amongst teachers and textbook writers, and was realized as the *functional syllabus:* that is, a syllabus that was not organized around the
traditional *grammatical* categories, such as the somewhat random items
of grammar–translation courses, or the carefully graded sentence patterns
of audiolingualism, but around communicative functions. This, in turn,
provided materials writers and teachers with a metalanguage to describe

256

what was happening in the different moves of any speech event. Thus, Byrne (1976) advocates using 'functional outlines' which can be used 'to build up a fairly extensive conversation' (1976: 73). For example:

(a) Exchange greetings
(b) Enquire about health
(c) Make a suggestion for a meeting
(d) Make an excuse
(e) Persuade
(f) Agree (but with some reservations)
(g) Confirm arrangements
(h) Exchange greetings

(Byrne, 1976: 73)

Combined with the notion of the *information gap*, in which the completion of a task requires the pooling of information among the interactants, these functional outlines formed the basis of the cued dialogue, a standard task type in early CLT coursebooks. For example:

Student A:	Student B:
1. Greet Student B	Greet Student A
2. Invite Student B somewhere	Refuse and make an excuse
3. Insist	Agree
4. Suggest a time to meet	Disagree
5. Suggest another time	Agree
6. Suggest a place to meet	Agree
7. Say goodbye	Say goodbye

The popularity of such activities was relatively short-lived, however, partly because of the management problems involved in setting them up, but more perhaps because the organization of language courses into communicative functions itself lost favour. Such an organization tended to reinstate an utterance-level view of language, based as it was on 'an overly simplistic tendency to equate speech-acts with particular linguistic formulae, a sort of "phrasicon" of speech acts, or "functions", as they were often popularly called' (McCarthy, 1998: 19). The functional syllabus survives, residually, as merely one strand in the present-day fashion for 'multi-layered' syllabuses, and often surfaces in those sections of coursebooks devoted to 'social English'.

However, the value of including such 'phrasebook' language has experienced a revival recently, primarily due to the promotion of 'the lexical approach' (Lewis, 1993). Lewis has popularized the belief (and one that we have repeatedly endorsed) that having such a stock of pre-fabricated and memorized chunks is the single most important guarantor of conversational fluency – far more important than having an extensive knowledge of the target-language grammar. Accordingly, many

257

ELT materials now incorporate a focus on 'chunk learning', variously called 'real language' or 'takeaway English' for example. Here is a section from *Innovations* (Dellar and Hocking, 2004: 86):

Real English: sort of / kind of

sort of and *kind of* are both very common in spoken English. They are often used when you cannot find the right word to express what you mean. Some people do not like these phrases, but they are extremely common even in educated speech.

It was kind of expensive-looking.
She was sort of annoyed with me.

8.6.2 Discourse analysis

At the level of *discourse*, the analysts of authentic speech has demonstrated that, like written language, spoken language also has texture and structure, and that conversation, far from being shapeless and unregulated, has patterns and regularities that distinguish it from both written language and other spoken genres. More recently, *genre analysis* has attempted to show how these patterns and regularities, far from being arbitrary, are socially determined and frequently become institutionalized over time. Both these disciplines have influenced the content and design of classroom speaking tasks.

The use of *discourse markers,* for example, to achieve cohesion across utterances and to signpost speakers' intentions, has been exploited in speaking exercises such as the following:

---

41. Seeing the Good Side

On the other hand,	OK, but . . .
But then again,	But in the long run,
Look at this way,	Very true, but . . .
Anyway,	To make up for it, . . .
Even so,	

Are you an optimist or a pessimist? This is an optimist's game! The class divides into two teams. Take turns to make complaints, starting with the ideas below. The other side must try to say something positive.

For example:

Team 1: Everything's so expensive nowadays, isn't it?
Team 2: Yes, but on the other hand, wages are much higher than
they used to be.

Each team take it in turn to make statements and to answer. The
answers must be introduced by one of the phrases from the list. Each
team has 10 seconds to answer. Play two or three 'rounds' with each
round lasting 5 minutes.

1. It's been raining now every day this month.
2. This coffee is really strong.
3. English is very difficult.
4. Grammar is really boring.
5. I hate learning to spell.
6. I've put on 5 kilos since Christmas.
7. Volvos are very expensive.
8. You can't park anywhere around here!
9. It can be very cold in Norway in winter.
10. I can't understand Pierre's accent.
11. Bill is very mean with money.
12. Liz is always late.
13. Joan can't dance. She's awful, isn't she!
14. Children have too much money these days.
15. Schools are far too liberal.
16. Teachers aren't strict enough.
17. I hate starting school at 8 in the morning.
18. It's wrong that people get paid for giving their blood.

('Seeing the Good Side', from Keller and Wamer,
Conversation Gambits, LTP 1988: 52)

Similarly, conversational routines, such as those that are used to open
and close conversational exchanges, to check and repair communication,
to provide listener feedback, to interrupt, and to change topic, are occasionally incorporated into classroom materials as discrete items to be
presented and practised in much the same way as the exponents of a
functional syllabus. For example:

D3 Which of the following are answers to good news and which to bad news? Put a tick (✔) for good news and a cross (✘) for bad news. (Two of them could be good or bad.)

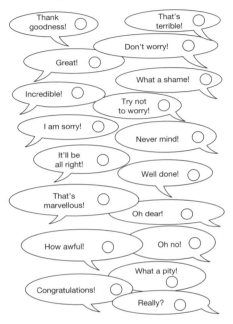

D4 Work in pairs. You are A or B. Cover up your partner's card. Your partner will tell you some news. Reply with one of the phrases in *D3*.

A Tell your partner that . . .

---

1 Your dog has just died.
2 You've passed your driving test.
3 You're worried about the exam tomorrow.
4 You've lost your passport and all your money.
5 You've won a free trip to Los Angeles.

B Tell your partner that . . .

---

1 You saw a UFO last night.
2 You've crashed your car.
3 You've just got engaged.
4 You've just got a new job.
5 You've scratched your partner's favourite record.

(Good news/bad news, from Black *et al.*, *Fast Forward 1*, OUP, 1986: 80)

The analysis of conversational exchange structures, including adjacency pairs, the way that the openings and closings are sequenced, and the fairly predictable structures of service encounters, have suggested exercise types such as the following:

Closing a conversation

In casual conversation in English we usually follow a series of steps when we want to end a conversation. The first step tells the other person that the conversation is about to close, we call this pre-closing. In this step we usually give a reason for closing the conversation. It seems rude if we close a conversation too abruptly. The final step closes the conversation. For example:

Pre-closing step

A: Well I suppose we'd better be off. We all have to get up early tomorrow.

Closing step

B: Yeah that's right I forgot. Well we'll see you soon then.
A: Yeah thanks for a great dinner.
B: Fine. See Ya. Bye.
A: Bye.

1   Read the phrases we can use to say goodbye. Tick if the phrase is a pre-closing phrase (PC) or a closing phrase (C). The first one has been done for you.

	PC	C
a. Look I've got to dash. I'm going to miss my bus.	☑	☐
b. I'll see you later.	☐	☐
c. Goodbye.	☐	☐
d. Oh look I've got to go now. I've got an appointment at 3.	☐	☐
e. Talk to you later.	☐	☐
f. I must go. The phone's ringing.	☐	☐
g. Thanks for the coffee.	☐	☐
h. I have to get to the shops.	☐	☐
i. See you next week.	☐	☐
j. I'd better go. I've got to collect the kids.	☐	☐

(Closing a Conversation, from Delaruelle, *Beach Street*, NSW AMES, 1998 37–8)

The kind of multi-layered analysis which is favoured by proponents of Systemic Functional Linguistics (Halliday, 1985; Martin, 1992) has also influenced the teaching of conversation. According to this view, the *texture* of conversation is analysed at various levels of delicacy, especially with regard to the way the contextual variables of field, tenor and mode motivate choices at the level of lexis and grammar. In an attempt to redress what is seen as a preoccupation with language *use* as opposed to form, proponents of a genre approach (especially in the Australian context) are committed to instructional approaches that 'help learners understand how the form of the language allows people to do things with language in social contexts. This means that the teaching of speaking is returning to an explicit teaching of the form of language and aligning this to using the language' (Burns and Joyce, 1997: 88). The example from *Beach Street*, cited above, demonstrates how an explicit focus on the structural features of conversation (i.e. pre-closings and closings) might be realized in classroom materials.

The influence of both sociolinguistics and pragmatics on the pedagogical treatment of appropriacy, including sensitizing learners to register factors and to degrees of politeness, can be seen in materials such as the following:

7.1   ASKING PEOPLE TO DO THINGS

Presentation

1 Why does the speaker ask for help in a different way in each picture?
2 In what *other* situations might you say 'I don't suppose you could help me get the washing in, could you?'

Practice

Work in pairs.

Student A: You are staying at your friend's house for the weekend. At various times you make the request below. Choose the most appropriate way of asking, from the expressions in the box.

Student B: Reply to each request in any way you like. If you refuse, give a *reason*.

Could you . . . ?	Would you mind . . . -ing . . . ?	I don't suppose you could . . . , could you ?
Would you . . . ?	Do you think you could . . . ?	
. . . , could you?		Do you think you could
. . . , would you?		possibly . . . ?

(Asking people to do things, from Doff *et al.*, *Meanings into Words Intermediate*, 1983: 44, Ex. 7.1)

Finally, awareness of crosscultural and gender differences in the ways casual conversation is structured and negotiated have found their way into teaching materials in activities such as this one:

Speaking: Small talk

1 Imagine you are at a formal party with people whom you are meeting for the first time. Which of the subjects below do you think are appropriate as topics for conversation in (a) your own country and (b) Britain? Complete the table below, adding any comments if you wish.

Topic	Own country	Britain
today's weather		
your opinions about marriage		
your religious beliefs		
how you got to the party		
your political views		
a recent sporting event		
the food and drink at the party		
your salary		

(Topic)	(Own country)	(Britain)

a TV programme you saw last night
the latest political crisis
the attractiveness of your host
a neighbour's sudden death
some physical symptoms you've got

2 Are these appropriate ways of starting a conversation with someone you don't know at a party?

   a Haven't we met somewhere before?
   b Do you come here often?
   c It's a bit chilly today, isn't it?
   d How much did those beautiful shoes cost?
   e Can I get you something to drink?
   f Where do you work?
   g What do you think of the Prime Minister?
   h Are you a friend of Jane's?
   i Would you like to dance?
   j Have you got a light?
   k This is a pretty boring party, isn't it?
   l How old are you?

Can you suggest any good ways of starting a conversation?

3 Work with a partner. Imagine that you are in one of the locations shown in the illustrations on page 125 and that you have never met each other before. Take it in turns to initiate a conversation and carry on the conversation as seems appropriate to you. When the conversation comes to a natural end, move on to a different location.

4 Follow these instructions.

   1 You are going to role play being at a formal party where few of the guests already know each other, a party in an embassy, perhaps.
   2 Your teacher will give you a card to describe the character of the person you are to be.
   3 Look at your card. How might that person behave at a formal party? What sorts of things would he or she talk about?
   4 Act your role. Try to move around the party speaking to as many people as possible.
   5 After the role-play, discuss what roles you felt the other students were playing.

(Small talk from O'Dell, *English Panorama*, 1997: Unit 18, p. 124)

8.6.2 Communicative competence

The idea that linguistic competence is subsumed within the broader notion of *communicative* competence has been far-reaching, occupying as it does a foundational place in communicative learning theory. By shifting the emphasis from accuracy to *fluency*, and by (re-)defining the latter as 'natural language use, whether or not it results in native-speaker-like comprehension or production' (Brumfit, 1984: 56), the architects of the communicative approach asserted the importance of freer speaking activities, preferably those that involve (or, at least, simulate) natural language use. What could be more 'natural' than conversation? Accordingly, Littlewood (1981) comments: 'The conversation session is sometimes regarded as a source of relief from more "serious" language work. This should not prevent us from recognising the important functions it can perform in helping to develop communicative ability' (1981: 46). For Littlewood classroom conversation is a *social interaction activity*, that is, one in which 'learners must pay greater attention to the *social* as well as the *functional* meanings that language conveys' (1981: 43). This has implications in terms of the roles of teacher and students: 'If the conversation session is to perform its proper role as social interaction activity, the teacher must perform as "co-communicator" rather than "director"' (1981: 47).

However, other writers working within the communicative paradigm are less convinced of the value of free conversation. Taylor and Wolfson (1978) go so far as to argue that 'class time devoted to having foreign students talk in a totally free and unstructured way is wasted' (1978: 31). Clearly influenced by developments in sociolinguistics, they claim that 'what students need most from a conversation class is not the opportunity to speak, but, rather, explicit instruction in what Hymes (1972b) has called the "rules of speaking"' (1978: 34). Accordingly, the fluency activity favoured by many communicative methodologists is not so much conversation as *role play*. Role play allows learners to explore the effects of different contextual factors – power relationships, setting, communicative purpose, etc. – on language. By pre-selecting speaker roles, the teacher is able to calibrate sociolinguistic factors and thereby provide the need for what Taylor and Wolfson call 'instruction in linguistic etiquette' (1978: 36). Moreover, 'role plays and games are important because they present learners with the opportunity to practise speaking under conditions that are as close as possible to those of normal communication' (Scott, 1981: 77). Role plays, of course, could be conversations, as in this example (from Swan and Walter, 1985: 79):

> Work with four or five other students. You are all in the same
> compartment on a long train journey. Act out a conversation in
> which you get to know one another.

More often than not, however, role plays tend to be transactional rather
than interactional, and tasks tend to be structured rather than free. The
following is a typical example of how a conversational structure is
mapped on to a transactional framework:

---

3 ⬚ [5.9] Work in pairs. Act out the conversation below. Then
listen to the real conversation.

Student A: you are phoning *Bank Direct* about a money
transfer you're expecting from the USA. You
want to speak to Sharon Elliot, your personal
banker, to find out what is happening.

Student B: you are the telephonist at *Bank Direct*. Sharon
Elliot is on the other line at the moment.

Student A	**Student B**
	↓
	answer the phone
ask to speak to Sharon Elliot	
	explain that Sharon Elliot is on the other line; ask if the caller wants to hold or if Sharon Elliot should call back
ask if she can call back	
	ask what it's about
explain what it's about	
	ask for the caller's number
give your number and say when you'll be there	
	say 'thank you' and end the conversation
say 'good-bye'	

(from Cunningham and Moor *Cutting Edge*, 1998: 57)

8.7 Task-based learning: Conversation as a task

In fact, structured transactional tasks, with clearly defined objectives, are defining features of *task-based language teaching* (TBLT), which in turn evolved as a 'strong form' of communicative language teaching. Early proponents of TBLT (e.g. Prabhu, 1987) argued that communicative competence might best be achieved if learners are focusing on communicating from the outset. Instruction should focus, therefore on 'the creation of conditions in which learners engage in an effort to cope with communication' (Prabhu, 1987: 1). To this end, task-based instruction is based around sequences of *tasks*, a task being, in Ellis's definition

> . . . a workplan that requires learners to process language pragmatically in order to achieve an outcome that can be evaluated in terms of whether the correct or appropriate propositional content has been conveyed. To this end, it requires them to give primary attention to meaning and to make use of their own linguistic resources . . . A task is intended to result in language use that bears a resemblance, direct or indirect, to the way language is used in the real world.
>
> (2003: 16)

It might be thought that, given this emphasis on pragmatic language processing and on meaningful, 'real-world' language use, *having a conversation* would qualify as a kind of task. However, the lack of any obvious, testable outcome has meant that having a conversation rarely if ever figures as a task type in task-based materials. Moreover, the use of the term 'workplan' in Ellis's definition would seem to disqualify conversation, since conversation is not normally considered a form of work (i.e. structured, goal-oriented activity) and therefore not amenable to the kind of planning implied in Ellis's term. (Of course, as McCarthy (1998) notes, conversation does have goals, but these are interpersonal rather than transactional.) It is this transactional focus that has led some writers, such as Cook (2000), to criticize task-based learning on the grounds that it is overly preoccupied with language work at the expense of language *play*. A more ludic conception of language learning might more comfortably accommodate casual conversation, with its jokes, puns and apparent triviality.

Task-based instruction also draws heavily on interactionist views of second-language acquisition (Long, 1985) which argue for the key role that *negotiation for meaning* plays in providing the psychological conditions whereby language *input* becomes *intake*, and thus available for mental processing and, ultimately, acquisition. It has been claimed that transactional tasks, such as information exchange, provide better opportunities for meaning negotiation than more 'open' language activities, such as conversation. This is because transactional tasks tend to be convergent (i.e. they are directed at a single, agreed outcome), a condition that is more likely to induce meaning negotiation than the divergent and seemingly aimless nature of conversation. Thus, the interactionist research agenda departed significantly from Hatch's original claim that 'language learning evolves *out of* learning how to carry on conversations' (1978: 404, see Chapter 6). As Block notes, researchers in the interactionist tradition 'were not interested in just any form or aspect of conversational interaction; rather, they adopted a fundamentally instrumental view of conversational interaction where the key was the exchange of information' (2003: 62). An exception is in Willis's formulation of task-based learning, in which she includes, as one of six generic task types, 'sharing personal experiences'. Here learners are encouraged 'to talk more freely about themselves and share their experiences with others' (1996: 27). She adds that 'the resulting interaction is closer to casual social conversation in that it is not so directly goal-oriented as in other tasks' but she cautions that such open-ended tasks 'may be more difficult to get going in the classroom' (1996: 27).

Another reason for the absence of conversation in task taxonomies is that, because of its primarily interpersonal function, conversation is not conducive to the use of those interactional moves, like clarification requests, that are believed to be crucial for acquisition. Pica (1987), for example, has argued that, if complex language is to be made comprehensible and accessible to learners, conversational adjustments in the form of *repair* are essential – they are the engine that drives interlanguage development forward. But, as Markee notes, 'an important reason why talk-in-interaction cannot be a sufficient locus for naturalistic L2 learning is that, whereas repair (rather like cod-liver oil) may be acquisitionally good for you, it is nonetheless potentially face-threatening' (2000: 113). Even in traditional information-gap activities, Foster (1998) found that, in classroom settings, many learners – when confronted with communication breakdown – often adopt a 'wait-and-see' strategy, rather than attempt to initiate repair.

The interactionist view has also gathered support from the argument, originally proposed by Swain (1985), that comprehensible *output* is a necessary condition for second-language acquisition. In contradistinction to Krashen's (1982) input hypothesis, which argued for the necessity and sufficiency of comprehensible *input*, Swain argued that learners need to be *pushed* to produce comprehensible output, that is, output that is not only accurate but appropriate and coherent. In other words, as Skehan succinctly puts it, 'to learn to speak we have to actually speak!' (1998: 16). Output serves a number of important functions that input on its own does not. One of these is to force syntactic processing; another is to test hypotheses (Swain, 1985); while a third is to develop automaticity. With regard to the first of these purposes, Skehan (1998) is sceptical as to the value of conversation. The elliptical and jointly constructed nature of conversation is not conducive to the production of well formed sentences, and speakers are able to 'bypass syntax' a great deal of the time. 'Since it is meanings that are primary, as long as the speaker feels that communication is proceeding satisfactorily, the need for precise syntax is diminished' (Skehan, 1998: 26). In Swain's terms, the speakers' output is not sufficiently *pushed*.

However, Skehan does concede that there are at least two functions of output in the form of conversation that may be beneficial. The first of these is the development of *discourse skills*, such as turntaking and conversational management: 'We cannot read about these skills, or even acquire them passively, but instead have to take part in discourse and realize how our resources are put to work to build conversations and negotiate meaning' (1998: 18). Finally, Skehan argues that output allows the learner 'to develop a personal voice': 'It seems inevitable that if one wants to say things that are important, one must have, during language learning, the opportunity to steer conversations along routes of interest to the speaker, and to find ways of expressing individual meanings' (1998: 18–19). This echoes a sentiment expressed many years earlier by Billows: 'We must teach a language through speech, to give each individual a personally fitted instrument which he [sic] can use and develop as part of himself. Our awareness of each pupil as an individual entity, our concern for him as a person, can only be developed through personal speech' (1961: 31).

In fact, such worthy aims are more commonly associated with those 'fringe' methodologies that owe allegiance to humanistic principles of learning (Stevick, 1980). Personalized talk is a defining characteristic of *Community* (or *Counselling*) *Language Learning* (CLL), for example, as developed by Curran (1976). Here the content of the language lesson is the jointly constructed and audio-recorded conversation of the learners themselves. While CLL shares many characteristics of TBLT, the two are seldom if ever mentioned in the same breath (but see Thornbury, 1997). Again, this may be due to the non-transactional nature of 'personalized talk'. (We will return to the topic of CLL in the next chapter.)

In balance, then, proponents of task-based learning see only a limited role, if any, for classroom conversation. However, the argument that conversation is an impoverished source for task-based learning opportunities has been challenged by Nakahama *et al.* (2001). In an admittedly small-scale study, they compared the way that meaning was negotiated in two types of tasks: two-way information-gap tasks of the type favoured by interactionist researchers, and relatively unstructured conversation. Using native-speaker and non-native-speaker pairs, they did in fact confirm the view that information-gap activities produce a greater number of repair negotiations than in the conversational interactions. But they also found that these repair negotiations differed in quality. In the information-gap task, negotiation cycles occurred locally and independently of one another, and were focused primarily on lexical issues. By contrast, in the conversation task, 'repairs focused on an overall understanding of the interlocutor's contributions' (2001: 388). This, in turn, had the effect that the conversations produced longer turns, more complex language, and a greater range of pragmatic markers than in the information-gap tasks. The researchers concluded that 'the work of clarifying information for the purpose of building mutual understanding may carry a much greater cognitive load in terms of processing the interlocutor's discourse and responding appropriately than information exchange about lexical items in an information-gap task' (2001: 397). These findings led the researchers to suggest that 'conversation should be studied in much more detail as a potential source of rich learning opportunities' (2001: 401), a sentiment that, we would add, has motivated the writing of this present book.

In the meantime, and until its potential as a locus for learning is more fully appreciated, conversation seems set to continue as just another form of fluency practice, playing only a marginal role in the development of overall linguistic competence. In that sense, we seem not to have moved far from the scepticism that Sweet voiced (1899, 1964, quoted above) to the effect that 'conversation is really not a means of learning new words and expressions, but only of practice in hearing and reproducing what we have already learnt' (1899, 1964: 75). In the next chapter, after reviewing key themes relating to the teaching of conversation, we will argue the case for a more central role for conversation in second-language learning.

Task

Here are some conversations taken from a variety of different coursebooks, published between 1980 and 2005.

(a) Try and put them in the chronological order of publication. What criteria influenced your choice of order?

(b) Evaluate each conversation in terms of its 'naturalness', i.e. to what extent does it display the characteristics of authentic conversational data?

(c) Natural or not, would they be useful models for teaching conversation? I.e. what features of conversation could each conversation serve to highlight?

270

1 Conversation

A:	It's terrible.
B:	The prices.
A:	Oh dear.
B:	Do you know potatoes are eighty pence a kilo?
A:	Eighty pence a kilo? In our supermarket they're eighty-five.
B:	It's terrible.
A:	Oh dear.
B:	Everything's so expensive.
A:	Do you know tomatoes are £6.00 a kilo?
B:	£6.00? In our supermarket they're £6.25.
A:	No!!!
A and B:	It's terrible.
A:	Milk's seventy-five pence a litre.
B:	Half a kilo of rump steak is £7.50.
A:	An orange costs 60p. One orange!
B:	And cheese!
A:	I know!
B:	Do you know, yesterday I was in Patterson's.
A:	Were you?
B:	Yes, and cheese was £8.30 a kilo.
A:	£8.30?
B:	Yes, and bananas were £2.25.
A and B:	It's terrible.

2 Conversation

Jane:	Hey Jane. What's up?
Kevin:	Oh, I've lost my mobile again.
J:	Lost or stolen?
K:	Lost.
J:	Oh, bummer. Hey. Have I ever told you about the time I was in Rome?
K:	No. What happened?
J:	Well, I was sitting outside a bar with my bag on the table and this guy ran past and grabbed it. I chased him but no luck.
K:	So . . . ?
J:	You'll never guess what happened next. I was walking home, a bit scared, wondering what to do and this other guy came and gave it back to me.
K:	Amazing. Was everything there?
J:	Nearly everything. Just the money was missing.
K:	Lucky!

J: Yeah, I reckon it was a trick. Someone steals something, you get it back, so you feel good and don't go to the police.

K: Yeah. Suppose so.

3 Conversation

Steve: Windy, isn't it?
Erika: Yes, it is.
Steve: Uuh. . . . Where are you going?
Erika: To Germany. I'm going home.
Steve: Oh, you're German.
Erika: Yes. You're English, aren't you?
Steve: Yes, I am.
Erika: Where are you going?
Steve: To Portugal.
Erika: On holiday?
Steve: No. I'm going to take some photographs.
Erika: Photographs?
Steve: Yes, I work for a travel magazine.
Erika: Aah.
Steve: What do you do?
Erika: I'm a student.
Steve: What are you studying?
Erika: Medicine.
Steve: Oh, my brother's a doctor.
Erika: Ah, really.
Steve: Cold, isn't it? Would you like a coffee?
Erika: Yes, I'd love one.
Steve: Let's go to the restaurant then.

4 Conversation

A: Hello?
B: Oh hello. Is that Sophie?
A: Yes?
B: Hi! This is Frank.
A: Frank! How are you?
B: Great! How are you?
A: Fine. I was going to phone you.
B: Listen. Have you heard about Anna?
A: Yeah, terrible, isn't it? What happened exactly?
B: Well, she went to the cinema and when she got back, they'd broken into her house.
A: Did they take much?
B: No, but it's a horrid feeling, you know, someone else

	in your house. Anyway, the worst thing is she doesn't feel comfortable there at night now.
A:	No. I can understand that. Of course, she could always stay here.
B:	Could she? I think she'd appreciate that.
A:	Well, I'll phone her. Why don't you come round later?
B:	OK, listen I'll bring dinner.
A:	Great. Right, well, I'll phone Anna now. See you later.
B:	OK fine. Bye.

9   Teaching conversation: Approach, design, procedure and process

Introduction

In the previous chapter we traced the history of the teaching of conversation up to the present day. In this history several key themes have surfaced repeatedly. For a start, the term *conversation* has been used at one time or another to embrace everything from controlled oral practice to uncontrolled chat, and the finer distinctions between dialogue, discussion, debate, free speaking, role play and casual conversation have been consistently blurred. As we attempted to show in Chapters 1 to 5, while conversation as a form of spoken language can incorporate a range of sub-genres, it can nevertheless be fairly narrowly defined in terms both of its purposes and of its characteristic features. As awareness of these purposes and features has grown, it has become no longer viable simply to treat conversation as synonymous with speaking.

Even when the term is used more precisely – to mean something like 'informal talk among friends' – conversation has for the most part been treated as a curricular 'add-on'. At times, in fact, it has been actively discouraged in classrooms. Only sporadically has it been highly prioritized, either as a primary learning objective, or, even, as the means by which language learning itself might best be achieved.

In this chapter we outline, in broad strokes, the pedagogical options available to teachers who have chosen to include the teaching of conversation as a curricular objective. The strokes are necessarily broad because no single approach to teaching conversation will be appropriate or even practicable in all teaching situations. Different configurations of context factors will determine the ultimate design and implementation of the program. Among these factors not the least important will be the age, level of proficiency, needs, expectations and preferred learning styles of the learners; the constituency of the class, e.g. whether or not they share the same L1; the size of the class; the resources available; and the skills and expertise of the teacher.

In our outline we adopt the three-level model for methodological description elaborated by Richards and Rodgers (1986). That is, we describe the options that seem viable at the level of the *approach*, i.e. the general theoretical position with regard to learning and language that

274

underpins the programme; the way these principles might be realized in the *design* of the programme, including its objectives, syllabus and materials; and, finally, the choice of *procedures* – i.e. the 'moment-to-moment techniques, practices, and behaviours' (1986: 26) that are consistent with both the design and the approach. We will also discuss how such a programme might be assessed and evaluated.

Finally, we address the issue of the role conversation might play in mediating instruction. That is to say, can (or should) conversation be part of the *process* of language learning, not simply the objective of certain classroom *procedures*?

9.1 Approach

9.1.1 Direct vs indirect

Which theories of language learning are directly relevant to the teaching of conversation? In Chapter 7 we reviewed the arguments for and against the claim that conversation is not so much learned as acquired, to use Krashen's (1982) distinction. We concluded that there is evidence to suggest that explicit instruction in certain features – such as formulaic routines – does help, especially where learners have little or no exposure to naturally occurring conversation. On the other hand, there are other features, such as intonation, which seem to be resistant to instruction and which may only be acquired. Classroom instruction that replicates natural acquisition processes – through simply 'doing' conversation – may provide the right conditions for the positive transfer of L1 conversation skills into the L2. It may however encourage negative transfer of L1 stylistic features, or even cause premature stabilization (also known as *fossilization*) of the learner's interlanguage systems, so some degree of teacher intervention, in the form of explicit instruction, may be necessary – again, depending on the learner's needs and the likely contexts of use.

The learning versus acquisition polarity underpins a distinction that Richards (1990) makes between two fundamental choices at the level of a teaching approach: whether to teach conversation *directly* or *indirectly*. The direct approach 'involves planning a conversation programme around the specific microskills, strategies, and processes that are involved in fluent conversation' (1990: 77). While stressing the importance of providing learners with opportunities to 'have conversations', the direct approach presupposes the need for a form-focused, instructional stage at some point in the lesson cycle.

An indirect approach, on the other hand, assumes that learners can acquire conversational competence simply by doing it. It is an approach 'in which conversational competence is seen as the product of engaging learners in conversational interaction' (Richards, 1990: 76–7), or, as Burns more narrowly defines it, where 'the essential focus is on tasks mediated through language, negotiation and the sharing of information' (1998: 103). This reference to the role of tasks aligns the indirect approach to task-based learning (see Chapter 8) which in turn derives from what Howatt (2004) calls the *strong* form of the communicative approach, where 'language is acquired through communication'. A characteristic expression of strong communicative language teaching (CLT) is All wright's claim that 'if the language teacher's management activities are directed exclusively at involving the learners in solving communication problems in the target language, then language learning will take care of itself' (1979: 170).

The same evidence in favour of explicit instruction (reviewed in Chapter 7) can be marshalled in support of the direct approach. As we saw, the features of second-language conversational competence that respond positively to instruction consist of routinized ways of realizing certain conversational move types appropriately. These may take the form of discourse markers and conversational 'gambits' such as conventionalized ways of opening and closing conversations, of turntaking, and of back-channelling etc. And they may take the form of conventionalized ways of performing certain speech acts, such as apologizing, requesting and thanking. As Aijmer (1996) points out, it is these routines in particular that create difficulty for learners 'because they are culture-bound and because their formal description and their situational frames are extremely complex (Yorio, 1980). Learners of the language are usually not aware that there are rules governing these expressions' (1996: 30).

However, the very fact that these conversational routines *are* culture-bound may in fact be an argument for *not* teaching them, especially for learners whose objective is English as an *international* language, as opposed to a second or a foreign language. We will return to this point when discussing course objectives below.

Proponents of an indirect approach argue that, apart from learning certain formulaic routines, some of which may be of doubtful utility, and the learning of lexical phrases in general, there is little concrete evidence in favour of the direct teaching of conversation. This is especially the case with regard to the higher-order conversational skills implicated in the global management of talk, such as turntaking, topic change, overall coherence, or the effective alternation between chat and chunk.

Moreover, since these higher-order features are universal features of conversation in general, they are (potentially, at least) transferable from the learners' L1. As Brown and Yule (1983) suggest, 'in language teaching it seems reasonable to assume that much of what the student has learnt about the nature of primarily interactional speech in his own language can be transferred to the foreign language' (1983: 23).

According to this argument, what learners principally lack is *language*. They know the tune, as it were, but not the words. This, at least, is the thinking that underlies Kellerman's (1991) scepticism about the wisdom of teaching communication strategies: 'There is no justification for providing training in compensatory strategies in the classroom . . . Teach the learners more language and let the strategies look after themselves' (1991: 158). Thus, awareness-raising exercises of the following type are arguably redundant.

Task

In conversation people take turns to speak. Two ways they do this are:
a The person who is speaking now selects (nominates) the next speaker: **nomination.**
b A listener decides to speak without being nominated: **self-selection.**
Look at the data in Task 1 again.
1 Compare how many times each speaker uses **nomination.**
2 In line 14 Sachiko uses **self-selection:** *Ah yes it's very exciting.*
Find another example of Sachiko using **self-selection.**
Find an example of Yoriko using **self-selection.**
3 The first part of the extract sounds a bit like an interview. Why?

(Geddes and Sturtridge, *Intermediate Conversation* 1994: 7)

The time spent 'teaching' these universal features of conversation would perhaps be better spent teaching and practising the language, including the exponents of specific conversational moves, without which these universals remain inert and non-transferable. As McCarthy (1991) puts it, 'it is not a question of telling learners that speakers take turns; they know this naturally from their own language. The problem is to make sure that activities generate the natural sorts of turn-taking that occur in the target discourse type and so not inhibit typical turn-taking patterns' (1991: 128).

It would seem, on balance, that there is a case for at least some indirect (or 'experiential') learning in the acquisition of conversational competence, and that this learning would typically involve exposure to a lot of conversational input – preferably authentic – from which learners would be able to extract lexical chunks, including conversational routines. Practice at having conversations would not only provide learners with opportunities to 'test-drive' these routines, but would allow the development and automization of communication strategies (which also partly rely on the knowledge of certain fixed expressions). It may nevertheless be the case that a certain degree of teacher intervention – e.g. by having students identify and categorize discourse markers, hesitation devices, etc., in a conversational extract – will promote the conscious 'noticing' (Schmidt, 1990) of how these exponents are realized, and thereby accelerate the processes of acquisition.

Current thinking tends to support a view of learning which combines features of indirect and direct learning in alternating cycles of performance and instruction. Proponents of task-based learning, for example, acknowledge the need for a periodic *focus on form*, whether pre-, during-, or post-task (see, for example, Doughty and Williams (1998)). Cazden (1992), coming from a 'whole learning' perspective, argues for the need for 'instructional detours' in order to shift attention, when necessary, away from the whole and on to the parts: 'The idea of a detour preserves what I believe to be essential: the prior establishment of a main road of meaningful language use, to which the detour is a momentary diversion when needed' (1992: 14). Cazden argues for what she calls 'whole language *plus:* ' . . . as people of any age learn to read and write, they need help in focusing attention on specific features of written language; they need deliberate, well-planned help in attending to parts as well as wholes' (1992: ix). The same could be said for the learning of conversation, which suggests that what might work best is alternating the experience of participating in conversation with periodic instructional detours. That is to say, an indirect approach *plus*.

9.1.2   Bottom-up vs top-down

The part versus whole dichotomy also has relevance in terms of the choice of *language* theory that might underpin a teaching approach to conversation. As we saw in the last chapter, a knowledge of grammar, lexis and phonology was traditionally considered a sufficient basis for conversational proficiency. In this so-called 'bottom-up' view of language, the smallest meaningful units of the language – its phonemes, words and sentences – are taught in isolation before they are combined into larger units and only finally put to work in real talk. One problem with this approach is that it may indefinitely prolong the teaching phase, at the expense of the talk, as both teachers and learners become overly concerned with the parts, rather than the whole, and with accuracy rather than fluency.

More recently, the discourse analysis, conversation analysis and genre analysis perspectives have enriched language description considerably. One implication of a discourse and genre perspective is that, rather than building conversational proficiency from the ground up through the learning of isolated bits of grammar and vocabulary, whole conversations themselves (or large chunks of them) should be the starting point of instruction. Such a model takes as axiomatic the view that meaning is conveyed and negotiated over stretches of extended discourse rather than at the level of single utterances. Moreover, such stretches of discourse tend to display patterns and regularities according to the degree to which they have become conventionalized in order to fulfil specific social purposes. Genre analysis attempts to identify these textual patterns and regularities and show how such text types (or *genres*) are determined by their contexts of use (see Chapter 5).

The starting point of a top-down, genre-driven model of instruction, therefore, is a context of use, and an authentic instance of real communication typical of such a context. This 'text' is then subjected to analysis (which may include analysis of its grammatical, lexical and phonological features, as well as of its overall discourse structure) before learners attempt to replicate these features in the production of their own texts. Figure 9.1 illustrates the three stages of such a teaching cycle.

First stage of the cycle	• activities build knowledge of a context of language use which relates to learner needs
	• activities involve visuals, realia, excursions, discussions, field-work and vocabulary-building
	• parallel activities build cross-cultural strategies and pronunciation or spelling skills
Second stage of the cycle	• involves a close investigation of the purpose and structure of a model of a text type which occurs in the context
	• students focus on the register and language features which are central to the text achieving its purpose
	• language features are studied at both whole text and clause level
Third stage of the cycle	• initial activities provide students with opportunities to use the text type with support
	• later activities gradually demand more independent performances

Figure 9.1   Example of the teaching/learning cycle (from Feez, 1998: 33)

But, as with bottom-up approaches, the danger of any approach that foregrounds analysis is that, in practice, the analysis stage can become the ends rather than the means of instruction. Moreover, in order that students are not overwhelmed by the processing demands involved in interpreting, deconstructing and reproducing authentic texts, this approach assumes students are already at a relatively advanced level, i.e. that they have sufficient grammatical and lexical knowledge to permit them to handle such texts. (Even native speakers find the reading of conversation transcripts a daunting task.) On the other hand, if the example texts are selected or simplified, not only is their authenticity compromised, but the criteria of selection or simplification (e.g. grammatical difficulty) may end up determining the syllabus, leading us back to what is essentially a bottom-up approach.

Nevertheless, the advantage of a top-down approach is that learners are immediately exposed to examples of language in use. Moreover, by attempting to relate texts to their contexts and functions, there is a better chance that the linguistic features of such texts will not be seen as arbitrary but socially and contextually determined. Especially for ESL learners (i.e. those learning English as a second language, in order to participate in an English-speaking culture) a genre-driven approach can provide insights into the shared cultural values that are embedded in spoken and written genres, and learners are thus better equipped to function in that society and to exploit the genres for their own purposes. And, as Hammond argues: 'if students are left to work out for themselves how language works . . . then a number of students are likely to fail' (1987: 176).

On balance, we would argue for providing learners with contextualized data where possible, in the form of audio or video recordings and their transcripts. This data can then be subject to varying degrees of analysis. A good example of such material is Carter and McCarthy (1997), which consists of 20 extracts of authentic spoken discourse covering a range of genres including casual conversation. Each extract is preceded by a task 'which normally involves students in an activity-based exploration of some aspect of language' (1997: 10). Information about the situational context follows, including the participants and setting. The extracts themselves are relatively easy to follow – some have been re-recorded using professional actors – and are transcribed 'rather like written text' (1997: 20) and with only the most essential paralinguistic information included. These are followed by a detailed commentary 'with line-by-line notes pointing out significant linguistic and related cultural features' (1997: 11). The authors note that these commentaries are by no means exhaustive, and that the major focus is on 'those aspects of grammar, vocabulary and discourse patterning judged to be of significance for learners of English' (1997: 11). Because these features were not pre-selected, but emerge naturally from the data, they do not distract from the essentially top-down nature of the approach.

The materials, however, are designed solely for receptive use, and the authors provide no guidance in terms of how the language features they have highlighted could be incorporated into production activities. Perhaps the assumption is that it is for teachers and learners to decide on what classroom procedures might be locally relevant and practicable. But without such guidance, materials like this and Crystal and Davy's earlier *Advanced Conversational English* (1975) are likely to have more applicability to academic, rather than language learning, contexts.

9.2 Design

9.2.1 Objectives

The teaching of conversation may form just one component of an instructional programme as, for example, when it comprises the social-skills element of a business-oriented language course. Or it may be an end in itself, as in specially programmed 'conversation classes'. In either case, the broader goal of achieving conversational fluency is typically broken down into sub-goals. The way these are formulated will largely reflect the particular theoretical paradigm underlying the design of the programme. In Chapter 1 we outlined a number of approaches that have informed descriptions of conversation, and which, in turn have influenced the design of teaching programmes. Thus, a conversation analysis (CA) bias will typically prioritize objectives such as the management of turntaking, including openings and closings, and strategies for repairing breakdown, as well as preference structure in adjacency pairs, and topic management. Sociolinguistic approaches are likely to foreground objectives such as sensitizing learners to context factors that in turn affect style and degrees of formality, as well as cultural differences that impact on conversational style. Programmes influenced by speech act theory will tend to focus on the learning of conversational routines and the ways that specific speech acts are realized in interactional talk. Pragmatics will foreground the co-operative nature of conversation, politeness strategies, and ways of avoiding face-threatening conversational behaviour. And a systemic-functional approach will seek to sensitize learners to the way the speaker's social identity is realized in conversation at different levels, including the lexical, grammatical, discoursal and generic.

More often than not, teaching programmes and materials will combine elements from more than one of these paradigms. Richards (1990), for example, provides a comprehensive list of possible objectives (see Figure 9.2) which is notable for its eclecticism in drawing on a range

---

- How to use conversation for both transactional and interactional purposes
- How to produce both short and long turns in conversation
- Strategies for managing turn-taking in conversation, including taking a turn, holding a turn, and relinquishing a turn
- Strategies for opening and closing conversations
- How to initiate and respond to talk on a broad range of topics, and how to develop and maintain talk on these topics
- How to use both a casual style of speaking and a neutral or more formal style
- How to use conversation in different social settings and for different kinds of social encounters, such as on the telephone, at informal and formal social gatherings
- Strategies for repairing trouble spots in conversation, including communication breakdown and comprehension problems
- How to maintain fluency in conversation, through avoiding excessive pausing, breakdowns, and errors of grammar and pronunciation
- How to produce talk in a conversational mode, using a conversational register and syntax
- How to use conversational fillers and small talk
- How to use conversational routines

Figure 9.2 Goals for a direct approach to teaching conversation (Richards, 1990: 79–80)

of theoretical bases. Keller and Warner (1988), however, focus almost entirely on conversational routines (or *gambits*), divided between *opening gambits* (such as formulaic ways of breaking into a conversation, and of changing the subject), *linking gambits* (e.g. ways of signalling topic cohesion) and *responding gambits* (such as ways of expressing agreement or disbelief).

A more exclusively top-down description of objectives, and one that is firmly anchored in a systemic-functional paradigm, is offered by Feez (1998). She points out that 'the objectives for a course based on a text-based [i.e. top-down] syllabus are always related to the use of whole texts in context' (1998: 23). Feez provides an example of how such an approach would be formulated in relation to teaching conversation (see Figure 9.3).

Finally, Burns and Joyce (1997) distinguish between objectives that are related to knowledge, such as *How spoken texts are organized to achieve particular social purposes*, and objectives which are related to skills, such

> **Goal**
> To enable learners to participate in a casual conversation in a work-place.
>
> **Objectives**
> The learners will:
> - understand the purpose of casual conversation in Australian workplace culture
> - know which conversation topics are appropriate in Australian workplaces
> - recognize and use the key elements of a casual conversation i.e. greetings and closures, feedback, topic shifts
> - recognize and use conversation chunks such as comments, descriptions or recounts
> - take turns appropriately within simple exchanges i.e. question/answer, statement/agreement, statement/disagreement
> - use language appropriate to casual conversation including politeness strategies, informal language, idiom
> - build pronunciation and paralinguistic skills and strategies, specifically in the areas of intonation and gesture

Figure 9.3 Unit of work: Casual conversation (Feez, 1998: 23)

as *Initiating conversations, giving feedback and backchannelling*, etc (1997: 75–6). It is not clear, however, whether in making this distinction the authors assume that learners need to be taught the skills themselves, or simply that they need to be given practice in ways of realizing these skills in the target language. As we argued, in our discussion of transfer in Chapter 7, time spent teaching learners skills that are already in place (such as back-channelling) may be time misspent, when what the learners need is the knowledge of specific back-channel routines in order to be able to transfer these skills into the L2.

9.2.2 Needs

Apart from the particular theoretical stance that is adopted, a determining factor in deciding objectives will be the specific needs of the target learners.

A good deal of conversation teaching makes the implicit assumption that learners will need conversation for social interaction with native speakers, and it therefore takes for granted that learners will need to be prepared for differences in cultural style. A common component of many conversation courses is a section on cultural taboos. For example, in their resource book, *Conversation and dialogues in action*, Dörnyei and Thurrell (1992) advise learners, 'There are so many culture-specific dos and don'ts that without any knowledge of these, a language learner is constantly walking through a cultural minefield' (1992: 113). In order to minimize potential injury in this minefield, the authors provide a list of conversational dos and don'ts for British (middle class) English:

INPUT 30 Some British (middle class) conversational and cultural dos and don'ts

Do not ask: how much someone earns; how much something they bought cost; about a stranger's political stance (or reveal your own directly); personal questions, such as how old someone is or whether they are married; do not mention toilet and sex too openly; do not respond to '*How are you?*' by starting to talk about your headache or digestion problems.

In conversation there is very little simultaneous talk or overlap between two speakers; some interruption is allowed, especially to ask for repetition or explanation, but too much is considered impolite.

Silences are to be avoided; a question should be followed by an answer without any delay; talking very little, not initiating topics, or giving very brief answers may imply unfriendliness or a lack of interest.

etc

(Dörnyei and Thurrell, 1992: 135–36)

However, for learners who need conversational skills primarily in order to interact with other non-native speakers – i.e. whose goal is *English as an international language* or EIL (McKay, 2002) – rules of conversational behaviour appropriate for interacting with middle-class Britons (or Canadians, or Australians, or Californians) may be largely irrelevant.

   The internationalization of English also has implications on the teaching of politeness strategies, conversational routines, and other pragmatic aspects of conversational competence. Much of the research in favour of explicit instruction that we have cited compares learners' use (or misuse, or lack of use) of certain conversational routines with the way native speakers use them. Recommendations for ways of teaching these routines is then extrapolated from the research. For example, Dunham (1992) outlines a strategy for teaching complimenting behaviour that includes: comparing how complimenting is done in the native culture with how it is done in the United States, classroom role plays to practise

United States complimenting behaviour, followed by projects in which learners must compliment native speakers.

But, as McKay points out, if learners are learning EIL, then 'there is no inherent reason why a native speaker model should inform the teaching of pragmatics' (2002: 74). The adoption of native-speaker norms may even be counterproductive. 'In fact, some studies suggest that there may be benefits in *not* conforming to native speaker pragmatics' (2002: 75, emphasis added). Not conforming may be a form of resisting cultural and linguistic submersion. Just as adult immigrants retain features of their mother-tongue accent, out of a sense of identity, so too may many non-native speakers choose not to adopt native-speaker pragmatic norms, so as not to be seen by their peers as having 'crossed over' to the dominant native-speaker community. As Norton (2000) reminds us, 'while it is important for language learners to understand . . . the "rules of use" of the target language, it is equally important for them to explore whose interests these rules serve. What is considered appropriate usage is not self-evident' (2000: 15). This is particularly acute with regard to conversation, which, as we have repeatedly said, is a site for constructing and asserting personal and group identity. Encouraging learners to adopt the conversational style of a group which they do not wish, or are not *allowed*, to become members of, may be futile and de-motivating.

Clearly, the use that is made of native-speaker models will depend very much on the learners' needs and contexts. As Judd (1999) points out, in addressing the question 'Is native-speaker pragmatic knowledge necessary?', 'if our students are now in an ESL [English as a second language] environment, they will certainly need to be exposed to and gain mastery of the pragmatic knowledge of the English that they will encounter on a daily basis . . . In an EFL [English as a foreign language] situation, . . . pragmatic accuracy may be less important, and in some cases may even be unnecessary' (1999: 160–61).

What may be more important than cultural competence (defined as competence in the cultural norms of one specific culture) is the capacity to achieve *intercultural competence* (Scollon and Scollon, 1995). Rather than assuming that access to insider cultural knowledge will help preempt misunderstandings, intercultural competence accepts that misunderstandings are an inevitable part of any communicative event, even in cases where cultural knowledge is shared, and that speakers need to be equipped with ways of dealing with these misunderstandings. Compilers of lists of the dos-and-don'ts type (as above) – in their well-intentioned desire to foreground the phatic purposes of conversation, and therefore to warn against any behaviours that might be considered antisocial – overlook the fact that one of the main purposes of any language activity is to explore and negotiate *difference*. If there were no difference, there would be no need to communicate at all. As Kress (1985) points out, 'difference is the motor that produces texts. Every text arises out of a particular problematic . . . Dialogues, whether conversations, interviews, or debates, are the clearest examples' (1985: 12). Rather than encouraging learners to avoid difference, teachers should be aiding them in developing the skills of *managing* difference.

Coping with difference and the potential for misunderstanding are the keys to successful intercultural communication, i.e. communication with members of other discourse systems – what Scollon and Scollon characterize as *outgroup communication*. In outgroup communication there are likely to be differences in knowledge, assumptions, values and forms of discourse, which may in turn lead to ambiguity and problems of interpretation. 'We must look for these problems, anticipate where they will arise out of our differences, and then plan our communications to be effective as outgroup communications' (1995: 251). Successful intercultural communication, then, is not so much the knowledge of what one does or does not do in X culture; rather it is the degree of skill one has at anticipating, recognizing and collaboratively negotiating difference.

A significant block to successful outgroup communication is ethnic, cultural and gender stereotyping, especially the sort that polarizes groups along a single, binary dimension of analysis, e.g. individualistic vs collectivist, or rational vs intuitive. Lists of dos and don'ts of the type: *Do not mention toilet and sex too openly* are also a form of stereotyping in that they promote a monolithic, static and even folkloric view of the 'host' culture, and one that has long been ridiculed (viz. the title of the West End show *No sex, please, we're English*). Such stereotyping, Scollon and Scollon argue, 'will blind us to the real differences that exist between the participants in a discourse' (1995: 158). They conclude:

> The American who is sure he knows all there is to know about communication with Chinese is doomed to failure. The Japanese who is certain she is adept at communication with Koreans will have difficulties. The man who feels he really, deeply understands women is likely to know very little at all. Such outgroup certainty is virtually always a signal of binarism and stereotyping. On the other hand, a person who understands the outlines of the pattern of differences and commonalities, but fully recognizes his or her own lack of membership and state of non-expertise, is likely to be the most successful and effective communicator.
>
> (1995: 252)

A teaching approach that provides the learners with the experience of coping with difference and diversity is likely to have more successful outcomes than one that deals simply in certainties.

9.2.3 Organization

There are a number of choices available in terms of the way the course objectives are realized in the course design. In general English courses, the conversation components are usually distributed throughout the course, and are subsumed under the superordinate heading 'Speaking'. These consist of either topic-related discussion tasks, or 'free practice' of a pre-selected grammar item. In many general English courses a section – called for example 'Everyday English' – is a regular feature of every unit, and typically includes both interactional and transactional talk, and is independent of the main grammar focus of the unit. In ESP courses, such as those targeted at business English, conversation is often dealt with under the heading 'Social English' or 'Small Talk'.

A topic-based organization is also favoured by free-standing conversation courses, i.e. those that specifically target conversation. Thus Geddes and Sturtridge (1994) devote one half of their book to such topics as *Talking about children, Talking about marriage* and *Talking about superstitions*. In a similar vein, Richards and Hull (1987) – who adopt a more transactional approach to conversation – organize their book around commonly encountered situations, such as *Choosing a restaurant, Giving advice to a tourist, Making arrangements for studying at a university*, etc. A functional organization is sometimes favoured: Dörnyei and Thurrell (1992) include a section called *Functions and meanings in conversation*, which looks at the way specific speech acts are realized, as well as ways of dealing with violations of Grice's cooperative principles. And, as noted earlier, Keller and Warner (1988) deal exclusively with the different conversational routines, or 'gambits', that realize specific conversational move types.

All the above organizations are essentially semantic and knowledge-based. That is, they attempt to meet the learners' need to *know* what to say to express specific *meanings*. This is often supplemented with a more formalist, skills-based, organization in which learners are presented with information about how conversations are *structured*. For example, Dörnyei and Thurrell devote the first two sections of their book to *Conversational rules and structure* and *Conversational strategies*. The former category deals with 'how conversation is organised, and what prevents conversations from continually breaking down into a chaos of interruptions and simultaneous talk' (1992: xi); conversational strategies, on the other hand, are 'ways and means of helping learners to overcome communication breakdowns, to deal with trouble spots, and to enhance fluidity' (1992: xi). Similarly, Geddes and Sturtridge (1994), focus on such 'conversation skills' as *Expanding what you say, Summarizing to show understanding* and *Going back to an earlier point*.

Finally, Nolasco and Arthur (1987) adopt a different organization altogether, and categorize their activities according to their pedagogic purposes, i.e. *controlled activities, awareness activities, fluency activities*, and what they call *feedback tasks*, i.e. tasks that enable learners to evaluate, and learn from, their own performance. They recommend that the teacher select a balanced 'diet' from these generic activity types for a conversation class, or, if the conversation component supplements a general English programme, that the conversation activities be integrated into the wider programme on the principle of 'little and often'.

9.2.4 Materials

In theory, no teaching materials should be necessary in order to initiate conversation in the classroom, since, in real life, conversation typically happens independently of any textual support. In practice, however (and given the fact that classrooms are *not* always conducive to spontaneous interaction), teachers have found certain materials useful either to provide input or to act as a stimulus, and we shall discuss these two types of material in turn.

Input materials are designed to model certain features of conversation for the purposes of conscious study and internalization. Typically these take the form of written transcriptions of conversational extracts, either specially written or authentic, with accompanying audio or video recordings. Two collections of such material that provide excellent sources of data, especially for teachers, advanced students, and researchers, and which have already been mentioned, are Crystal and Davy (1975) and Carter and McCarthy (1997).

Apart from collections such as these, teachers have normally had to rely on scripted dialogues of the type that appear in most textbooks, and which have been criticized by researchers for their lack of many features of naturally occurring conversational data. For example, Bardovi-Harlig *et al.* (1991) looked at the way conversational closings are effected in textbook dialogues and in authentic conversational data, and found that the former 'do not provide natural, or even pragmatically appropriate, conversational models for learners' (1991: 4). Similarly, Wong (2002) found that naturally occurring features of telephone conversations, 'such as summon–answer, identification, greeting, and how-are-you sequences . . . are absent, incomplete, or problematic in the textbook dialogues' that she studied. Such criticisms seem to have prompted at least some writers into providing more authentic-sounding conversational models for learners, even if still scripted. For example, the following dialogue (from Kay and Jones, 2001) demonstrates the way closings consist in large part of formulaic language, and redresses a tendency of textbook conversations to finish very abruptly:

The long goodbye
(A = Ann, B = Bob)
A: I'd better be going.
B: It's been lovely to see you.
A: Thanks for having me.
B: Thanks for coming.
A: I'll be off then.
B: Give my regards to your family.
A: I will.
B: Give me a ring.
A: Okay. I really must be off now.
B: Take it easy.
A: See you.
B: Look after yourself.
A: Bye for now.
B: Safe journey.
A.   Love you.
B: Missing you already.

(Kay and Jones, 2001: 151)

The distinction between authentic and non-authentic is less clear in practice, however. Even the process of transcription involves a degree of simplification, since many features, especially non-linguistic ones, have to be excluded from the transcription for the sake of clarity. Moreover, strict authenticity may not always be practicable. Conversations are notoriously hard to capture on tape, and even harder to listen to, especially in the absence of contextual information. In the interests of intelligibility, authenticity may need to be sacrificed in favour of simulated conversations, although we would recommend that these should not be pre-scripted. Rather, speakers should be recorded talking about a topic (or a number of topics) without being told exactly what to say in advance. This way there is more likelihood of capturing naturally occurring features of conversation such as hesitations, fillers, false starts, overlaps, etc. The following extract is from the transcription of a conversation, made by two teachers, the theme being a birthday present:

Rob: Piet, it's my dad's birthday soon and I just don't know what to get him. Got any ideas?
Piet: Umm, it kind of depends on what his interests are. What does he like doing?

289

> Rob: Well, he's a keen gardener, umm, but they've got all the bits and pieces they need for the garden.
>
> Piet: Umm, what about sort of music and books? Does he like reading?
>
> Rob: Oh yeah, but he's a very specialist sort of reader and he likes poetry mainly and he collects antique books. Well, I can't possibly get him one of those.
>
> Piet: Gosh. Kind of tricky, isn't it?

Note that even this short segment includes such features of spoken language as ellipsis, fillers, vague language (*kind of . . . sort of . . .*), discourse markers (*well, oh*), and question tags.

In order to raise his learners' awareness of the use of discourse markers and other lexical phrases in conversation, Hobbs (2005) describes how he made recordings of native speakers performing tasks from a coursebook. He was motivated to do this by the failure of his learners to use such phrases spontaneously, and the relative paucity of such phrases in the coursebook dialogues. The transcripts of these recordings were used, along with the recordings themselves, as part of a task-based instructional cycle. Having performed the coursebook task themselves, learners then studied the transcripts of the native speakers performing the same task and answered questions that directed their attention to the discourse markers, vagueness expressions, and other lexical phrases, in the texts. Jones (2001) describes a similar procedure for raising awareness about spoken narrative structures (see Chapter 5). Learners are supplied with two transcribed versions of a narrative, one which is simply a 'bald narrating of events' (2001: 158) and the other a more elaborated version incorporating evaluative comments, discourse markers and back-channel devices. Both versions are compared and contrasted, and the learners' attention is directed to features of the more natural-sounding text through the use of prepared questions.

A study by Takahashi (2005) suggests that learners notice salient features of transcribed talk even when their attention is not formally directed to these features. In an earlier study (Takahashi, 2001), which had focused on the acquisition of complex bi-clausal request forms (e.g. *Would it be all right if . . . ?*), it was found that, when Japanese learners had been asked to identify 'interesting' features of native (-like) usage in transcripts of native speakers performing role plays, the learners 'tended to attend more often to idiomatic expressions and discourse markers such as "you know" and "well" than to the target bi-clausal request forms' (Takahashi, 2005: 91). The subsequent study confirmed these findings: learners attended more closely to the pragmatic markers than they did to other features of the transcripts, possibly because 'the novelty of the interactional features may have lent them special salience in the learners' perception and engaged their attention to them' (2005: 111). Moreover, the study showed that the degree of interest in these idiomatic features correlated less with their language level than with their intrinsic motivation. Like the Hobbs study mentioned previously, this study suggests a useful awareness-raising role for authentic conversation data in the classroom. Basturkmen (2001) makes a similar case for the use of authentic data to teach the features of questioning routines: 'Text-focused description and instruction offers a way of opening up talk, such as questioning, to higher-level learners, and of showing features of interactive spoken discourse neglected by conventional approaches' (2001: 4).

An alternative to either authentic conversation data, textbook dialogues and home-made texts are conversational extracts from films or television dramas. While these are invariably scripted, they can sometimes be surprisingly naturalistic, in terms of their features, and have the advantage of being both audible and entertaining. Grant and Starks (2001) compared conversational closings as portrayed in textbooks with closings as enacted in a New Zealand television soap opera, and found that, although the soap opera conversations were far from ideal, they provided a better source of data than most textbook examples.

Materials designed to stimulate (as opposed to model) conversational interaction can take the form of:

- questions to discuss
- situations, role cards and flow diagrams
- texts to read and respond to

The website http://iteslj.org/questions/ offers hundreds of discussion questions grouped according to topic. For example, under the topic *Friends* appear the following questions (among many others):

- What things should friends never do?
- Why do you like your best friend?
  - What are some things you like about your best friend?
- Where is a good place to meet new friends?
  - Where is a good place to meet a new boyfriend/girlfriend?
- There is a proverb that says, 'A friend in need is a friend indeed.' Do you agree?

Questions such as these can form the basis of a discussion, which while being somewhat artificially constrained by this externally imposed agenda, is still likely to share many of the features of casual conversation. One way of using the questions productively is to write each one on to a separate card: the group discusses each question in turn, giving as much – or as little – time to the question as they require. Cards are moved to the bottom of the pack once they have been dealt with. An alternative to questions is a list of statements which the students respond to. Summarizing the discussion, either in writing, or as a report to the class, adds an element of formality which, in theory, encourages some attention to linguistic form (Willis, 1996).

Another variant is to provide individual students with cards, each with a different topic written on it. For example: *Football*; *The Royal Family*; *Dieting*; *Pets*; etc. The students are told that the topic is their personal 'obsession' and the idea is to have a conversation, during which each person tries to work the talk around to their obsession.

A teacher in Japan, Kindt (2000) has developed a classroom approach based around his students' own conversation cards (SOCCs). These take the form of index cards which students prepare in advance of paired conversation practice in the classroom. The teacher selects a theme and supplies a rubric, for example:

> For this card, think of 3 of your favourite movie scenes and draw or glue pictures of the scenes onto your card. Then write a few sentences using the phrases 'I like the scene when . . .' or 'I like it when . . .' to help explain your favourite scenes. . . .

In class the students use the cards as both stimuli and mnemonics for conversations of at least five minutes duration. These are staged to include a greeting, some small talk, plus discussion of the subject at hand, and a closing. The backs of the cards are used to record names of conversational partners and a self-evaluation.

Situations that describe such contextual features as the setting and the relationship between speakers can be used to prompt conversations, such as this one:

> Read the situations below and make phone calls to other students. Begin like this:
>
> A: Oh hello. Is that (+ her/his name)?
> B: Yes.
> A: Hi! This is (+ your name)

> Student A: Phone and invite Student B to come and stay with your family some time soon. Explain some of the things you'll be able to do together.

> Student B: Answer the phone. Find out what Student
> A has been doing lately and tell her/him about your
> own activities. Accept his/her invitation and find out
> as much as possible about the suggested visit.

(Mohamed and Acklam, 1995: 91)

Role play cards are simply more elaborated situations, i.e. ones where the social relationships and other relevant factors, such as job, age, gender, etc., of the speakers are made explicit, and where therefore a degree of simulation is required. The role play will usually specify the purpose of the exchange, and may even suggest specific conversational moves. On the other hand, it may simply stipulate the conversational style of each interactant, as in these examples:

The Contradictor: You *always* disagree with what anyone says.

The Story Teller: You are always looking for an opportunity to tell a personal anecdote or joke.

The Obsessive: You are obsessed by a topic (you choose) and you want to talk about it constantly.

The Curious Person: You are interested in everything everyone is saying, and you have lots of questions.

The Conciliator: You try to make the conversation pleasant for everyone by agreeing, and trying to make the others agree.

The Topic Changer: You are always looking for opportunities to change the topic – it doesn't matter what.

A variant of the role play is the 'flow diagram', which displays diagrammatically the conversational moves as they are expected to unfold. In this example, the students are given some choice with regard to situational factors, but the basic move structure is pre-selected:

D Role play: asking favours

1 **Work in pairs. You are going to write and act out a dialogue in which Student A asks Student B a favour. Choose one thing from each of the boxes below. Spend about fifteen minutes writing and practising your dialogue.**

293

Who are you?
- parent and child
- two friends/colleagues
- boss and employee
- husband and wife

Where are you?
- on the phone
- at home
- at work
- in the pub/a restaurant
- somewhere else?

What favour does Student A want?
- help with filling in an important form or writing an important letter (what?)
- to borrow something (£100/an item of clothing, etc.)
- to have a lift somewhere (where)
- someone to look after your pet/baby / plants, etc.
- someone to mend your radio/washing machine, etc.

Why?
- you're going on holiday
- you've got an appointment
- you can't do it yourself
- you haven't got any money
- you're really worried about it
- another reason?

What problem does Student B have?
- you're tired/ill/busy yourself at the moment
- you have to be somewhere else at that time
- you're fed up of Student A asking you to do things

Conclusion
- How does Student A try to persuade Student B?
- What is agreed in the end?

2 Act our your dialogue to the rest of the class. Listen to other students' dialogue and try to answer the questions in the boxes above.

3 ⊡[2] You are going to hear some native speakers in two of the situations above. Listen and answer the questions in the boxes. Did they use any words/phrases which might have been useful in your dialogue? Listen again to check.

(Cunningham and Moor, 1998: 89)

Finally, texts can act as springboards for conversation, and it is common practice in textbooks to include a discussion task in the sequence of tasks that follow on from a reading or listening text. For example, after listening to a text in Mohamed and Acklam (1995) about bungee-jumping, students are set the task:

Talk to other students about their hobbies. Who has the most similar hobbies to you? (1995: 7)

9.3 Procedure

9.3.1 Procedures and techniques

Earlier in this chapter we suggested that classroom practice should be based on the principle of 'indirect teaching *plus*', i.e. that learners should have plentiful opportunities for exposure to, and participation in, authentic conversation, but that at strategic points in the process some explicit instruction will be useful (see Figure 9.4).

This three-part instructional model echoes recommendations made by other writers. For example, Judd (1999), advocates a programme for the teaching of pragmatic competence that includes the following elements:

• cognitive awareness [raising]
• receptive skill development
• productive use

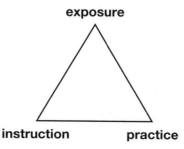

Figure 9.4. Elements of a pedagogy of conversation

Likewise, Dörnyei and Thurrell (1994) advocate an approach to the teaching of conversation which is essentially communicative, in that it prioritizes fluency tasks, but into which is incorporated an explicit focus on language data, and consciousness-raising activities.

The three elements in our model – instruction, exposure and practice – have been arranged in the form of a triangle so as not to pre-suppose a single sequence. The following sequences all have precedents in language-teaching methodology:

- exposure → instruction → practice: e.g. learners listen to conversation extracts; study specific features in transcripts of these extracts; attempt to incorporate these features into their own conversations;
- instruction → exposure → practice: e.g. learners are given explicit instruction in a feature of conversation; they observe how this feature works in context, before going on to practise it themselves;
- exposure → practice → instruction (→ practice): e.g. learners listen to conversations; they attempt similar conversations; they are given instruction, e.g. in the form of feedback, in those features they failed to incorporate, and repeat the practice stage; and
- practice → exposure → instruction (→ practice): e.g. learners attempt a conversational task, then witness proficient speakers performing the same task, noticing the difference between these and their own conversations ('noticing the gap') and receiving some instruction in these features, before repeating the practice task.

In fact, questions of sequencing are probably of less importance than the fact that all three elements are included at least somewhere in the instructional programme.

Exposure

One logical starting point is *exposure*, in the form, for example, of listening to audio recordings, accompanied, or followed, by the reading of a transcript. Alternatively, students could try to reconstruct the transcript themselves. Nolasco and Arthur suggest a way that coursebook dialogues could be exploited this way:

1. Divide the students into groups of three and ask them to sit around a cassette/tape recorder.
2. Ask them to select a piece of listening material for a coursebook they are using. Ideally they should not have gone through the dialogue in class, but weaker students may prefer this.
3. Ask one student to act as the prompter who is allowed to consult the tapescript, if necessary.

4. The other two students take a part each and try to repeat what they hear on the tape. Tell them that they should start by doing this on a line-by-line basis and try to progress through to repeating the whole dialogue. Having got the form, they should concentrate on rhythm, intonation and pronunciation.

(1987: 29)

Instruction

Whether provided by the teacher, or reconstructed by the students, conversation transcripts are then available for a focus on specific features of the data, such as the use of discourse markers, or of appraisal language, or the way anecdotes are structured. Alternatively, video extracts (including the use of segments of film or TV drama, see above) could be used, along with their accompanying transcriptions. As we indicated earlier, the value of transcripts cannot be overestimated. Willis and Willis (1996) point out that 'using transcripts allows learners time to notice features that may not be noticed for a long time if only heard in the flow of real time conversation' (1996: 75–6). They recommend a 'consciousness-raising' approach, using a sequence of language-focused questions based on the transcript, such as:

> Find these words in the conversation : *And, But, So, Well*. What do they all have in common?
> What might you say in your language for each of them?
> What about the function of the words *Right, Yeah*, and *Mhm* and *Mm*?

(1996: 75)

Burns and Joyce (1997) suggest that the following features of spoken language could be subjected to study by means of transcripts:

- the style of interaction
- the relationship of the interactants
- the purpose of the interaction and whether it was achieved
- the strategies adopted by the interactants
- the turn taking and turn type patterns
- the sociocultural values which informed the interaction

(1997: 87)

Classroom tasks associated with the use of transcripts include: underlining and/or counting instances of a particular feature; gap-filling while listening, in order to draw attention to the feature; gap-filling as a post-reading and/or post-listening task, in order to test recall of a feature; marking phonological features, such as pausing and prominence; and reading the transcript – or parts of it – aloud. Because all these techniques focus attention on specific aspects of the text, they count as conscious-ness-raising tasks, and, in turn, constitute a form of instruction.

Transcriptions of the learners' own conversations can also be used as a vehicle for instruction. Kindt (2000), for example, asks learners to record and transcribe some of the conversations that are prompted by their conversation cards. They are asked to leave a space in the left-hand margin for teacher's comments and their own self-corrections. Lynch (2001) describes how a group of learners transcribed two-minute extracts from recordings of themselves performing a role play. These transcripts were then self-corrected and submitted to the teacher for further reformulation. Lynch notes that the students noticed, and cor-rected, many of their errors themselves, suggesting that the transcribing process 'appears to offer a productive route to noticing' (2001: 131). Encouragingly, the students also seemed to find the transcribing task useful, and showed no signs of getting bored.

In a similar vein, Clennell (1999) reports a study in which a group of EAP (English for Academic Purposes) students carried out interviews with native speakers on campus. In advance of the interviews, the learn-ers were coached in specific communication strategies and pragmatic skills (such as different ways of initiating an interview). These interviews were then transcribed, and the transcriptions presented to the rest of the class in the style of an academic presentation, where significant pragmatic features of the transcripts were available for comment and discussion.

More explicit instruction might usefully focus on the learning and memorization of formulaic language. As we saw in Chapter 6, fluency is largely a function of being able to mobilize a repertoire of memorized pre-fabricated 'chunks' in order to reduce processing time. Preparation for fluency, then, can involve the learning and controlled practice of chunks, especially those with 'high surrender', i.e. those that can be used imme-diately and often. In EFL contexts, these often take the form of metalin-guistic phrases that can be used in the classroom, and are often displayed in classrooms in the form of signs or posters on the wall: *Excuse me? Can you say that again? I don't understand. What does X mean?* etc. The idea is sometimes extended to 'process language', i.e. the language learners need to participate in classroom tasks, such as *Whose turn is it? I'll start. What did you put for number 1?* etc. It could of course be extended further to include commonly used conversational formulae, such as *by the way; . . . do you know what I mean? I don't believe it! Go on*, etc.

More elaborated lists, including social formulae, discourse markers, sentence frames, and conventionalized speech act routines, can be found in conversation-teaching texts, such as Keller and Warner (1988) and Dörnyei and Thurrell (1992). In a sense, this is a return to the 'phrase-book' approach that dates back to the 16th century (see Chapter 8). In fact, learners could do worse than memorize a stock of these phrase-book-type chunks. The problem with most contemporary travellers' phrasebooks, however, is that they are seldom if ever based on corpora of naturally occurring data, and therefore often have a rather stilted and old-fashioned flavour. An enterprising publisher might consider the usefulness of a 'conversational phrasebook' for language learners, based on attested examples of high-frequency lexical chunks.

Including high-frequency chunks in textbook dialogues for memorization is another option. In the following dialogue, from an elementary course (Dellar and Walkley, 2005), common idiomatic chunks, collocations and social formulae have been italicized:

> A: Hello. *Is this seat free?*
> B: Yes. *Go ahead. Sit down.*
> A: Are you going to Glasgow?
> B: Yes.
> A: *Me too.*
> B: *Where are you from?*
> A: Germany.
> B: *Oh right.* How long have you been here?
> A: *Not very long.* I arrived in London last Thursday.
> B: Your English is very good.
> A: Thanks.
> B: So, what are you doing here? Is it *business or pleasure?*
> A: Business, really. I work for an export company.
> B: *Oh right.* Do you enjoy it?
> A: Yes, *it's OK.* I like travelling, *so that's good.*

(2005: 126)

In the same course, students are encouraged to maintain an 'expression organiser': 'This section helps you to record and translate some of the most important expressions from each unit. It is better to record expressions than single words . . .' (2005: 146). As an example, the following expressions are listed for Unit 4:

> What're you doing tonight?
> What're you doing this weekend?
> I'm going to go shopping.
> I'm going to go swimming.
> on my own
> with a friend from work
> I'm going to the cinema.
> Do you want to come with me?
> Yes, OK. That'd be nice.
> Maybe some other time.
> I don't really like that kind of thing.

> It sounds really interesting.
> It sounds really boring.
> Entrance is free.
>
> (2005: 147)

In arguing for a more lexical approach to teaching language, Lewis (1997) advocates the use of 'lexical chants', that is, rhythmic chants that are composed entirely of lexical phrases. If these are dialogic in form, such as the following (written by one of the authors), they can be chanted by alternating groups:

Group A:	*Group B*:
I was going to say . . .	Do go on.
I meant to tell you . . .	Don't mind me.
A funny thing happened . . .	Take your time.
You'll never believe it . . .	I entirely agree.
And the funny thing was . . .	What do you mean?
How can I put it?	I haven't a clue.
Believe it or not . . .	Sorry, I'm lost.
Do you see what I mean?	Not at all. Do you?

The use of such chants may suggest a return to the somewhat mindless and hence discredited techniques associated with audiolingualism. However, there is growing evidence supporting the value of repetition of 'chunks'. N. Ellis (2005), for example, describes 'ways that chunking and sequence repetition lead to the consolidation of memorized whole utterances' (2005: 333).

Practice

The challenge for the teacher is to provide practice opportunities that target both accuracy and fluency. Some tasks will aim at encouraging accurate production of the language features that learners have been focusing on in the consciousness-raising tasks referred to in the previous section. Others will need to provide opportunities for free-flowing talk in real operating conditions. Nolasco and Arthur (1987) distinguish between controlled activities and fluency activities. They argue that 'although conversational competence can only come from fluency activities or natural language interaction outside the classroom, there is an argument for the use of controlled activities which help students develop confidence as well as the ability to participate in and maintain simple, commonly encountered conversations' (1987: 23).

One such controlled activity is improving written dialogues by adding, for example, back-channel devices, or discourse markers. Nolasco and

Arthur offer the following dialogue as a candidate for improvement in this way:

A   Hello, where are you from?
B   From Singapore.
A   Why did you come to London?
B   To study.
A   Oh, what are you studying?
B   Accountancy.
A   How long are you planning to stay?
B   Two years.
A   When did you arrive?, etc

(1987: 41)

A more elaborated way of adapting dialogues, aimed in this instance at the teaching of fillers, is described by Dörnyei and Thurrell (1992). Any coursebook dialogue can be used.

1. Begin by asking students questions such as, '*What were you doing last Friday at 11:15 am?*' or '*Where did you spend the summer seven years ago?*' They are unlikely to be able to answer immediately and will probably stammer, laugh, lapse into silence or say '*I don't know*'.
2. One way to react to difficult questions is to use certain filling words or phrases to gain some time to think. Demonstrate this by answering one of your own difficult questions using several fillers. Ask someone what fillers they know, and list them on the board/OHP along with the ones you have selected.
3. Get the students to ask each other difficult questions so that they can practise using fillers. Point out that a combination of several fillers sounds more like a native speaker and gives them more time to think! [. . .]
4. Students get into pairs/groups and prepare a version of the [coursebook] dialogue in which all the speakers are terribly uncertain and hesitant and use lots of fillers.
5. Students perform the new versions of the dialogue and the audience notes all the different fillers that were used. Which were the most popular?

(1992: 45)

In a similar fashion, Jones (2001), in his report on teaching conversational storytelling, mentioned earlier, suggests 'giving students the script of "bare bones" stories . . . and have them discuss in pairs how they could make the story more "tellable"' (2001: 161). He also suggests 'asking students to examine newspaper stories of the "strange but true" type, and discussing how they might retell the story to a friend in a pub or coffee shop' (2001: 161).

301

A logical follow-on to this kind of activity is for learners to improvise their own conversations and stories, incorporating the targeted feature(s) appropriately. In actual fact, the demands of online processing in spontaneous face-to-face conversation often mean that newly learned language items are overlooked. Ways of encouraging their integration include such techniques as asking learners to write the target expressions onto cards or slips of paper, to place these face up when they are talking, and to turn each one over once they have 'used' it. Another technique is to 'slow conversation down', by, for example, writing rather than speaking it, in the manner of online chat or text-messaging. Learners can be set the task of having a 'paper conversation', for example, whereby they work in pairs or small groups and 'talk' to each other by writing onto a shared piece of paper.

Audio-recording of conversations, line by line, is another slowing-down technique, and is standard practice in *Community Language Learning* (CLL, or *Counseling-Learning*). Stevick (1996) describes the basic procedure:

> Learners sit in a circle and engage in a free conversation.
> Utterances may originate either in the new language [i.e. the L2] or in the native language. In the latter case, the teacher (called in Counseling-Learning the "knower") supplies the equivalent in the new language, and the learner repeats it. . . . The new-language parts of these proceedings are recorded on tape. The recording then becomes the source for activities in the remaining phases.
>
> (1996: 224)

The remaining phases include an *analysis* phase, in which the conversation is played back in its entirety and then transcribed. It is then available for some kind of focus-on-form. It is also possible that, at this stage, the conversation could be subjected to the kind of adaptations suggested above, e.g. the addition of appropriate discourse markers, back-channel devices, appraisal lexis, etc., although this is not part of the orthodox CLL procedure. Here, for example, is the 'raw material' that resulted from a CLL session with a small class of teenagers in Barcelona:

S1: Did you go to the cinema this weekend, Miguel?
S2: No, I didn't, but probably I'll go next week. And you. Did you go to the cinema last week?
S1: No, I didn't.
S3: Did anybody go to the cinema this weekend?
S4: Yes, me. Twice. On Friday I went to see 'The Legends of Fall' and on Saturday morning I went to see 'Little Women'.
S3: Which film did you prefer?

S4:	I liked them both because in 'The Legends of Fall' the actor Brad Pitt was very handsome, and in 'Little Women' I knew the story and also I like Winona Ryder very much.
S3:	What's 'Little Women' about?
S4:	It's the story of a family whose father went to the Independence War.
S5:	Is it sad?
S4:	Yes.
S3:	Did you cry?
S4:	Yes, a lot.
S3:	And in 'Legends of the Fall'?
S4:	Yes, not as much. Albert? Did you play football, Albert?
S6:	Yes, I did. Tomorrow Spain is playing Belgium.
Teacher:	And who do you think will win?
S6:	I expect Spain will.
S2:	What's your favourite music group, Carla?
S1:	Not a special group. And what do you like, Albert?
S6:	Green Day.
S3:	I think that this conversation is a bit silly.
S1:	Why don't we finish this conversation?
Teacher:	OK.

The techniques described so far are designed to achieve a measure of accuracy, and are therefore deliberately controlled so as to allow learners to allocate attention to the language they are using. However, learners also need to achieve fluency in conversation. That is, they need to be able to cope with demands of real-time interaction. There are a number of generic activity types that aim to provide the experience of real-time interactive language processing, and these include:

- role plays and simulations
- discussions and debates
- games

Ur (1981), Porter Ladousse (1987) and Klippel (1984) offer a rich menu of fluency activities of the above types. However, most of these activities are not focused on casual conversation specifically, but on more formal or more transactional language, so they are likely to benefit conversational competence only indirectly, by providing an opportunity to develop oral fluency. One of the problems with providing opportunities for *real* conversation in the classroom is that, as Bannink (2002) points out, conversation resists planning: 'Genuine conversational interactions cannot be the outcome of preplanned lesson agendas, they have to *emerge* – and so, by definition, cannot be planned' (2002: 271).

Teaching conversation: Approach, design, procedure and process

Nevertheless, there is some evidence that 'programmed' conversation is feasible. Ernst (1994), for example, describes the stage of a conversation class that she calls the 'talking circle':

> The talking circle is a total group activity that generally takes place at the beginning of the 45-min conversational English class. Almost every day, teacher and students gather in the talking circle to share and discuss experiences, anecdotes, news, special events, introduce the weekly theme, and the like. Although the teacher might open the discussion by suggesting a general topic, the overriding assumption is that the talking circle provides a place and an audience for students to discuss anything of interest to them.
>
> (1994: 299)

Ernst notes that these talking circles 'provide rich opportunities to practice the L2 and to engage in direct and meaningful interaction' (1994: 294). It may be that the best fluency practice that learners can have is when the pre-lesson chat is 'ritualized' in this way, i.e. when it is incorporated into the lesson as a regular feature.

9.3.2 Assessment

Conversational interaction is notoriously difficult to quantify, and hence, to test. Since it involves multiple and overlapping skills and knowledge bases, it is virtually impossible to separate these out in order to test them individually, while a more holistic assessment runs the risk of being overly subjective. Moreover, the same paradox mentioned above with regard to planning 'unplanned' conversation in the classroom applies equally, if not more so, to testing. How do you test spontaneous and informal interaction in circumstances that are not at all conducive to spontaneity and informality?

Moreover (and as we have seen), by virtue of its spontaneity and informality, spoken language is characterized by such performance phenomena as hesitations, repetitions, false starts, incompletions and non-standard grammatical forms. A detached and judgmental listener of such dysfluencies (or reader of them, in the case of transcripts) might not rate the speaker's competence very highly. As Hughes (2002) notes, 'it takes a considerable change in preconceptions about language proficiency for, for example, single word answers to be regarded as "good"' (2002: 77).

Then there is the issue of the interactive and interpersonal nature of conversation. If candidates in tests of oral interaction are tested in face-to-face interactions with an examiner, the lack of symmetry in the relationship both precludes a two-way exchange of information, and constrains the talk in terms of its tenor and field. The conversation is less

304

a conversation than an oral interview (van Lier, 1989). And, even in the case of interactions with a peer, as in student–student interactions, it is difficult to eliminate the effect that one speaker has on the other.

Many of these problems are common to the testing of speaking in general, but they are exacerbated by the particular nature of conversation. In the light of these difficulties, van Lier (1989) suggests that a viable approach might be to diversify oral testing so that it includes a *range* of performance tests, one of which is casual conversation. This multi-genre approach is in fact the approach adopted by Cambridge ESOL in its suite of English language examinations, all of which include an oral component. For example, the specifications for the Speaking component (the fifth of five papers) of the Certificate of Advanced English (CAE) is as follows:

> The Speaking Test assesses candidates' ability to interact in conversational English in a range of contexts. It contains four parts, including an interview section, individual long turns, a collaborative task and a discussion. Candidates are provided with stimulus materials such as photographs and drawings. Candidates normally take the Speaking Test in pairs.

Assessment is made on the basis of four discrete categories, as well as on a 'global achievement scale'. The four categories are:

- Grammar and vocabulary (including range, accuracy, and appropriacy)
- Discourse management (including coherence, extent, and relevance)
- Pronunciation (including stress and rhythm, intonation, individual sounds)
- Interactive communication (including initiating and responding, hesitation, turn-taking)

The descriptors for both *Discourse management* and *Interactive communication* – the categories that are arguably most relevant to the ability to engage in casual conversation – include, at the top end of the scale:

Discourse management:
- Contributions are relevant and coherent, and are effective in developing discourse.
- Contributions are consistently of an appropriate length.

Interactive communication:
- Interaction is sustained and developed fully and effectively by initiating and responding appropriately.
- Hesitation is minimal and does not interfere with the interaction.
- Sensitivity to turn-taking is shown throughout the test.

	CONVERSATION
C2	*Can converse comfortably and appropriately, unhampered by any linguistic limitations in conducting a full social and personal life.*
C1	*Can use language flexibly and effectively for social purposes, including emotional, allusive and joking usage.*
B2	*Can engage in extended conversation on most general topics in a clearly participatory fashion, even in a noisy environment.* *Can sustain relationships with native speakers without unintentionally amusing or irritating them or requiring them to behave other than they would with a native speaker.* *Can convey degrees of emotion and highlight the personal significance of events and experiences.*
B1	*Can enter unprepared into conversations on familiar topics.* *Can follow clearly articulated speech directed at him/her in everyday conversation, though will sometimes have to ask for repetition of particular words and phrases.* *Can maintain a conversation or discussion but may sometimes be difficult to follow when trying to say exactly what he/she would like to.* *Can express and respond to feelings such as surprise, happiness, sadness, interest and indifference.*
	Can establish social contact: greetings and farewells; introductions; giving thanks. *Can generally understand clear, standard speech on familiar matters directed at him/her, provided he/she can ask for repetition or reformulation from time to time.* *Can participate in short conversations in routine contexts on topics of interest.* *Can express how he/she feels in simple terms, and express thanks.*
A2	*Can handle very short social exchanges but is rarely able to understand enough to keep conversation going of his/her own accord, though he/she can be made to understand if the speaker will take the trouble.* *Can use simple everyday polite forms of greeting and address.* *Can make and respond to invitations, suggestions and apologies.* *Can say what he/she likes and dislikes.*
A1	*Can make an introduction and use basic greeting and leave-taking expressions.* *Can ask how people are and react to news.* *Can understand everyday expressions aimed at the satisfaction of simple needs of a concrete type, delivered directly to him/her in clear, slow and repeated speech by a sympathetic speaker.*

Figure 9.5 Descriptions for Conversation, from *Common European Framework of Reference for Language*

Of course, descriptors such as these are difficult both to formulate and to apply, and they raise as many questions as they answer (what, for example, makes a contribution coherent? What is an appropriate length of utterance? and so on), but they have the merit of counterbalancing traditional concerns for grammatical accuracy. Moreover, the standardizing process involved in training and monitoring testers is rigorous, involving the use of video-taped interviews

For a checklist of skills relating solely to conversation, the performance-related, competence-based descriptors in the *Common European Framework of Reference for Languages* (Council of Europe, 2001) are also useful (see Figure 9.5). They are phrased as 'can do' statements, rather than as discrete areas of knowledge. Again, such statements are not unproblematic, but, by focusing on what learners can do, rather than what they can't, they may encourage a more benevolent attitude on the part of testers (and, because of backwash, on teachers) than do most rating scales. This is consistent with the view that to demand native-like standards of language proficiency of learners who do not have native-like goals is unrealistic and, in the end, counterproductive.

9.4 Process

So far we have been considering the teaching of conversation as a set of procedures nested within the larger framework of the discourse of the lesson. Now we will consider the case for making the discourse of the lesson itself a conversation, for learning *through* conversation. Or, put another way, we will argue for conversation not as a teaching procedure, but conversation as the teaching *process*.

In Chapter 6 we reviewed the arguments for making the educational process more conversational. According to sociocultural theory, conversation provides a natural context for verbal scaffolding and is therefore an effective medium for learning. By extension, a conversational approach to teaching a second language would seem to offer two distinct advantages. When lessons themselves are 'long conversations' not only do learners get the benefit of engaging directly in conversational discourse, and thereby become better conversationalists, but also the long conversation that is the lesson embeds learning opportunities by means of which the learners' overall language competence improves. Or, as Ellis puts it, 'There are two reasons for claiming that learners need the opportunity to engage in conversational discourse: (1) it enables them to develop discourse competence and (2) it facilitates the development of linguistic competence. It has also been argued . . . that the two are inextricably linked. That is, through the process of developing discourse competence learners come to extend their linguistic resources' (1990: 92). In short, they learn conversation, and they learn *through* conversation.

In Chapter 7 we contrasted classroom talk with conversation, and argued, on sociocultural grounds, for the 'conversationalization' of classroom talk. What, then, is the effect of classroom talk that is more conversational in style? Research into question types and topicalization is suggestive. Brock (1986), for example, found that referential questions elicit significantly longer and syntactically more complex responses than do display questions. Slimani (2001) found that, on the basis of what learners claimed to have learned in any one lesson (the 'uptake'), 'learners benefited much more from their peers' rare instances of topicalisation than from the teacher's' (2001: 297). That is, the topics raised by their classmates made a more durable impression than those raised by the teacher.

In classroom organizations, such as pair and group work, where the teacher-led, IRF-type discourse structures no longer operate, researchers have found a marked improvement both in the quality and quantity of language produced. Ellis (1994), summarizing the findings, comments that 'it seems reasonable to conclude that interaction between learners can provide the interactional conditions which have been hypothesized to facilitate acquisition more readily than can interaction involving teachers' (1994: 599). These interactional conditions include repair negotiation, which Porter (1986) found to be present in learner–learner interactions during task-centred discussions in ESL classrooms.

These results, though, have to be balanced against Foster's (1993) finding that, in classroom conditions – as opposed to laboratory conditions – learners do not always take information-exchange tasks seriously, with the result that the quality of talk actually deteriorates. It may be that such tasks are simply not 'conversational' enough. In her analysis of the 'talking circles' (see above), Ernst (1994) compared the kind of talk that such circles generated with the more teacher-led phases of the lesson. The amount of student-generated talk increased markedly during these phases. Ernst also found that when students have control over the topic of conversation 'they are more likely to use a variety of communication strategies to overcome problems of communicating with limited L2 resources' (1994: 316). And in a comparative study of repair negotiation during two kinds of speaking activities – two-way information gap tasks, and 'relatively unstructured conversation' – Nakahama *et al.* (2001) found that the native speaker–non-native speaker dyads negotiated communication problems in both kinds of tasks, but that 'in information gap interaction, negotiation cycles occurred locally and independently of one another . . . . In conversation, on the other hand, they negotiated meaning in order to achieve coherence in the entire interaction' (2001: 400).

Moreover, the conversational activity generated longer and more syntactically complex utterances, and a higher incidence of pragmatic markers, leading the researchers to conclude that 'conversation should be studied in much more detail as a potential source of rich learning opportunities' (2001: 401). Since this study was based on native-speaker–non-native speaker interaction, it suggests that teacher–learner talk might offer similar learning opportunities, so long as it is conversational in style.

All these findings support the argument advanced by Ellis that 'opportunities need to be created for learners to control the discourse' (1998: 166), because when they do, not only is the quantity and quality of student talk increased, but learning opportunities are maximized. 'Discourse control', however, need not preclude the teacher. In fact, the teacher's role may be critical in terms of guiding and prompting learners, even when they have discourse control, in order to extend their competence, by providing the kind of scaffolding discussed in Chapter 7. In Ernst's talking circles, 'the teacher's role involved supporting students' conversations by encouraging, acknowledging, and extending their contributions' (1994: 301). Likewise, in a study by Ko *et al.* (2003), in which the researchers attempted to account for improvements in students' story-telling tasks over two tellings, they found that 'the teacher, although not the sole factor in improving stories, was a critical player' (2003: 320). The teacher helped scaffold the story re-telling, by listening for places in the stories which lacked essential information, and by leading the storytellers to provide it. They were also sensitive to cultural assumptions the storytellers were making, which might have made their stories difficult to follow, and they encouraged other learners to ask questions in order to clarify doubts. Finally, they supplied missing lexical items and corrected pronunciation. The researchers conclude that 'if one wanted to list specific teacher behaviours in line with current conceptions of effective ESL teaching, these interactional moves would very likely find a place on the list' (2003: 320).

In fact, these interactional moves are very much in the spirit of the notion of *instructional conversation*, as outlined in Chapter 6, or of *dialogic inquiry* as proposed by Wells (1999). In an extended study of classroom interaction, Johnson (1995) urges teachers to expand the patterns of classroom interaction, and one way they can do this is by enacting verbal and instructional scaffolds so that learners can 'participate in social interactions that are beyond their current linguistic ability level' (1995: 155). It is through such means, where new language is embedded in the familiar, that learning opportunities are maximized. For van Lier (1996), conversational interaction, because it is 'contingency work', provides the best means for doing this: 'Conversation, or any language use which plays with contingencies (storytelling for example), can . . . be expected to be the most stimulating environment for learning. Conversational interaction naturally links the known to the new. It creates its own expectancies and its own context, and offers choices to the participants. In a conversation, we must continually make decisions on the basis of what other people mean. We therefore have to listen very carefully . . . and we also have to take great care in constructing our contributions so that we can be understood' (1996: 171).

How does such contingent classroom talk work in practice? Ulichny (1996) examined sequences of teacher–learner talk in which teachers were ostensibly chatting with learners about their out-of-class activities, but were at the same time using such conversations as an opportunity to embed form-focused instruction. She studied one teacher in particular, who routinely started each class with a chat episode.

> Within this larger speech event, the teacher interrupts the casual conversation numerous times to engage the whole class in correction and, possibly, instruction (. . .) Thus the teacher puts the original conversation on hold for either a correction-by-repetition routine or an instructional routine.
>
> (1996: 744)

Here, for example, is a typical sequence, with the chat in the left-hand column, and the correction and instructional asides in columns two and three respectively:

	Conversation	Correction/ conversational replay	Instruction
T:	You were delivering mail to the patients?//		
K:	yah//		
T:	how many times did you go//=		
K:	=no no//the I should go but I didn't go//		
T:		I was SUPPOSED to go//	
			that's a good one//. I was SUPPOSED to go [taps table rhythmically while repeating]//everyone
A:			I was SUPPOSED to go//

Conversation	Correction/ conversational replay	Instruction
T:		again//
C+:		I was SUPPOSED to go//.
T:		but I couldn't//. but I couldn't=
C−:		= but I couldn't//
T:		(ev?) again//
A:		but I couldn't//
T:		I was supposed to go but I couldn't// again//
C+:		I was supposed to go but I couldn't//
T:		I was supposed to go but I DIDN'T// you can also say but I DIDN'T//
	uh-huh [rising intonation]// because the baby's sick//	
	aah// is the baby still very sick?// what's the matter//	
K:	(he?) don't know//	
T:	[expressive breath in take indicating possibly surprise, sympathy] oh// (that's a problem then?)//	

Key:
K = Katherine
T = Ms Towers (teacher)
A = members of class and Ms Towers
C+ = members of the class participating chorally
C− = a few members of the class, not functioning in unison

// end of an idea unit, not necessarily a pause
= latched contributions, no beat between exchange of speakers

(Ulichny, 1996)

311

Ulichny argues that such sequences – of conversationally embedded instruction – are an attempt by teachers to resolve the dual demands of their students, 'demands for opportunities to negotiate meaning authentically through interaction with their classmates and for explicit instruction and controlled practice' (1996: 741). Such insertions represent what we earlier termed *instructional detours* (Cazden, 1992).

Ulichny adds that 'there are obvious motivational and language reasons for building the instruction on "real" interaction' (1996: 758). However, she is sceptical as to its overall worth: 'The double purpose embodied in this complex classroom speech event – to serve as both a conversation and an instructional activity – may have made it difficult for the class to appreciate either activity' (1996: 759–60). It's true that there is a fine line between intervention and interruption, and the teacher's interaction in the sequence quoted above looks suspiciously like the latter.

Nevertheless, there is considerable evidence to suggest that expert teachers are capable of exploiting learning opportunities in conversational discourse, without subverting the learners' own communicative agenda. One way they do this is by reformulating their learners' contributions in such a way as to align these contributions more closely to what has been said, and also to provide a springboard into the next stage of the talk. Cullen (2002) shows how one teacher achieves this through her skilful use of the F (follow-up) move in the traditional IRF routine (see Chapter 6). In this sequence, taken from a recording of an English lesson in a government secondary school in Tanzania, the teacher is preparing the class (of some 40 girls) to read a text about a plane hijacking:

T: Now suppose you were inside the plane and this was happening. What would you do? You have to imagine yourself now, you are in the plane.
      Now I'll give you two minutes to discuss it with your friend.
      Two minutes. OK. Yes, please?
S8:   I shall pray my God because I know it is my final time. [laughter]
T: She says she's going to kneel down and say, 'please God, forgive my sins'. [laughter]
T: Yes?
S9:   I won't do anything. I'm going to die.
T: She won't do anything. She'll just close her eyes [laughter] and say, 'take me if you want. If you don't want, leave me'.
T: Yes?
S10: I will shout.

T: You will shout. Aagh!
     [laughter]
     I don't know if Heaven will hear you.
     [laughter]

(Cullen, 2002: 121)

Cullen comments that 'the teacher's follow-up moves play a crucial part in clarifying and building on the ideas that the students express in their responses, and in developing a meaningful dialogue between teacher and class. In doing so, the teacher supports learning by creating an environment which is rich in language and humour' (2002: 126). Cullen identifies at least four specific strategies that the teacher uses in her follow-ups: *reformulation, elaboration, comment* and *repetition*. A reformulation is a more accurate or more appropriate rewording, by the teacher, of the learner's utterance (also called a *recast*). An elaboration extends or embellishes the reformulation (as in the teacher's second turn in the above extract). A comment, on the other hand, is the teacher's own personal response to the learner's utterance, as when the teacher in the above extract comments: *I don't know if Heaven will hear you*. The purpose of repeating a learner's utterance (sometimes called, disparagingly, *echoing*) is 'to confirm, question, or express surprise' (2002: 125).

Cullen also identifies a quality that characterizes all the teacher's follow-up moves, which (following Jarvis and Robinson, 1997) he labels *responsiveness*, i.e. 'the general quality the teacher exhibits of listening and responding meaningfully, and with genuine interest, to the *content* of what the student is saying' (2002: 125, emphasis added).

In a similar vein, Gibbons (2003) studied the way teachers' interventions helped transform students' command of the specialist discourse of their science classes. She identifies at least four ways that teachers mediate language learning: through the use of *recasts*, by *signalling to learners how to reformulate*, by *indicating the need for reformulation*, and by *recontextualising personal knowledge*. (Unlike Cullen (2002), Gibbons distinguishes between *recasting* and *reformulating*, the former being the teacher's rewording of the learner's meaning, while the latter refers to learner-initiated modifications of a previous utterance.) She comments that 'central to such interactions is the notion of *contingency*, the way an adult judges the need and quality of assistance required by the learner on the basis of moment-to-moment understanding' (2003: 267). But she adds that such judgements are largely intuitive. Nevertheless, 'teacher education courses might usefully pay more attention to developing teachers' understandings of the role of discourse in mediating learning' (2003: 269). This is a view echoed by Walsh (2002). 'There is a need to understand more fully the qualitative aspects of language use in the L2 classroom with

313

a view to arriving at a set of guidelines which constitute "good practice" in language use in the classroom' (2002: 20).

Such guidelines already exist. Kramsch (1985), for example, makes the following recommendations:

Turns-at-talk

In group-oriented interaction the teacher should systematically encourage the students to take control of the turn-taking mechanism, by following the five rules of natural turn-taking:

1. Tolerate silences; refrain from filling the gaps between turns. This will put pressure on students to initiate turns.
2. Direct your gaze to any potential addressee of a student's utterance; do not assume you are the next speaker and the students' exclusive addressee.
3. Teach the students floor-taking gambits; do not always grant the floor.
4. Encourage students to sustain their speech beyond one or two sentences and to take longer turns; do not use a student's short utterance as a springboard for your own lengthy turn.
5. Extend your exchanges with individual students to include clarification of the speaker's intentions and a negotiation of meanings; do not cut off too soon an exchange to pass on to another student.

Topic Management

If students are to take an active part in interactions, they must be shown how to control the way topics are established, built and sustained, and how to participate in the teaching and learning of lessons. The following three rules of natural discourse can be useful here:

1. Use the foreign language not only to deal with the subject matter, but also to regulate the interaction in the classroom. You will thus offer a model of how to use interactional gambits in natural discourse.
2. Keep the number of display questions to a minimum. The more genuine the requests for information, the more natural the discourse.
3. Build the topic at hand together with the students; assume that whatever they say contributes to the topic. Do not cut off arbitrarily a student's utterance because you perceive it to be irrelevant. It might be very relevant to the student's perception of the topic.

Repair Tasks

Natural forms of interaction in the classroom would . . . require that the teacher frequently observe the following rules of natural repair:

1. Pay attention to the message of students' utterances rather than to the form in which they are cast (. . .). Keep your comments for later.
2. Treat the correction of linguistic errors as a pragmatic or interactional adjustment, not as a normative form of redress.
3. Leave students a choice in the linguistic form of their utterances, e.g., if they are not sure of their subjunctive, allow them to avoid this form and to find alternatives.
4. Make extensive use of natural feedback ("hmm,/interesting/I thought so too") rather than evaluating and judging every student utterance following its delivery ("fine/good"). Do not overpraise.
5. Give students explicit credit by quoting them ("just as X said"); do not take credit for what students contributed, by giving the impression that you had thought about it before.

(Kramsch, 1985)

As an instance of this kind of programme in action, here is an extract of classroom talk recorded in an EFL classroom in Barcelona:

Text 9.1: 'Barranking'

1.	S	What about go to mountains?
2.	T	What about . . .?
3.	S1	What about going to mountains, we can do 'barranking'. [Ss laugh]
4.	T	What's 'barranking'?
5.	S	Is a sport.
6.	T	Yes, but what do you do exactly?
7.	S3	You have a river, a small river and [gestures]
8.	T	Goes down?
9.	S3	Yes, as a cataract.
10.	T	OK, a waterfall. What's a waterfall, Manuel? Can you give me an example? A famous waterfall.
11.	S1	Like Niagara?
12.	T	OK. So what do you do with the waterfall?
13.	S4	You go down.
14.	T	What? In a boat?
15.	S4	No, no, with a . . . ¿cómo se dice 'cuerda'? (How do you say 'rope'?)
16.	S3	Cord.
17.	T	No, rope. A cord is smaller, like at the window. Look.
18.	S4	Rope, rope, you go down rope in waterfall.
19.	S	You wear . . . 'black clothes' [mispronounced].
20.	T	Black clothes. Repeat. This sounds dangerous. Is it dangerous?
21.	Ss	No no.
22.	S3	Is in summer, no much water.
23.	T	Sorry?
24.	S3	Poco, poco . . . little water, river is not strong.

25.	T	OK. And you have done this? What's it called in Spanish?
26.	S4	Barranquismo. In English?
27.	T	I don't know. I'll have to ask somebody.
28.	S2	It is good, you come? Com es dìu? (How do you say it?) Let's go together.
29.	T	I don't think so. [laughs]
30.	S4	Yes, yes, you come. We can go in summer
31.	T	Well, in the summer. Not now. It's too cold
32.	Ss	No no.

(from Thornbury, 2002)

The extract demonstrates well how classroom talk can achieve the contingency of naturally occurring conversation, while at the same time it can incorporate an explicit instructional component. That is, it refutes Sweet's scepticism (quoted in Chapter 8) that 'conversation is really not a means of learning new words and expressions' (1899: 75). Rather, conversation (of this instructional kind) embeds real 'learning opportunities' (Allwright, 2005), and thereby constitutes what Kumaravadivelu (2003) terms a viable *macrostrategy* for language teaching:

> One way of maximizing learning opportunities in the classroom is to seriously 'listen' when language learners speak, and build on what they say . . . Recognizing the learners' voice also means recognizing their attempt to create learning opportunities for themselves and for other participants in class. When learners ask a question or say something, even if it appears to be far removed from the topic at hand, they might possibly be creating learning opportunities. They may also be indicating that they are capable of not only contributing to the classroom discourse but also navigating it in a direction not anticipated by the teacher.
>
> (2003: 48–9).

Text 9.1 ('Barranking') is a single instance of learners 'navigating' the classroom discourse. Most experienced teachers will be familiar with these often infrequent and somewhat random moments of learner-generated chat. But to what extent can the curriculum be designed so as to maximize opportunities for conversation of this type to occur?

To answer this question, a practising teacher (Jones, 2003) reports a sequence of lessons in which she attempts to put into practice the principles of the 'Dogme ELT' teacher development group. This group originated in Thornbury's (2000) critique of materials-driven teaching, in which he co-opted the principles (and name) of the Dogme 95 film collective. Dogme 95 is pledged to rid cinema of an obsessive concern for technique and rehabilitate a cinema which foregrounds the story, and the inner life of the characters. By analogy, Thornbury argues for a pedagogy that is grounded in the concerns and needs of 'the people in the room', and whose primary content is the talk that is generated by these people: essentially, teaching through conversation.

In a sequence of six lessons, the teacher explored the potential – and the problems – of such an approach with a group of 14 'pre-advanced' learners of mainly East Asian origin, who were preparing for the IELTS examination in a further education college in the UK. After struggling with the 'tensions' of an approach that devolved considerable responsibility onto the students in terms of the content and direction of the lesson, she experienced a breakthrough in the fourth lesson:

> On entering the class I sat at a desk with the students and waited. For a while the students chatted amongst themselves. A student then asked me what we were going to do; I said, 'you tell me.' He looked surprised but then asked me if he could ask a question. He wanted to know where he could play basketball. Another student told him that there was a sports centre nearby where he could play. The conversation continued until all of the male students had decided that they should go to the sports centre and play together. During this conversation I sat back, listened and made notes, concentrating on the interaction between the students and how involved they seemed to be. Until this point it seemed that the female students were not particularly involved but then one girl suggested they organise a basketball tournament. Another suggested that some girls might like to be included in the teams so they should have mixed teams. One of the usually more reserved students told the class about how he had organised a football tournament at his university in Japan and that he would like to do the same here. And so the discussion developed.

> At the end of this lesson I realised that students can define their own content and goals and still learn a great deal. During these two hours I was called upon to supply formulations for the language gaps students encountered which I have termed 'just-in-time' input. This is surely a more effective and meaningful way of giving new language to students and it overcomes the tension of natural language versus forced pedagogy.

Two lessons later she reported:

> On the penultimate day of term I decided to discuss the forthcoming summer holidays with the students. Again I was determining the topic but found that on this occasion the students were genuinely interested and all of the students were involved. All students had made plans for their holidays and were all excited to talk about what they were going to do.

> I realised on this occasion that . . . it is possible to include all students most of the time if the teacher knows her students well

317

and plays the part of a director, directing the students to follow a path which most or all students are willing to take.

This class showed me that more dominant students will try to direct the conversation but when the less dominant students are genuinely interested and feel they have something to contribute the more dominant students can be reined in.

During these two hours I was just another member of the group, of course I was someone who was more knowledgeable in the target language but I only intervened in order to facilitate the group's common purpose – to extend their second language.

(Jones, 2003)

This small-scale study supports the view that a conversation-as-process approach to language instruction is achievable. Without necessarily going so far as van Lier (2001) does in suggesting that such talk ('the organic, self-regulating process of contingent interaction' (2001: 102)) is a sufficient condition for language development to occur, we would nevertheless argue that it is a viable pedagogical option and a necessary component in a 'postmethod pedagogy' (Kumaravadivelu, 2003).

Conclusion

'Conversation in a foreign language,' wrote Henry Sweet in 1899, 'may be regarded from two very different points of view: (1) as an end in itself, and (2) as a means of learning the language and testing the pupil's knowledge of it. But there is, of course, no reason why the second process should not be regarded as being at the same time a preparation for the first' (Sweet, 1899: 210). Over a century a later, that is the position we have been arguing in this chapter. To Sweet's original formulation we can now add the insights gleaned from the wealth of research into spoken language – from linguistic, sociolinguistic, psycholinguistic, functional systemic linguistic, and corpus linguistic perspectives – over the last 50 years in particular. It is not so obvious, in the light of these findings, that classroom discourse and conversation really do share a great many features in common. Conversation-as-medium, as construed by Sweet and his contemporaries, was a far remove from conversation-as-talk, as described in this book, for example. Yet it is our view that, in the right circumstances, and with sufficient preparation, teachers can achieve a close match between conversation-as-talk and conversation-as-medium-for-instruction, such that the second process is at the same time a preparation for the first. We hope that this book has contributed to the realization of that goal.

318

Tasks

A. Here are some coursebook tasks that target aspects of the teaching of conversation.

1. Identify (a) the aspect of conversation that is targeted; (b) the general approach, e.g. direct or indirect, bottom-up or top-down.

2. Evaluate the likely effectiveness of the material in a context that you are familiar with.

7

Look at the pictures below and try to imagine the stories. The expressions below will help you tell the stories. Work with a partner. Use one expression from each group and plan how to tell each story.

A. Introducing your story
Did I ever tell you about the time I . . .
I must've told you about the time I . . .
Did I ever tell you about this friend of mine who . . .

B. Giving background details
A few years ago, when this friend of mine was . . .
Last August when my family was on holiday in . . .

C. Introducing the problem
All of a sudden, . . .
Then suddenly, . . .

D. How the problem was solved
Well, what happened in the end was . . .
Eventually, . . .
Luckily, . . .

E. Finishing off the story
It was one of the funniest/silliest/strangest/worst things that's ever happened to me!
Looking back on it, it was all very exciting/interesting/strange/upsetting.
It seems funny now, but it didn't seem like that at the time!

(Dellar Walkley and Hocking, *Innovations Upper Intermediate* 2004: 78)

---

1 Complete the following conversation with the most appropriate expression from the lists below. (Most help to convey the personal point of view of the speakers.)

EVE:	You sound a bit out of breath. Are you OK?	
DEBRA:	I'm exhausted!	
EVE:	Another tough work-out in the gym —(1)—.— (2)— I think that kind of thing is a waste of time.	
DEBRA:	The company insists on it —(3)—. We even have a gym at work.	
EVE:	—(4)— they give you time off to go there.	
DEBRA:	You're kidding! We're expected to go at lunchtime. It's not too bad, though. —(5)— I get to see Tony. — (6)— he's in pretty good shape, given how much he eats.	
EVE:	—(7)— you're not still seeing him, are you?	
DEBRA:	—(8)—, we've become very close recently.	
EVE:	—(9)— dear Debra, I think you're mad. He's not worth it. He's —(10)— seeing someone else anyway.	

	A	B	C
1	generally	I suppose	really
2	To my mind	Personally	Naturally
3	undoubtedly	seriously	unfortunately
4	Honestly	Broadly speaking	Presumably
5	Frankly	At least	In my opinion
6	Surprisingly	Perhaps	Obviously
7	Certainly	Surely	I imagine
8	Eventually	Consequently	Actually
9	To be honest	Hopefully	Evidently
10	anyhow	strictly speaking	probably

Now answer the following questions.

a) What do you think Eve is trying to persuade Debra to do? Could she have personal reasons of her own?
b) How will Debra respond?

2 Find at least one attitude word or expression in the box below that can be used when you want to:
a) contradict someone.
b) express your opinion forcefully.
c) express surprise.

as a matter of fact   definitely   clearly   apparently   luckily
as far as I know   as far as I'm concerned   between you and me
amazingly   curiously   funnily enough   strangely

3 Write a conclusion to the conversation in Exercise 1. Use at least
   five attitude words or expressions from Exercises 1 and 2.

   (Bell and Gower, *Upper Intermediate Matters*, 1992: 110

Often we want to give ourselves thinking time before we answer
a question, especially if we don't understand it! Here are four
techniques:

Techniques	Examples	Advantages	Disadvantages
Pretend you haven't heard	*Pardon?* *Sorry?* *Eh?*	Simple – only one word to remember.	Everyone does it.
Repeat the question	*You mean . . . what is forty-five divided by nine?*	Lots of thinking time.	Can you remember the question?
Use delaying noises	*Well . . .* *Um . . .* *Er . . .*	You can use them several times in the same sentence.	If you use them too often you sound stupid.
Use *it depends*	*It depends.* *It depends on (the situation).*	You will sound intelligent. (Stroke your chin at the same time).	You can only use it when there is more than one possible answer.

Don't forget that you can use more than one technique.

*Sorry? You want to know what I think about this? Well . . . um . . .
it depends, really.*

Ask your partner questions. You partner tries to get thinking time.
You can ask:
– mathematical questions *What's five hundred divided by twenty?*

- factual questions *What's the capital of Mongolia?*
- moral questions *Should we kill animals for their fur?*
- personal questions *Do you believe in Father Christmas?*

(Viney and Viney, *Handshake: A Course in Communication*, 1996: 79)

Casual conversations do not have a fixed structure. They tend to
- be open ended
- be about subjects which the speakers know about
- cover a range of topics.

Topic changes are sometimes indicated by the use of certain words eg

OK   *Oh well*   *Anyway*   *Oh by the way*   *Well um*

They can tell us that a speaker is moving onto a different aspect of the same topic or a new topic altogether.

1 Listen to the cassette. The topics Helen and Eduardo discuss are listed on the table. Write the statement or question which begins each new topic in the right-hand column. The first one has been done for you.

	Topic	Question or statement
a	Pram	*Can I give you a hand with that pram?*
b	Settling in	
c	Location of the flats	
d	Baby	
e	Girls starting school	
f	Taking children to school	
g	Shopping	

2 What is most common way that Eduardo and Helen begin a new topic? Tick the correct answer.

A statement ☐   A question ☐

3 Are any of these words used before a topic change? Listen again.
  a. Tick the words you hear.
     OK ☐   Oh ☐   Anyway ☐   Oh by the way ☐   Well um ☐

  b. Which words were used most often in this conversation?

(Delaruelle, *Beach Street*, 1998: 6–7)

D Role play

1 Work in pairs. Imagine that you are two passengers sitting next to each other on a long flight. Spend two or three minutes reading the cards below and thinking about what you will say.

> **STUDENT A**
> You are flying home to your own country. Invent some details about yourself (your name, age, job, family, interests, etc.) Student B is a tourist who has never visited your country before. Chat with him/her about yourself, and recommend places to visit and things to do during your visit.

> **STUDENT B**
> You are a tourist visiting Student A's country for the first time. Invent details about yourself (your name, age, job, family, interests, reason for visiting, etc.) Chat to Student A about yourself, and ask him/her questions about himself/herself. Also ask about his/her country (places to visit, things to do, etc.)

2 **You are ready to have your conversation. It is fifteen minutes until lunch is served, so try to keep talking for all of that time. Remember you can use short questions (*Do you?*, *Are you?*, etc.) to show interest.**

(Cunningham and Moor, *Cutting Edge*, 1998: 47)

B: In the following extract, a teacher is interacting with a small group of Spanish-speaking adult elementary learners.
1. Identify any instances of:

      reformulation
      elaboration
      comment
      repetition

What are the functions of the teacher's repetitions, do you think?

2. Evaluate the teacher's *responsiveness*, and the overall *contingency* of the extract.

3. To what extent does the teacher's talk fulfil the recommendations made by Kramsch (on page 314)?

4. To what extent is the above extract an instance of 'conversationally embedded instruction'? How might it have been made more so?

(1) T:	How many, uh, how many meals do you eat a day?
(2) S1:	In general or personally?
(3) T:	Personally.
(4) S1:	Two.
(5) T:	Only two?
(6) S1:	Mm-mm.
(7) T:	What? What meals?
(8) S1:	*Es difí . . . Es difícil, pero . . .*
(9) T:	What? It's *difícil*?
(10) S2:	Difficult.
(11) S1:	Yes. Two, two. And one coffee.
(12) T:	OK.
(13) S2:	I, I eat more.
(14) T:	What about – how many meals do you eat?
(15) S2:	Five.
(16) T:	Five!
(17) T:	What is, what's the biggest meal? What's the biggest meal of the day?
(18) S4:	Here? Here? The big? . . . the lunch.
(19) T:	Lunch. Yeah. I think so . . . usually in America, and I think Britain as well, dinner is the big meal . . . the biggest meal.
(20) S4:	*¿Sí? Es que . . .* why?
(21) T:	Why? Uh. . . . I don't know why. Tradition.
(22) S4:	Is, is bad .. . . . for the sleeping.
(23) T:	Hmm, yeah, but = =
(24) S4:	= = Is very bad.
(25) T:	uh, usually we eat dinner earlier than, uh = =
(26) S2:	= = You eat what?
(27) T:	We eat dinner earlier . . . so . . . [several students speaking simultaneously]
(28) S1:	I think, uh, they . . . work . . . uh, early . . . and come back . . . home earlier . . . and . . . *se reunen, ¿cómo se dice?* [*They come together, how do you say it?*]
(29) T:	They . . . eat together.
(30) S1:	Yeah.
(31) T:	They come together.
(32) S1:	The family together.
(33) T:	Exactly.
(34) S1:	Take, uh . . . lunch.

(35) S2:   In Spanish.
(36) S3:   *El marido . . . [The husband . . .]*
(37) S1:   In the lunch . . . everybody work in the city . . . than
(38) T: Exactly. That's true.
(39) S2:   The food = =
(40) S1:   = = the food a sandwich.
(41) T: Yeah, and because in America we don't have a siesta,
           we don't have three hours.
           [laughter]
(42) S4:   Is cheaper.
(43) S2:   And, and one hour for . . .?
(44) T: Yeah . . . or half an hour. Yeah . . . OK, so these are the
           things. Yeah. Usually these are kind of the main meals,
           are like breakfast, lunch, and dinner. We talk about
           usually three meals. These are kind of . . . snacks. We
           have snacks, usually, between meals. Alright? A snack
           between lunch and dinner and a snack between
           breakfast and lunch maybe . . .
           Tell you what. Now I'm gonna tell you a little bit
           about, uh, *my* eating habits . . .

                                              (Authors' data)

Task key

Chapter 1

Evidence of spontaneity:

- back-tracking: *over a year, oh, well over a year ago*
- repetition: *about, about a year ago, About yeah well over a year ago*
- false starts: *But you never actually, did you know people in common?*
- (self) repair: *. . . the peop . . . person*

Evidence of reciprocity:

- back-channelling: *Oh really?*
- question–answer (adjacency pair): *. . . did you know people in common? Yes.*
- discourse markers and interactional signals: *yes, yes definitely, but, well, and*

Evidence of interpersonality:

- topic focus on 'human interest'
- appraisal language: *. . . I couldn't believe it; It's incredible . . . No doubts, yeah*
- humour and laughter
- parallel utterances (suggesting empathy): *Adam used to think there were these strange people next door . . . And now we KNOW there were strange people next door.*

Chapter 2

1. *Lexical density*: If fillers (*um*) and interactional signals like *yeah* are counted as function words, there are 140 function words compared to 117 content words in the transcript, giving a (low) lexical density of 45% (the proportion of content words to total words).
2. As a measure of *lexical variety*, the type–token ratio is 0.35, indicating a lot of repetition.
3. There are eight low-frequency words, i.e. words outside the 2,000

most frequent words band: *feature, buttery, couch, darling, gorgeous, smart, terrific,* and the proper name *Lesley.*

4. Candidates for *keyword* status include: *wall, blue, bold, fifties, paint, painted, yellow, terrific* (three mentions each), and *feature, couch, pink* and *gorgeous* (two mentions each).

5. Derived forms: *paint, painted*; synonyms: *fairly, quite*; *nice, lovely, gorgeous, beautiful*; *great, terrific, smart*; *bold, strong, hot*; (near) antonyms: *uncomfortable*; *terrific*; co-hyponyms: *(hot) pink, (buttery/bright) yellow, (royal) blue,* plus superordinate term: *colour*; lexical set: *room, wall, couch, bedroom.*

6. Cross-turn repetitions: *something bold – something fairly bold*; *back to the fifties – what do you mean 'back to the fifties'?*; *feature walls – feature wall.*

7. Vague language: *too too*; *something fairly bold*; *a sort of a buttery yellow.*

8. Fillers: *(but) um*; stallers : *she's got this you know this terrific one wall . . . that's you know that's*

9. Discourse markers: *I think, well, cause, oh, and, and then, but then* interactional signals: *yes, yeah.*

10. Lexical phrases/conversational routines: *I think; I find it; the most . . . in the world; what do you mean?*

11. Bundles – two words: *I think; you know, she's got; sort of; it looks; I like*; three words: *I'm going to; in front of; in the world*; four or more words: *I thought I'd just; what do you mean? as long as it's not.*

12. Appraisal language: *nice, quite like it, find it too too, lovely, terrific, gorgeous, great, beautiful, most uncomfortable, fairly bold, I like, quite smart.*

Chapter 3

A.

1. Most of the turns consist of clausal units, e.g., *We have to maybe dismantle the sauna; I don't know about that; But how sort of if we don't calculate the kids; you're probably looking at roughly thirty people having dinner.* The following are examples of syntactic non-clausal units: *Like a horseshoe. A horseshoe type thing. Not very interesting.* The following are inserts: *Well. No. But see. Yeah, Oh good. Oh yeah. Mmm. Yes.*

2. Heads: ***But the spa**, you might want to use it; **And the kids**, I think the kids need to be . . . **And with the speeches** – it's not for the kids . . .*

Task key

Tails: *you might want to use it,* **you know**; *Just in case we need some more room* **or whatever**; *it's not very nice* **is it?** *it's not for the kids* **not very interesting.**

3. Deictic language: personal deixis is expressed in the personal pronouns (*we, I, you* etc.); examples of spatial deixis include: *where is that going to be moved to? sticking out the side* **there**; *have something in the middle for people* **here**, . . . *coming down* **there**; **here** *at least everyone can see* . . . one example of temporal deixis is: *this week.*

4. Questions: *What are you using as tables?* = interrogative, *wh*-question; to elicit information; *Are you going to hire like a type of . . .?* = interrogative, *yes/no* (polarity) question; to elicit information; *They sort of bring the tables?* = declarative; to elicit confirmation; *You thought having people on opposite sides then might be a bit much?* = declarative; to elicit confirmation; *Yeah, it's not very nice is it?* = question tag; to elicit agreement.

5. Modality – turn 1: *have to* (intrinsic; obligation); turn 3: *probably* (extrinsic; probability); turn 4: *could* (extrinsic; ability/probability); *would* (extrinsic; hypothetical possibility); turn 6: *can* (extrinsic; theoretical possibility); turn 7: *might* (extrinsic; probability); turn 10: *have got to* (intrinsic; obligation); turns 11, 12, 15: *going to* (intrinsic; intention/volition); turn 15: *don't have to* (intrinsic; negative obligation); turn 17: *could* (extrinsic; probability); turn 20: *will* (extrinsic; predictability); turn 23: *might* (extrinsic; probability); turn 24: *can* (extrinsic; ability); turn 27: *need to* (intrinsic; necessity); *have to* (intrinsic; obligation); turns 29 and 31: *probably* (extrinsic; probability); turn 34: *won't* (extrinsic; predictability).

B. The speaker uses the past simple to situate the event in past time (*we were burgled*) and the past continuous (*I was breastfeeding*) to provide ongoing background information. She uses the past continuous again (*I was getting up*) to provide a frame for the series of events that constitute the robbery, narrated in the past simple (*came in, went, helped themselves*, etc.). She uses the past perfect (*we'd been burgled*) to report events that happened retrospective to the point in time when the burglary was discovered (*I got up* . . .). She uses the 'future-in-the-past' (*we were going up to Cairns . . . we'd be away . . .*) to report future plans as seen from the viewpoint of the past (*we knew*), and a series of past simple events to describe what happened subsequently (*they came back, they took . . .*).

C. 1. Reporting verb *said* followed by direct speech (*before you go to France . . .*); reporting verb *said* followed by direct speech introduced with a discourse marker (*okay . . .*); reported thoughts introduced with discourse markers: *okay, right I'm ready . . .*

2. Reporting verb *said* followed by direct speech (*I'd like to join; Have you got anything published?*); reporting verb *said* followed by direct speech introduced with discourse marker (*well, how will we join you under? well, yes . . .; we'll, we'll join you . . .*).

Chapter 4

Task 1:

Examples of grammatical cohesion

- Reference: *I*; *it*; *this*; *that*; *she*; *you*
- Conjunctions: *and*; *then*; *but*

Examples of lexical cohesion:

- room: the side wall
- colour: this terrific bold bright
- room: house
- colour: pink and yellow; hot pink; royal pink
- couch: couch
- bold: bold
- room: middle wall
- fifties: fifties
- middle wall: feature walls

Task 2:

i) Examples of adjacency pairs:

CRAIG:	Kate I must say this fish is cooked beautifully.	complement	First pair part
MOTHER:	It's lovely darling.	complement	Insertion sequence
KATE:	Thanks. Thank you Craig so much for saying so.	response	Second pair part
CRAIG:	Grab the pan.	instruct	First pair part
JANE:	Oh no I'll grab the pan I think.	receipt	Second pair part
KATE:	Oh.		
JANE:	Oh no no. It's I'm sorry.	receipt	Post-sequence
FATHER:	Is that electricity is it?	question	First pair part

CRAIG:	It's gas.	answer	Second pair part
KATE:	Mum you're not enjoying your dinner are you?	question	First pair part
MOTHER:	I am.	response	Second pair part
CRAIG:	She is. Her fish. Look at these chefs they're so sensitive aren't they.		Insertion sequence
MOTHER:	But you know that I have a very small appetite.		Post-sequence
JANE:	Turn it down.	request	First pair part
CRAIG:	She says she prefers cigarettes to fish.		Insertion sequence
JANE:	Oh shut up. I didn't say ==that.		Insertion sequence
MOTHER:	==Well that's a fair comment.	grant	

ii) Exchange structure analysis with different move types classified:

CRAIG:	Kate I must say this fish is cooked beautifully.	Initiating move: Statement
MOTHER:	It's lovely darling.	Initiating move: Statement
KATE:	Thanks	Response: Acknowledge:
KATE:	Thank you Craig so much for saying so	Response: Acknowledge:
CRAIG:	Grab the pan.	Command
JANE:	Oh no I'll grab the pan I think.	Response to command
KATE:	Oh.	Response: Acknowledge
JANE:	Oh no no.	Tracking move: Clarify
JANE:	It's I'm sorry	Initiating move: Statement
FATHER:	Is that electricity is it?	Initiating move: Question
CRAIG:	It's gas.	Response: Answer
KATE:	Mum you're not enjoying your dinner are you?	Initiating move: Question
MOTHER:	I am.	Response: Answer 1
CRAIG:	She is. Her fish.	Response: Answer 2
CRAIG	Look at these chefs they're so sensitive aren't they.	Initiating move: Statement
MOTHER:	But you know that I have a very small appetite.	Challenging move

JANE:	Turn it down.	Initiating move: Command
CRAIG:	She says she prefers cigarettes to fish.	Challenging move
JANE:	Oh shut up. I didn't say ==that.	Response to challenge
MOTHER:	==Well that's a fair comment.	Response to challenge 2

iii) Describe the different types of feedback in the transcript and the role that these perform in this conversation.

iv) Describe the ways the speakers introduce, develop and change topics in this conversation.

Extract 2: "Bandon Grove"

		Feedback	Topic management
CRAIG:	Kate I must say this fish is cooked beautifully.		Craig introduces topic of Kate's cooking
MOTHER:	It's lovely darling.		
KATE:	Thanks. Thank you Craig so much for saying so. Jane Jane's not happy.		Kate develops the topic by introducing Jane's dislike of fish
JANE:	Mine's cold and [**general laughter**]	Non-verbal vocalizations	
MOTHER:	You're having me on. [inaudible overlap]		
KATE:	Well Jane think of smoked salmon.		
CRAIG:	Grab the pan.		
JANE:	**Oh no** I'll grab the pan I think.	Assessment (Jane indicates engagement with Craig's command, by indicating that she should do it instead	
KATE:	**Oh.**	Continuers (Kate is signalling to Jane to continue)	
JANE:	**Oh no no.** It's I'm sorry.	Assessment (Jane indicates engagement with Craig's	

331

		Feedback	Topic management
		command, by indicating that she should do it instead)	
CRAIG:	Mmm. Mine is sensational. Sensational.	Acknowledgement (Craig indicates understanding of Jane's utterance)	
JANE:	It's alright Kate. Oh the pan's been washed has it.		
CRAIG:	It hasn't has it. God mine's terrific. Do you know how to turn the stove on? Look everybody watch this is the this is the stove turning on demo. Stand back so you can see. Turn it to the right. Turn it on like that press the button. Very easy.		
FATHER:	**Oh** automatic.	Continuers (Father is signalling to Craig to continue)	
CRAIG:	You don't even need a match.		
KATE:	**Mmm.**	Acknowledgement (Kate indicates agreement of Craig's utterance)	
FATHER:	Is that electricity is it?		
CRAIG:	It's gas.		
KATE:	Mum you're not enjoying your dinner are you?		Topic recycle (from the stove back to discussing the food)
MOTHER:	I am.		
CRAIG:	She is. Her fish. Look at these chefs they're so sensitive aren't they.		

		Feedback	Topic management
MOTHER:	But you know that I have a very small appetite.		
			Topic shift (from fish to a small appetite)
KATE:	Si.	Acknowledgement (Kate indicates understanding of what Mother said)	
MOTHER:	Si.	Acknowledgement	
[. . .]			
JANE:	Oh dear. I'm very . . . [whispers] I absolutely hate the smell of fish cooking.		Topic shift (from Mother's small appetite to the smell of fish)
MOTHER:	What?		
JANE:	Turn it down.		Topic change
CRAIG:	She says she prefers cigarettes to fish.		Topic shift (from fish to cigarettes)
JANE:	Oh shut up. I didn't say ==that.	Assessment (Jane indicates disagreement of Craig's utterance)	
MOTHER:	==Well that's a fair comment.		
CRAIG:	Oh so.	Assessment	
CRAIG:	Oh so.	Assessment	
KATE:	Just leave her alone.		
CRAIG:	Oh.	Acknowledgement	
KATE:	Nothing worse than bloody . . .		
CRAIG:	Vigilantes.		
KATE:	Non smokers.		
JANE:	Oh look will you all shut up.	Acknowledgement	
CRAIG:	[laughs]	Non-verbal vocalisations	
JANE:	I really do hate the smell of fish.		Topic recycle
CRAIG:	Well we'll stop cooking it now.		
MOTHER:	Well we won't do it again.		

(OZTALK)

333

Task key

Task 2 (iv):

The different cultural assumptions to explore are:

- the familiarity of the participants and how this influences not only what is talked about but how it is talked about. For example, criticizing the food that has been served is only appropriate in these cultural contexts because the participants are close family members.
- the generational differences: the mother plays a placating role, for example; *Well that's a fair comment* and *Well we won't do it again*. There is no noticeable use of deferential language to the mother or the father.
- the gender differences: the cooking is shared and so are the tasks in the kitchen; Craig humourously does a stove demonstration.
- Teasing each other occurs in the context of high familiarity as does disagreement and bantering. For example when Craig teases Jane about smoking; and she argues back:

Craig: She says she prefers cigarettes to fish.
Jane: Oh shut up. I didn't say ==that.

Chapter 5

Task 1: Schematic structure of Extract 1:

STAGES	SPEAKER	TRANSCRIPT
Abstract: Orientation:	RICHARD:	I'll tell you one thing when we moved to London and we'd been here for about a month and we were just driving around looking at the sights and we were driving past Buckingham Palace right and Chloe's in the back of the car right
Remarkable Event:		this is so funny um and she said there it is there's Buckingham Palace woah woah oh we should open the window oh and the Queen lives there oh look the flag's up the Queen's in there now and she said is that the Queen's house then? and we said yeah she said ooh fancy building a palace next to the main road

STAGES	SPEAKER	TRANSCRIPT
Reaction:	RAJ, R & J:	(*laughter*)
	JUDY:	on the main road (*laughs*) which is logical
	RICHARD:	which is very observant absolutely why did they do that she said and actually I couldn't think, because the road was probably there when they built it although there wouldn't have been cars on it
Coda:	RAJ:	I hope you praised her for making a good point
	RICHARD:	well we fell apart

What micro-features of a conversational anecdote does it display?

Stages	Transcript	Language Features
Abstract signals that a story is about to be told	I'll tell you one thing	signals the onset of the story; and implicitly encodes evaluative comment
Orientation introduces characters and sets them in time and place	when we moved to London and we'd been here for about a month and we were just driving around looking at the sights and we were driving past Buckingham Palace right and Chloe's in the back of the car right	introduces character and sets them in time and place encodes circumstantial information (London; driving around looking at the sights; driving past Buckingham Palace)
Remarkable Event temporally orders actions outlining a remarkable event of which the narrator wants to share his reaction	this is so funny um and she said there it is there's Buckingham Palace woah woah oh we should open the window oh and the Queen lives there oh look the flag's up the Queen's in there now and she said is that the Queen's house then? and we said yeah she said ooh fancy building a palace next to the main road	'this is so funny' provides a break in the storyline and by doing so creates an expectation that something unusual is about to happen event sequenced in time temporal links are implicit, the text follows events in time use of reported speech which is a feature of retelling anecdote featuring a third party

Stages	Transcript	Language Features
Reaction evaluation of the events establishes significance of story	RAJ, R & J: (laughter) JUDY: on the main road (laughs) which is logical RICHARD: which is very observant absolutely why did they do that she said and actually I couldn't think because the road was probably there when they built it although there wouldn't have been cars on it	jointly constructed outburst of laughter (in amusing anecdotes) often occurs after remarkable event.
Coda makes point about text as a whole returns text to present	RAJ: I hope you praised her for making a good point RICHARD: well we fell apart	evaluation of the whole event and the use of attitudinal lexis, such as *praised*; *good* and *fell apart*. return to the present

Task 2: Schematic Structure of gossip:

Setting:

Participants: Debbie, aged 13, Australian; Francesca, aged 13, Australian; Christina, mother of Olivia

Context: The conversation takes place at Olivia's home in Sydney. The two girls attend school together and have been close friends all their lives. They are discussing two other girls who go to the same school.

Speaker	Schematic Structure	Transcript
Francesca:	Third Person Focus	You know, okay you know at lunchtime today when Susan says like, "Oh! DP likes you Liv" and I'm like, "Oh sure, Susan!" and she's like "No no no seriously!" He likes a girl who had her hair up at um at ==the play
Debbie:	Pejorative Evaluation	==Yeah Annie's like, "but yeah but I had my hair up half way through"==
Francesca:	Substantiating Behaviour	== And we're like "Well no you didn't Annie!" and she's like, "Yes I did" Well and Susan's like, and Katelan's like,

Speaker	Schematic Structure	Transcript
		"No you didn't!" And then, then she, anyway you know, Su- and then no, she'll say, and then all of us says, "No you didn't Annie!" And she's like, "Yeah I did, I put it up in the middle of the play no one just saw!" OK? Oh it's so sad.
Christina:	Probe	Was this the SCEGGS concert?
Francesca:	Pejorative Evaluation	It was then - do you know then, you know, she was like, "He's not even hot!" and oh my god "He's so ugly!" And I'm just like "Oh okay."
Debbie:	Pejorative Evaluation	She's so weird. Like, I don't get her sometimes.
Francesca:	Wrap-up	I kind of like her but then, then she's just being, she's not – but she seems really upset at school lately have you noticed that? Like not as in like. She's really strange.

Chapter 6

A. 1. In the first extract, in which Mark's language is syntactically and morphologically still very simple, he relies on repetition to maintain topic cohesion, and to connect his turns to his mother's. He shows some awareness of how to repair misunderstandings (as in *Mummy's flower?*). But he is still very reliant on his mother's scaffolding to maintain the conversational flow, and on the immediate external world to provide the topical content. In the second extract, Mark is able to control the direction of the conversation much more assertively, principally through his ability to ask questions, and to use question forms and imperatives in order to make requests, give commands, and as confirmation checks. He is much less reliant on his mother, and only at one point (*Break it up*) does he resort to direct repetition to connect turns; no repair is necessary and the conversation is both coherent and contingent, harmonizing with the ongoing activity that the two speakers are involved in, while also making occasional reference outside the immediate here-and-now (*I made this puzzle*).

2. The mother's talk, especially in the first extract, is characterized by clarification checks (*A man walked down there?*), confirmations (*Oh*

yes), elaborations (*Oh yes, the bonfire*), and continuing moves (*It will burn, won't it?*). In the second extract, where Mark is a more assertive conversational partner, she has to do less scaffolding work, and her role is more to direct the conduct of the task than to manage the construction of the talk.

B. Extract 1 consists entirely of IRF exchanges, where the teacher initiates by asking display questions, nominates the student who is to respond, and follows up the response with evaluative feedback, often involving a direct repeat of the student's response. There are no student-initiated turns; the teacher has complete control of the topic and the direction of the discourse, and also has much longer turns than the students. In Extract 2 the teacher's interventions serve less to check what the students already know than to help them construct (or *scaffold*) their developing understanding of the subject under discussion. This involves asking clarifying questions about the state and origins of the students' knowledge (*HOW do you know? . . . So, you're – you think it doesn't need food during THIS stage . . .?*) The few display questions (e.g., *What would the food be? Where does it come from?*) act as prompts to the formation of concepts, and the teacher's feedback is more 'conversational' (*uh-huh, yeah*). The students' turns are correspondingly longer, on average, than in the first extract, and they initiate more.

Chapter 7

Overall, the fluency, as indicated by length of turns, repetitions and hesitations, varies considerably. S1's turns, for example, are short, repetitious, sometimes incomplete, and seem hesitant and somewhat disconnected (*In my time when I go to sleep . . . These people is very good*). S2, on the other hand, not only helps scaffold S1's talk by recasting and elaborating his/her utterances (e.g, *You can't say, because if you say, maybe you will feel different*), but also uses S1's topic to embark on one extended, apparently fluent, turn in which he/she holds the floor even in the face of interruptions. S2 also responds to the other speakers' turns by backchannelling (*No good. Yeah, that's no good*, etc.). S4 also sustains a relatively long turn, although shows more evidence of dysfluency (*But I . . . it's difficult*). S5 has to be invited to talk, but is able to tell a coherent anecdote, involving direct speech, and a coda. S3's few contributions seem the least relevant (*Independence . . . those people probably very protective*), and, at least on this evidence, seems the least conversationally competent of the five.

Both S2 and S5 seem to be able to command some basic discourse markers, including *of course* and *for example*, and S4 uses *you know* both as an utterance head and a tail. S2 and S4 use indefinite pronouns (*anything, something*) and adverbs (*sometime*) to express vagueness and also, perhaps, as a communication and production strategy, so as to avoid time-consuming word searches. There is not a lot of evidence of formulaic and idiomatic language, although S2's *you might get upset, in my place*, and S4's *little bit hard* might qualify. Overall, the turntaking is reasonably fluid, and utterances are topically connected and contingent – in some cases, explicitly so, as when S1 incorporates S3's *You don't like it* to produce *I don't like it*, or when S2 responds to S4 (*It's difficult*) with *It's a difficult*. The couple of bursts of laughter also indicate a degree of conversational harmony and empathy. Only S1's rather abrupt nominating move (*Sarah, you tell*) reminds us that this is a group work, classroom task, rather than casual talk amongst friends.

Chapter 8

(a) The actual order of publication is as follows: 3. (Webster and Castañon, 1980); 1. (Swan and Walter, 1984); 4. (Mohamed and Acklam, 1995); and 2. (Betterton and Leigh, 2005).

(b) The coursebook conversations reflect naturally occurring conversation in these respects: (1) topic focus, i.e. prices, shopping; repetition of formulaic appraisal language (*It's terrible*; *oh dear*); reactive and supportive back-channelling (*No!!!*; *I know*); use of repetition in contingent utterances, e.g. B: *Do you know potatoes are eighty pence a kilo?* A: *Eighty pence a kilo? In our supermarket they're eighty-five.* (2) informal, colloquial style (*What's up? Oh bummer.* etc); narrative; use of discourse markers (*well*), and interactional signals (*hey! yeah*), continuing moves (*What happened? So . . .?*) and evaluative back-channelling devices: *Amazing. Lucky!* (3) opening moves (*Windy, isn't it?*); back-channelling (*Ah, really*); ellipsis (*To Germany*; *On holiday?*); repetition as a continuing move (*Steve: I'm going to take some photographs. Erika: Photographs?*); question-and-answer routines; question tags; topic management and topic shift; social formulae and adjacency pairs (*Would you like a . . .? Yes, I'd love one.*) (4) telephone openings and closings; formulaic language (e.g. *see you later*); appraisal language (*terrible*; *the worst thing is . . .*); interactional signals (*listen*; *great*; *right*) and discourse markers (*well, anyway, you know, of course*); responding moves using echo questions (*could she?*). The recordings of all four conversations might also display typical prosodic features of conversation, such as the use of intonation in questions and question tags, and the use of high key to initiate new topics.

Task key

(c) As models of the above features, all four conversations could usefully be exploited in the classroom, both in their recorded and their written forms.

Chapter 9

A. 1. The extract from *Innovations* targets the telling of conversational narratives; the approach is direct and it focuses on both top-down (i.e. macrostructure) and bottom-up features (i.e. discrete exponents of narrating). The second extract (from *Upper Intermediate Matters*) focuses on what are called *stance* (or attitude) markers. The approach is direct and bottom-up. The extract from *Handshake* targets ways of "buying time", e.g. by filling pauses, in conversation; again, the approach is direct and bottom-up. The extract from *Beach Street* highlights topic shift, and the discourse markers that signal a change in topic; the approach is direct and focuses both on top-down features of conversation, namely, topics, as well as the bottom-up indicators of topic shift. Finally, the role play takes an indirect, top-down approach to sustaining a conversation between strangers, although students are reminded to include some discrete, bottom-up items in the form of echo questions.

B. 1. Reformulation: turn 19; turns 29 and 31; elaboration: turn 19; comment: turns 21, 25, 27 and 41; repetition: turns 5, 9 and 16. Turn 5 and 16 show surprise; turn 9 is perhaps designed to elicit a repair in the form of the English word *difficult*.

2. The teacher is generally responsive, showing he is aware of what students are saying, and responding to their questions, although misses some opportunities to draw the students out (e.g. at turn 16), and seems to be intent on getting to the vocabulary teaching point (in turn 44) where his purpose is to itemize the meals.

3. At the level of turns-at-talk, the teacher does not always "encourage students . . . to take longer turns" but he does attempt to clarify and negotiate their meanings, as in the sequence from turn 28 to turn 41. At the level of topic management, he asks referential questions rather than display questions, and allows the students a measure of topic control, indicated by the number of questions they themselves ask (turns 2, 20, 26 and 43). Likewise, the teacher seems to be attending to the message, rather than the form, of the students' utterances, which is indicated by the few corrections and recasts, and he makes "extensive use of natural feedback".

4. The extract provides a context for the teacher to focus on key, topic-related words, such as *lunch* and *dinner*, and, in turn 44, he usefully sum-

340

marizes this vocabulary, as well as introducing the term *snack*. He translates a couple of student L1 utterances, but the relatively low number of recasts and corrections, and the fact that students are not prompted to self-correct, underlies the fact that there are few embedded instructional "asides". There are a number of points (e.g. turns 23, 33 and 38) where the learners' utterances could have been exploited for a focus on accuracy or idiomaticity.

References

Adolphs, S. and Schmitt, N. 2003. Lexical coverage of spoken discourse. *Applied Linguistics* 24: 425–38.

Aijmer, K. 1996. *Conversational Routines in English: Convention and Creativity*. Harlow: Longman.

Alesi, G. and Pantell, D. 1962. *First Book in American English*. New York: Oxford Book Company.

Alexander, L. 1967a. *First Things First*. London: Longman.

Alexander, L. 1967b. *First Things First: Teacher's Book*. London: Longman.

Allwright, R. 1979. Language learning through communication practice. In Brumfit, C. and Johnson, K. (eds.) *The Communicative Approach to Language Teaching*. Oxford: Oxford University Press.

Allwright, R. 2005. From teaching points to learning opportunities and beyond. *TESOL Quarterly*, 39, 9–32.

Andersen, E. 1978. Lexical universals of body-part terminology. In Greenberg, J. H. (ed.) *Universals of Human Language*, vol. 3 *Word Structure*. Stanford, CA; Standford University Press.

Anderson, A., Clark, A. and Mullin, J. 1994. Interactive communication between children: Learning how to make language work in dialogue. *Journal of Child Language*, 21, 439–63.

Austin, J. 1962. *How to Do Things with Words*. Cambridge: Cambridge University Press.

Bachman, L. 1990. *Fundamental Considerations in Language Testing*. Oxford: Oxford University Press.

Bachman, L. and Palmer, A. 1996. *Language Testing in Practice*. Oxford: Oxford University Press.

Bannink, A. 2002. Negotiating the paradoxes of spontaneous talk in advanced L2 classes. In Kramsch, C. (ed.) *Language Acquisition and Language Socialization*. London: Continuum.

Bardovi-Harlig, K. 2001. Evaluating the empirical evidence: Grounds for instruction in pragmatics? In Rose, K. and Kasper, G. (eds.) *Pragmatics in Language Teaching*. Cambridge: Cambridge University Press.

Bardovi-Harlig, K., Hartford, B., Mahan-Taylor, R., Morgan, M. and Reynolds, D. 1991. Developing pragmatic awareness: Closing the conversation. *ELT Journal*, 45, 4–15.

Basturkmen, H. 2001. Descriptions of spoken language for higher level learners: The example of questioning. *ELT Journal*, 55, 4–13.

Bell, J. and Gower, R. 1992. *Upper Intermediate Matters (Student's Book)*. Harlow: Longman.

References

Berger, P. and Luckmann, T. 1966. *The Social Construction of Reality: A Treatise in the Sociology of Knowledge.* New York: Doubleday.

Berlitz, M. 1906. *First Book for Teaching Modern Languages: English. Part for Adults.* Berlin, etc.: Berlitz.

Betterton, S. and Leigh, K. 2005. *Platform 2 (Student's Book).* Madrid: McGraw-Hill.

Biber, D., Johansson, S., Leech, G., Conrad, S. and Finegan, E. 1999. *Longman Grammar of Spoken and Written English.* Harlow: Longman.

Billows, F. L. 1961. *The Techniques of Language Teaching.* London: Longmans, Green.

Black, V., McNorton, M., Maldarez, A. and Parker, S. 1986. *Fast Forward 1, Classbook.* Oxford: Oxford University Press.

Block, D. 2003. *The Social Turn in Second Language Acquisition.* Edinburgh: Edinburgh University Press.

Bloom, L., Rocissano, L. and Hood, L. 1976. Adult–child discourse: Developmental interaction between information processing and linguistic knowledge. *Cognitive Psychology* 8, 521–52.

Blum-Kulka, S. 1991. Interlanguage pragmatics: The case of requests. In Phillipson, R., Kellerman, E., Selinker, L., Sharwood Smith, M. and Swain, M. (eds.) *Foreign/Second Language Pedagogy Research.* Clevedon: Multilingual Matters.

Blum-Kulka, S. 1997. *Dinner Talk: Cultural Patterns of Sociability and Socialization in Family Discourse.* Mahwah, NJ: Lawrence Erlbaum.

Borkin, A. and Reinhart, S. 1978. Excuse me and I'm sorry. *TESOL Quarterly,* 12 (1), 57–69.

Bouton, L. 1999. Developing nonnative speaker skills in interpreting conversational implicatures in English: Explicit teaching can ease the process. In Hinkel, E. (ed.) *Culture in Second Language Teaching and Learning.* Cambridge: Cambridge University Press.

Brazil, D. 1995. *A Grammar of Speech.* Oxford: Oxford University Press.

Brazil, D. 1997. *The Communicative Value of Intonation in English.* Cambridge: Cambridge University Press.

Brock, C. 1986. The effects of referential questions on ESL classroom discourse. *TESOL Quarterly,* 20, 47–59.

Brown, G. and Yule, G. 1983. *Discourse Analysis.* Cambridge: Cambridge University Press.

Brown, P. and Levinson, S. 1987. *Politeness: Some Universals in Language Use.* Cambridge: Cambridge University Press.

Brumfit, C. 1984. *Communicative Methodology in Language Teaching: The Roles of Fluency and Accuracy.* Cambridge: Cambridge University Press.

Bruner, J. 1974. *Beyond the Information Given: Studies in the Psychology of Knowing.* London: Allen & Unwin.

Burns, A. 1998. Teaching speaking. *Annual Review of Applied Linguistics,* 18, 102–23.

Burns, A. and Joyce, H. 1997. *Focus on Speaking.* Sydney: NCELTR.

Burns, A., Joyce, H. and Gollin, S. 1996. *'I see what you mean'. Using Spoken Discourse in the Classroom: A Handbook for Teachers.* Sydney: NCELTR.

References

Bygate, M. 1987. *Speaking.* Oxford: Oxford University Press.

Byrne, D. 1976. *Teaching Oral English.* Harlow: Longman.

Cadorath, J. and Harris, S. 1998. Unplanned classroom language and teacher training. *ELT Journal,* 52, 188–96.

Cambridge Advanced Learner's Dictionary. 2005. (2nd edition.) Cambridge: Cambridge University Press.

Canale, M. 1983. From communicative competence to communicative language pedagogy. In Richards, J. and Schmidt, R. (eds.) *Language and Communication.* Harlow: Longman.

Canale, M. and Swain, M. 1980. Theoretical bases of communicative approaches to second language teaching and testing. *Applied Linguistics* 1 1–47.

Carter, R. 2004. *Language and Creativity: The Art of Common Talk.* London: Routledge.

Carter, R. and McCarthy, M. 1995. Grammar and the spoken language. *Applied Linguistics,* 16: 141–58.

Carter, R. and McCarthy, M. 1997. *Exploring Spoken English.* Cambridge: Cambridge University Press.

Carter, R. and McCarthy, M. 2006. *The Cambridge Grammar of English.* Cambridge: Cambridge University Press.

Cash, C., Aherne, C. and Normal, H. 2002. *The Royle Family: The Complete Scripts.* London: Granada Media.

Cazden, C. 1992. *Whole Language Plus: Essays on Literacy in the United States and New Zealand.* New York: Teachers College Press.

Chambers, F. 1997. What do we mean by fluency? *System,* 25, 535–44.

Channell, J. 1994. *Vague Language.* Oxford: Oxford University Press.

Cheepen, C. 1988. *The Predictability of Informal Conversation.* London: Pinter.

Chomsky, N. 1965. *Aspects of the Theory of Syntax.* Cambridge, MA: MIT Press.

Clark, R. 1974. Performing without competence. *Journal of Child Language 1,* 1–10.

Clennell, C. 1999. Promoting pragmatic awareness and spoken discourse skills with EAP classes. *ELT Journal,* 53, 83–91.

Coates, J. 1995. The role of narrative in the talk of women friends. Paper presented at The University of Technology, Sydney.

Coates, J. 1996. *Women Talk: Conversation between Women Friends.* Oxford: Blackwell.

Coates, J. 2003. *Men Talk.* Oxford: Blackwell.

Cohen, A. 1996. Speech acts. In McKay, S. and Hornberger, N. (eds.) *Sociolinguistics and Language Teaching.* Cambridge: Cambridge University Press.

Cohen, A. 1997. Developing pragmatic ability: Insights from intensive study of Japanese. In Cook, H., Hijirida, K. and Tahara, M. (eds.) *New Trends and Issues in Teaching Japanese Language and Culture.* Honolulu: Hawai'i University Press.

Collins' COBUILD English Dictionary. 1995. London: HarperCollins.

Cook, G. 2000. *Language Play, Language Learning.* Oxford: Oxford University Press.

Cope, B. and Kalantzis, M. (eds.) 1993. *The Powers of Literacy: A Genre Approach to Teaching Writing.* London: Falmer.

Coulthard, M. 1985. *An Introduction to Discourse Analysis.* (New edition.) Harlow: Longman.

Coulthard, M. and Brazil, D. 1981. Exchange Structure. In Coulthard, M. and Montgomery, M.M. (eds.) *Studies in Discourse Analysis.* London: Routledge.

Council of Europe. 2001. *Common European Framework of Reference for Languages: Learning, Teaching, Assessment.* Cambridge: Cambridge University Press.

Coupland, J. 2000. *Small Talk.* London: Longman.

Crystal, D. 1980. Neglected grammatical factors in conversational English. In Greenbaum, S., Leech, G. and Svartvik, I. (eds.) *Studies in English Linguistics for Randolph Quirk.* London: Longman.

Crystal, D. 1987. *The Cambridge Encyclopedia of Language.* Cambridge: Cambridge University Press.

Crystal, D. 2001. *Language and the Internet.* Cambridge: Cambridge University Press.

Crystal, D. and Davy, D. 1975. *Advanced Conversational English.* Harlow: Longman.

Cullen, R. 1997. Teacher talk and the classroom context. *ELT Journal*, 52, 179–87.

Cullen, R. 2002. Supportive teacher talk: The importance of the F-move. *ELT Journal*, 56, 117–27.

Cunningham, S. and Moor, P. 1998. *Cutting Edge. Intermediate (Student's Book).* Harlow: Longman.

Cummins, J. and Swain, M. 1986. *Bilingualism in Education.* Harlow: Longman.

Curran, C. 1976. *Counseling-Learning in Second Languages.* Apple River, Ill; Apple River Press.

Dalton, C. and Seidlhofer, B. 1994. *Pronunciation.* Oxford: Oxford University Press.

Dechert, H. 1983. How a story is done in a second language. In Faerch, C. and Kasper, G. (eds.) *Strategies in Interlanguage Communication.* Harlow: Longman.

de Cock, S., Granger, S., Leech, G. and McEnery, T. 1998. An automated approach to the phrasicon of EFL learners. In Granger, S. (ed.) *Learner English on Computer.* Harlow: Longman.

Delaruelle, S. 1998. *Beach Street: An English Course for Adults (Student's Book 2)* Sydney: AMES.

Dellar, H. and Hocking, D. 2004. *Innovations Upper Intermediate.* (2nd edition.) London: Thomson Heinle.

Dellar, H. and Walkley, A. 2005. *Innovations Elementary.* London: Thomson Heinle.

de Saussure, F. 1916/1974. *Cours de linguistique générale.* Lausanne: Librairie Payot. Reprinted as *Course in General Linguistics.* Glasgow: Fontana/Collins.

Doff, A., Jones, C. and Mitchell, K. 1983. *Meanings Into Words. Intermediate (Student's Book).* Cambridge: Cambridge University Press.

References

Dörnyei, Z. 1995. On the teachability of communicative strategies. *TESOL Quarterly*, 29, 55–83.

Dörnyei, Z. and Thurrell, S. 1992. *Conversation and Dialogues in Action*. Hemel Hempstead: Prentice Hall.

Dörnyei, Z. and Thurrell, S. 1994. Teaching conversational skills intensively: Course content and rationale. *ELT Journal*, 48, 40–9.

Doughty, C. and Williams, J. (eds.) 1998. *Focus on Form in Classroom Second Language Acquisition*. Cambridge: Cambridge University Press.

Douglas, M. 1975. *Implicit Meanings*. London: Routledge & Kegan Paul.

Dunbar, R. 1996. *Grooming, Gossip and the Evolution of Language*. London: Faber and Faber.

Dunham, P. 1992. Using compliments in the ESL classroom: An analysis of culture and gender. *MinneTESOL Journal*, 10, 75–85.

Eggins, S. 1994. *An Introduction to Systemic Functional Linguistics*. London: Pinter.

Eggins, S. and Martin, J. 1997. Genres and registers of discourse. In van Dijk, T. (ed.) *Discourse Studies: A Multidisciplinary Introduction. Volume 1: Discourse as structure and process*. London: Sage.

Eggins, S. and Slade, D. 1997. *Analysing Casual Conversation*. London: Equinox (previously published by Cassell).

Ellis, N. 1998. Emergentism, connectionism, and language learning. *Language Learning*, 48, 631–64.

Ellis, N. 2005. At the interface: Dynamic interactions of explicit and implicit language knowledge. *Studies in Second Language Acquisition*, 27, 305–52.

Ellis, R. 1990. *Instructed Second Language Acquisition*. Oxford: Blackwell.

Ellis, R. 1992. Learning to communicate in the classroom. *Studies in Second Language Acquisition*, 14, 1–23.

Ellis, R. 1994. *The Study of Second Language Acquisition*. Oxford: Oxford University Press.

Ellis, R. 1997. *Second Language Acquisition*. Oxford: Oxford University Press.

Ellis, R. 1998. Discourse control and the acquisition-rich classroom. In Renandya, W. and Jacobs, G. (eds.) *Learners and Language Learning*. Anthology series 39. Singapore: RELC.

Ellis, R. 2003. *Task-based Language Learning and Teaching*. Oxford: Oxford University Press.

Ernst, G. 1994. 'Talking Circle': Conversation and negotiation in the ESL Classroom. *TESOL Quarterly*, 28, 293–322

Fairclough, N. 1992. *Discourse and Social Change*. London: Blackwell.

Fairclough, N. 1995. *Critical Discourse Analysis*. London: Longman.

Feez, S. 1998. *Text-based Syllabus Design*. Sydney: NCELTR.

Firth, J.R. 1957. *Papers in Linguistics 1934–51*. Oxford: Oxford University Press.

Fishman, P. 1980/1990. Conversational insecurity, in Giles, H. *et al.* (eds.) *Language: Social Psychological Perspectives*. Oxford: Pergamon Press. Reprinted in Cameron, D. (ed.) 1990. *The Feminist Critique of Language*. London: Routledge & Kegan Paul.

Fletcher, P. 1988. *A Child's Learning of English*. Oxford: Blackwell.

Forster, E. M. 1990. *Aspects of the Novel*. London: Penguin.

Foster, P. 1998. A classroom perspective on the negotiation of meaning. *Applied Linguistics, 19*, 1–23.

Foster, S. 1990. *The Communicative Competence of Young Children.* Harlow: Longman.

Fraser, B. 1978. Acquiring social competence in a second language. *RELC Journal, 9*, 1–26.

Gairns, R. and Redman, S. 2002a. *Natural English: Intermediate Teacher's Book.* Oxford: Oxford University Press.

Gairns, R. and Redman, S. 2002b. A spoken syllabus. *English Teaching Professional, 25*, 5–7.

Gardner, R. 1994. (ed.) *Spoken Interaction Studies in Australia.* Special Volume of *Australian Review of Applied Linguistics*, Series S, Number 11.

Garfinkel, H. 1967. *Studies in Ethnomethodology.* Englewood Cliffs, NJ: Prentice Hall.

Geddes, M. and Sturtridge, G. 1994. *Intermediate Conversation.* Hemel Hempstead: Prentice Hall.

Gibbons, P. 2003. Mediating language learning: teacher interaction with ESL students in a content-based classroom. *TESOL Quarterly, 37*, 247–74.

Givón, T. 1979. *On Understanding Grammar.* New York: Academic Press.

Goffman, E. 1986/1974. *Frame Analysis: An Essay on the Organization of Experience.* (Rpt. edn.) Boston: Northeastern University Press.

Goffman, E. 1976. Replies and responses. *Language in Society, 5*, 254–313.

Goffman, E. 1981. *Forms of Talk.* Philadelphia: University of Pennsylvania Press.

Grant, L. and Starks, D. 2001. Screening appropriate teaching materials. Closings from textbooks and television soap operas. *IRAL* (Berlin, Germany), 39, 39–50.

Grice, H. P. 1975. Logic and conversation. In Cole, P. and Morgan, J. L. (eds.) *Syntax and Semantics 3: Speech Acts.* New York: Academic Press, 41–58.

Gumperz, J. 1982. *Discourse Strategies.* Cambridge: Cambridge University Press.

Gumperz, J., Jupp, T. and Roberts, C. 1979. *Crosstalk: A Study of Cross-cultural Communication.* Southall, Middlesex: National Centre for Industrial Language Training.

Gumperz, J. and Roberts, C. 1980. *Developing Awareness Skills for Interethnic Communication.* Singapore: Seameo Regional English Language Centre, Occasional papers: 12 April.

Halliday, M.A.K. 1975. *Learning How to Mean: Explorations in the Development of Language.* New York: Elsevier.

Halliday, M.A.K. 1978. *Language as Social Semiotic: The Social Interpretation of Language and Meaning.* London: Edward Arnold.

Halliday, M.A.K. 1985. *Spoken and Written Language.* Geelong, Vic: Deakin University Press (Republished 1989 by Oxford University Press).

Halliday, M.A.K. 1994. *Introduction to Functional Grammar.* (2nd edition.) London: Edward Arnold.

Halliday, M.A.K. and Hasan, R. 1976. *Cohesion in English.* London: Longman.

Halliday, M.A.K. and Hasan, R. 1985. *Language, Context and Text: Aspects of*

347

Language in a Social-semiotic Perspective. Geelong, Vic: Deakin University Press (Republished 1989 by Oxford University Press).

Halliday, M.A.K. and Matthiessen, C. 2004. *An Introduction to Functional Grammar.* (3rd edition.) London: Hodder and Stoughton.

Halliday, M.A.K., McIntosh, A. and Strevens, P. 1964. *The Linguistic Sciences and Language Teaching.* London: Longman.

Hammond, J. 1987. An overview of the genre-based approach to the teaching of writing in Australia. *Australian Review of Applied Linguistics*, 10, 163–81.

Hasan, R. 1996. *Ways of Saying: Ways of Meaning.* London: Cassell.

Hatch, E. 1978. Discourse analysis and second language acquisition. In Hatch, E. (ed.) *Second Language Acquisition: A Book of Readings.* Rowley, MA: Newbury House.

Haycraft, J. 1978. *An Introduction to English Language Teaching.* Harlow: Longman.

Higgs, T. and Clifford R. 1982. The push towards communication. In Higgs, T. (ed.) *Curriculum, Competence, and the Foreign Language Teacher.* Skokie, Ill: National Textbook Co.

Hillier, H. 2004. *Analysing Real Texts.* Basingstoke: Palgrave Macmillan.

Hobbs, J. 2005. Interactive lexical phrases in pair interview tasks. In Edwards, C. and Willis, J. (eds.) *Teachers Exploring Tasks in English Language Teaching.* Basingstoke: Palgrave Macmillan.

Hoey, M. 1991. *Patterns of Lexis in Text.* Oxford: Oxford University Press.

Hoey, M. 2005. *Lexical Priming.* Oxford: Routledge.

Holmes, J. 1995. *Women, Men and Politeness.* Harlow: Longman.

House, J. 1996. Developing pragmatic fluency in English as a foreign language. *Studies in Second Language Acquisition*, 18, 225–52.

Howatt, A. 2004. *A History of English Language Teaching.* (2nd edition.) Oxford: Oxford University Press.

Hübscher, J. and Frampton, H. 1947. *A Modern English Grammar, 1,* Lausanne: Librairie Payot.

Hughes, R. 2002. *Teaching and Researching Speaking.* London: Longman.

Hughes, R. and McCarthy, M. 1998. From sentence to discourse: discourse grammar and English Language Teaching. *TESOL Quarterly*, 33, 263–87.

Hutchby, I. and Wooffitt, R. 1998. *Conversation Analysis.* Cambridge: Polity Press.

Hymes, D. 1972a. Models of the interaction of language and social life. In Gumperz, J. and Hymes, D. (eds.) *Directions in Sociolinguistics: The Ethnography of Communication.* New York: Holt, Rinehart & Winston.

Hymes, D. 1972b. On communicative competence. In Pride, J. and Holmes, J. (eds.) *Sociolinguistics: Selected Readings.* Harmondsworth: Penguin.

Itoh, H. and Hatch, E. 1978. Second language acquisition: A case study. In Hatch, E. (ed.) *Second Language Acquisition: A Book of Readings.* Rowley, MA: Newbury House.

Jarvis, J. and Robinson, M. 1997. Analysing educational discourse: An exploratory study of teacher response and support to pupils' learning. *Applied Linguistics*, 18, 212–28.

Jefferson, G., Sacks, H. and Schegloff, E. 1987. Notes on laughter in the pursuit of intimacy. In Button, G. and Lee, J. (eds.) *Talk and Social Organisation*. London: Multilingual Matters.

Johnson, Karen. 1995. *Understanding Communication in Second Language Classrooms*. Cambridge: Cambridge University Press.

Johnson, Keith. 1996. *Language Teaching and Skill Learning*. Oxford: Blackwell.

Jones, E. 2003. Developmental Record. Assignment submitted as part of the Trinity Diploma in TESOL, at City College Manchester (England).

Jones, R. 2001. A consciousness-raising approach to the teaching of conversational storytelling skills. *ELT Journal, 55*, 155–63.

Judd, E. 1999. Some issues in the teaching of pragmatic competence. In Hinkel, E. (ed.) *Culture in Second Language Teaching and Learning*. Cambridge: Cambridge University Press.

Kasper, G. and Rose, K. 2001. Pragmatics in language teaching. In Rose, K. and Kasper, G. (eds.) *Pragmatics in Language Teaching*. Cambridge: Cambridge University Press.

Kasper, G. and Rose, K. 2002. The role of instruction in learning second language pragmatics. *Language Learning (Supplement) 52*, 237–74.

Kay, S., and Jones, V. 2001. *Inside Out, Upper Intermediate (Student's Book)*. Oxford: Macmillan Heinemann.

Keller, E. and Warner, S. 1988. *Conversation Gambits*. Hove: Language Teaching Publications.

Kellerman, E. 1991. Compensatory strategies in second language research: A critique, a revision, and some (non-)implications for the classroom. In Phillipson, R., Kellerman, E., Selinker, L., Sharwood Smith, M. and Swain, M. (eds.) *Foreign/Second Language Pedagogy Research*. Clevedon: Multilingual Matters.

Kindt, D. 2000. *Don't Forget Your SOCCS! Developing Communication Skills with Students' Own Conversation Cards*. Nagoya, Japan: Department of British and American Studies, Nanzan University.

Klippel, F. 1984. *Keep Talking: Communicative Fluency Activities for Language Teaching*. Cambridge: Cambridge University Press.

Ko, J., Schallert, D. and Walters, K. 2003. Rethinking scaffolding: Negotiation of meaning in an ESL storytelling task. *TESOL Quarterly, 37*, 303–24.

Kramsch, C. 1985. Classroom interaction and discourse options. *Studies in Second Language Acquisition, 7*, 169–83.

Krashen, S. 1982. *Principles and Practice in Second Language Acquisition*. Oxford: Pergamon.

Kress, G. 1985. *Linguistic Processes in Sociolinguistic Practice*. Geelong, Victoria: Deakin University Press.

Kumaravadivelu, B. 2003. *Beyond Methods: Macrostrategies for Language Learning*. New Haven: Harvard University Press.

Labov, W. 1972. *Language in the Inner City*. Oxford: Basil Blackwell

Labov, W. and Waletzky, J. 1967. Narrative analysis: Oral versions of personal experience. In Helm, J. (ed.) *Essays in the Verbal and Visual Arts*. Seattle: University of Washington Press.

Levelt, W. 1989. *Speaking: From Intention to Articulation*. Cambridge: Cambridge University Press.

References

Lewis, M. 1993. *The Lexical Approach*. Hove: Language Teaching Publications.
Lewis, M. 1997. *Implementing the Lexical Approach*. Hove: Language Teaching Publications.
Littlewood, W. 1981. *Communicative Language Teaching: An Introduction*. Cambridge: Cambridge University Press.
Long, M. 1983. Native speaker/non-native speaker conversation and the negotiation of meaning. *Applied Linguistics*, 126–41.
Long, M. 1985. Input and second language acquisition theory. In Gass, S. and Madden, C. (eds.) *Input in Second Language Acquisition*. Rowley, MA: Newbury House.
Long, M. and Sato, C. 1983. Classroom foreigner talk discourse: forms and functions of teachers' questions. In Seliger, H. and Long, M. (eds.) *Classroom Oriented Research in Second Language Acquisition*. Rowley, MA: Newbury House.
Longman Dictionary of Contemporary English. 1995. (3rd edition). Harlow: Longman.
Lynch, T. 2001. Seeing what they meant: transcribing as a route to noticing. *ELT Journal*, 42, 124–32.
MacLure, M. and French, P. 1981. A comparison of talk at home and at school. In Wells, G. 1981. *Learning Through Interaction: The Study of Language Development*. Cambridge: Cambridge University Press.
Markee, N. 2000. *Conversation Analysis*. Mahwah, NJ: Lawrence Erlbaum.
Matsumuru, S. 2003. Modelling the relationships among interlanguage pragmatic development, L2 proficiency, and exposure to L2. *Applied Linguistics*, 24, 465–91.
Martin, J. 1984. Language, register and genre. In Christie, F. (ed.) *Children Writing: A Reader*. Geelong, Vic: Deakin University Press.
Martin, J. 1989. *Factual Writing: Exploring and Challenging Social Reality*. Oxford: Oxford University Press.
Martin, J. 1992. *English Text: System and Structure*. Amsterdam: John Benjamins.
Martin, J. 2000. Beyond exchange: Appraisal systems in English. In Hunston, S. and Thompson, G. (eds.) *Evaluation in Text: Authorial Stance and the Construction of Discourse*. Oxford: Oxford University Press.
Martin, J. and Rose, D. 2003. *Working with Discourse: Meaning Beyond the Clause*. London: Continuum.
McCarthy, M. 1988. Some vocabulary patterns in conversation. In Carter, R. and McCarthy, M. (eds.) *Vocabulary and Language Teaching*. Harlow: Longman.
McCarthy, M. 1991. *Discourse Analysis for Language Teachers*. Cambridge: Cambridge University Press.
McCarthy, M. 1998. *Spoken Language and Applied Linguistics*. Cambridge: Cambridge University Press.
McCarthy, M. 1999. What is a basic spoken vocabulary? *FELT Newsletter*, 1 (4), 7– .
McCarthy, M. 2003. Talking back: 'small' interactional response tokens in everyday conversation. *Research on Language in Social Interaction*, 36 (1): 33–6.

McCarthy, M. and Carter, R. 1995. Spoken grammar: What is it and how do we teach it? In *ELT Journal*, 49:3, 207–18.

McCarthy, M. and Carter, R. 1997. Written and spoken vocabulary. In Schmitt, N. and McCarthy, M. (eds.) *Vocabulary: Description, Acquisition, and Pedagogy*. Cambridge: Cambridge University Press.

McCarthy, M. and Carter, R. A. 2001. Ten criteria for a spoken grammar. In Hinkel, E. and Fotos, S. (eds.) *New Perspectives on Grammar Teaching in Second Language Classrooms*. Mahwah, NJ: Lawrence Erlbaum.

McCarthy, M., Matthiessen, C. and Slade, D. 2002. Discourse Analysis. In Schmitt, N. (ed.) *An Introduction to Applied Linguistics*. London: Edward Arnold.

McCarthy, M. and O'Keeffe, A. 2003. 'What's in a name?' Vocatives in casual conversations and radio phone in calls. In Leistyna, P. and Meyer, C. (eds.) *Corpus Analysis: Language Structure and Language Use*. Amsterdam: Rodopi.

McCarthy, M. and O'Keeffe, A. 2004. Research in the teaching of speaking. *Annual Review of Applied Linguistics* 24: 26–43

McKay, S. 2002. *Teaching English as an International Language*. Oxford: Oxford University Press.

McTear, M. 1985. *Children's Conversation*. Oxford: Basil Blackwell.

Mercer, N. 1995. *The Guided Construction of Knowledge: Talk Amongst Teachers and Learners*. Clevedon: Multilingual Matters.

Mitchell, T.F. 1957. The language of buying and selling in Cyrenaica: A situational statement. *Hespéris* XLIV: 31–71.

Mohamed, S. and Acklam, R. 1995. *Intermediate Choice (Student's Book)*. Harlow: Longman.

Mulkay, M. 1988. *On Humour*. London: Polity Press.

Myers, G. 1999. Functions of reported speech in group discussions. *Applied Linguistics* 20, 376–401.

Nakahama, Y., Tyler, A. and van Lier, L. 2001. Negotiation of meaning in conversational and informational gap activities: A comparative discourse analysis. *TESOL Quarterly*, 35, 377–406.

Nation, I.S.P. 1990. *Teaching and Learning Vocabulary*. New York: Newbury House.

Nattinger, J. 1988. Some current trends in vocabulary teaching. In Carter, R. and McCarthy, M. (eds.) *Vocabulary and Language Teaching*. Harlow: Longman.

Nattinger, J. and DeCarrico, J. 1992. *Lexical Phrases and Language Teaching*. Oxford: Oxford University Press.

Nelson, G., Carson, J., Al Batal, M. and El Bakary, W. 2002. Cross-cultural pragmatics: Strategy use in Egyptian Arabic and American English refusals. *Applied Linguistics*, 23, 163–89.

Nolasco, R. and Arthur, L. 1987. *Conversation*. Oxford: Oxford University Press.

Norrick, N. 1993. *Conversational Joking: Humor in Everyday Talk*. Bloomington, IN: Indiana University Press.

Norrick, N. 2000. *Conversational Narrative: Storytelling in Everyday Talk*. Amsterdam: John Benjamins.

Norton, B. 2000. *Identity and Language Learning: Gender, Ethnicity and Educational Change.* Harlow: Longman.

Nunan, D. 1987. Communicative language teaching: Making it work. *ELT Journal* 41, 136–45.

Nunan, D. 1989. *Understanding Language Classrooms.* Hemel Hempstead: Prentice Hall.

Nunan, D. 1990. The language teacher as decision maker. A case study. In Brindley, D. (ed.) *The Second Language Curriculum in Action.* Sydney: NCELTR.

Ochs, E. 1979. Planned and unplanned discourse. In Givón, T. (ed.) *Syntax and Semantics, Vol 12: Discourse and Semantics.* New York: Academic Press.

Ochs, E. 1983. Conversational competence in children. In Ochs, E. and Schieffelin, B. (eds.) *Acquiring Conversational Competence.* London: Routledge & Kegan Paul.

Ochs, E. 1997. Narrative. In van Dijk, T. (ed.) *Discourse Studies: A Multidisciplinary Introduction. Volume 1: Discourse as Structure and Process.* London: Sage.

O'Dell, F. 1997. *English Panorama, 1 (Student's Book).* Cambridge: Cambridge University Press.

Odlin, T. 1989. *Language Transfer: Cross-linguistic Influence in Second Language Acquisition.* Cambridge: Cambridge University Press.

O'Neill, R. 1970. *English in Situations.* Oxford: Oxford University Press.

Orton, J. 1976. *The Complete Plays.* London: Eyre Methuen.

Oxford Advanced Learner's Dictionary. 2000. (6th edition.) Oxford: Oxford University Press.

Palmer, H. 1940. *The Teaching of Oral English.* London: Longman.

Pawley, A. and Syder, F. 1983. Two puzzles for linguistic theory: Nativelike selection and nativelike fluency. In Richards, J. and Schmidt, R. (eds.) *Language and Communication.* Harlow: Longman.

Peccei, J. 1999. *Child Language.* (2nd edition.) London: Routledge.

Peters, A. 1983. *The Units of Language Acquisition.* Cambridge: Cambridge University Press.

Pica, T. 1987. Second language acquisition, social interaction, and the classroom. *Applied Linguistics*, 8: 3–21.

Picture it! Sequences for Conversation (1981). New York: Regents Publishing Company.

Pinter, H. 1967, 1991. *Tea Party and Other Plays.* London: Faber and Faber.

Plum, G. 1988. Text and contextual conditioning in spoken English: A genre-based approach. Unpublished PhD dissertation, University of Sydney.

Porter, P. 1986. How learners talk to each other: input and interaction in task-centred discussions. In Day, R. (ed.) *Talking to Learn: Conversation in Second Language Acquisition.* Rowley, MA: Newbury House.

Porter Ladousse, G. 1987. *Role Play.* Oxford: Oxford University Press.

Prabhu, N.S. 1987. *Second Language Pedagogy.* Oxford: Oxford University Press.

Pridham, F. 2001. *The Language of Conversation.* London: Routledge.

Prodromou, L. 1997. From corpus to octopus. *IATEFL Newsletter*, 137, 18–21.

Prodromou, L. (forthcoming) 'You see, it's sort of tricky for the L2 user': the puzzle of idiomaticity in English as a Lingua Franca. Unpublished PhD dissertation, University of Nottingham.

Ramsey, R. 1967. *English Through Patterns*. Barcelona: Editorial Teide.

Raupach, M. 1984. Formulae in second language speech production. In Dechert, H., Möhle, S. and Raupach, M. (eds.) *Second Language Production*. Tübingen: Gunter Narr.

Richards, J. 1990. Conversationally speaking: approaches to the teaching of conversation. In Richards, J. *The Language Teaching Matrix*. Cambridge: Cambridge University Press.

Richards, J. and Hull, J. 1987. *As I Was Saying: Conversation Tactics*. Tokyo: Addison Wesley.

Richards, J. and Rodgers, T. 1986. *Approaches and Methods in Language Teaching*. Cambridge: Cambridge University Press.

Richards, J. and Schmidt, R. 1983. Conversational analysis. In Richards, J. and Schmidt, R. (eds.) *Language and Communication*. Harlow: Longman.

Richards, J. and Schmidt, R. (eds.) 2002. *Dictionary of Language Teaching and Applied Linguistics*. (3rd edition.) Harlow: Longman.

Richards, J. and Sukwiwat, M. 1983. Language transfer and conversational competence. *Applied Linguistics*, 4: 113–25.

Rivers, W. 1968. *Teaching Foreign-Language Skills*. Chicago: University of Chicago Press.

Roberts, C. 2001. Language acquisition or language socialisation in and through discourse? Towards a redefinition of the domain of SLA. In Candlin, C. and Mercer, N. (eds.) *English Language Teaching in its Social Context: A Reader*. London: Routledge.

Rowe, M. 1986. Wait time: Slowing down may be a good way of speeding up. *Journal of Teacher Education*, 37, 43–50.

Sacks, H. 1972a. An initial investigation of the usability of conversational data for doing sociology. In D. Sudnow (ed.) *Studies in Social Interaction*. New York: Free Press.

Sacks, H. 1972b. On the analysability of stories by children. In Gumperz, J. and Hymes, D. (eds.) *Directions in Sociolinguistics*. New York: Holt, Rinehart and Winston.

Sacks, H. 1974. An analysis of the course of a joke's telling in conversation. In Bauman, R. and Sherzer, J. (eds.) *Explorations in the Ethnography of Speaking*. Cambridge: Cambridge University Press.

Sacks, H. 1978. Some technical considerations of a dirty joke. In Schenkein, J. (ed.) *Studies in the Organization of Conversational Interaction*. New York: Academic Press.

Sacks, H. 1992. *Lectures on Conversation*, vol II. Cambridge, MA.: Blackwell.

Sacks, H., Schegloff, E. A. and Jefferson, G. 1974. A simplest systematics for the organisation of turn-taking for conversation. *Language* 50: 696–735.

Sacks, O. 1985. *The Man Who Mistook His Wife for a Hat*. London: Picador.

Schegloff, E. and Sacks, H. 1973/74. Opening up closings. In Turner, R. (ed.) *Ethnomethodology*. Harmondsworth: Penguin. First printed in *Semiotica* 8, (3/4): 289–327.

References

Schenkein, J. (ed) 1978. *Studies in the Organization of Conversational Interaction*. New York: Academic Press.

Schiffrin, D. 1987. *Discourse Markers*. Cambridge: Cambridge University Press.

Schiffrin, D. 1994. *Approaches to Discourse*. Oxford: Blackwell.

Schmidt, R. 1983. Interaction, acculturation and the acquisition of communicative competence. In Wolfson, N. and Judd, E. (eds.) *Sociolinguistics and Second Language Acquisition*. Rowley, MA: Newbury House.

Schmidt, R. 1990. The role of consciousness in second language learning. *Applied Linguistics*, 11, 129–58.

Schmidt, R. 1992. Psychological mechanisms underlying second language fluency. *Studies in Second Language Acquisition*, 14, 357–85.

Schmidt, R. and Frota, S. 1986. Developing basic conversational ability in a second language: A case study of the adult learner of Portuguese. In Day, R. (ed.), *Talking to Learn: Conversation in Second Language Acquisition*. Rowley, MA: Newbury House.

Schmidt, R. and Richards, J. 1980. Speech acts and second language learning. *Applied Linguistics*, 1, 129–57.

Schmitt, N. 2000. *Vocabulary and Language Teaching*. Cambridge: Cambridge University Press.

Schmitt, N. and McCarthy, M. (eds.) 1997. *Vocabulary: Description, Acquisition and Pedagogy*. Cambridge: Cambridge University Press.

Schonell, F.J., Meddleton, I.G. and Shaw, B.A. 1956. *A Study of the Oral Vocabulary of Adults*. Brisbane: University of Queensland Press.

Scollon, R. 1976. *Conversations with a One-Year Old*. Honolulu: The University of Hawai'i Press.

Scollon, R. and Scollon, S.W. 1995. *Intercultural Communication: A Discourse Approach*. Oxford: Blackwell.

Scott, M. 1999. *WordSmith Tools, Version 3*. Oxford: Oxford University Press.

Scott, R. 1981. Role play. In Johnson, K. and Morrow, K. (eds.) *Communication in the Classroom*. Harlow: Longman.

Searle, J. 1969. *Speech Acts: An Essay on the Philosophy of Language*. Cambridge: Cambridge University Press.

Seedhouse, P. 1996. Classroom interaction: possibilities and impossibilities. *ELT Journal*, 16–24.

Sinclair, J. and Brazil, D. 1982. *Teacher Talk*. Oxford: Oxford University Press.

Sinclair, J. M. and Coulthard, R. M. 1975. *Towards an Analysis of Discourse*. Oxford: Oxford University Press.

Skehan, P. 1998. *A Cognitive Approach to Language Learning*. Oxford: Oxford University Press.

Slade, D. 1996. *The Texture of Casual Conversation: A Multidimensional Interpretation*. Unpublished PhD Dissertation, University of Sydney.

Slimani, A. 2001. Evaluation of classroom interaction. In Candlin, C. and Mercer, N. (eds.) *English Language Teaching in its Contexts: A Reader*. London: Routledge.

Snow, C. 1977. The development of conversation between mothers and babies. *Journal of Child Language*, 4, 1–22.

Sorhus, H. 1976. To hear ourselves – implications for teaching English as a Second Language. *ELT Journal*, 31, 211–21.

Soriano Escolar, C. 2000. La repetición: sus valores en el relato conversacional y la iconicidad interraccional. Unpublished MA dissertation. Universidad de Barcelona.

Sperber, D. and Wilson, D. 1990. *Relevance*. Oxford: Basil Blackwell.

Stenström, A-B. 1994. *An Introduction to Spoken Interaction*. Harlow: Longman.

Stern, H. 1983. *Fundamental Concepts of Language Teaching*. Oxford: Oxford University Press.

Stevick, E. 1980. *Teaching Languages: A Way and Ways*. Rowley, MA: Newbury House.

Stevick, E. 1996. *Memory, Meaning & Method: A View of Language Teaching*. (2nd edition.) Boston: Heinle and Heinle.

Stubbs, M. 1983. *Discourse Analysis*. Oxford: Blackwell.

Stubbs, M. 1996. *Text and Corpus Analysis*. Oxford: Blackwell.

Svartvik, J. and Quirk, R. (eds.) 1980. A Corpus of English Conversation. Lund: Gleerup. (Lund Studies in English 56.)

Swain, M. 1985. Communicative competence: some roles of comprehensible input and comprehensible output in its development. In Gass, S. and Madden, C. (eds.) *Input in Second Language Acquisition*. Rowley, MA: Newbury House.

Swales, J. 1990. *Genre Analysis: English in Academic and Research Settings*. Cambridge: Cambridge University Press.

Swan, M. and Walter, C. 1984. *Cambridge English Course, 1*. Cambridge: Cambridge University Press.

Swan, M. and Walter, C. 1985. *Cambridge English Course, 2*. Cambridge: Cambridge University Press.

Sweet, H. 1899. *The Practical Study of Languages. A Guide for Teachers and Learners*. London: Dent. Republished by Oxford University Press in 1964, ed. R. Mackin.

Takahashi, S. 2001. The role of input enhancement in developing pragmatic competence. In Rose, K. and Kasper, G. (eds.) *Pragmatics in Language Teaching*. Cambridge: Cambridge University Press

Takahashi, S. 2005. Pragmalinguistic awareness: Is it related to motivation and proficiency? *Applied Linguistics*, 26, 90–120.

Tannen, D. 1984. *Conversational Style*. Norwood, NJ: Ablex Press.

Tannen, D. 1989. *Talking Voices: Repetition, Dialogue and Imagery in Conversational Discourse*. Cambridge: Cambridge University Press.

Tannen, D. 1990. *You Just Don't Understand: Men & Women in Conversation*. New York: Morrow.

Tarone, E. 1980. Communication strategies, foreigner talk, and repair in interlanguage. *Language Learning*, 30, 417–31.

Tarone, E. 1981. Some thoughts on the notion of communication strategy. *TESOL Quarterly*, 15, 285–95.

Tarone, E. 1983 On the variability of language systems. *Applied Linguistics*, 4, 143–63.

References

Taylor, B. and Wolfson, N. 1978. Breaking down the conversation myth. *TESOL Quarterly*, 12, 31–39.

Taylor, T. and Cameron, D. 1987. *Analysing Conversation: Rules and Units in the Structure of Talk*. Oxford: Pergamon Press.

Tharp, R.G. and Gallimore, R. 1988. *Rousing Minds to Life: Teaching, Learning, and Schooling in Social Context*. Cambridge: Cambridge University Press.

Thomas, J. 1983. Cross-cultural pragmatic failure. *Applied Linguistics*, 4, 91–112.

Thornbury, S. 1996. Teachers research teacher talk. *ELT Journal*, 50, 279–89.

Thornbury, S. 1997. Reformulation and reconstruction: Tasks that promote 'noticing'. *ELT Journal*, 51, 326–35.

Thornbury, S. 2000. A Dogma for EFL. *IATEFL Issues, 153*, 2.

Thornbury, S. 2002. Training in instructional conversation. In Trappes-Lomax, H. and Ferguson, G. (eds.) *Language in Language Teacher Education*. Amsterdam: John Benjamins.

Towell, R., Hawkins, R. and Bazergui, N. 1996. The development of fluency in advanced learners of French. *Applied Linguistics*, 17, 84–119.

Tsui, A. 1992. A functional description of questions. In Coulthard, M. (ed.) 1992. *Advances in Spoken Discourse Analysis*. London: Routledge.

Tsui, A. 1994. *English Conversation*. Oxford: Oxford University Press.

Ulichny, P. 1996. Performed conversations in an ESL classroom. *TESOL Quarterly*, 30, 739–64.

Ur, P. 1981. *Discussions that Work: Task-centred Fluency Practice*. Cambridge: Cambridge University Press.

Ure, J. 1971. Lexical density and register differentiation. In Perren, G. and Trim, J. (eds.) *Applications of Linguistics: Selected Papers of the Second International Congress of Applied Linguistics, Cambridge 1969*. Cambridge: Cambridge University Press.

van Lier, L. 1988. *The Classroom and the Language Learner*. Harlow: Longman.

van Lier, L. 1989. Reeling, writhing, drawling, stretching and fainting in coils: Oral proficiency interviews as conversation. *TESOL Quarterly*, 23, 489–508.

van Lier, L. 1996. *Interaction in the Language Curriculum: Awareness, Autonomy and Authenticity*. Harlow: Longman.

van Lier, L. 2001. Constraints and resources in classroom talk: Issues of equality and symmetry. In Candlin, C. and Mercer, N. (eds.) *English Language Teaching in its Social Context: A Reader*. London: Routledge.

Viney, P. and Viney, K. 1996. *Handshake: A Course in Communication (Student's Book)*. Oxford: Oxford University Press.

Vygotsky, L.S. 1978. *Mind in Society: The Development of Higher Psychological Processes*. Cambridge, MA: Harvard University Press.

Vygotsky, L. S. 1986. *Thought and Language*. Cambridge, MA: MIT Press.

Wagner-Gough, J. 1975. Comparative studies in second language learning. *CAL-ERIC/CLL Series on Language and Linguistics 26*.

Walsh, S. 2002. Construction or obstruction: teacher talk and learner involvement in the EFL classroom. *Language Teaching Research 6*, 3–23.

References

Webster, M. and Castañón, L. 1980. *Crosstalk*. Oxford: Oxford University Press.
Wells, G. 1981. *Learning through Interaction: The Study of Language Development*. Cambridge: Cambridge University Press.
Wells, G. 1987. *The Meaning Makers: Children Learning Language and Using Language to Learn*. London: Hodder and Stoughton.
Wells, G. 1999. *Dialogic Inquiry: Towards a Sociocultural Practice and Theory of Education*. Cambridge: Cambridge University Press.
Wennerstrom, A. 2001. *The Music of Everyday Speech: Prosody and Discourse Analysis*. Oxford: Oxford University Press.
West, M. 1953. *A General Service List of English Words*. London: Longmans, Green.
West, M. 1960. *Minimum Adequate Vocabulary*. London: Longman.
Widdowson, H. 1978. *Teaching Language as Communication*. Oxford: Oxford University Press.
Willis, D. 1990. *The Lexical Syllabus*. London: Collins ELT.
Willis, J. 1996. *A Framework for Task-based Learning*. Harlow: Longman.
Willis, D. and Willis, J. 1996. Consciousness-raising activities in the language classroom. In Willis, J. and Willis, D. (eds.) *Challenge and Change in Language Teaching*. Oxford: Heinemann.
Wilkins, D. 1976. *Notional Syllabuses*. Oxford: Oxford University Press.
Wolfson, N. 1983. Rules of speaking. In Richards, J. and Schmidt, R. (eds.) *Language and Communication*. Harlow: Longman.
Wong, J. 2002. 'Applying' conversation analysis in applied linguistics: Evaluating dialogue in English as a Second Language textbooks. *IRAL* (Berlin, Germany), 40, 37–60.
Wray, A. 1999. Formulaic language in learners and native speakers. *Language Teaching*, 32, 4.
Wray, A. 2000. Formulaic sequences in second language teaching: Principle and practice. In *Applied Linguistics*, 21/4, 463–89.
Yorio, C. 1980. Conventionalized language forms and the development of communicative competence. *TESOL Quarterly*, 14, 433–42.
Yule, G. 1998. *Explaining English Grammar*. Oxford: Oxford University Press.

Author index

Acklam, R. 293, 295
Adolphs, S. 41, 42, 43
Aijmer, K. 62, 63, 64, 276
Alexander, L. 252, 253, 254
Allwright, R. 276, 316
Andersen, E. 203
Anderson, A. 204
Alesi, G. 252
Arthur, L. 288, 296, 300
Austin, J. 31

Bachman, L. 187, 223
Bannink, A. 244, 245, 303
Bardovi-Harlig, K. 223, 288
Basturkmen, H. 291
Bell, J. 321
Berlitz, M. 248, 250
Biber, D. 2, 12, 21, 40, 42, 44, 49, 59, 65,
    75, 76, 78, 80, 82, 86, 88, 89, 90, 92, 95,
    97, 98, 176
Billows, L. 253, 269
Black, V. 260
Block, D. 268
Bloom, L. 200
Blum-Kulka, S. 204, 223
Borkin, A. 228
Bouton, L. 232, 234
Brazil, D. 11, 33, 76, 90, 149, 238
Brock, C. 308
Brown, G. 276
Brown, P. 230
Bruner, J. 201
Burns, A. 181, 262, 282, 297
Bygate, M. 220, 222
Brumfit, C. 265
Bryne, D. 254, 257

Cadorath, J. 242
Cameron, D. 116
Canale, M. 186
Candlin, C. 256
Carter, R. 43, 44, 45, 53, 54, 58, 75, 84,
    97, 159, 179, 182, 280, 288
Cash, C. 170
Cazden, C. 278, 312
Chambers, F. 216

Channell, J. 43, 54, 55
Cheepen, C. 151, 172, 178
Chomsky, N. 74, 186
Clark, R. 192
Clennell, C. 298
Clifford, R. 236
Coates, J. 136, 137, 169
Cohen, A. 229, 232, 233, 234, 237
Cook, G. 267
Cope, B. 181
Coulthard, M. 33, 90, 224
Curran, C. 269
Crystal, D. 9, 12, 25, 49, 50, 74, 159, 160,
    161, 162, 166, 167, 224, 255, 281, 288
Cullen, R. 242, 312, 313
Cummins, J. 227
Cunningham, S. 266, 295, 323

Dalton, C. 11
Davy, D. 9, 12, 50, 74, 159, 160, 161, 162,
    166, 167, 255, 281, 288
de Cock, S. 219
DeCarrico, J. 12, 62, 63, 70, 102, 234
Dechert, H. 218
Delaruelle, S. 261
Dellar, H. 258, 299, 319
Doff, A. 263
Dörnyei, Z. 221, 222, 233, 234, 284, 287,
    296, 298, 301
Doughty, C. 278
Dunbar, R. 21
Dunham, P. 232, 234, 284

Eggins, S. 23, 34, 35, 67, 69, 89, 95, 97,
    98, 117, 119, 121, 161, 167, 169, 171,
    172, 173, 178
Ellis, N. 235, 300
Ellis, R. 198, 216, 217, 219, 222, 223, 235,
    267, 307, 309
Ernst, G. 243, 244, 304

Fairclough, N. 1, 36, 146
Feez, S. 279, 282, 283
Firth, J.R. 33, 253
Fishman, P. 136
Fletcher, P. 199

Forster, E.M. 157
Foster, P. 268, 308
Foster, S. 189, 197, 198, 200, 1990
Frampton, H. 73
Fraser, B. 230
French, P. 205
Frota, S. 194, 214, 215, 216, 218, 235, 237

Gairns, R. 102
Gallimore, R. 208, 245
Gardner, R. 132
Garfinkel, H. 114
Geddes, M. 277, 287
Gibbons, P. 313
Givón, T. 101
Goffman, E. 114, 163, 229
Gollin, S. 181
Gower, R. 321
Granger, S. 219
Grant, L. 291
Grice, H.P. 32, 200, 287
Gumperz, J. 134, 135

Halliday, M.A.K. 13, 20, 25, 34, 51, 75, 76, 77, 109, 117, 118, 146, 147, 200, 201, 202, 253, 262
Hammond, J. 280
Harris, S. 242
Hasan, R. 51, 109, 110, 146, 147
Hatch, E. 1, 195, 196, 198, 268
Haycraft, J. 254
Higgs, T. 236
Hillier, H. 25
Hobbs, J. 290, 291
Hocking, D. 258, 319
Hoey, M. 42, 51
Holmes, J. 54, 88
House, J. 231, 234, 235
Howatt, A. 247, 249, 254, 276
Hübscher, J. 73
Hughes, R. 304
Hull, J. 287
Hutchby, I. 161
Hymes, D. 29, 186, 228, 256, 265

Itoh, H. 195, 196

Jarvis, J. 313
Jefferson, G. 27, 114, 124
Johnson, Karen 309
Johnson, Keith 218, 219, 234
Jones, E. 316, 317, 318
Jones, R. 290, 301
Jones, V. 289
Joyce, H. 181, 262, 282, 297
Judd, E. 285, 295
Jupp, T. 134, 135

Kalantzis, M. 181
Kasper, G. 224, 229, 233, 241
Kay, S. 289
Keller, E. 64, 259, 282, 287, 298
Kellerman, E. 277
Kindt, D. 292, 298
Klippel, F. 303
Ko, J. 309
Kramsch, C. 314, 315
Krashen, S. 230, 268, 275
Kress, G. 286
Kumaravadivelu, B. 316, 318

Labov, W. 30, 81, 91, 146, 148, 149, 151, 152, 172
Levelt, W. 1
Levinson, S. 230
Lewis, M. 102, 257, 300
Littlewood, W. 265
Long, M. 238, 267
Lynch, T. 298

Markee, N. 268
MacLure, M. 191, 205
Martin, J. 35, 66, 67, 68, 117, 119, 144, 146, 181, 262
Matthiessen, C. 34, 108
McCarthy, M. 16, 41, 42, 43, 44, 45, 47, 48, 53, 54, 58, 75, 76, 82, 84, 93, 94, 97, 98, 107, 132, 150, 159, 179, 182, 257, 267, 277, 280, 288
McEnery, T. 219
McIntosh, A. 253
McKay, S. 43, 284, 285
McTear, M. 191, 203, 204
Mercer, N. 2, 208, 212
Mitchell, T.F. 147
Mohamed, S. 293, 295
Moor, P. 266, 295, 323
Myers, G. 156, 159, 163, 164, 166

Nakahama, Y. 269, 270, 308
Nation, I.S.P. 42, 43
Nattinger, J. 12, 62, 63, 70, 101, 102, 234
Nelson, G. 230
Nolasco, R. 288, 296, 300
Norrick, N. 153
Norton, B. 285
Nunan, D. 238, 239, 246

O'Dell, F. 264
O'Keeffe, A. 82
Ochs, E. 101, 169, 200
Odlin, T. 229
O'Neill, R. 253, 254

Palmer, A. 187
Palmer, H. 1, 251

Author index

Pantell, D. 252
Pawley, A. 62, 102, 193, 218
Peccei, J. 195, 199, 201
Peters, A. 193, 195
Pica, T. 268
Plum, G. 152, 156
Porter, P. 233, 234, 308
Porter Ladousse, G. 303
Prabhu, N. 267
Prodromou, L. 101, 219, 235

Quirk, R. 124

Raupach, M. 218
Redman, S. 102
Reinhart, S. 228
Richards, J. 20, 227, 229, 230, 231, 236,
    249, 274, 275, 276, 281, 282, 287
Rivers, W. 252
Roberts, C. 134, 135
Robinson, M. 313
Rodgers, T. 249, 274
Rose, D. 66, 67
Rose, K. 224, 229, 233, 241
Rowe, M. 206

Sacks, H. 27, 114, 115, 123, 124, 131, 157
Sacks, O. 168
Sato, C. 238
Sauveur, L. 249
Schegloff, E.A. 27, 114, 124, 131
Schiffrin, D. 57, 150, 162, 163, 165
Schmidt, R. 20, 194, 214, 215, 216, 218,
    222, 223, 227, 230, 231, 235, 236, 237,
    278
Schmitt, N. 41, 42, 43
Schonell, F.J. 42
Scollon, R. 197, 285, 286
Scollon, S.W. 285, 286
Scott, M. 41, 50, 51
Scott, R. 265
Searle, J. 31
Seedhouse, P. 242, 243
Seidlhofer, B. 11
Sinclair, J. 33, 238
Skehan, P. 101, 220, 222, 234, 268, 269
Slade, D. 23, 67, 69, 89, 108, 117, 119,
    120, 121, 126, 152, 157, 169, 171, 172,
    173, 174, 178
Slimani, A. 238, 308
Snow, C. 189
Sorhus, H. 62
Soriano Escolar, C. 225
Sperber, D. 32
Starks, D. 291
Stenström, A-B. 56, 58, 90
Stern, H. 248, 252

Stervens, P. 253
Stevick, E. 269, 302
Stubbs, M. 1, 44
Sturtridge, G. 277, 287
Sukiwat, M. 229
Svartvik, J. 124
Swain, M. 186, 227, 268, 269
Swan, M. 74, 265
Sweet, H. 250, 270, 318
Syder, F. 62, 102, 193, 218

Takahashi, S. 290
Tannen, D. 17, 30, 52, 53, 137, 163, 169,
    194
Tarone, E. 219, 220
Taylor, B. 236, 265
Taylor, T. 116
Tharp, R.G. 208, 245
Thomas, J. 227, 228
Thornbury, S. 269, 316
Thurrell, S. 284, 287, 296, 298, 301
Towell, R. 216
Tsui, A. 86

Ulichny, P. 310, 311, 312
Ur, P. 303
Ure, J. 44

van Lier, L. 2, 208, 240, 241, 242, 243,
    305, 309, 318
Viney, K. 323
Viney, P. 323
Vygotsky, L. 207

Wagner-Gough, J. 217
Waletzky, J. 30, 148, 149, 151, 152
Walkley, A. 299
Walsh, S. 313
Walter, C. 74, 265
Warner, S. 64, 259, 282, 287, 298
Wells, G. 190, 191, 198, 200, 201, 202,
    204, 205, 206, 207, 208, 209, 210, 213,
    309
Wennerstrom, A. 235
West, M. 43
Widdowson, H. 256
Williams, J. 278
Willis, D. 102, 297
Willis, J. 268, 292, 297
Wilson, D. 32
Wolfson, N. 229, 236, 265
Wong, J. 288
Wooffitt, R. 161
Wray, A. 12, 62, 63, 192, 218

Yorio, C. 276
Yule, G. 100, 276

Subject index

abstract (narrative) 148–57, 159–60
accuracy, grammatical 237, 254
acquisition (vs. learning) 230, 275
acts 33
adjacency pair 29, 86, 114–17, 125, 131, 199, 224, 261, 281
anecdote 152, 154–6
appraisal language 23, 66–9, 70, 180
aspect 90–94, 160–61
assessment 304–7
assisted performance 207
asynchronous communication 25
audiolingualism 251–2

back-channelling 23, 58, 131, 224, 283, 290, 300
back-tracking 11
Birmingham School 33, 114, 117
bundle, lexical 65, 176

'chat' sequences 144–5
child-directed speech 190–91
chunk, lexical 12, 24, 62–5, 102, 192, 218, 234, 257, 277, 290, 298–9
classroom talk
    see teacher talk
closings 130–31, 224, 261, 281, 288–9, 291
coda (of narrative) 148–9, 168, 226
coherence 52, 199–200
cohesion 51–2, 108–13, 198–9
collocation 41, 299
colloquial speech 20
common underlying proficiency (CUP) 227
communication strategies 219–22, 233–4, 236, 277, 298, 308
communicative approach, the
    see communicative language teaching
communicative language teaching (CLT) 256–67, 276
Community Language Learning (CLL) 269, 302
competence (vs. performance) 74, 186
competence, communicative 186–7, 204, 256, 265
competence, conversational 188, 214, 231
competence, discourse 187

competence, grammatical 187, 214–15
competence, intercultural 285–6
competence, pragmatic 187, 203, 223–4
competence, sociolinguistic 187, 203, 233
competence, strategic 187
complexity, syntactic 75–80
computer mediated communication (CMC) 8, 23–5
concordance 37, 38
concordancing software 41
conjunct
    see linker
consciousness-raising 297–8
context 14, 107–8
context of situation 253
contingency 16, 110, 200, 208, 240, 250, 309–10, 313
contractions 21
conversation, definition of 5, 8, 25
Conversation Analysis (CA) 27, 114–16, 123, 281
conversation, instructional 208, 245, 250, 309
conversationalization 1, 308
Co-operative Principle (Grice's) 32, 200, 287
coordination 13
co-text 108
core lexicon 48
corpora 16, 37, 40, 75
corpus linguistics 37, 40–41
Counselling Language Learning
    see Community Language Learning
Critical Discourse Analysis (CDA) 36, 146
cross-cultural variation 134–5
C-unit 78

deixis 14, 44, 48, 70, 85–6, 102, 150
delexical verbs 48
density, lexical
    see lexical density
dialogic inquiry 309
dialogue 190, 202
dialogue (teaching) 247–8, 253, 294, 299, 301
'direct approach' 275 ff

361

Subject index

Direct Method 248–51
discourse analysis 33, 107, 256, 258, 278
discourse management 305
discourse markers 16, 24, 35, 48, 56, 57–61, 66, 70, 77, 82, 99, 111, 165, 180, 198, 225, 258, 278, 290, 297
discourse strategies 130–37
discussion (classroom) 254, 303
display question 205, 238, 240, 242, 249, 314
dual-mode processing 194
dysfluency 12, 304

ellipsis 15, 24, 78, 83–5, 110, 198, 220, 290
English as an International Language (EIL) 43, 276, 284–5
ethnography of speaking 29
evaluation (in narrative) 148–9, 166–8, 169
exchange 121
exchange structure 33, 121, 261
exemplum 152, 156–7
expletives
see swearing

false starts 11, 12, 220
feedback 131–3, 136
see also back-channelling
field 34, 253
filler 12, 56–7, 66, 70, 220, 234, 290, 301
fluency 12, 214–17, 234, 237, 254, 257, 265, 282, 298, 300, 303
focus on form 278, 302
formal speech 20
formulaic language 62, 192–4, 218–19, 220, 289, 298–9
fossilization 236, 275
frequency, word 41, 45–9
function, communicative 31, 256–7
function, speech 118, 200–202
functionalism 256–7

gambit, conversational 64, 126, 231, 276, 282, 287
gender 54, 88, 98, 128, 132, 136–7, 169, 263
genre 29, 36, 145–82, 200, 262, 279
genre analysis 147–50, 258, 278
gossip 21, 55, 122, 128–30, 170–82

head 13, 80–82
hesitation 12, 56, 216, 220, 234
holophrase 192
horizontal construction 197–8
humour 22, 23, 67

ideational meaning 34
identity 21

incorporation strategy 195, 217
informal speech 20, 23
information gap 257, 268, 269–70, 308
initiation – response – follow-up (IRF) 33, 205, 238–42, 308, 312
inserts 44, 60, 78
insertion sequence 29, 116
instructional conversation 208, 245, 250, 309
interaction 15, 113 ff.
interactional function 20, 52, 200, 240, 268, 282
interactional signals 16, 24, 58, 70, 82
interactional sociolinguistics 30, 134
interactionist theory (of SLA) 198, 207, 267–8
interjections 23, 58, 60
interlanguage 101, 215, 222, 223–4, 238, 268, 275
interpersonal function 17, 20, 26, 39, 52
interpersonal meaning 35
interview 17, 26
intonation 9, 10
involvement, high/low 11, 17, 25, 66–9, 169

jokes 22, 91, 128, 224

key (in speaking) 29–30
key, high/mid/low 10, 11, 17
keywords 50

language-in-action 44, 84
lexical approach, the 101–2, 257, 300
lexical density 13, 43–4
lexical pattern 51
lexical phrase
see chunk, lexical
lexical phrase knowledge 70
lexical variety 44–5
linker 111

metafunction 20
modal verbs, modality 48, 94–8, 102, 256
mode 8, 34, 253
mood 95, 97, 118
move 117–21, 224
move, continuing 190
move, challenging 119–20
move, discretionary 118–20
move, initiating 19, 117–21
move, responding 19, 118–21, 231
move, tracking 119–20
move complex 120
multilog 15, 26
multi-word phrase
see chunk, lexical

narrative structure 30, 36, 81, 148, 152–4, 201, 225–6
non-clausal elements 15, 77
noticing 237, 278, 296, 298

orientation (narrative) 148–50, 160–61, 226
openings 130–31, 261, 281
output, comprehensible 268
overlaps 4, 15, 123, 126, 133, 224
overtures 59

parataxis 150
passive (voice) 94
pause filler
    see filler
performance (vs. competence) 74, 186
phatic function 20, 285
play, language 267
politeness 22, 223–4, 229–30, 262, 281, 284
pragmatic knowledge 187, 223
    see also competence, pragmatic
pragmatic markers 58, 290
pragmatics 32–3, 203–4, 232–3, 235, 281, 284
presentation-practice-production (PPP) 254–5
production strategies 220
probe (in gossip) 173
pronoun 14, 44, 150
prosody 8, 9, 235

questions 31, 86–90, 103, 120, 205
quotative 99, 103, 180, 227

reciprocity 15, 39
recount 152, 157–8
reference 109–10
reformulation 313
register 35, 253, 262
relevance theory 32
relexicalization 53
repair 12, 17, 28–9, 203, 220, 241, 268, 270, 282, 308, 314–15
repetition 17, 43, 113, 194–6
repetition, lexical 49–54, 112–13, 199
reporting (speech) 98–100
ritual constraints 229
role play 254, 264, 265, 284, 290, 293, 303
routine, conversational 62–5, 70, 219, 231, 276, 277, 282, 284

scaffolding 191, 196–7, 202, 207, 307, 309
schema 52, 202
schematic structure (of genres) 146
sentence builder 63, 66

sentence frames 12
service encounter 19, 26, 253, 261
setting 29
side-sequences 15
situational approach, the 252–4
size, lexical 42
slang 20
social formulae 64, 66
sociocultural (learning theory) 206–9, 307
sociopragmatic failure 228
speech act 200, 224, 228, 229, 257
Speech Act Theory 31, 33, 281
spontaneity 12, 26, 39
stories 23, 91, 128, 136, 151, 168–70, 224
strategies
    see communication strategies, production strategies
subordination 13
substitution 110, 199
swearing 20, 23, 60, 66, 67
symmetry 19, 26, 240
syntax, development of 197–8
Systemic Functional Linguistics (SFL) 33, 34, 114, 117, 146, 262, 281, 282

tag 60, 66
tag, question 61, 81, 88, 290
talking circle 243, 304, 308
tail 13, 60, 66, 80–82, 179
task-based language teaching (TBLT) 267–8, 276, 278, 290
teacher talk 204–9, 238–45, 313–15
tenor 17, 34, 97, 253
tense 90–94, 150, 161, 162–4, 177, 180, 226
textual meaning 35, 52
theme 13
tone unit boundary 9
topic 112, 127–30, 199–200, 224, 244, 314
topicalization 238, 244, 308
transactions 33
transactional function 19, 20, 240, 266, 267, 282
transcription 3, 289, 298
transfer (from L1 to L2) 224–6, 232
turn 15, 24, 28, 123–6
turn-constructional unit (TCU) 117, 123–6
turntaking 27, 123–6, 188–90, 192, 204, 224, 269, 281, 282, 314

utterance launchers 12, 59, 64, 66

vague language 43, 54–6, 70, 219, 290
variation theory 30

Subject index

variety, lexical
  see lexical variety
vernacular grammar 21
vertical construction 197–8
vocative 78, 82

wait time 206
word family 42

zone of proximal development (ZPD) 207